Moral Literacy

Moral Literacy

Barbara Herman

Harvard University Press

Cambridge, Massachusetts

London, England

First Harvard University Press paperback edition, 2008.

Library of Congress Cataloging-in-Publication Data

Herman, Barbara.
  Moral Literacy / Barbara Herman.
    p.   cm.
  Includes bibliographical references and index.
  ISBN: 978-0-674-02467-0 (cloth : alk. paper)
  ISBN: 978-0-674-03052-7 (pbk.)
    1. Kant, Immanuel, 1724–1804.   2. Ethics.   I. Title.
BJ21 .H47 2007
22.170 22   2006049779

Contents

Preface

Before we come to moral philosophy, we know some morally significant things about ourselves and about the social world in which we act. We know that we are imperfect, psychologically complex, and only partly in control of the effects of that complexity on our moral responses and actions. We also know that we live in and through social institutions that shape our moral lives, sometimes in ways that empower us and sometimes in ways that challenge our will to act well. If we are reflective, this is practical knowledge.

Moral philosophy depends on an accurate account of what we are like as agents: our range of motivations, the structure of our practical thinking, the different ways we respond to and are affected by circumstances. Often, however, the idea of agency in use within moral philosophy, and especially within formal, rationalist theory, is denatured, abstract, simplified, as if the details of what we are like or the circumstances in which we act could not be relevant to fundamental moral questions. That surely cannot be right.

Now, since avoidance of the obvious can look like resistance, one might ask: what would happen if the moral theory were open to facts about our psychology and the framing effects of social institutions? One possibility is that it would survive, changed and improved in interesting ways; another is that the theory would be shown to be less compelling as an account of the morality of human beings. The essays collected here were conceived with the first, more attractive conjecture in mind. The idea throughout is to let the phenomena in; the hope is that by dissolving resistance we can liberate untapped theoretical power.

In this book, the moral theory that is either explicitly or implicitly on the line is Immanuel Kant's. It is widely seen as the archetype of a theory resistant to shaping by contingent psychological and social facts, and long criticized for emptiness as the result. Although this view is deeply entrenched, it depends on a tradition of criticism that is, I believe, based on mistakes of interpretation and a certain narrowness of philosophical imagination. Faced with a theory that prizes formality of principle, necessity of duty, and an account of motivation that transcends psychology, readers of Kant since Hegel have mistaken metaphysics for ethics, regarded the relationship between principle and duty as deductive rather than deliberative, and assumed that our rationality could be regulative of choice and action without transforming any of what it regulated.

The project undertaken here is not so much rehabilitative as exploratory: I believe that the resources of Kantian moral theory are much more extensive than has been thought, even in the recent, more Kant-friendly philosophical environment. By asking questions that Kant did not consider and trying to answer them sometimes in terms that can only afterward be shown to fit with fundamental Kantian values and principles, we get a fuller idea of what the theory can be asked to do. Some of the essays involve explicit Kant interpretation that aims to overcome narrow readings and conventional assumptions that impede understanding. Other essays are prompted by questions at the ground level. How should we think about moral character given what we know about the fault-lines produced in normal development? The morality of ordinary life is saturated by the content of all sorts of local institutions; how can our accounts of moral obligation and judgment accommodate this? What is it like at the intersection of moral and political reasons, especially when they conflict? As the questions are filled out, they can be used to put pressure on resistant theoretical positions.

Because these questions are not about fanciful possibilities but about the way people actually manage to live morally, or fail to, it has seemed to me imperative to proceed, where possible, using real examples that capture moments of moral difficulty. There are advantages and risks in doing this. Examples of psychological or moral or political disorder are rich with detail that reveals some of the occluded dynamics of moral practice. They are also potentially confusing in their detail, their significance perhaps limited to time and place. I see these as reasons for caution, not reasons to avoid the attractive messiness of real cases. The goal is to develop methods of casuistry that are sensitive both to the way moral events happen and to the resources of moral theory that can account for or explain them. The resulting dynamic may lead us to think about the events differently; it may also prompt us to extend or modify the moral principles we bring to the task. In the last essay of the volume, there is an extended trial of this casuistical ambition. I discuss the South African Truth and Reconciliation Commission with an eye to questioning the familiar assumption that in times of urgent social conflict, appeals to political necessity provide sufficient justification to set morality aside. Reading the historical record closely, one finds instead a compelling example of people trying to use familiar moral tools to do something new. If they were successful, it wouldn't show that justification by political necessity is never called for, but it can show us that the terms of moral justification need not be constrained by the terms in which such a conflict is standardly or initially presented. Whether and how moral innovation might be possible is exactly the kind of question a real case can force us to consider.

What makes an enlarged version of Kantian theory especially useful for this sort of investigation is that it offers an account of obligation and duty that is essentially deliberative, anchored both in agents' articulated grasp of their social world *and* in norms of correctness for choice and action. For the agent, these together constitute a kind of moral literacy: an ability to recognize and interpret moral facts that is a necessary condition for moral action and criticism, as well as the possibility of our together making reasoned moral progress.

However, viewed this way, moral reasoning starts in the socially available moral knowledge we use to interpret our circumstances of action. Moral theory then has to provide the content for premises of interpretation as well as the evaluative principles we use in judgment about choice and action, given an understanding of what's at stake. And this means that a deliberative theory cannot be merely formal: it must ·offer a substantive account of moral value to serve as the basis of the work of moral interpretation. The more theoretical essays in this volume take on different parts of the task of showing where in Kant's theory this is to be found. The resulting account of moral premises and moral value is not only consistent with the more familiar elements of Kantian theory but is also, I argue, the missing condition of the theory's general applicability.

Nine of the thirteen essays collected here were previously published. Despite my respect for the historical record, I have taken the liberty of revising all but one of them. Sometimes the revisions are cosmetic; sometimes they are more substantial, either to improve an argument or example or to make the essay fit better with those it now lives among. I have left Chapter 9, "The Scope of Moral Requirement," intact since it was first published in an easily accessed journal. The rest of the essays were published in volumes derived from conferences, festschrifts, and other hard-to-find books. It was the thought that this volume would turn out to be the volume of record for those essays that to my mind justified taking the liberty of revision.

There are two pairs of essays in this volume: a pair of Tanner Lectures (Chapters 4 and 5) and a pair of Whitehead Lectures (Chapters 11 and 12). Each chapter is distinct, but the second element in the pair clearly builds on the first. In general, there is progression across the essays in this volume. Although the line is not always direct, ideas only entertained in earlier essays become the subject-matter of later ones.

Versions of most of the essays were presented to audiences of colleagues and friends who provided thoughtful criticism and a supportive willingness to suspend disbelief, at least for a while, about the directions in which I claimed Kantian theory could be taken. For helpful public responses to some of this work I am grateful to Seyla Benhabib, Frank Michelman, Martha Nussbaum, Samuel Scheffler, and David Sussman. Ruth Gavison and Carol Voeller have provided valuable insights; each of them has seemed to understand parts of my work better than I. I am especially indebted to Seana Shiffrin, who has been a generous friend and greatly valued critic and interlocutor. More times than I can remember, Mickey Morgan has carved time out of his own extremely demanding life to work through drafts with me, demanding clarity and structure where I was vague, raising objections that made the work better, and all from within a keen philosophical appreciation of the project.

During the past twelve years, it has been my good fortune to be a member of an exceptional group of philosophers at UCLA who possess and value the intellectual virtues I most admire. There is a shared belief that philosophy is very hard: its central problems demand understanding from the ground up. Solutions must make real sense, and cleverness is no substitute for getting things right. It is a demanding ethos, but it keeps one's sights high and bolsters confidence that all the work is worth it.

—1—

Making Room for Character

In the course of the very productive encounter between Aristotelian and Kantian ethics, some things seem to have been established. In particular, from the Aristotelian side, it has been argued and is now widely accepted that moral judgment is not a practice of applying fixed rules to particulars in the manner of a legal system.[1] There is, on the one hand, the recognition that what is right to do *here* is often, if not typically, a function of what is specific to the given situation,[2] and on the other, the requirement of salience—much of the work of moral judgment takes place prior to any possible application of rules in the eliciting of the relevant moral facts from particular circumstances. Indeed, one of the great successes of revitalized virtue theory has been to shift philosophical attention away from the mechanics of a rule-based practical syllogism to the ways in which the conditions for moral judgment involve the complexities of a developed moral character.[3] Having a virtuous character, we see different things, or see them in ways that have different practical significance, than we would if our character were vicious or in some lesser way defective. And because of the way we come to see what we see, we are moved to act.

This seems to me exactly right, and to present a feature of moral judgment that *any* sound moral theory must be able to accommodate. The central difficulty it poses for Kantian theory comes from the identification of the aspect of character that makes moral judgment possible with a capacity that

---

1. Not that it is so obvious how, even given fixed laws, judgment is to proceed.

2. Sometimes this fact is taken to show "noncodifiability"—the thesis that the moral features of circumstances of action cannot be described by rules. But noncodifiability does not follow from context-dependence.

3. The most powerful and challenging version of this sort of account is to be found in the work of John McDowell.

involves, or requires for its development, the nonrational faculties. But if we are ever to have a Kantian ethics liberated from its excess noumenal baggage, this is just the sort of fact that must be accommodated. It is one thing to reject the idea that moral perception flows directly from a nonrational faculty—the sophisticated virtue theorist rejects this too—and quite another to resist the role of the nonrational in our capacities for judgment and action. I believe that the key to getting this right involves rethinking the basic relation between desire and motive: the way desires are or can be the occasion for motives and the way rational motives in turn affect the structure or natural history of desire.[4] Mistakes here open an unnecessary chasm between reason and character in Kantian ethics.

In making room for character, however, other issues emerge. One might be concerned that judgment that relies on character may have a tendency to be normatively static, especially when it involves the development of special perceptual capacities. Character-based judgment is good at explaining how an agent "gets it right," and why, in getting it right, there is no separate question of motivation. But the task of moral judgment often requires the resolution of practical perplexity in circumstances where part of getting it right requires being able to recognize and evaluate unfamiliar moral phenomena. Here, I think, the initial advantage may go the other way: certain features of a Kantian conception of moral judgment accommodate moral perplexity and its practical resolution, especially in changing circumstances of judgment. Classical virtue theory seems to me less flexible. Not *in*flexible, but in its nature less open to the tumult of competing values and ways of life that characterize the contemporary moral scene. This may be more a legacy of its historical origins than any permanent defect. That will be for others to say. My ambitions here are limited to describing some of the resources that might be drawn on to develop a Kantian idea of character and to indicate, briefly, some of its advantages for moral judgment.

I

The first step to take in introducing a robust conception of character into Kantian theory involves a rethinking of the place of desire in a naturalistic story of moral motivation. This is because much of the problem about

4. For Kant, desires are incentives that are available for a rational agent to act on as motives, just in case she judges that acting to satisfy a particular desire is in some sense good. Desires are not, of course, the only incentives a rational agent has.

desire—and so about character—for Kantian ethics comes from the ways desire is thought about elsewhere under the influence of one or another kind of naturalism. When it is simply taken that desire, or some other original (unmediated or noncognitive) spring of activity, lies behind action as a cause, the resulting story of motivation in a rational agent tends to be one of direction or redirection of an activity-producing force.[5] An agent's practical rationality—her access to motivating reasons—extends the array of actions that are possible for her, given a set of desires (or desire-like states). She expresses her rationality in action by doing what she does out of a sense of its fit with something she wants. She may desire food; she may desire pistachio ice cream. How she should act is a function of judgment and circumstantial orientation: what is at hand and how she might proceed to acquire an object not presently available. No very special explanation is required for the possibility of acquiring a taste for pistachio ice cream; no explanation of any sort is required for the reason-giving force of hunger. Nor do we require explanation of the move to means: we define a rational agent as one who can act via a representation of an object of desire *as* a possible effect of her acting. What does require special explanation according to this story, what appears to be most strange, is a moral motive that is not tied to natural desires (such as self-interest or sympathy). To the extent that the moral motive seems to come from nowhere, it calls not for explanation, but to be explained away, or reduced to something else. That is why the standard Kantian account of moral motivation seems so unhelpful. It asserts as true just the thing that does not seem possible.

Most reductive strategies for explaining moral motivation orient themselves to providing an account of reliable causes of moral outcomes. Knowing what moral agents are to do (treat strangers with honesty and respect, honor agreements, etc.), and what "natural" materials a theory may draw on, the task is to explain how the moral concern of the normal agent is assembled from these nonmoral materials. Where the cause of our moral interest is itself not obscure—suppose it is sympathy—its relative priority and limited scope require correction (sympathy is neither strong nor general; it does not reach to justice). If there are no natural desires that can support a moral motive directly, one posits various mechanisms to account for the transfor-

5. It is a story that Kant seems to endorse to explain the motivating effect of every source of action *but* the motive of duty. I do not think this is correct. In this chapter, however, I am more concerned with setting out a different view than with proving that it is, or could have been, Kant's.

mation of a morally indifferent affective state into a moral motive (reflective self-interest, for example). The emergent motive may require correction so that its independently defined (moral) object is more reliably and predictably its output. But lack of fit is of no grave concern to the theory since the point was to show the possibility of motivating moral action at all.[6]

Not every naturalistic account of moral motivation looks to independently defined moral outcomes in its explanation of moral motivation. For example, Samuel Scheffler has explored psychoanalytic theory as a possible explanatory framework because it includes the moral capacity as one of the emergent mechanisms by which a young child resolves what is perceived to be a life-threatening parental response to the aggressive and sexual desires of the Oedipal situation.[7] But though this story can account for the emergence of a capacity for moral action and concern, it leaves the moral character of the individual shrouded by the obscurity of its prerational development. For Freud, the hidden origins of moral character had explanatory power. Once uncovered, they could explain a subject's (possibly correct) perception that her moral convictions were not good for her.[8] However, what is an advantage to psychoanalytic treatment may not be advantageous for moral theory. This is especially so given the fact that the deep structure of personality dictates no more than the form of the moral: cost-sensitive rules and ideals relevant to negotiating intimacy and separation. The range of normal development does not thereby rule out morally noxious content.[9]

It is most likely because reductive theories are prompted by the perceived strangeness of the moral motive—by the need, in effect, to explain it away—that they have a high toleration for indirect or self-effacing solutions. It is thought not to matter if our interest in morality is the inscrutable product of a complex process or a mask for other, themselves unexamined, interests. What counts is that our having a moral disposition is explained, and in that limited sense, justified. I think this is a mistake. It very much does matter that the moral motive—and so our moral character—have

6. It is, not surprisingly, very difficult to disentangle such accounts from a rule-based conception of morality.

7. Samuel Scheffler, *Human Morality* (New York: Oxford University Press, 1992), chap. 5.

8. Of course, the value of such explanation was not limited to the individual and her symptoms. It also figured in accounts of mass hysteria, the rise of charismatic leaders, and other social pathologies.

9. Scheffler's theoretical program would not be disturbed by this. What he is exploring at this point is the possibility of natural moral motivation that is not tied to the promotion of some end (the well-being of others, self-interest), and so not defeated when morality fails to support the end. He offers other sorts of argument to constrain moral content.

some available transparency with regard to its origins. This is not to say that we must be able to recover and endorse all the developmental steps that produce our character. But the structure of character that is the product of this process should have reflexive connection with moral content. It is not neutral. When subjected to reflective pressure, the conditions of our caring about morality affect the resources we have available for moral response.

If the range of "moral outcomes" is uncertain, if new facts or changed circumstances can require changes in the way the moral agent ought to respond and act, lack of available connection between the roots of moral attachment and the moral motive can be the occasion of serious moral failure. We tend to mistake the nature of the motivational stability morality requires. It may not be so much a matter of steadfastness in the face of temptation to transgress as it is openness to continuity of development in response to various demands. In this sense, an agent's reflective self-understanding can be a vital component of an agent's moral character.[10]

Support for this mistake comes from the acceptance of two views that are often connected: skepticism about the possibility of a nonreductive (or pure) moral motive and a contemporary version of motivational internalism—one that makes the defining issue for morality, for the range of moral reasons, depend on what can be motivating for an individual at a time. The sites of contention are then restricted to the range of possible causal links practical reason can deliberatively make available, and the possibility of some nondeliberative, yet rational transformation, that is nonetheless anchored in an agent's current motivating interests.[11]

10. One might say: transparency is to morality what publicity is to justice.

11. Christine Korsgaard argues that there is nothing in the internalist requirement as such that argues against a substantive conception of practical reason ("Skepticism about Practical Reason," *Journal of Philosophy* 83 [January 1986]: 5–25). John McDowell adds to this the possibility of something like conversion—a kind of "transcendence of the mere facts of individual psychology"—that can bring an agent into position to deliberate correctly. He imagines the possibility of some nondeliberative process that could, say, by exposure, "bring . . . reasons within the person's notice." Importantly, these can be reasons that we will want to say, and that he may want to say, were reasons for him all along, even though there was no deliberative process that brought him to see what he now takes to be vividly relevant. McDowell's example is of coming to appreciate twelve-tone music—something it is not irrational for agents per se not to like on first notice. But for some agents, with some backgrounds in music, exposure or a description or an understanding of the history may move them—change what they hear. Such a process of making something available is not nonrational for being nondeliberative. See John McDowell, "Might There Be External Reasons?" in J. E. J. Altham and Ross Harrison, eds., *World, Mind and Ethics: Essays on the Moral Philosophy of Bernard Williams* (Cambridge: Cambridge University Press, 1995), pp. 77–78.

It seems to me that one should be able to accept that a moral theory must be constrained by the facts of human motivation without also having to hold that moral reasons must be capable of motivating each agent within their scope at all relevant times through a connection, however attenuated, with the agent's interests. This last is such an implausible position that the most steadfast internalist almost always supplements the connection, adding full information, clear deliberative connections, absence of distraction, depression, and so on. The real puzzle is why such a form of internalism has a lock on moral theory. If, as John McDowell suggests, it is in part to stave off a kind of predatory move by the partisans of universal, denatured Reason, then as a strategy, its cost to the claims morality would make on human character may be unacceptably high.[12] Given the cost, it is worth considering our options.

Suppose, instead, we divided the question of reasons an agent has or could have here and now from the question of the possibility conditions for morality. We might then think there is an internalism requirement for normative moral theory that is different from the requirement when addressed to an agent's reasons for action. The area of concern for theory-internalism would be the nature and point of different possible directions of human development. Morality as a normative enterprise is then not restricted to what an individual at a time is capable of doing. It can be, indeed it often ought to be, subjectively transforming, not just with respect to its demands at a particular moment, but about the kind of person one comes to be. It will be consistent with this sort of internalism to view the facts of human nature as constraining the shape of a moral life, without determining it. We should even be able to talk of possible directions for moral growth and development without having to argue for any strong teleological idea of human flourishing. Experiences, especially moral experiences, create possibilities of character.[13] I believe that Kantian moral theory can not only help itself to

12. Not everything can be accomplished through a more robust account of practical rationality; and even if "conversion" is a possibility, some nontrivial background conditions need to be in place. Saul was not just taking a walk to Damascus when he became Paul. See John McDowell, "Two Sorts of Naturalism," in Rosalind Hursthouse, Gavin Lawrence, and Warren Quinn, eds., *Virtues and Reasons: Philippa Foot and Moral Theory* (Oxford: Oxford University Press, 1995), and "Might There Be External Reasons?"

13. Something like this is to be found in John Rawls's idea that the effect of a public culture of a certain sort will be that citizens come to be motivated by a concern for fairness. It is also, I believe, central to Mill's argument in his *Utilitarianism*. There is, Mill argues, a course of education and civilization through which the good of others comes to be for each person "a thing naturally and necessarily attended to, like any of the physical conditions of our exis-

this idea, it can contribute the next bit through the conception of character it offers, based on the transformative role of the moral motive in the structure of agents' intentions and maxims.

II

I want to return now to the claim I made earlier: that the key to a Kantian account of moral development and moral character is in the relation between motive and desire. Let us take desire, in the most general sense, to refer to those states of an organism that dispose it to activity. This includes desires in the colloquial sense (for drink, fame, companionship), as well as what we think of as instincts (governing flight, reproduction, etc.). The defining Kantian claim is that desires, in this general sense, do not directly support reasons for action. Desires may move us to activity; they may provide the occasion for reasons for action (and for reasoning about action). They are nonetheless not reasons, and they do not on their own give agents reasons to act.

The Kantian claim is about what there is: in a world without rational agents whose reason is effectively practical, there could be active beings, even beings who choose means for their ends, but no reasons for action.[14] Reasons are evaluative. An agent has a reason when she is thereby in a position to judge that acting (in a particular way) is in some sense good. She acts for a reason when her activity is governed by such a judgment. Judgment about reasons for action need not involve deliberation or ratiocination. It necessarily involves evaluating an action or possible action, under a description, as it is or promotes something itself judged to be of value.

In Kant-speak, to say that an agent has and acts on a reason is to say she acts on a maxim. It is to present the agent as having a practically effective evaluative attitude toward the sources of activity she encounters—within and outside herself.[15]

tence" (*Utilitarianism,* chapter 3). It is this possibility, built on natural sympathy and developed through the unifying experience of successful cooperative activity, reinforced by education and religion, that is the ground of the possibility of utilitarianism as a moral way of life.

14. Here, on Kant's behalf, I am accepting the internalism requirement on what a reason can be.

15. Some have argued that desires are evaluative: to desire X is to see it as in some way good or attractive. I think there is much to be said for such accounts, but not in the space of this chapter. I will have more to say about the question of whether evaluation can be captured in notions of *n*th-order desires in Chapter 7.

That said, there is nonetheless something right in the view that a full account of human actions must include desires; indeed, that the presence of
desire is in some sense a condition for its being the case that an agent has an
effective reason for action. We are that sort of organism. The question is,
what follows from such a concession? I want to explore the thesis that there
is some primitive desire or desire-connected state in the genealogy of what
moves us, even when we act for Kantian kinds of reasons. Such complex
desire-connected states are the normal product of human development;
they are also, I believe, the natural solution to the supposed Kantian problem with desire.

It is important to be clear about what I do and do not want to claim. My
acceptance of a "priority of desire" account is not nominal: it is not a case of
merely widening the range of things to be called "desire" to "whatever moves
us." In speaking of desire-connected states I mean affective, practical states
derived in some way from such primary desires as desires for nourishment,
erotic bonding, and so on. (It will matter, though not now, just what we
imagine the cast of original desires to be.) I want to accept *both* that there is
a difference between reason and desire *and* that even rational action depends
on desire. However, I also want to argue that a full explanation of what
moves us to action in a given instance need not appeal to primary desires.
Not only may there be no recognizable traces of these desires in our motives,
the content and object of what moves us may be "from reason."

Kant is often saddled with the view that all action based on desire is both
mechanistic in its structure and crudely pleasure- or satisfaction-seeking in
its end. As I argue elsewhere, this is not Kant's view.[16] As rational agents, we
take the presence of desires to be occasions (or grounds) for reasons to act.
That our action is to yield satisfaction (of desire) is not to mark the single
end of all action-on-desire but to say something about what desire is (we
have acted successfully when our desire is no longer unsatisfied; it is different with moral action). Since Kant's primary concern is to distinguish
autonomous from heteronomous willing, the fact about desire that he
most often attends to is that reasons that look to desires are ultimately derived from contingent facts alien to the rational will. He can ignore the fact

---

16. For more on this see Chapter 8, "Rethinking Kant's Hedonism," and Chapter 10, "The
Will and Its Objects." For a different way of sorting out these issues, see Andrews Reath, "Hedonism, Heteronomy, and Kant's Principle of Happiness," *Pacific Philosophical Quarterly* 70
(1989): 42–72.

that the relations between reason and desire in a person are quite complex. But if our interest is in developing a Kantian conception of character, we cannot.

Consider a possible Kantian thesis about the relation between reason and desire. What it means for us to be practically rational beings is that we are by nature disposed to have desires that develop and are modified in accordance with the requirements of practical reason. Normal human development is reason-responsive. This is not to say that we have an original desire to conform to rational principle. I think we could have no such original desire. Where it seems reasonable to expect such a desire is in a mature and moderately reflective person whose life has proceeded in a roughly normal—that is, noncatastrophic—way. We take it to be normal that a person come to recognize the value not only of acting according to reason but also of having rational desires; we expect the development of a general (or second-order) desire to conform to reason. There is neither inevitable completeness nor developmental necessity in this. One might come to value rationality in some areas of one's life and not in others, and to value some aspects of rationality, not others.

The claim that our development is originally reason-responsive, as opposed to reason-following, is a claim about what it is to be a rational-being-with-desires. It involves, among other things, the idea that we have a distinctive kind of mechanism for learning, one such that at least some of the information acquired in our earliest stages is archived in a way that is available to emerging cognitive function. The potential for rationality in us must be expressed in prerational structures of perception, recognition, memory, and the like. One would expect that such structured information contributes to the epigenetic causes of the emergence of higher cognitive function. We should then think of the defining features of rational agency—self-consciousness, judgment, rule-following—as later stages in a complex process of development. Other sorts of creatures with desires will have different learning and developmental mechanisms. Instinct in animals, we might suppose, will play a greater role, more tightly constraining the form of information acquired and the possible development of desires.

The *principles* of rationality are in this sense descriptive of our kind of activity and development; they are also normative (in a reflexive sense) for our success as the kind of being we are. Whether they are effective guides for our individual flourishing or well-being is a contingent and local matter, depending on circumstances (personal, physical, and social) and, of course, good fortune. They are nonetheless the tools we possess; no other principles can be systematically normative for us.[17]

What I am trying to do here should be plain. I want to describe—in a lightly speculative way—a natural fact about us as rational beings that is resonant with both a Kantian view of practical reason and an Aristotelian view of the nonrational part of the soul that "shares in reason." I would continue in an Aristotelian vein this way: Obedience to reason is possible for some desires because they *can* develop in certain reason-related ways, though they need not do so. That is why a child needs guidance based in the reason of others: when desires are to be satisfied and when frustration is tolerable; when there is a range of substitution for objects of desires and for which desires this is so; and so on. Such instruction is possible because the system of desires already has a certain structure—one that places (some) desires on a developmental track that leaves them open to transformation through the effects of training and new knowledge carried on the threads of intimacy and early bonding.[18]

Now some will surely think that such a claim of resonance for a naturalistic account of reason with the Kantian project is impossible to support—perhaps even showing the Kantian project's fatal weakness. In this mood, if there is any concession to a story of moral development, it is of the emergence of a kind of rational musculature, a special power capable of providing sufficient motivation for morally correct action even in the face of recalcitrant desires. Moral learning is a matter of refinement of judgment: the cognitive capacity to discern morally salient features of one's circumstances and to select relevant action. What happens in the system of desires is of no deep moment: the moral life will be easy if desires are cooperative, hard if they are not. Indeed, nothing that could happen in the system of desires could be deeply relevant to the moral project since the fundamental Kantian moral fact is, after all, that the ground of obligation in us cannot involve desires. However, the inference drawn from this foundational claim to the developmental conclusion—to the practice of moral judgment and action—is suspect.

The question comes to this: Must it follow from the fact that the founda-

17. The fact that an inspired guess hits the target careful calculation misses gives no reason to abandon calculation for guessing. Though one of the attractions of this modified rationalist story is that it can account for real inspiration—i.e., that it is not just a matter of lucky guesses.

18. This partly explains why, although rationality is a defining characteristic of individuals, its expression is social.

tion of morality—the determining ground of the will—can only be in pure practical reason, that (1) the motive of the morally worthy agent must be extra-material (a miracle every time), or that (2), the desirable purity of the motive of duty is in its complete separation from the empirical life of the human agent? I think that we can hold with Kant that the application of the moral law (to us or to any rational being) cannot be empirical, in the sense that the condition of its claim to be the law of the will of any rational being must be "completely a priori and independent of any sensible data,"[19] only if we interpret this to be a claim about authority, not efficacy. That is, the moral law—morality—applies to us, is legitimately regulative of our willings, without regard to the state of our desires or inclinations. This is the condition that secures universal validity. But our motivating under-standing of the moral law, what I would call our effective moral motive, need not be pure in that way.[20] What it must involve essentially is the ac-knowledgment of the normative order of incentives.[21]

In the main moral texts, Kant is not often concerned with the fact or the way morally developed or rationalized desire becomes part of the practical provisions of the mature moral agent. But even here we should be wary of exaggeration. Kant has a lot to say about moral education, and when he does attend to practical matters, he shows far greater moral sensitivity than the usual quoted remarks suggest.[22] Probably the most important argument to mark on this issue is, somewhat paradoxically, the discussion of moral

---

19. Immanuel Kant, *Critique of Practical Reason* (hereafter abbreviated *KpV*) (1788), in *Practical Philosophy*, trans. and ed. Mary J. Gregor (Cambridge: Cambridge University Press, 1996) 5:91.

20. In most cases, the context of remarks about the purity of the moral motive is the dan-ger of confusing motive and ground in moral theorizing: the requirement of purity keeps us focused on the nature and scope of moral obligation, avoiding the "laxity, or even mean cast of mind, which seeks its principle among empirical motives and laws." Immanuel Kant, *Groundwork of the Metaphysics of Morals* (hereafter abbreviated *G*) (1785), in *Practical Phi-losophy*, trans. and ed. Mary J. Gregor (Cambridge: Cambridge University Press, 1996), 4:426.

21. See Immanuel Kant, *Religion within the Boundaries of Mere Reason* (1793), in *Religion and Rational Theology*, trans. and ed. George di Giovanni and Allen W. Wood (Cambridge: Cambridge University Press, 1996), 6:26–36.

22. A good example of this is his remarks on the need to exercise and train the natural mo-tive of sympathy by seeking out the environments (sickrooms and debtors prisons) where our feelings will be aroused and challenged. Immanuel Kant, *The Metaphysics of Morals* (1797), in *Practical Philosophy*, trans. and ed. Mary J. Gregor (Cambridge: Cambridge University Press, 1996), 6:457.

incentives in the *Critique of Practical Reason* (5:71–82).[23] Here is Kant in his most puritanical-sounding voice, describing the moral law as thwarting inclination, striking down self-conceit (self-love taken "arrogantly" as a first principle of action). The moral law brings about a humbling of the material self through the emergence of feelings of respect for the law: in acknowledging morality's supreme authority one at the same time accepts the lesser status of the natural desire for happiness (in the condition he calls "rational self-love"). Overall, this double action leads to feelings of sublimity directed at the self. What I wish to note is that underneath the high rhetoric is a view of the desires, and of the claims made on behalf of the faculty of desire, as responsive to, in a certain sense resonant with, the moral law. There is no a priori necessity that the effect of striking down desire (or our pretensions on its behalf) should be an elevated feeling—one that draws us to morality—rather than merely pain and resistance. But we do not seem to be organized the latter way. What we desire, what we understand to be the value of our desiring, is affected by the normative claims in the situation in which we find ourselves. This is a fact about our system of desires itself: it can be humbled.[24] It is also a fact about us as rational beings with a system of desires that this is not the end of the story.

The general Kantian picture is that both theoretical and practical reason provide form for material that is given from external sources (external to reason). So far as we accept the authority of the rules of logic as the correct form of thought regardless of our feelings, we thereby acknowledge our capacity to accept a logical conclusion that we have no interest in, or even have every interest in denying. *Modus ponens* is, free association is not, an authoritative form for discursive thought. The moral law offers a comparable compelling form to our practical maxims of action.[25] Why we are motiva-

---

23. For a more extended discussion of the issues raised here, see Barbara Herman, "Transforming Incentives," in Åsa Carlson, ed., *Philosophical Aspects of the Emotions* (Stockholm: Thales, 2005).

24. One might think: perhaps we respond this way to systematic thwarting because of a tendency to identify with the "oppressor" (the Patty Hearst syndrome). I'm not sure this would pose a problem. It is not part of my argument that reason-responsiveness is part of the telos of desires. But also, one might think that the Patty Hearst syndrome was itself a sign of a failure or incompleteness of development, much in the way we think that certain rigidities about planning can signal a developmental stall on the way to a capacity for delayed gratification.

25. Consider the Kantian argument to mutual aid. The moral law requires that we recognize the needs of others as making claims on our resources. One could think of this as the imposition of a new end, one added by reason (alone) to the ends we already have. But the

tionally responsive to either formal constraint is not a simple matter: in both cases the answer involves some kind of appeal to conditions for our inhabiting an ordered world.[26]

III

The framework for adding an account of moral development to Kant's ethics must take as fundamental the idea of the moral law as the principle of autonomy of the will. The effect of the moral law as a principle of autonomy is to preclude all inclinations from having a *direct* determining influence on the will.[27] This is what has seemed to force desire to the side where moral action is concerned. But if we are no longer restricted to a rigid oppositional model—if the system of desires is itself reason-responsive—the content of desires need not remain unaffected by our developing moral and rational capacities, and the exclusion of all desire from moral action will not follow so easily.

This moves the discussion beyond the old issue of the overdetermination of motives. We are not now limited to the claim that the presence of desire may be benign, so long as the incentive that is the agent's motive is respect for the moral law. It is open to explore the idea that the strict separation of desire from the reason-connected motive of duty may not be necessary, or even appropriate, given the possibility of deep connection between reason and a human being's developing system of desire. Just how desire can change and what role it may play in moral action consistent with the autonomy of the will are the questions that need to be taken up next.

In thinking about the role of desire, given developmental changes in the system of desire, what is to be rejected—really superseded—is the simple

---

nature of the argument suggests we instead view the obligatory end as the resultant of a formal constraint on the ends we naturally adopt: according to the Moral Law it follows from acknowledging my own status as a dependent being with needs that I must recognize the claim-supporting status of the needs of others. The latter view is the key to the structure of character in Kantian ethics.

26. "For, how a law can be of itself and immediately a determining ground of the will (though this is what is essential in all morality) is for human reason an insoluble problem and identical with that of how a free will is possible. What we shall have to show a priori is, therefore, not the ground from which the moral law in itself supplies an incentive but rather what it effects (or, to put it better, must effect) in the mind insofar as it is an incentive." *KpV* 5:72.

27. *KpV* 5:71.

version of the desire-belief model of action. I am thirsty; I see that there is fresh water in that glass; putting the desire and belief together, I drink the water. It is not that this can't happen. It can. The problem arises when such examples are used to represent the building blocks of complex, rational action. If we are to understand the way rationality exhibits itself in action and judgment, we should begin from the other end: from the complex practical judgments of the mature agent. It will be from getting it right about them that we can intelligibly ask, for example, how an inclination such as thirst can both move someone to act and not influence her will directly when she drinks. When we start with the inclination as the primitive element, the most reasonable account of mature action is unavailable.

"Thirst" seems a likely candidate for a possible primitive feature of the system of desires. It certainly has the role of being last in an explanatory chain of reasons: we do not need to appeal to anything else for a complete explanation of drinking. But that fact, and it is a fact, is misleading. That something can be last in an explanatory chain does not show that it is a primitive element in the system of desires. Consider: In what sense can a neonate have thirst or, stranger still, desire for drink? Certainly there is the physiological condition of fluid deficit, and no doubt a mechanism to trigger sucking (the source of that interesting original confusion of nourishment and intimacy). But this state—hardly distinct in its original form from hunger—is not the thirst that plays a role in explaining purposive drinking action. It lies in its origins; it is part of the natural history of thirst. This is because the physiological condition is not yet an intentional state of the organism: it has no object. There is a condition of agitation; there are mechanical responses. In the natural environment for neonates, nursing or feeding reduces the agitation and gives pleasure. Thirst—a desire for *drink*—can only emerge much later.[28]

Rather than suppose a picture of a set of primal or primitive desires whose objects are in some sense present from the outset and then refined as knowledge and experience are acquired, it seems truer both to our beginnings and to the outcome in the normal agent to work with a model that starts with what we might call "original orectic states" that are developmentally open to the kind of cognitive and volitional capacities our kind of agent has. (It will be no accident that "this feeling" comes to be associated

---

28. I am not just claiming that development is required for there to be the concept of drink and so *desire for* drink. It seems unlikely that thirst, as a distinct felt need, is primitive either.

with "that object"—drink.) Now the fact that most or all of our desires have a history (and to some extent a natural history) does not imply that in explanations of action the most complete explanation must look to the originating orectic state. We would surely lose the sense of a reason for action if we replaced an explanation given in terms of a desire for an orderly workplace with the primal need to forge boundaries between self and other, even if it were true that the latter belonged to the essential history of the former.

Sometimes, of course, the fact that desires have a history does indicate an explanatorily relevant geology of desire. We commonly explain irrational behavior, urges, and cravings by appeal to something primitive or developmentally undigested, as when the source of addictions is attributed to residual infantile needs, or when self-defeating patterns of behavior call for an investigation into the desire behind a desire (as when the desire for order interferes with work that needs to be done).

The fact that desires have a history (and a natural history), combined with the fact that in human development they are reason-responsive, alters the way we should think about deliberation and judgment. In the mature agent, objects of judgment (puzzles about what to do, questions about what is right) will present themselves already laden with deliberative and evaluative content. We get it wrong about children if we suppose their harmful demands must rest on some error concerning the relative importance of, say, health and pleasure. Manipulative temper tantrums aside, the frenzied intensity of a young child's demands, the sense of life on the line, is better understood as the product of unmediated desire—desire whose importance is still a direct function of its momentary strength. It is for this reason that small children cannot be rational. They may or may not lack knowledge; their wills are certainly not weak. What is missing, or only present to a very limited degree, is the co-development of their desires and rational understanding.

By contrast, the accurate representation of judgment and deliberation in the normal rational adult requires a model that exhibits the enmeshed development of the system of desires and the capacity for effective practical rationality. The transformation of orectic states into desires with objects takes place in an environment regulated by a wide range of evaluative concepts. The desire for drink becomes a desire for safe and pleasant (not dangerous or unpleasant) drink, and also a desire for an available (not otherwise possessed) drink. The desire itself becomes socialized.

This point may seem less strange if we consider weightier objects of desire such as children or expensive consumer goods. My desire for a new computer or car does not (because it ought not) range over those already owned by others; a desire to have a child does not include a desire for anyone else's child. Something has gone tragically wrong when it is otherwise. I think it is reasonable to say that what has gone wrong is something about the desire itself—how it has, or has failed to, develop.

There are, of course, other ways of representing the phenomena. One might tell a story of competing desires, one for drink, another for not taking what belongs to someone else, and of rational development looking toward the regulative superiority of the second, either through its increased strength or through the emergence of a second-order desire that selects respect for property as the desire whose satisfaction is a condition for satisfying other desires. What seems wrong here is not that this fails to describe something that could happen, but the implicit idea that the desires themselves, in the normal cases, remain unaffected by the regulative space in which they live or, if affected, more beaten down than transformed.[29]

What would a more adequate account be like? It should be able to capture the complexities of desires that emerge at the intersection of distinct paths of orectic development and be sensitive to the ways that primitive orectic residues remain and become part of the urgency for or insistence behind a developed desire. A model in which desires form a system independent of regulative principle, or one in which desires are seen as descending from each other primarily via instrumental pathways, cannot readily cope with what is so often in our experience and our explanations an elaborate architecture of desire. Further, insofar as we are rational beings, we come to have certain kinds of desires and interests because the developmental path from primitive orectic states to complex desires is partly structured by the principles of practical rationality. The fact that we are capable of learning and eventually capable of conscious and principled self-regulation should be represented as part of the environment in which desires emerge.[30]

29. The abnormal cases are important. There are tragic cases where despair at childlessness has led to desperate actions. And it matters whether we characterize these desires as unmediated or unprincipled, or just so intense that they swamp the second-order commitment to moral constraint. The caution I urge is that we not use the explanation that seems to make best sense of moral failure as the model for normal action. The relation may not be so simple: failures of some kinds may indicate that development has not been normal, either in general or with respect to some subset of desires.

30. It is possible to describe much of this in terms of the neural complexities of brain function: the way patterns are laid down in the system of thalamus and cortex. Neurobiology, or a certain strain of it, seems to be the current legatee of transcendental idealism.

The deliberative or evaluative location of a desire will therefore not always be external to it. Unlike the desire to go to sleep after one has had a bad night—a desire that plays against the deliberative current of the day, needing to be ignored, resisted, dosed with coffee—other, more derived desires carry their relative value with them. My desire to go to the movies or to drink wine with good food does not need to be constrained when I set to work in the morning. These desires are in some sense present then, for they enter in planning for the rest of the day. But their content is complex and expressive of various regulative norms that I accept: somewhat stodgy norms of using the mornings to get work done, of commitment to the priority of familial and professional obligations, and so on. Because these norms have a certain structural priority in my life, the value that my desires express is different from what it was when I was an *n*th-year graduate student or hanging out in Paris (the *value* is different, the object may be the same). There is no necessity or fixity in this; I can decide to go to an 11 A.M. movie tomorrow. My point is rather that we will likely misdescribe the desire if we insist on an evaluatively neutral "desire to go to the movies," constrained today, released into action tomorrow. Again, it could be that way; it is possible that the pressure to go to the movies is always there—it is what I would almost always rather do and so I have to keep my desire in check in order to go about my business. That possibility does not generalize, however. Because the neutral description ignores the array of ways one may have a desire for an object or activity, it masks the way derived desires can function in the deliberation and choices of mature rational agents.

The desires of a mature human agent normally contain, in addition to a conception of an object, a conception of the object's value—for itself, as determined by its fit with other things valued, and as its satisfaction, in general as well as in a given case, comports with the principles of practical reason. We might say that desires so conceived have been brought within the scope of reason, or that the desires themselves have been rationalized, or, to the extent that an agent's system of desires has evolved in a reason-responsive way, that she has, at least in these respects, the character of a rational agent. Of course the normal agent does not, indeed cannot, have a wholly rational character: not all of our desires are reason-responsive (or wholly so), nor does the natural history of human desire, even if reason-responsive, follow a rational plan.[31]

---

31. If Kant saw order even here, it was in the potential for the species as a whole.

IV

Suppose we accept such a developmental account of desires—that they do develop, and that the system of desires is reason-responsive. Its advantage to Kantian moral theory should be obvious. It plainly offers a way to mitigate the hostility between reason and desire, something attractive in itself. It is also, and equally plainly, necessary if Kantian theory is to support any reasonable account of moral virtue, insofar as it invites a rethinking of the relations of reason and desire in the structure of moral motivation.

On the standard Kantian account, the rational agent acts for ends, not directly from desires—neither as impulsions or urgings nor as the necessary independent condition of the attractiveness of ends. The presence of a desire provides an occasion for action, an incentive. There are other incentives. The question for a rational agent is whether acting in response to a given incentive is good (or justified). As she judges that it is, she has a reason, other things being equal, to adopt the relevant end (and so have a maxim), and then to act.[32] I would add: An incentive is available for purposes of *deliberation* as and to the extent that acting for its sake is judged to be in some sense good. It is only then, and in that sense, to be regarded as a possible "motive." Thus the judgment that "acting to satisfy this desire is good" is part of a motive for action, making the connection between motive, end, and action more than a matter of causal adequacy. That is why, for a rational agent, competing incentives need not always present the threat of competing motives.

I use the device of a "deliberative field" to represent the space in which an agent's rational deliberation takes place.[33] It is constructed by the principles and commitments that express her conception of value. Desires and other incentives are present for purposes of deliberation only as they can be located in the field. To say that such incentives are then possible motives is to say that part of what being a rational agent involves is having the motivational capacity to take desires *as valued* as reasons for action. More complex structures of value generate complex motives, setting further conditions on the satisfaction of desires.

32. In this account, freedom and the capacity for practical rationality are one.

33. The idea is introduced in "Obligation and Performance," and developed further in "Agency, Attachment and Difference," in Barbara Herman, *The Practice of Moral Judgment* (Cambridge, Mass.: Harvard University Press, 1993).

An incentive is present in the deliberative field in what we might call a normalized or rationalized form—as a possible motive—to the extent that its representation and affective significance have been transformed from that of an impulse or an intentional disposition into a rational value. Some incentives that "present" to the deliberative field can already be, to some extent, rational—that is, their development can have been partially shaped by rational principle. Others come as they are, as it were, gaining entry with the condition added that their satisfaction be dependent on the nonviolation of rational principle. Thus, from the moral point of view, many things can happen to an incentive. An incentive can be only partially transformed; an agent can have internalized some but not all of the constraints of the deliberative field and, even, some of them in the wrong way.

Consider some ways the motivation to be moral can be awry. The prudent criminal, as well as the timidly obedient agent (who adheres to morality out of fear of the consequences of doing otherwise), has motives that are partly responsive to moral constraints, though in the wrong way. For them, moral constraints function as externally imposed or passively encountered limits, rather like the misplaced stop sign in my neighborhood that gives me no reason to stop except for the fact that the local sheriff's deputies like to lurk nearby and give tickets (a cost I am not willing to risk). For other agents, morality may be experienced as a quasi-physical barrier, more like a taboo or a phobia than a reason—something that incentives cannot get past. In none of these cases is the agent's motive directly or correctly responsive to the moral features of her circumstances. This is not a matter of whether moral norms apply; it is the very different question of the evaluative content of the motives responsible for a rational agent's moral action.

Even where there is more appropriate motivational connection to morality, it may not be an all-or-nothing thing. Some features of morality may be separated off, as when a person is sensitive and motivationally responsive to actions and situations that introduce risk of physical harm to others, but indifferent to psychological risk and injury, or concerned about immediate injury but not about injustice. The possibility of a moral form of aspect blindness has posed special difficulties for Kantian theory. Failure to recognize the fact and salience of injustice is not just a mistake about what follows from the categorical imperative (CI), and it has not been clear what other resources Kantian theory has to provide a more satisfactory explanation or response. This is not the sort of issue that interested Kant, but it is one that ought to concern anyone interested in refurbishing Kantian theory for contemporary purposes. One of the advantages of making the story about motivation both natural and complex is that it gives room and sense to such possibilities. In particular, it allows for talk of moral defects of character impinging on moral judgment.

Earlier I spoke of the history and architecture of desire—shaped by, among other things, the principles of rationality to which the system of desire is developmentally responsive. More recently I have been talking about motives: incentives to action that gain standing in the deliberative field as they survive evaluation and/or transformation by the principles of practical reason. Developed desires and motives should not be confused. While an evolved desire can have internalized moral content—for example, where it is part of the concept of the object of desire that its pursuit not involve violation of moral restrictions—it lacks the *deliberative* content of a rational motive. That is, while it may be the case that because of good upbringing, one's material desires do not range over others people's possessions, one may still be, in acting for such a desire, acting on a maxim of satisfying one's strongest desire. It is only when one's maxim of desire-satisfaction contains the full deliberative framework (one will act for this evolved desire only as and because doing so conforms with prudential *and* moral principle) that one has a (fully) rational motive.

The formation of a motive—the way an incentive gains entry to the deliberative field—involves a process of judgment and evaluation. The pair of the incentive and the range of possible objects of action that match it (object or end) are judged to be good and are accepted as grounds for possible action because they are good. Since the principles of practical reason describe the domain of evaluation (the Good), the resulting motive draws content both from practical principles and from the original incentive. Such a motive may yield the same action one would have taken based on the original incentive (and, say, a principle of satisfying my strongest desire), but now the action is performed with and from a different and regulative conception of its value. There is a different maxim.

Here is the new claim. When and to the extent that agents have desires that have evolved in a reason-responsive way, the incentives themselves are open to further, more principled, rationalization. There is, on the one hand, a possible conceptual convergence between motives and developed incentives, and on the other, the practical possibility of the transformation of desire. The evolution of desire is in this way the condition for having a moral character that does not necessarily involve the segregation (or oppression) of one's affective life in general by one's commitment to morality.

But what has happened to the Kantian motive of duty? In all this talk of complexity, development, and the transformation of incentives, it seems to have been lost—its work done by other structures and motives. My thought is this. In an agent with a moral character, the motive of duty is *dispersed* in the motives that satisfy the constraints of the deliberative field. It need not be a separate motive that produces actions on its own, or a motive that must be added on to differently determine an already complete intention to act.[34] The idea, then, is that when we act "from duty," we can act on a maxim (a conception of our action) whose principle has the form of universal law, but that this conception need not be motivationally separate from the way we specifically conceive of the action and its desired end as a justified whole.

Neither the idea of a deliberative field nor this way of thinking about rational character belong in any special way to Kantian ethics. I believe that both are useful devices for representing the structure of our practical lives when one takes the fact that we are rational agents to be part of the developmental history of our desires and interests (however one fills out the norm or norms of rationality). They are especially appropriate devices for working with Kantian ethics because they exhibit the way principles of rationality can constitute a structure of value in a rational agent's motives. This structure is essential to understanding the connection between the CI as a principle of practical reason and the motive of duty as a possible motive of an empirically situated rational agent—that is, a person.

There are considerable practical advantages to a motive of duty understood in this way—as dispersed in the rational agent's motives for action. For example, if we think that practical conflict is a matter of an agent unable to satisfy competing incentives (desires or interests), the primary deliberative problem will be establishing terms of commensurability— finding bases of comparison for urgently felt personal needs, the present relevance of longer term goals, the current demands of greater and lesser moral requirements, and so on. There is no deep mystery about why so many philosophers who present the range of sources for practical inter-

---

34. Agents whose motives are fully normalized to the principles of the deliberative field act on maxims with moral content: they express the agent's autonomy. Agents whose maxims contain a principle of deference to desire (or any other incentive), make a mistake of valuation: they take themselves to be justified when they are not.

ests in this way tend toward some kind of utilitarian calculus (whether of consequences, preferences, or even connection to identity-defining ground projects).

The contra-utilitarian alternative that appeals to situationally specific judgment obscures more than it clarifies. It is no doubt true that I can know that in a particular circumstance it is better for me, more important, to spend time with long absent friends than to keep some trivial promise. And one may want to agree that no deeper or more encompassing knowledge is required. But from this it is said to follow that there is no principle that determines when friendship trumps obligations. One comes to have situated knowledge, acquired through experience, of when it is appropriate to do one sort of thing and when another, and that's the end of the matter.

I think it is misleading, however, to represent such judgments as relying on no deeper content. For if one is wrong, as one surely may be, about the relative value of the two options, an explanation belongs to the way one learns from mistakes. It is not like correcting for the wind when one tries to hit a target: you sight a bit to the right, and then a bit more if your first judgment was wrong, and then a bit to the left if you overcorrect. But where you have mistaken the relative importance of obligation and interest, the mistake may not be one of location on some map of ordered pairs. There is something amiss in the picture one would have: that in these circumstances, one had valued friendship too much and the obligation too little, but without any view that there was some value (or principle) that made sense of the difference between correct and mistaken judgment.

The idea of the motive of duty as dispersed—as (ideally) a component of the motive in all maxims of action—changes the look of moral conflict. When the connection between incentive and action is mediated by rational motives, deliberation depends neither on a situation-specific "read" nor on importing a standard that is alien to the values already expressed in an agent's maxim. If I cannot attend to a friend because of the demands of some prior obligation, I need not view myself as subordinating friendship to morality, or valuing friendship less, or differently. The way morality can make demands is part of the structure of mature friendship; it is why we have reason to believe a true friend will understand.

It will be helpful to consider, in this light, what happens to self-interest. The Kantian brief against self-interest is not that it is inherently contrary to morality; it need not be. The problem lies in its tendency to be presumptive. We are inclined to give special weight to our advantage; we implicitly accept a principle of self-interest as one of the determining grounds of our will. On the standard Kantian account, morality constrains self-interest, offering (through the motive of duty) a kind of counterweight in the contest of reasons. However, if the motive of duty is not merely something that enters into a balance of reasons, but is instead part of the structure of the agent's reasons in general, not only will the account of moral reasons look different, so does the account of self-interest. The fully rational *motive* of self-interest does not carry a presumption of independent authority in the agent's deliberative field. It is not that the moral agent ignores her interests or her advantage. Rather, her conception of self-interest has developed, been shaped or altered, in a reason-responsive way. That is why (some) interests of a self can rebut a moral presumption: it may be permissible to break a trivial promise for matters of great personal importance, but only if the agent's concerns have and are conceived of as having moral standing (Kant would say they must express different grounds of obligation). It is in this sense that the agent's self-interest is not what it was or would have been outside the deliberative field.[35]

As it should, character shapes moral judgment. When I don't pocket the funds entrusted to me at a PTA meeting, it is not that I don't know the advantage in having some extra money, I simply do not regard this money *as available.* This is not because honesty involves a habit of overlooking advantage, or because a commitment to morality sets up a barrier such that the voice of advantage cannot be heard. In these circumstances there is no advantage to be had, no appeal to interests that support a reason. This is what is supposed to follow from having a moral character—here, one in which the moral law belongs to the framework within which desires and interests develop and gain access to the deliberative field.

---

35. Kantian grounds of obligation are deliberative principles that set normative presumptions about reasons for action. For example, the categorical imperative's rejection of deceitful maxims (in the standard *Groundwork* example, 4:422) sets a deliberative presumption against deceit for reasons of personal advantage. Likewise, the rejection of a maxim of nonbeneficence establishes that one cannot reject the claim of "true needs" of others on grounds of lack of concern or interference with one's projects. It does not follow that one may never not help or deceive. But a maxim of deceit or not-aiding can rebut a deliberative presumption only if its justificatory basis is something other than self-interest. A fuller account of this way of interpreting Kantian principles of deliberation can be found in "Moral Deliberation and the Derivation of Duties," in Herman, *The Practice of Moral Judgment*, chap. 7.

At the outset of this chapter I set the task of describing a model of Kant-ian moral judgment and action that drew on a conception of character that included nonmoral desires. The developmental account I have sketched— from incentives to rational motives—shows a way to do this that I believe is consistent, on the one hand, with the natural history of desires and, on the other, with the Kantian strictures about moral motivation. I have accepted as noncontroversial that a human agent can be "moved" to action only by reasons that are connected, in some way, with her desires. However, I have suggested that we complicate the desire story two ways. First, through an appeal to the idea of a natural history or "geology" of desires: what we take to be desires are already highly evolved intentional dispositions, drawing on various original sources for their force, and extensive learning for their con-tent and array of possible objects. Second is the idea that as rational beings, it is part of our nature that the evolution of our desires will be, to varying degrees, reason-responsive. These architectural or structural features of hu-man development are sufficient to accommodate a Kantian picture of moral judgment and action, and to provide natural space for the motive of duty.

V

It may seem natural at this point to ask whether the fact that we *can* make room for character in a naturalized Kantian moral psychology provides any advantage, beyond the rapprochement between the Aristotelian and Kant-ian projects. At the outset of this chapter I suggested that one useful thing that comes from the distinctively Kantian elements is the right kind of room for moral perplexity. In this last section, I will be able to do little more than introduce the issue and offer some reasons for the claim of advantage. It is a large topic that deserves more extensive discussion.

The questions that tend to be central to moral philosophy often reflect concerns that are external to normative ethics. Questions about the relation between reason and motives (the domain of internalism) have made the paradigm case of moral action seem to be one where an agent recognizes that some action is morally significant (obligatory, forbidden, desirable) so that what remains problematic is the connection to motivation. And puzzles about the nature of the necessity that obligation purportedly carries make conflict of duties the canonical example of moral uncertainty.

What gets lost in the strategic maneuvering at the level of theory is the hard work of moral deliberation that is central to a moral life: the engagement with multiple moral considerations present in an agent's current or anticipated circumstances of action. The range of moral perplexity is much greater than the central examples moral theory works with suggest, and need not typically involve the agent in finding ways of balancing or weighing competing moral considerations. It may be plain, for example, that a helping action is called for, but problematic how one is to help in a way that preserves the recipient's dignity. A concern to honor standards of equal treatment may appear compromised by evidence that girls perform better in sex-segregated school environments. When a group of California parents objected to the inclusion of a passage from an Alice Walker short story on a statewide exam on the grounds that it is "anti-religious," an issue was raised whose moral complexity is not adequately captured in terms of a conflict between freedom of speech and discrimination against local religious values.[36] Because we live in complex and intersecting communities that endorse different standards of injury and offense, we require not only a way of determining when, say, toleration is appropriate, but we also need ways of engaging substantively with distinct local values that threaten or compete with our own. Some local values that can be threatened by public actions should be protected (penalizing students for religious observances can impose an unjustified cost), while others should not (banning religious benedictions at public school graduations protects a more important range of interests).

Of course not all interesting examples of moral perplexity involve public institutions or competing local values in a liberal, pluralistic state. There are hard adjustments of autonomy and legitimate interference (just ask any adolescent); all sorts of problems that follow from the decision to break a promise (how responsible one is for subsequent effects; issues for establishing future reliance and credibility in different social and personal contexts). The chief advantage of focusing on the social cases is the clarity there of the

36. Jean Merl, "State Yanks Academic Test Question, Sparks Outcry," *Los Angeles Times,* February 26, 1994. Students were asked to write their feelings about the following passage from Alice Walker's story "Roselily": "She cannot always be a bride and a virgin, wearing robes and veil. Even now her body itches to be free of satin and voile. . . . She wonders what it will be like. Not to have to go to a job. Not to work in a sewing plant. . . . Her place will be in the home, he has said, repeatedly, promising her rest she has prayed for. But now she wonders. When she has rested, what will she do? They will make babies—she thinks practically about her fine brown body, his strong black one. They will be inevitable. Her hands will be full. Full of what? Babies. She is not comforted."

range of moral issues a responsible agent may confront. However well one is brought up, however complete the internalization of a regulative moral motive, what one will have to know, or how one may have to rethink one's own values, cannot be predicted. There is thus reason internal to the moral phenomena to want a characterization of moral life that supports a certain degree of flexibility in both judgment and motivation.

This seems to me to be a reasonable point of concern for the revival of an Aristotelian conception of character as the basis for moral judgment and motivation. Much moral work can be done by a sensitivity that is both world-regarding and motivationally secure. Agents are able to see what is to be done through a fine appreciation or reading of what is morally salient in their circumstances. The sensitivity that is the judgment side of character is the product of upbringing, training, practice, and some amount of reflection. And since it is also a function or expression of a motivational state, there is, in a virtuous agent, no separate question of motivation, given a judgment of what to do. What raises a question about the flexibility of this arrangement of judgment and motivation is the apparent absence at the limit of a way (for the agent) to criticize the sensitivity itself—for it to take itself as the object of its own critical regard.

The flexibility I find in the revised Kantian theory comes from the distinctness in kind between motives, on the one hand, and interests and desires, on the other. The process of normalization to the deliberative field transforms interests and desires into motives that are internally responsive to the deliberative requirements of rational principle. It yields a different conception of how having a moral character affects judgment. When formal regulative norms become internal to the agent's conception of her ends, her sense of what morality demands can more readily include an acknowledgment that ways of life taken for granted, that are part of her developed desires and interests, may turn out to depend on practices or traditions that are not acceptable. The priority of principle secures this.

Let me offer a slightly more detailed example of the kind of thing I have in mind. Many elite academic institutions represent their hiring practices as exemplary in their openness to quality, regardless of gender, race, and so on. But if the world in which they operate is racially stratified, and persons of color do not have equal access to the same resources as others do, then a deeper fairness may be required that might not only be uncomfortable, but institutionally or personally transformative. Suppose we came to think that our profession was racially unbalanced. And suppose further that graduate admissions and hiring processes, though procedurally fair, do not turn up many qualified candidates of color. One response might be sincere regret—that having done what we ought, the results were so meager. But were our commitment open to a deeper fairness, then we might wonder whether institutions have a responsibility to go beyond procedural fairness. There are many things they could do. They could, for example, have departments develop standing relations with their peers at historically black colleges, or other racially isolated institutions, in order to learn how to better evaluate students from institutions whose faculty are (in present circumstances) unfamiliar; they might possibly provide training opportunities, spend resources on visiting scholar and exchange programs, and so on. But more than appreciation of the need for new means may be involved here. As one comes to see the deeper difficulties in devising fair procedures, one's understanding of what the value of fairness amounts to changes, perhaps making one for a time less confident in one's immediate judgments. To the extent that one has a developed moral character, one ought to be prepared for this—for the fact that accepting instrumental changes can alter familiar terrain of action, and even one's sense of the value of what one takes to be right.

The resources available to a person of good moral character on the Kantian model seem to me well-suited for such eventualities since the motives and interests that shape her character are internally connected to deliberative procedures and outcomes. Thus changed, understanding is possible independent of one's best sensitivity, and yet it can still generate practical acceptance. Of course, that's in the ideal case. As with any complex motive that arises through psychologically complex processes, the elements of an effective moral motive may not be wholly separated from their structurally more primitive bases, or fully reason-responsive. But what we do have, even in the face of affective failure, are terms of moral criticism whose authority of application is secured.

Now I have no argument to show that an Aristotelian ethics of character cannot develop comparable resources.[37] Indeed, I have a suggestion for the

37. One might, for example, draw on the aesthetic analogy that has been used to explain part of what is involved in the link between so-called noncognitive dispositions and moral knowledge. If moral character is at all like either aesthetic enjoyment or artistic activity, there are various stories about how standing norms of excellence or beauty change. Kant, for example, thinks that art requires norms and standards for enjoyment, but that artistic genius is the capacity to create convincing examples of new standards. Perhaps the true moral exemplar has such a kind of genius.

way it might do this. If the notion of character it deploys explains the way we register morally salient facts, we might think of the problem an ethics of character needs to address as the problem of *new* saliences: how to see that the moral facts have changed. Where the moral world is unpredictable, the moral agent needs to be something of a cosmopolitan explorer. Not everything she encounters will be of equal value; not every value she brings with her will survive in its original form. The openness to conceptual change that comes from a commitment to the (now much maligned) Enlightenment value of Reason seems to be useful equipment to bring along.

Of course, the resourcefulness of non-Kantian character theorists is not really the issue. There is a more important methodological lesson to be drawn. The pressures on Kantian moral theory arising from the challenges of the virtue theorists have been entirely salutary. We should expect a reciprocal effect. A theoretical position arises out of the need to answer a challenge, and in so proceeding, will typically ignore issues that have other sources. The Kantian theorist needs to make room for character, but without abandoning the primacy of rational principle. The Aristotelian theorist has to find a way to move beyond the virtuous agent's repertoire of rich evaluative concepts to make room for a flexibility of judgment answerable to a standard of correctness, but not one that is external to the agent's outlook.

— 2 —

Pluralism and the Community of
Moral Judgment

It is now widely acknowledged that social pluralism—the presence in a society of distinct traditions and ways of life—vastly complicates the project of liberal political thought.[1] The permanent presence of different and often competing systems of value challenges the ideal of civic culture on which liberal principle depends. Conceptions of equal citizenship or of universal human rights can be seen to have protected deep-reaching structures of inequality and domination that are damaging to women and other subordinate groups. The complementary separation of public and private intended to secure a univocal sphere of civic culture paid insufficient attention to the fact that the values governing people's daily lives are not ones they are willing to cabin off from decisions that affect the culture in which their lives take place. It was certainly a vain hope that the effects of continuing religious division would spend themselves in a private sphere of worship—a fact we see played out in the present struggle over gay rights and abortion. About the only thing one can confidently say is that there is no easy bridge between the need to secure uniform principles of reasonable public agreement and the social consequences of deep pluralism.

The hard questions that come with the acknowledgment of the fact of social pluralism are not restricted to liberal political theory. If the elements of pluralism are deep, if persons of different ethnic and religious commit-

---

1. In his later work, John Rawls talks about "the permanent fact of pluralism." He does not have in mind social and ethnic diversity as such, but rather the probable fact that philosophical argument will not demonstrate the truth of any single comprehensive conception of the good. That is why he thinks that the strongest available justification of principles of justice is found in an "overlapping consensus." The pluralism of views he has in mind coexists with deep social homogeneity. In this essay, the pluralism at issue is social, ethnic, and racial diversity in the familiar sense.

ments, different races, men and women, all bring different structures of value to bear on the problems of their lives and shared institutions, then this should affect our understanding of the norms and conditions of morality as well.

In much moral philosophy, however, the significance of social pluralism is seen in its potential for introducing ultimate moral disagreement: a challenge to morality's claim to objectivity. I believe that this characteristic response is mistaken in its view of the nature of the moral challenge deep pluralism poses. To explore this claim, I want to examine the much less attended-to and prior question of moral judgment: the practical task of engagement with actions and practices embedded in distinct or opposing systems of value. There are very good reasons to begin here: an impoverished account of moral judgment is not only inadequate to the moral complexity of ordinary life, it also impedes our understanding of the theoretical issues pluralism introduces. One of the things I will try to show is that a primary route to the standard epistemological worry depends on a certain obliviousness to what an adequate account of moral judgment involves.

I

In moral theory influenced by classical liberal values, toleration is sometimes offered as a reasonable strategy of response to a wide range of moral disagreements in circumstances of pluralism. Its value is defended as both pragmatic and instrumental: it does not require the resolution of all moral disagreements, and it enables other liberal values such as autonomy, pursuit of truth, and privacy. It also supports an argument for a sphere of legal and social noninterference that, apart from contested issues of harm, requires formal neutrality (a public suspension of moral judgment). But toleration is not a morally or politically neutral response to pluralism, insofar as it permits continued private moral hostility toward the values and activities that are the objects of toleration. If, for example, we are to be tolerant of diversity in private consensual sexual conduct, our tolerance is compatible with private disdain for or abhorrence of some of the tolerated activity. This can have (and has had) profoundly negative consequences for recognizing legitimate political claims for equality and civil rights. Moreover, widespread disdain for certain sexual preferences can create a moral culture of oppression.[2] The dynamic of toleration and oppression, while hardly in-

2. There is in this a reason to be cautious about the move from moral relativism to a social-

evitable, is, I believe, sustained by the morally minimal and instrumental nature of liberal toleration.[3]

It will be useful in this regard to mark two general features of liberal toleration. First, the object of toleration has negative value to the tolerator: one tolerates what one dislikes or disapproves of. What I tolerate, I need not mind—indeed I might want—that it cease to be. Second, toleration is not in itself chosen as a good; one comes to it as the result of balancing competing considerations. One accedes to the continued existence of something one objects to either because its continued existence contributes to something else one values, or because the costs of interfering with it are too high. Someone who exemplifies the virtue of toleration thus need not approve of, be interested in, or be willing to have much to do with the objects of her toleration. It is a laissez-faire virtue. If I must tolerate the public speech of minority groups because suppression of speech is politically dangerous over the long run, I do not have to listen. If we may not prevent groups with special histories and traditions from continuing objectionable practices, we do not have to live with them among us. (Though we may not be able to pass restrictive zoning, we can move.)

It is a condition of liberal toleration that the objected-to differences (in ways of life, activities) not be harmful, or not harmful to interests that must be protected. But whether a practice or set of values is harmful has to be to some extent an open question in circumstances of pluralism. An action may be benign in one social context and not in another; the harmfulness of an action may arise from its contingent and local support of objectionable values. A generalizable claim of "no harm" requires that we can show that an action or practice cannot harm regardless of social context. Where circumstances of pluralism obtain, then, to investigate any claim about harm we must not only be able to locate the fit of the questioned action or practice in its own sphere of value, we must be able to judge whether the action or practice contributes to a system of value that is itself morally possible—that is, one that does not generate impermissible actions or support practices inconsistent with persons' moral standing. Determinations of harm can

contractarian resolution of disagreement. This accepts too easily the need for a political solution to a moral problem. (Gilbert Harman is tempted this way; see "Moral Relativism Defended," *Philosophical Review* 84 [1975]: 3–22.)

3. That oppression might follow on toleration may also reflect a power asymmetry. The weak are not normally in a position to tolerate the strong. Nietzsche's *Genealogy of Morals* provides a delicate exploration of the complex strategies and attitudes involved in reversing this.

therefore require the possibility of context-sensitive, cross-group moral judgment. Of course it is not enough to show that an action or practice harms to justify interference with it. The harm involved must be grave or impermissible or one that persons have a right not to receive. Such determinations also require a high level of contextually sensitive engagement with the object of judgment.

The demand for context-sensitive judgment leads to an awkward impasse. In conditions of deep social pluralism, the moral attitudes liberal toleration permits (and that are part of the values it supports) are inhospitable to the conditions on judgment necessary for justifying toleration. In encouraging a partition between moral attitudes and moral judgment, liberal toleration can be, in a practical sense, self-defeating.[4]

To understand the scope of this problem, we will need a fuller characterization of what engaged moral judgment involves. Much of what I want to say about moral judgment in the circumstances of pluralism is quite general in its import. But because a more theoretically informed guide is sometimes necessary, I develop the account of engaged moral judgment within a Kantian framework. Traditional interpretive misgivings notwithstanding, I believe the Kantian framework provides the reasoned balance between objectivity of judgment and sensitivity to the particular that is necessary to acknowledge pluralism without succumbing to across-the-board relativism.[5]

---

4. It is not much of an objection to claim that the conditions of judgment do not have to be satisfied by each agent because what is and is not to be tolerated is a public or political decision. We would have to give up a great deal to accept that persons who are required to tolerate or permitted to interfere could not know or appreciate the supporting moral reasons.

5. Before continuing, I should note that Kant's explicit discussions of toleration do not indicate that he saw any connection with the problems posed by social pluralism. (Kant's extended discussions of toleration are to be found in the essays "What Is Enlightenment?" and "Theory and Practice." The best treatment of Kant on toleration is Onora O'Neill, "The Public Use of Reason," in *Constructions of Reason* [Cambridge: Cambridge University Press, 1989].) On religious toleration, Kant is consistently liberal—with a twist. The lack of certainty about all religious claims makes groundless hatred and persecution of other religions. Further, because religions are historically embedded and limited practices, it is only as they express (independent) morality that their tenets are normative at all.

Kant does have striking views about political toleration—especially about the necessity of free speech as the public use of reason. He holds that "[r]eason depends on this freedom for its very existence. For reason has no dictatorial authority; its verdict is simply the agreement of free citizens, of whom each one must be permitted to express, without let or hindrance, his objections or even his veto" (*Critique of Pure Reason* A738/B766, trans. N. K. Smith [London: Macmillan, 1933]). Nothing follows directly from this understanding of toleration that connects with the moral effects of social pluralism. What can be drawn on is the ideal of public

II

First, what are the facts of social pluralism to which moral judgment might need to attend? Consider some possibilities. Membership in a group or class of persons could be morally relevant to one's moral standing, claims, or obligations.[6] The fact that there are such groups may in turn alter the moral terrain of others who interact with them, directly or via participation in shared social institutions. Persons who belong to a group may identify themselves or be partly constituted by a cluster of distinct (or distinctly arranged) values. This will show in matters of character, dispositions, vulnerabilities, conceptions of the good life. Acting with and toward persons so identified may require different sorts of knowledge and sensitivities than are required when one is "at home." And last, membership in a group may be a practically necessary means for identifying morally relevant facts that apply to a person, especially when the facts are a function of the group's history.[7] There may be other relevant facts; these may be inadequately described. But some such set of facts must be what is claimed to obtain if the occurrence of social pluralism is significant for moral judgment. Let us assume, then, that the moral relevance of social pluralism is manifested in these ways.

It would seem that any moral theory that had the resources even to acknowledge such parochial values would run the risk of inviting practical failure: different agents in different cultures (or subcultures) arriving at different conclusions (about themselves, about how they should regard and act toward others) in what seem to be relevantly similar circumstances, on valid grounds that are inaccessible to each other. In the face of this one might well think that the best strategy is to develop some most widely acceptable neutral notion of impermissible harm, and about other moral matters, accept that we are limited to our own point of view. That this can look to be the only available response depends on holding onto a model of moral judgment that regards local values as fixed objects of local judgment. One of the reasons for employing a Kantian model of moral judgment is that it can acknowledge the distinct claim of local values without regarding them as fixed.

reason: a formal, normative construction of the space of moral judgment that can provide room for the expression of distinct values in conformity with the standard of practical reason.

6. Since the topic is social pluralism, I am not considering the special problems for moral judgment posed by nonhuman groups.

7. The contrast I have in mind is with cases where knowledge of group identity is merely convenient for identifying something to which we have or could have independent access (e.g., susceptibility to a genetic disorder).

Kantian moral judgment attends to agents' maxims: the subjective principles that show actions in the form a rational agent wills them. Maxims thus represent the subjective justification of agents' choices, including their sense of means-ends fit, consistency with other ends, and judgments of permissibility or obligatoriness. The full relevance to agents of their perceived context of action—their different connections and commitments—is thus reflected in their maxims and available for moral assessment. So, choices that are justified in ethnic or racial terms will have maxims whose content reflects those specific value commitments. If the fact that I am a woman or an ethnic European enters my understanding of, and so my reason for, acting in a particular way, my maxim will include these facts. It is an essential part of Kantian moral judgment to provide a method for assessing such maxims, since they contain agents' sincerely proffered justifications.[8] And surely *some* of the facts agents appeal to can make a difference in moral judgment. Being a member of a historically oppressed race might justify some actions or claims that being of Polish extraction cannot (and, perhaps, vice versa). It is because it has resources to register such possibilities that the Kantian model of moral judgment is well suited to the circumstances of pluralism.

The more comprehensive the claims of a way of life are, the more pervasive its values will be in agents' maxims. Consider the possible diversity of willings involved in child-rearing practices, recreation, conjugal relations, and caring for the homeless. Something as ordinary as choices in clothes may be dictated by slavishness to fashion, whim, religious discipline, or cultural identification. Quite precise facts about cultural commitments, pride, and the connection to personal taste need to be understood in order to determine the rationality—or even to appreciate the sense—of a given choice.

It is no different for maxims with explicitly moral content. Acts of beneficence or charity will be differently understood depending on an agent's view of the resources to be distributed. If wealth is regarded as deserved private possession, charity may be more personal (giving what is one's own) than if one views possessions as common goods held in trust for all (giving as a required redistribution). An account of moral judgment that could not register these differences in willing would plainly be inadequate.

Thinking about Kant here one might object: if we have obligations to the poor (or to those in need), then what morality requires is that we give what

8. There are general arguments that support this assumption in Barbara Herman, "Moral Deliberation and the Derivation of Duties," in *The Practice of Moral Judgment* (Cambridge, Mass.: Harvard University Press, 1993).

is necessary, and do that according to a conception that we are doing what morality requires (this is the motive of duty in its reason-giving form). Anything else in one's maxim of beneficence diminishes its moral content or purity. On this picture there is *one* correct maxim of beneficence for all agents in comparable circumstances of giving. But this is a picture we have reason not to accept. What is necessary, indeed what counts as giving, cannot be determined independent of context.

We act from the motive of duty in circumstances of need by acknowledging the claim of need as a presumptive (conditionally sufficient) reason for action. The motive of duty, however, does not exhaust the value texture of our action and choices. If I view my level of wealth as a contingent feature of class and good fortune, and have a conception of wealth as joint social product, I can act as morality requires, fully acknowledging the claim of need as a sufficient reason for action, while acting on a maxim of trusteeship. Much of moral importance would be lost if this maxim of giving could not be distinguished from an act of giving *as charity*.

Kant himself adds to the duty to aid the further requirement that acts of charity be performed in ways that do not demean their recipients.[9] His point is not that we should give aid *and* act respectfully—that we should do two things—but that the aid given should be conceived of and expressed in a respectful way. This is a moral, not a conceptual point. And it is a moral point that can have far-reaching moral consequences. The further requirement on acts of charity might give reasons to favor an institution with a conception of property as trusteeship insofar as it supports a moral climate of ownership that avoids both arrogance and servility.

The importance of particular contexts and a morally complete conception of an action is not limited to circumstances that involve institutions. Moral judgment in general requires a fuller conception of action than what might be deemed sufficient to capture a singular performance. One of the things one wants (or ought to want) from a moral theory is an account of moral judgment and deliberation that can underwrite agents' confidence in each other's moral practice. Knowledge that someone has done or intends to do the right thing is obviously important, but it is often also shallow knowledge. We may in addition need to know what the action meant to someone, how it fit with other things she is doing—questions that have implications about how she would "go on." This is often the case because circumstances of

9. Immanuel Kant, *The Metaphysics of Morals* (1797), in *Practical Philosophy*, trans. and ed. Mary J. Gregor (Cambridge: Cambridge University Press, 1996), 6:452.

action are not in automatic one-to-one correspondence with judgment. The decision to act in the requisite way—even if correct—may not provide closure. Where resources are limited, an act of charity may put strain on other obligations. Or the act of charity itself may promote dependency. Some possible effects of an action can and should be anticipated. But some of an action's effects arise from the unexpected (and unexpectable) actions, reactions, and decisions of others. It is a substantive requirement on an agent's maxim that in acting she recognize and where possible anticipate likely outcomes. She must also act with and from the recognition that it is only in rare circumstances (and, perhaps, philosophical discussions) that a single action is a sufficient response to a complex moral situation.[10]

Further, the moral adequacy of an action can depend on the structure and content of the maxims of other persons. That I act from a maxim of beneficence does not guarantee that I act beneficently. If the recipient of my good will is insulted by what I would do, and if this response is at all reasonable, then my action has failed to be the kind of action I willed. This is not a challenge to my moral worth; it calls into question the efficacy of my agency in my action. What makes this of special concern is the possibility that the efficacy of my agency may depend on factors over which I have no complete control and into which I have no automatic insight.

It is a normal feature of action and willing to be concerned with the conditions of effective agency. I do not will as I should when I ignore my own limits of skill and resources. Likewise, my maxims of action must be formed on the basis of some knowledge of how others act and react. If I had no idea about how another agent understands or reacts, the possible maxims of interaction I could responsibly adopt would be minimal. Much of this we take for granted because we assume that the other is like us: needing food when hungry and help when injured, being susceptible to guilt and shame, responsive to disrespect, and so on. And to a very large extent we are warranted in this assumption: others *are* pretty much like us. But even in the normal range of cases we are attentive to relevant differences. We do not treat children as we do adults; we recognize that gross physical or psychological differences can alter what counts as morally significant need. But because we tend to live among others whose similarities to ourselves we take for granted, and because patterns of ac-

---

10. Because the required nature and degree of such further response is not a matter of individual choice, an adequate moral theory must have resources to develop such standards. And they need to be *developed,* for what counts as adequate preparation in one situation may be woefully unsuited to another. This may be an especially acute matter when the context of action involves agents with different or culturally diverse conceptions of what is at issue.

tion become routine, most of us are rarely challenged—in our private lives, anyway—to acknowledge differences that are deep or make us uncomfortable.

Recent lessons about gender and race in the workplace warn of ways this ordinary fact may support culpable complacency. When apparently sincere and decent people infer from the removal of formal institutional discrimination that the barriers to the advancement of women and persons of color have been removed, it becomes easy to regard remaining complaints of discrimination as matters of insensitivity or delicate feelings, residues to be dissolved over time, aided by the accumulated effects of good intentions. One of the lessons of pluralism—of moral claims based in facts about groups and their relations—has to be sensitivity to the *moral* fault in such attitudes. Facts about institutions that favor white males, as well as facts about women and racial minorities that make them especially vulnerable to informal barriers, need to be acknowledged in maxims of action in relevant contexts. Educational practices and policies that have the effect of disabling women or racial minorities are not morally neutral.

The possibility of such moral complexity enjoins moral agents to develop a morally tuned sensitivity to the effects of their sincerely intended actions and to the interplay between what they intend and the social or institutional contexts in which they act. There must be intelligent anticipation about failure and subsequent response built into the initial maxims of claim and response. This cannot be restricted to some after-the-fact check. It is rather a morally required feature of judgment and deliberation—of agents' maxims—the effects of which will show in the way agents respond to morally complex circumstances and context-specific claims.

Special burdens of moral judgment are present whenever social circumstances are such that first-order sincerity is morally insufficient. This fact is perspicuous in, though hardly unique to, complex institutional settings. A labor negotiator's maxim with respect to wage claims includes more than a precalculated scale of offer and counteroffer. It presupposes a shared understanding of responsive action based on the institutional facts of good-faith bargaining, including the conditions for strikes, lockouts, and so on. Part of the work of responsible labor organizing is to educate union members about the structure of collective bargaining. Wildcat strikes, for example, often provide more direct expression of workers' grievances. But they can be inappropriate, arguably morally inappropriate, where fair procedures for settling labor and wage disputes exist.

The same kind of sensitivity and responsibility for the actions of others is plainly not required of agents in all circumstances. Members of a profoundly egalitarian, ethnically and racially homogeneous society would for the most part be able to rely on their first-order sincere intentions. The absence of traditions of persecution and dominance, plus public knowledge of the adequacy of institutions, create a context of deliberation and action in which each may be confident of what others' intentions are and of what they will do if the effects of their actions are untoward. Justified public confidence (in a well-ordered society) allows for a certain shallowness of agents' maxims.

III

In complex social circumstances, especially ones involving inequalities of power, in which differences in history (or class or race) produce competing systems of local value, if agents on both sides of an issue are to include in their maxims claims (or responses to claims) that express local values, there must be principles that provide deliberative guidance. Their task is twofold: to reconcile the content of local maxims with objective moral principle and to provide resources for the presentation of differences that allow for moral conversation and real disagreement. A moral conception is deficient to the extent that it restricts agents to negotiated agreements from within their separate spheres of value. The preservation of mutual opacity forces terms of agreement that track power and trading advantage.[11] Fair procedural constraints on negotiation can eliminate abuse, but they cannot be relied on to be adequately responsive to relevant local claims. The procedural ideal of a level playing field implicitly assumes the irrelevance of differences—or that differences, if ineliminable, need only to be balanced or handicapped. This misses the point in those cases where it is acknowledgment of the significance of difference, or of a claim based on difference, that is the issue. Treating pregnancy as a disability is a good example of this mistake.

To move different systems of local value to a position where disagreements can be resolved through some other means than advantage-negotiation, a moral theory must either provide rules of value translation, so that disputes can be resolved through single-scale balancing or weighing, or must establish mediating regulative principles that, while neutral, do not efface relevant dif-

11. This is Gilbert Harman's picture, I believe. It is what John Rawls's original position blocks through constraints on information, justified by the goal of constructing principles on which all could reasonably agree. The Kantian alternative I am sketching takes the task to be one of elaborating the moral structures required for deliberation and conscientious action in circumstances of pluralism supported by complex social and cultural differences.

ferences when applied. I think there are many reasons to avoid rules of value translation, chief among them being the difficulty of establishing commensurability. But the deciding advantage of mediating regulative principles is that they better fit the issue at hand. If difference is potentially of the essence of a local value claim, value translation would be self-defeating in a practical sense when agents advancing local value claims have good reason to want their claims acknowledged, as far as possible, in their own terms.

Although the point of regulative principles is to secure fair placement of local value claims in a shared deliberative framework, this often involves costs. Again, the conditions of good-faith collective bargaining provide an instructive example. They demand a certain level of respect for organized labor on the one side and recognizing the claims for profit and capital accumulation on the other. Claims that all corporate profits are the illegitimate expropriation of the value created by labor power cannot be encompassed by the regulative principles of collective bargaining. Excluded on the same grounds is the presumption that a fair wage is measured by the price labor can get for itself in an open world labor market. This does not imply that each side must view the other in a sympathetic way. Accusations of greed, stubbornness, misplaced class solidarity are within bounds as appropriate, and can be part of the process of constructing common ground. It is where the conditions of good-faith collective bargaining do not obtain, where they are not yet established or have broken down, that there may be no alternative to unmediated assertions of local value and advantage-driven settlements.

The effect of regulative principles in mediating local value claims is to constitute a community of moral judgment. Membership in such a community is a necessary condition for the various forms of moral colloquy: agreement in moral judgment, disagreement, even shared confusion. I do not mean to suggest that each person is necessarily a member of only one such community or that a single community of moral judgment can encompass all the relevant moral value claims of its members. I do want to suggest that all moral judgment in fact takes place within the framework of a community of moral judgment. The rules of salience that identify the features of our circumstances that require moral attention, as well as the regulative principles that set the deliberative framework, are social rules acquired through participation in a moral community. Even the most basic moral facts—what counts as a harm that sets a moral claim, what counts as conditions for a valid agreement—are functions of social practice.[12]

12. This does not mean that persons from different backgrounds and cultures cannot have

It is reasonable to suppose that every valid moral conception will have a standard of harm and rules for agreement, and it may be that, given the kinds of beings that we are, certain harms will always establish a claim and certain conditions always invalidate agreement. But, as I noted earlier, general standards do not exhaust the array of reasonable claims and conditions. A culture or group may find nonphysical pain difficult to accept as real injury, and so not a candidate for harm. Another may hold that no pain is worthy of attention until it is named by its professional medical establishment. For them, incapacitating sadness or sorrow may not have moral standing until it is medically indexed as "depression." In such a culture, energy must be expended to influence medical institutions in order to make socially credible the moral standing of certain real phenomena.[13] This may seem to us perverse and even abusive. And it may be. But although it may be wrong to allow the medical establishment the power to stipulate what is morally real—what has moral standing—some such institutional mediation of suffering, and so harm, is inevitable. Pain does not speak until it is a social fact, and it is *as* a social fact that it enters moral colloquy.

The general point is this. Neither agents' moral circumstances nor their obligations can be understood without locating them within a social setting. This is not in any way an aberration or something ideal moral theory might avoid. Even universal grounds of obligation will have local instantiation. But to note the social bases of moral facts is not yet to see the way that regulative principles constitute a community of moral judgment. The question is thus not about the fact or role of a community of judgment, but about what impact the fact of pluralism has on its structure.

IV

Regulative principles constitute a community of moral judgment through the creation of what I will call a shared deliberative field. An agent's deliberative field is the normative space constructed by the principles she

fruitful moral debate. A shared moral root (religion, for example) makes possible overlapping principles. Powerful transcultural communities are created by international commerce and some deep similarities in forms of oppression. I have doubts, though, about how deep or ranging such moral colloquy can be.

13. This can work in both directions. For example, the attempt to make sexual preference a medical or biological fact can be seen as part of a morally questionable program to create inflexible sexual categories.

accepts—usually an ordered array of moral and nonmoral principles. What she values or wants is judged to be reason-giving as it satisfies the ordered principles and fits with other values or wants already present in the field. On a Kantian account, the ordered set of principles of practical rationality constrain the whole. (This does not imply that other principles and values, aesthetic ones, for example, cannot also have global scope.)

One role of regulative principles is as gatekeepers to the deliberative field. This is a general feature of practical reasoning. Without some developed conception of prudence or well-being, desires and interests cannot even raise deliberative questions. Consider the way pain gives rise to reasons. Its normally central status in a deliberative field derives from the fact that pain is typically a sign of injury or damage. If pain did not have this role, it is not clear we would have reason (or the same reason) to prevent its occurrence. Formally, it is no different with desire. That I want something is not in itself a reason for me—or for anyone else—to act to procure it. Desire becomes potentially reason-supporting through connection with permissible ends and values that refine the structure of an agent's deliberative field. Some desires (for some persons) have no deliberative place (the desire to drink for a recovering alcoholic, for example).[14] It is because it goes without saying (or thinking) that eating is a good thing that the desire to eat can be taken to be reason-giving. But this is misleading, of course, for once in the deliberative field, the desire to eat now supports a reason to eat *now* only if there is time, if I have not just eaten, if there are not more pressing things to do, and so on.

Not all positions in the deliberative field are equal—some interests weigh more than others, some trump some (or all) others. Principles of prudence may indicate that where a course of action is life-threatening, its avoidance has other-things-equal priority over the immediate end it promotes. But other things may not be equal: the loss of the immediate end may be of greater significance than the avoidance of the threat to life (or even to the loss of life). There are issues of balancing and weighing here. By contrast, principles of morality (Kantian ones, anyway) will require a different kind of reckoning. That one's principle (maxim) of action involves disregard for the moral status of another person condemns acting on that maxim, regardless of the value of the end that so acting would promote.

14. This is the reverse of the usual reason-desire connection. It is usually argued that there are no reasons without supporting desires. The claim here is that the presence of a desire does not by itself support reasons.

The practical principles that structure the deliberative field not only permit local interpretation, they require it. Even Kantian respect for persons (ourselves and others) as rational agents is empty if we cannot introduce, under interpretation, local experiences. In a culture that values individual autonomy, the pain of separation from a parent may be a stage of growth, not a sign of injury, and so does not provide a justifying reason to keep a child at home. In a different culture, one that values strong intergenerational bonds, it might be that the pain of separation indicates the absence of an important developmental stage and so gives good reason to resist institutional pressure for early schooling. Assuming that both developmental paths are normal, we cannot be respectful of the growing child or the concerned adult unless we know how these matters are worked out.

The interpreted principles of the deliberative field construct a sensibility that gives practical sense to our experiences. Essential to the nature of this sensibility is that it is shared. In part this is because the interpretations of practical principles must be taught; normal development is otherwise not possible. Children must learn how and in what sense their feelings and experiences have practical significance. They learn to value some feelings and to discount others. These values must be socially available, both in the sense that people around them hold and act on them and in the sense that circumstances permit their acquisition.

It is not just the role of socialization that explains why the sensibility must be a shared one. There are also social determinants of judgment in the usual sense: particular institutions of contract and property bring objects and the potential for relying on agreements into the moral sphere. Their mediation of our conceptions of what we can effectively desire and do is an integral part of moral deliberation and judgment. They explain why, if we live among persons, membership in civil society is both not optional and partly constitutive of a community of moral judgment.

Kant is quite explicit: The moral point of such institutions is not to compensate for our own and others' deficiencies (of goodness, strength, capacity to trust, etc.); they arise as the necessary social framework in which human beings can exercise and express their rational natures as free and equal persons.[15] Kant argues that, given the conditions of human life, there are things we each *must* be able to do that are not morally possible absent certain coer-

---

15. This is the argument of Kant's *Rechtslehre,* part 1 of *The Metaphysics of Morals,* 6:245–270.

cive political institutions. Our need to have exclusive use of things introduces a moral requirement for (and so justification of) a coercive political
institution of property; our need to rely on (have a moral interest in) the ful-
fillment of commitments calls for an institution of contract. The needs reflect conditions for effective human agency; the move to civil institutions is
necessary because we cannot have what we need without enforceable rights
against each other—that is, without legitimate coercive force.

In neither of these cases, however, is the content of the justified coercive
institution fully determined by its justifying argument. Kant's argument for
an institution of property is not an argument for any particular system of
property, private or communal. It is an argument to the conditions of intelligibility of the moral idea of property or right. The argument is not, however, neutral with regard to all systems of property. If property is justified as
the necessary condition for effective rational agency, no institution of property that excludes some persons or groups of persons from ownership can
be justified.

The Kantian deliberative framework is thereby able to conjoin contingent local institutions and principles of judgment in a way that preserves
local value without sacrificing objectivity. The condition of moral legitimacy of coercive institutions—that they make possible the expression of
free rational agency—makes it the case that even though moral judgments
may make sense only within a particular culture, when they are expressions
of legitimate institutions, local moral judgments can be fully objective. If
this shows that objectivity does not require universality, it also explains why
objectivity may not be the cure for moral disagreement.

The legitimate institutions of civil society add essential components to
the shared sensibility that both identifies what is morally salient in a wide
sphere of circumstances of action and gauges its standing in moral judgment.[16] As articulated, these institutions give the social world many of its
moral features. Living in a post-industrial capitalist economy, I will directly
see manufactured objects of a certain size or kind, such as tennis rackets or

16. Thus although it is the principle of manipulation of agency in Kant's famous maxim of
deceitful promising that makes it impermissible, what makes it a maxim of deceitful promising is a function of the prevailing institutions of promise and contract. This is not a deep
point. Whether an expression of future intentions in a context of possible cooperative activity constitutes a commitment depends on conventions; it does not follow from the internal
logic of the utterance. In similar fashion, the terms of legitimate possession and so of misap-
propriation are social, not natural.

sports cars, as having the property of being privately owned, just as I directly see these objects as having a certain color. While there is no necessity to this arrangement of possession (sports cars might have been like the famous white bicycles of Amsterdam in the 1960s were said to be—universally available for use), what is necessary is that such objects be *some* kind of property, under some kind of legal constraint.

In similar fashion, the community of moral judgment determines the relevant properties of morally salient desires and attitudes. Some desires have no standing at all: their satisfaction is not good, their frustration not in itself to be regretted. Sadistic desires, for example. The principles that exclude other desires may or may not be local. Desires to dominate other persons, to possess them materially or sexually have no right of entry in any agent's deliberative field. What may be more of a local matter is determining when these are the desires in question. Is someone's emphatic solicitude reasonable parental care or a possessive wish to prolong dependency? The answer might not be available through scrutiny of psychological states alone. Correct identification of an agent's intentions can require interpretation through local institutions. When it is that control over another's choices expresses impermissible possessiveness may be a function of a community's conception of what an adult is. This is not to say that every conception of an adult is morally acceptable, only that more than one may be, and that the threshold for autonomous choice (or autonomous choice in some spheres) may be a region in which there is permissible variation.

V

That the terms and moral properties necessary for moral judgment have their origins in a community of moral judgment is not a view specific to Kantian ethics. What Kantian ethics adds to this is the claim that local values can support objective moral judgments only insofar as they are mediated by moral principle (specifically, the categorical imperative). In different Kantian terms: local value has moral standing as it does or can express the value of rational agency. A given institution—of, say, property or family life—satisfies this role if it makes the expression of rational agency in action possible (for those within the orbit of the institution) *and* when the connection to the conditions of rational agency is or can be an essential part of the available cultural understanding of the institution (its structure and requirements). We might say that local values satisfying this condition support translation or reconfiguration in the terms of moral principle. Values that cannot accept translation have no legitimate deliberative place.

Thus "family values" that support spousal rape (or other forms of abuse) would be condemned: there is no possible translation of these values into terms that accept or express the regulative priority of support for rational agency. Other local values that are not condemned might not have the standing in the deliberative field that they claim in their own terms. For example, some ethnic and religious traditions, in addition to specific practices, make claims of ultimate authority over their members' ways of life and sometimes even their beliefs. The translation of local value may leave religious or ethnic practices unperturbed while rejecting the authority of the tradition that supports them. There is room for only one supremely regulative value in the Kantian deliberative field.

Because the location of local values in a structured deliberative field cuts them off to some degree from their original source of authority, they will be regarded as *possible* sources of value, subject to regulative principle and constraints of fit. Local community values are thus treated, in a formal sense only, on a par with desires and interests. They provide sources for reasons: they are not reason-giving on their own. This is not to say that all possible sources of value are reduced to mere interests, competing with each other and with interests in general for normative space. Much of the interior structuring of a life that religion or ethnicity may provide can be preserved. But this is not because there is something special about local values. Complex personal ends—career choices, attachments, political commitments, and the like—all provide substructures in the deliberative field that guide choice and perception. What makes this possible is the indeterminateness of shape of the deliberative field. Kantian morality does not designate a morally (or rationally) preferred way of life. The great variety of human interests and traditions, coupled with the fact that choices to pursue certain kinds of activities tend to preclude the pursuit of others, suggests that from the point of view of rational agency, there cannot be only one way to live.

Not just normative authority but also the content of local values may be affected by their relocation in the Kantian deliberative field. It is a constitutive principle of the deliberative field that no maxim of action may be inconsistent with the principle of respect for persons. This normative constraint not only rules out certain kinds of actions that local value supports, it requires the transformation of local values concerning the kinds of reasons they provide. If it is a rule in my community that women's place is in the home, the practice of female homemaking may survive, but not as something women must see as their morally ordained place.

In general, where practices survive and where the values that support them gain entry into the deliberative field, they will be to a greater or lesser extent transformed along the dimensions of authority, content, and value-based reasons. This might in some cases undermine a local value; it will in other cases affect what counts as satisfaction of a value.

Although this is not the place to try to say what sorts of local values could survive translation to the terms of the Kantian deliberative field, or what they would look like if they could, some projection is possible. For example, it is not clear whether Kantian notions of autonomy permit vesting any person or group with ultimate deliberative authority, whether fathers, councils of elders, or experts. What I think we can say is that *if* deliberative authority is permissible, it must be justified by reasons that are consistent with deliberative norms: deference to expertise that cannot be easily shared, the necessity of efficient and final decision-making in emergencies, and so on. Claims of authority are subject to deliberation-relative justification, and thus permanently open to rebuttal. A certain kind of critical practice is therefore necessary to maintain the legitimacy of authority. So, for example, to the extent that modern medicine relies on the obscurity of unnecessary Latin and the absence of generally accessible medical education, its authority is morally suspect.

Ways of life whose constitutive values resist transformation by moral principle can nonetheless contain virtues we admire. The courage and grace of a warrior class, the exquisite taste encouraged by great wealth or a hereditary nobility, or the self-sacrificial passion for justice in a revolutionary vanguard are unlikely to be present in a deliberative framework structured by Kantian principle. But the fact that from the moral point of view we cannot endorse everything in which we can see some good is not in itself an argument against the authority of moral principle.

VI

The range of differences that can be included in a single community of moral judgment is a function of the requirements for ongoing moral colloquy. Although neither consistency with moral principle (the values of rational agency) nor openness to reconfiguration in moral terms is sufficient to guarantee that two local values can be in the same community of moral judgment, there is reason to think that many encounters between initially incompatible systems of value need not conclude in mutual opacity and exclusion. The Kantian account, as I have reconstructed it, resists a kind of value stasis in judgment that encourages systems of value to remain disengaged from one another.

There is again an analogous deliberative problem for an individual. One can regard interests and commitments as making separate claims for deliberative attention and priority. Sometimes competing interests cannot be adjusted to each other: devotion to a fast-track corporate career conflicts with the desire to be a committed and available parent. Although a choice has to be made, its terms need not be dictated from the fixed perspective of either interest. If interests are denied authority independent of their place on a deliberative field, the exclusionary claim of a given interest is subject to re-examination, and it can be re-established on different terms. There is nothing compelling in the picture that describes the choice to move to a different career track or a different model of successful parenting as a choice to gain one thing at the expense of another. This is to accept the idea that our interests have some independent standing in our lives, some autonomous claim to expression. One could equally view one's life as involving in an essential way the development and mutual adjustment of a variety of interests. One does not know at any given point exactly how things will go, what one may come to care about, or how what one cares about may change as one comes to care about other things.[17] Practical rationality is a permanent task.

The point of the analogy is to underscore the conditional status of the interests and values that constitute a life or a community at a given time. Interests and values are to be adjusted to principles of practical rationality as well as to each other. The analogy breaks down over what drives each system toward higher degrees of unity and integration. One can exaggerate the unifying effect of being a person as a single locus of activity—we are all too able to adopt and pursue conflicting projects—but there is clearly something in the idea of a prudential need to live one life that is absent from the circumstances of multiple communities of moral judgment.

Kant argued that where "a multitude of persons" live in such a way that they "affect one another," they are under moral necessity to enter together

---

17. That this is a normal fact does not exonerate those institutions that force such adjustments when they are not necessary.

into civil society.[18] This is because the absence of common institutions of property and contract, with enforceable rights, is an impermissible hindrance to the effective expression of human rational agency. I think it can be argued that we are similarly obliged to enter and sustain a community of moral judgment, not to secure enforceable rights, but to bring about the conditions for moral development and colloquy: the conditions necessary to secure what Kant calls the "public use of reason." This provides the moral impetus to unity in circumstances of pluralism. It also explains the inappropriateness of tolerance as a first moral response to pluralism. Since toleration is at issue only where people can affect one another, where the conditions for toleration obtain, there is already in place a prior moral requirement to a more inclusive community of moral judgment.

While the moral necessity of civil society justifies coercing entry, the community of moral judgment cannot be brought about by compulsion. The obligation to enter and sustain a community of judgment sets agents a task of understanding and accommodation: a constraint on maxims. It is the practical expression in judgment of the kingdom of ends as a cosmopolitan ideal.

VII

Suppose one faces a community of moral judgment different from one's own—where, by definition, one is in moral disagreement either with the community's justifying reasons or with the outcomes of its sincere moral judgments.[19] In circumstances governed by the model of liberal toleration, I maintain a position of judging outsider, attempting to assess in my own terms whether the area of disagreement meets the conditions warranting intervention. If it does not, having made my critical judgment, there is only the private matter of attitude, continued proximity, and so on. That is why toleration can be a matter of public policy.

If instead I act under the obligation to extend the community of moral judgment, my task is both more complex and more demanding. Because one needs to determine the possibility of moral colloquy, the task of judgment requires substantial engagement with the values in question, not just to deter-

18. Immanuel Kant, *Toward Perpetual Peace* (1795), in *Practical Philosophy*, trans. and ed. Mary J. Gregor (Cambridge: Cambridge University Press, 1996), 8:358; Kant, *Metaphysics of Morals*, 6:252–255.

19. To simplify matters, I am ignoring the fact that it is from within a group that one encounters other communities of judgment.

mine consistency with moral principle but to consider the potential areas of mutual adjustment that may be necessary to make the community of moral judgment more inclusive. It can be difficult, for example, to determine whether one is facing a distinct community of judgment or whether moral deviance is masking itself as difference. Different questions arise depending on whether the focus of judgment is a subgroup within a pluralistic society or, as Kant imagined, groups encountered through travel and commerce.

Judgment that uses the conditions of moral colloquy to determine local legitimacy of ways of life must take care that difference per se is not read as grounds for exclusion. Correct judgment is dependent on the particular facts and norms of the institution or practice in question. Although, we might conjecture, the value of polygamous marriage as it functioned in the historical community of Latter-day Saints is not one that could be mediated by Kantian principle (because of its institutionalized subordination of women), nothing follows from this about other patterns of multiple-spouse marriage. The issue is not the pattern of marriage per se, but the moral meaning that comes with its mode of spousal relation.

Imagine two communities demanding local control over education, one seeing it as a necessary means for the preservation of its language and customs, the other wanting to protect its children from exposure to material that displays other systems of value in a favorable or even neutral light. Both demands may be in conflict with the dominant culture's value of uniform public, liberal education. In the United States, this sort of issue is usually discussed as it raises constitutional questions about the separation of church and state. But it is also, and perhaps first, a moral issue. The values involved and the practices they support are different in morally significant ways. Partial separation from the standard pattern of civic socialization in order to preserve a cultural identity need not threaten the conditions of moral colloquy. By contrast, because the proposed instantiation of the values of the second community promotes parochial intolerance, their case for preserving cultural identity (in this way) does not carry moral weight. This is not because their practice will lead to wrongful interference with others; it might not. Education to intolerance undermines the conditions for participation in an inclusive community of moral judgment.

The fact that a community would not survive the loss or change of a condemned value neither alters the terms of inclusion nor gives reason to shift to a model of toleration. Communities as such do not have rights of survival. However, where local values can be successfully mediated and the conditions for public dialogue and reasoning are secured, a community's interest in preserving local value—in preserving itself—would seem to be determinative. The legitimate interests of the larger community are limited to the satisfaction of the membership conditions in the community of moral judgment. But this description concedes too much to the dominant group. The conditions of co-membership in a community of moral judgment demand positive engagement with nonmajority systems of local value. The issue is not whether one can put up with ways of life one does not like, or whether other values one has are promoted by noninterference. That is the question of toleration. Rather, one needs to know that, and on what terms, there is a possible community of moral judgment. And this may require changes in one's own values. Not all values will satisfy the terms of entry, and not all values that survive will do so unchanged. If there are costs of entry to a community of moral judgment—costs to the local values themselves—it cannot be that the dominant community always decides who pays. Engaged moral judgment requires an openness in both communities to the point and role of value differences and a willingness to modify local values (even if at some cost to the continuity of community tradition) in order to achieve mutual accommodation.

In short, the obligation to inclusion does not leave everything as it would have been absent the fact of pluralism.[20] In conditions of pluralism, parochialism is not acceptable. If we follow Kant, it is a violation of our duty to enter and maintain (or, if necessary, to create) a cosmopolitan moral community.[21]

20. It is possible that there are no a priori limits to the modifications in values that may be required. But the losses involved should not be exaggerated, and the potential benefits not ignored. It will be the task of future work to explore this claim.

21. There is no guarantee, of course, that such efforts will succeed. Failure of the project of inclusion could have various sources. Systems of value might not be able to survive proximity: their encounter can lead to the demise of one (or both) of them. There need be no fault here. The conditions of co-membership do not guarantee sustained coexistence. Further, attempts at inclusion may fail if defining social institutions are incompatible. Some institutions are more generous than others. Within the system of liberal property, for example, it is permissible to have a range of private arrangements that express different values: families, private corporate entities, and utopian communities may operate within the dominant system according to their own rules of possession. To be sure, private arrangements exist on the sufferance of the public, and there must be recognized authority to resolve system-based conflicts. It is a suggestive thought that those institutions are best that can accept the greatest range of normalized variants.

— 3 —

A Cosmopolitan Kingdom of Ends

There is an often unspoken assumption at work in modern moral philosophy that morality is in important ways independent of social and political institutions. The intuitive idea is that whatever morality requires of us as individuals, it will be something that we are, as individuals, able to do, or able to do to the degree that we are virtuous or good. The assumed moral effect on us of political and social institutions is either, positively, to provide us with a set of benefits and burdens, the enjoyment and discharge of which may give us occasion for moral action, or, negatively, if we hold political office or have some role with special responsibilities, to sometimes call for compromise with moral principle in order to do what is politically or institutionally necessary.

Kant's ethics has often seemed the exemplar of such a "separate spheres" conception of ethics and politics. Social and political institutions are presumed to arise as the necessary strategy for negotiating the natural lawlessness of collective life. Morality, by contrast, has its source in the a priori requirements of practical reason. It is thus both independent of and prior to politics. Moral action, accordingly, is a matter of bringing the will into conformity with a priori principles of practical reason. What calls for philosophy is the demonstration that this is possible.

The complement to this view of morality is a conception of the moral person as an autonomous individual acting under the burden of practical reason (in particular, the necessitation of the categorical imperative). Much of the attractiveness of traditional Kantian ethics derives from the dignity it accords the individual person because of her capacity to act both freely and as reason requires, as well as from the moral equality of persons that follows from locating the basis of moral status in each agent's own practical reason.

51

Unhappily, the same attractive features present serious obstacles to the perceived adequacy of the theory—both as an account of what morality is, and as the basis of an adequate account of moral agency. For instance: if autonomy is a source of dignity, it seems equally to be the source of a kind of autarchic individualism, supporting a conception of persons as radically separate from one another. Social connections appear to be morally contingent, if not arbitrary; at most they are the result, not the condition, of obligation. The paradigm moral encounter or relationship looks to be the one between strangers, persons who cannot assume common interests but who are rationally compelled to acknowledge limits on their mutually affecting actions in virtue of their common humanity. One might say that it is the moral theory fit for the modern city, and not the town, or village, or extended family. In those locales, the pervasiveness of local knowledge and the bonds of shared life make the austerity of a morality for autonomous individuals appear sterile and unresponsive to salient particularity. Kantian moral autonomy, so understood, is in general incompatible with conceptions of morality or virtue or the moral life that depend on excellence at a social role. One is therefore likely to be drawn to applaud Kantian morality where it rejects hierarchical or excluding social connections that we abhor, and then to condemn it for heavy-handedly refusing moral standing to connection per se, since there are areas, like the community or the family, where we find it attractive.

My purpose here is not to argue directly for or against the merits of such sweeping assertions. The point of rehearsing them is to bring to mind a sense of familiarity about these or analogous descriptions of the power and the limits of the Kantian account of morality and moral agency. I think such views have been accepted as almost uncontroversially true by friends and critics of Kantian ethics alike. The former prize its securing moral relationship between persons as such; the latter fault the theory for its eschewal of the moral importance of attachment and place. The conditions on morality that each supports are surely correct. That it does not seem possible to have both autonomy and deep social connection within Kantian ethics is to be explained by the fact that *both* camps endorse what I believe is a mistaken view of Kantian moral agency and judgment.[1]

---

1. That they do not seem to be possible co-conditions for any possible ethical theory likely comes from misunderstanding both the demands of rational cosmopolitanism—what it means to regard another as a rational agent per se—and the constraints of the local—how it is that particular values have standing in a general moral framework.

There is a different place one might begin. The Kantian rational agent need not and should not be conceived as an isolated individual whose autonomous self-legislation is to bridge the gap from her own concerns to a regard for others as equal, rational, and autonomous. The "other" is not by conceptual necessity alien: a burden, a limit to be negotiated by reason. Some would even argue that, for Kant, to be a human rational agent is to be one among others in relations of rational colloquy.[2] It is not just morality that compels us to acknowledge other persons as equal and authoritative sources of reasons; insofar as we are rational, the other is integral to—even partly defining of—our rational activity. And if there is no valid conception of the individual rational agent qua rational agent without other persons, there is no gap that starts a skeptical argument, requiring some special reason to take other agents' reasons into account. No principle I offer on rational grounds requires a further step in order to engage the assent of the other as a condition of rational justification. Nonetheless, this deep fact of sociality does not by itself secure the principles of rational coordination necessary for rational agency. It is not just that we lack instincts for rational coordination, though that is true.[3] The difficulty is that the necessity of the project does not translate into a determinate solution. There is a task of construction for normative principles that can command rational assent. So understood, the social basis of agency and judgment is no threat to our autonomous rationality (a condition that as rational beings we must, or must wish to, overcome) but is the natural and inescapable arena for its expression.[4]

Nothing in this alternative conception of rational agency alters the primary task of moral philosophy: namely, giving an account of the nature and possibility of obligation. What does change is our sense of the primary task of Kantian moral *theory*: it is more plausibly seen as elaborating the practical consequences of the fact that the basic norms of rationality for autonomous agents are social. In what follows, I want to think about the kingdom of ends as a small piece of the moral theory project so understood. It would seem to be the obvious place to look if one wants to consider the place of the social as constitutive of the conditions and constraints

2. See Onora O'Neill, *Constructions of Reason* (Cambridge: Cambridge University Press, 1989) chap. 1; and Christine M. Korsgaard, *The Sources of Normativity* (Cambridge: Cambridge University Press, 1996), lecture 4.

3. This is O'Neill's point.

4. Nietzsche seems to have understood Kant this way. To go beyond good and evil is to act on principles others cannot endorse.

on moral agency and judgment.[5] The kingdom of ends appears to represent persons qua moral agents as (legislative) members of a possible social order. We are, in some sense, to consider our maxims as possible principles of an order of co-legislating beings. It is surely significant, and should be more puzzling than it is usually taken to be, that the representation of the principle of moral agency—the Categorical Imperative (hereafter CI)—has the form of a social order.

Within the *Groundwork*, the kingdom of ends is given several roles: as an ideal, as a further formula for representing the CI (and therefore as a distinct or complementary route to moral judgment), and as a component of the "complete determination of all maxims" that "brings an idea of reason closer to intuition (in accordance with a certain analogy) and thereby to feeling,"[6] useful "to provide access for the moral law" (*G* 4:437). The kingdom of ends also provides the framework for the discussion of price and dignity that precedes the so-called "summary of the argument." It would be nice to have an account of the kingdom of ends that explains the unity of these roles (if they are distinct) as well as explaining why the social dimension the kingdom of ends introduces is important to them. My plans for this essay, however, are more modest. I want to consider some basic questions about the idea of a kingdom of ends, and then, with some preliminary answers in hand, to begin exploring the sort of resource it provides for moral judgment, particularly in circumstances of social pluralism. This is an important focus for obvious moral reasons, but also because the effort to accommodate social pluralism brings to center stage the role that social institutions play in moral judgment in general.

5. That the expression of rational nature as in some way social is part of the idea of a kingdom of ends is not exactly news. Interesting elaborations of this idea figure in the work of Onora O'Neill and Christine Korsgaard, and especially of Thomas Hill, who has used the kingdom of ends as the centerpiece of what he calls a "constructivist" interpretation of Kantian ethics; see Thomas E. Hill Jr., *Dignity and Practical Reason in Kant's Moral Theory* (Ithaca, N.Y.: Cornell University Press, 1992). This body of work makes a convincing case for the importance and usefulness of the notion of a kingdom of ends. It certainly shows that the role of the kingdom of ends in the *Groundwork* argument had to be more than a conclusory high-toned moral ideal. However, it does not satisfactorily resolve the role the kingdom of ends is supposed to have, either as an element in the *Groundwork* argument or as an idea with practical import connected to the main line of Kantian deliberation and judgment.

6. Immanuel Kant, *Groundwork of the Metaphysics of Morals* (1785) (hereafter abbreviated *G*), in *Practical Philosophy*, trans. and ed. Mary J. Gregor (Cambridge: Cambridge University Press, 1996), 4:436.

I

If the idea of a kingdom of ends plainly gives expression to some sort of social element in Kant's account of moral judgment and obligation, it is not clear what the dimensions of the sociality might be or, therefore, what the significance of this social dimension is in our understanding of the nature and obligations of the autonomous rational agent. I want to approach this issue indirectly, by way of a set of more immediate, text-related questions. There is reason to be puzzled about the kingdom of ends as a formulation of the CI (if it is one) and about its relations to the other formulations; there are intriguing questions about the representation of persons in the kingdom of ends; it is not at all clear why or in what sense the kingdom of ends is an "ideal"; and there are, as I noted above, questions about the "strategy" of introducing a social dimension—what it means, what role it plays—that will affect our understanding of both persons in the kingdom of ends and the kingdom of ends itself as or as part of a formula of the CI.

The plan for this section is, first, to situate the kingdom of ends in the *Groundwork* argument, and then to begin an interpretation of it by raising and discussing two basic issues: whether the kingdom of ends is or contains the idea of a union of good wills, and the related matter of what is to be included as an end in the kingdom of ends. Since some of what I wish to do is to make some things puzzling that are not generally thought to be so, the discussion proceeds though a series of interpretive forays that will set some constraints on further interpretation, and raise more questions than they answer.

Consider the moment of introduction of the idea of a kingdom of ends (at G 4:433). It occurs immediately after the generation of the three formulae of the one CI, and so at a point when we know quite a lot about Kant's moral project. We know that there can be only one supreme moral principle, and that what it requires is the conformity of maxims to the principle of universal law-giving. We also know that it in some way supports a derivation of ordinary duties (although the reasons that support these duties may not be so ordinary). Left to be shown is that this principle (the CI) is a necessary law for all rational beings—indeed that it is even possibly such a law. This possibility hinges, Kant argues next, on the existence of an objective end: that is, an end that depends on motives valid for every rational being *and* that determines the will to act in conformity to the principle of universal law-giving. "Rational nature as an end in itself" is offered as the unique candidate for this role. However, rational nature can be an objective end—have standing as a regulative reason independent of agents' contingent and merely subjective interests—only if the rational will is, and conceives of itself as, an autonomous source of reasons. As beings with an autonomous will, we must be able to regard ourselves as subject to an objective norm whose authority is in no other place than "the idea of the will of every rational being as a will giving universal law" (*G* 4:431).

With this, Kant completes the stage-setting for the metaphysical arguments of *Groundwork* III. The possibility of a categorical imperative has been shown to depend on proving that the will of a rational agent is autonomous: capable of determining itself to action through a principle whose authority is independent of contingent interest.[7] But before taking up the metaphysical argument, Kant introduces "the very fruitful concept" of a kingdom of ends (*G* 4:433). I want to think about why he does this.

It has been said that with the formula of the kingdom of ends we can see a completion of the "perspective set" of the CI: of the agent in the formula of universal law, of the recipient in the formula of humanity, and of a citizen in a cooperative social order (a legislative perspective) in the formula of the kingdom of ends.[8] The last shift tells us that morality, through the CI, directs us to act on maxims whose principles could constitute the public rules of a possible social order of autonomous (human) beings.

The difficulty here is not that these ideas are somehow objectionable or un-Kantian. On the contrary, they are plausible, compelling, useful, and plainly expressive of central Kantian themes. The difficulty is in understanding how they could arise from the argument of the *Groundwork*. For if we have not correctly understood the point and place of the kingdom of ends in the argument of *Groundwork* II, despite the power of the ideas, we may doubt whether this interpretation gives us adequate access to the concept's intended fruitfulness.

The problem, as I see it, is this. *Starting* with the thought that the kingdom of ends represents morality in terms of an ideal social order is misleading, just in the way that taking "respect for persons" to be a first-order interpretation of treating humanity in persons as an end in itself is. There are surely connections and resonances between the two notions in both pairs, but using the ordinary notion to interpret the Kantian idea not only begs the interpretive question, it draws us away from core features of Kant's argument.

7. It is the object of *Groundwork* II to argue that this principle is "the principle of every human will as a will giving universal law through all its maxims" (*G* 4:432).

8. For one version, see John Rawls, *Lectures on the History of Moral Philosophy*, ed. Barbara Herman (Cambridge, Mass.: Harvard University Press, 2000), pp. 181–183.

Take the formula-of-humanity pair. If it seems that the formula of humanity is Kant's representation of respect for persons—an idea with moral content—it can be tempting to think that respect for persons as ends in themselves can operate in moral judgment independently of the formula of universal law (that the formula of humanity is a distinct principle of judgment). Certainly many of the canonically immoral actions are not respectful of persons in any sense. But the *Kantian* idea behind the deployment of the concept of respect is that it is the appropriate practical regard for beings who are end-setters of a certain sort, and whose status as rational beings is a limiting condition on what we can (rationally) will. It is this fact that sets the requirement to act only on maxims and for ends that others, as ends in themselves, can share or hold. And what that means, I believe, is that we are to act only on maxims that have the form of universal law (or law-giving). That is, when the Kantian argument is spelled out, we come to understand what respect for persons is: we respect persons *as ends in themselves* when our maxims of action satisfy the constraints of the CI in its first formulation. It is thus not inappropriate to talk of respect for persons as what the formula of humanity is about. But to use the notion of respect to interpret the Kantian argument gets the order of concepts reversed.

The situation is the same with the kingdom of ends. If it is a notion that has something to do with rational natures in a social system, the order of explanation must not be *from* the idea of a social union of rational beings *to* the kingdom of ends. Rather, since the kingdom of ends, as it bears on judgment, must be formally equivalent to the formula of universal law, the only thing that can make a principle a possible principle of an order of rational beings (that is expressive of their rational natures) is that it has the form of universal law-giving. What it signifies about us—that we (might possibly) belong to such an order—is what needs to be worked out.

The merit of this order of explanation will be manifest in sorting out many of the difficulties encountered in producing a satisfactory reading of the *Groundwork* presentation of the kingdom of ends. Whatever new element the kingdom of ends brings to the moral story will be visible only after we fix the connections with the argument that has come before. It is time to look at the text.

A kingdom *(Reich)* is "a systematic union of various rational beings through common laws" (*G* 4:433). Since, as Kant points out, ends are of two kinds, "rational beings as ends in themselves and . . . the ends of his own which each may set for himself" (*G* 4:433), we get to a kingdom of ends this way: "Now since laws determine ends in terms of their universal validity, if we abstract from the personal differences of rational beings as well as from all the content of their private ends we shall be able to think of a whole of all ends in systematic connection . . . ; that is, one can think of a kingdom of ends which is possible according to the above principles" (*G* 4:433). Assuming that "the above principles" are the three formulations of the one categorical imperative, one might suppose that the kingdom of ends is the law-governed union of rational beings that would follow just in case they all acted in conformity with the CI (made the CI the principle of their willing).[9] This looks like a union of good wills. It is worth walking through the reasons why this cannot be right.

It is true that a set of persons with good wills would, in that respect, be persons under one law. They would act in a single, lawful way with respect to all ends (other persons and particular ends). Would they thereby constitute "a systematic union of different rational beings through common laws?" Surely, yes, if "systematic union" just means "under one law." But why, we might ask, is this worth saying? What question might it answer?

The idea of the end-in-itself is brought in to answer the question of the end of maxims for agents for whom the moral law is the determining ground of their willing. Autonomy responds to the worry that this end might be given "externally," through some contingent interest; that the moral imperative might not be categorical. There is no comparable gap that the good wills interpretation of the kingdom of ends fills. Moreover, the "aforesaid principles" are principles of *all* rational wills, not just good ones. It is the rational will that is autonomous; not just the good will. And rational nature as an end in itself "is the supreme limiting condition of the freedom of action of *every* human being" (*G* 4:431, emphasis added). Indeed, immediately after the introduction of the concept of a kingdom of ends (in the passage I quoted), Kant sounds this same inclusive theme. He says: "For, all rational beings stand under the *law* that each of them is to treat himself and all others *never merely as a means* but always *at the same time ends in themselves.* But from this arises a systematic union of rational beings through common objective laws" (*G* 4:433). The sense in which *the law* constitutes a social union "of rational beings through common objective laws" remains to be worked out.

Some puzzles: Why would Kant have us "abstract from personal differences" in order to think of rational beings in systematic union? And what are we to make of the fact that the kingdom is a kingdom of *ends,* not just of rational beings? The law that is constitutive of the kingdom brings ends

---

9. Could the "principles" be the principles of the three kinds of imperative: assertoric, apodeictic, and categorical? This does not seem possible. Only the principle of the categorical imperative is a law.

of both sorts—the ends of agents and agents as ends (in themselves)—into systematic union. Why are private ends included at all? And in what sense, if we must abstract from their content?

We need to be wary of the ease with which we now accept the idea that the appropriate representation of persons, especially for purposes of moral deliberation, requires abstraction from differences. If the kingdom of ends is supposed to extend our understanding of the CI, the potential members of the kingdom of ends ought to be particular agents with maxims. The CI does not address abstract persons.[10] Abstraction from personal differences more reasonably marks the condition of *membership* in a kingdom of ends: a union of persons qua rational beings whose personal differences are not relevant to their status as members. This fits a general procedure for re-garding classes of things under law, as when we abstract from the particu-lars of size and shape in giving an account of which objects are brought into systematic union by the law of gravity. However, not all conditions of mem-bership indicate the defining character of members: though birthplace or naturalization can be the conditions of citizenship—for a union of persons under law—the conditions do not specify what it is to be a citizen, and surely not what it is to be a good citizen. If we are *members* of a kingdom of ends just insofar as we are rational beings, the particular facts about what we will must be irrelevant, just as our size or gender or nationality would be. But it does not follow from the fact that abstraction from personal dif-ferences reveals our membership qualification that the representation of persons within the kingdom of ends is as abstract persons.

Next there is the puzzling matter of private ends. Why are private ends (in abstract form) given equal play as constituent ends of the kingdom of ends? It would seem that if you abstract from the content of private ends, you get the mere concept of a private end: a state of affairs valued as a pos-sible effect of willing. But since under such abstraction all private ends are the same, in what nontrivial sense can they be in systematic union?

There are other ways to abstract from the content of private ends. We might take the lawful union of private ends-as-such to be a system of (all?) possible permissible ends, or perhaps as the somewhat stronger notion of a system of permissible compossible ends (permissible ends whose joint

10. If the model for a kingdom of ends is some kind of social order, then you do not want to abstract from all differences in picturing the union of persons under law. You want an idea of the differences that are morally compossible. Some differences matter, and it is an impor-tant moral question what they are. (Some rational beings are children; others are materially dependent; and so forth.)

satisfaction is possible). There are problems with both options. The set of all permissible ends—all ends that are neither obligatory nor forbidden—surely offers too minimal a conception of order to fit an idea of systematic union. Think of the jumble of things persons might do or bring about, all on maxims that satisfy the CI. (Part of the practical necessity that supports a coercive system of *Recht* is precisely the need to secure order among permissible ends.) Although a standard of compossibility gives a more robust sense of system, it seems arbitrarily restrictive to privilege only ends that can be jointly satisfied.[11] There may be an argument that shows why ends that are inherently or even contingently conflictual are morally problematic, but nothing like that is in place at this stage of the *Groundwork*.

One might think that, given a Kantian account of value, a more reasonable interpretation of the system requirement on private ends would be compossible permissible *willings* of ends. (If not everyone can satisfy the end of winning X, everyone can will—as in try or attempt—to win X). This picks up the essential fact that, for Kant, an end is not a state of affairs, but that which serves the will as the "ground of its self-determination" (G 4:427): that is, a rational agent's conception of what is choiceworthy (possibly, a representation of a possible state of affairs). Private ends are grounds of the will's determination that are not valid for all rational beings (what Kant calls "merely subjective ends"). Their abstracted-from-content inclusion further elaborates the membership condition of the kingdom of ends: it is a systematic union of ends-willing-ends. If this is right, abstraction from personal differences and from the content of private ends makes it possible "to think of a whole of ends in systematic union" only in an entirely formal sense. That is, when we think of persons qua rational agents and ends qua ends of their willing, we can say that both agents and their ends are under—in the sense of "governed by"—a single universal law (the CI): the law that determines universal validity for ends of both sorts.

Now to say that material objects are governed by the law of gravity or that cows are governed by the laws of their bovine nature is to say that there is a law that describes what they do qua object or cow. Material objects are subject to certain forces; cows to certain principles of growth and change. Neither law wholly determines behavior, for neither law works alone. Similarly with rational wills. There is a law describing the activity of such a will qua rational will, but it is not a law that wholly determines behavior. There are

---

11. Even in the natural world, order is measured by system and subsystem, not by the success of any given organism or activity.

other influences. And there is an important difference, because the law of the rational will is a different kind of law. Cows cannot grow into horses, but humans can act like beasts. It is no less true, when they do, however, that their wills are law-governed (and by the law of rational wills). It is rather that it is the nature of the human will to be both law-governed and free. Whether or not an agent wills well, the moral law *is* the law of her rational nature. It is the basis of her dignity (a status she does not lose on occasions of willing badly).

The basic idea here is this. Just as our wills are autonomous when we act contrary to the moral law, so we will remain members of the kingdom of ends however "irrational" our willing is. The kingdom of ends, like autonomy, is not something to be realized through the excellent activity of rational agents. We belong to a kingdom of ends just insofar as we are rational agents. But unlike autonomy, which is an essential property of a rational will, the kingdom of ends is a way of thinking about rational agents under law. We will have to see whether the formal idea of "systematic connection" that it introduces is rich enough to do any work.[12]

---

12. At three points, Kant says things that might seem to run counter to this line of argument. When he says that "morality consists . . . in the reference of all action to the lawgiving by which alone a kingdom of ends is possible" (G 4:434), one might read this as a claim that morality (moral action or good willing) is the means whereby a kingdom of ends may be brought about. I don't think it is. "Morality" names the authoritative relation of the CI to all willed actions of rational beings. It is the legislation that makes beings like us members of a possible kingdom of ends—a systematic union of rational wills under law. That is why in acting according to the moral law (in making the CI the principle of our actions) we can think of ourselves as giving expression to a "higher law" than the law that governs the realm of things. Failure to act lawfully, however, does not constitute freedom from the law. Kant also describes the kingdom of ends as "an ideal" (G 4:433), which suggests a concept of moral perfection: the way things would be if only we acted well (with a good will). Again, I think this is not correct. The sense of "ideal" that Kant has in mind is nothing so simple. "Ideal" is a technical term in the vocabulary of critical philosophy. It is a particular way of representing a concept of which we can have no experience. There are connections with notions of perfection, but they are epistemic, not utopic. (I examine this notion of the ideal in section 3.) And last, when (at G 4:438) Kant says that "a kingdom of ends would actually be realized through maxims whose rule is prescribed to all rational beings by the categorical imperative, if these maxims were universally obeyed," he seems to be describing how the kingdom of ends comes about—through good willing. But in the context of the passage, I think it is plain that we should take "realized"—*vorschreibt*—to mean "instantiated" or "inscribed" in *this* world, the "kingdom of nature." We are, he says, already members of "a world of rational beings" (*mundus intelligibilis*) as a kingdom of ends, because of the legislation belonging to all persons as members" (G 4:438).

II

The kingdom of ends is not the only lawful order to which we belong. Insofar as we are rational beings, we are subject to the law that is expressed by the CI. Insofar as we are material beings, we are also subject to the empirical laws of the natural world. But toward one of the realms to which we belong—the realm of ends—we are said to stand as both subject and legislator ("[t]he concept of every rational being as one who must regard himself as legislating universal law by all his will's maxims"; G 4:433). That is, belonging to the concept of rational agency is the idea of an agent subject to a law (the CI) that applies to her because she legislates it for herself. This complicates the story about membership conditions in the kingdom of ends. Here is what Kant says.

> A rational being belongs as a *member* to the kingdom of ends when he gives universal laws in it but is also himself subject to these laws. He belongs to it as *sovereign* when, as law-giving, he is not subject to the will of any other.
>
> A rational being must always regard himself as lawgiving in a kingdom of ends possible through freedom of the will, whether as a member or as sovereign. He cannot, however, hold the position of the sovereign merely by the maxims of his will but only in case he is a completely independent being, without needs and with unlimited resources [*Vermögen*, "power"] adequate to his will. (G 4:433–434)

Although all rational beings must regard themselves as law-giving (or as legislators) in a kingdom of ends, rational beings like ourselves are dependent beings and so mere members *(Glieden)*. An independent being *(unabhängiges Wesen)* is sovereign *(Oberhaupt)*, because as legislator *(gesetzgebend)* he is "not subject to the will of any other." The implication is strange: how could *we*, as law-givers, be subject to the will of *any* others consistent with our autonomy?[13]

Kant says that for a sovereign member of a kingdom of ends, it is not enough that he give universal law through his maxims; he must also be "a completely independent being without needs and with unlimited power adequate to his will" (G 4:434). I take the fact that the sovereign member is with-

13. There is no shifting of terms here: *unterworfen* is the term for being subject to the law and subject to the will of another.

out needs to imply that he cannot have private ends—his ends follow from his rational nature (they are necessary ends).[14] Further, he has the power to realize these ends without dependence on either contingent material conditions or the support of other rational agents. By contrast, we are dependent beings: we have needs (and so private ends) and lack power or resources adequate to our will. But how does it follow that we are subject to the wills of others? Certainly one of the reasons why our power is not adequate to our wills is that others may interfere with us. So perhaps we are subject to the wills of others in the sense that our ability to will effectively is conditional on some degree of noninterference. But if independent wills are *not* subject to the wills of others in the sense of "subject to" in which all rational beings are subject to the laws of a kingdom of ends, the permanent possibility of interference does not seem to be what makes us subject to the wills of others.

Just before the member–sovereign distinction is made, Kant remarks that the systematic union of rational beings may be called a kingdom of ends because the common law that constitutes the kingdom has in view "the relation of these beings to one another as ends and means." That is: beyond external noninterference, the moral law regulates the conditions and terms of human cooperation. We may not subject others to our will in certain ways: we may not enslave others, act to control or manipulate their willings for our purposes, and so on. But this sense of "subject to" does not explain why we remain "subject to" the will of others when our use of them as means is constrained by our conception of them as ends in themselves, nor does it explain the sense in which we are "subject to" the will of others when we are treated as an end.

We are subject to the wills of others when we are subject to their authority: as citizen, institutional subordinate, and the like. This is a condition we are in, one might suppose, because we are beings with needs for whom hierarchical social roles provide useful, even necessary, means.[15] On similar grounds the *Groundwork* argument for a duty of mutual aid holds that the help of others is a condition of our successful agency that we cannot rationally reject. In both cases, our limited powers lead to compromised empirical autonomy (independence). Because we have needs and only limited power, we are not, even as legislators, independent of the wills of others.

14. Since needs individuate empirical selves, no sovereign could have reason to adopt ends that were not a function of his rational nature.

15. The *Rechtslehre* can be seen as finding its moral place here in what is for us a noncontingent need.

We can take this idea another step. We are, in an extended sense, dependent on the wills of others insofar as the conditions of our agency are social. As our needs determine private ends, so also the particular and social conditions of our agency partly determine what we can will.[16] This is a social fact beyond the requirements of cooperation or noninterference. Thus although the principle of our willing is the self-legislated principle of autonomy, because we have needs that are mediated by social structures, what we will—the content of our maxims—is not.[17] On this interpretation, a being would be "subject to" the will of no other if and only if there was never sufficient reason to have the content of its willing determined by the content of the willings of others. We are not and cannot be in that position.

One final aspect of sovereignty needs attention: the sense in which the sovereign is a sovereign. This is the question of power. We know the sovereign's negative power: he is subject to the will of no other. But what can he bring about? If we are already legislating members of a kingdom of ends in virtue of our autonomous wills, what remains to be "realized" is precisely a kingdom of good wills and, beyond that, the highest good (the general condition in which virtue prevails and happiness is exactly proportioned to virtue, in direct response to it). Each of *us* lacks two relevant powers: to bring it about through our own good willing that others will also act well, and to make it the case that our virtue is rewarded (or even that our willings be effective: that we accomplish what we will). Even the "best" sovereign lacks the former power (concurrent good willing is a necessary condition for a union of good wills). Of course a *community* of sovereigns would have no need of either power: their maxims necessarily conform with the objective principle of rational beings as giving universal laws (G 4:434), and they have no needs.[18] Our condition might be compared to that of a government in exile: possessing a constitution and legitimacy but lacking the power to "realize" just rule. What a supreme being could do is bring the kingdom of nature into harmony with a kingdom of ends (make nature friendly to virtue). But it could alter neither the conditions of the objective reality of a

16. So the desires for sexual gratification, stable intimacy, and procreation are channeled by social institutions into a need for a spouse. Neither the conjunction nor the heterosexual demand are necessary.

17. Perhaps this tracks part of the elusive difference between the holy will and the merely good will.

18. They would also, I assume, have no virtue that calls for reward.

kingdom of good wills (that each act according to self-legislated universal law) nor the conditions of "worth" of its members. The kingdom of ends is a kingdom of limited sovereignty.

III

If, then, the kingdom of ends is just a way of representing an order of beings falling under the moral law, it remains to be seen what it contributes to the moral story. Does the order it represents bring to the practice of judgment any robust, normative sense of the social? Or does it merely represent the metaphysical fact that *as rational beings,* we are under self-given common law: the law of our autonomous rational natures?

Indeed, we might ask, what *could* follow from the mere fact of thinking of ourselves and all rational beings as under common law? Not that we are therefore to reject maxims that are not possible public rules of a *single* social order of rational persons. For if the principle of order just is the moral law—the principle of the CI—any maxim that has the form of universal law is consistent with the constitutive principle of a kingdom of ends. The set of all permissible maxims does not have the form of a social order, much less a unique order.[19]

Alternatively, one might suppose that the role of the kingdom of ends is to extend the reach of the CI to public rules, doing the work (on the moral side) of a principle or conception of justice. Only those laws or practices that could be laws for an order of rational beings (that is, consistent with the principle of their rational nature) are morally legitimate. I have no substantive objection to this extension; I can see good use that might be made of it. But I don't see where in the *Groundwork* discussion of the kingdom of ends there is support for this application.

Along these lines, one might think there is a prior question. Is it the case that insofar as rational natures constitute a realm under a law of autonomy, it must therefore be possible for any group of rational natures to exist as a real social order according to principles consistent with their status as rational natures? That is, the idea of a kingdom of ends is the solution to the possibility question of a moral social order. But why should it be? Why

---

19. If we say that it rules out maxims that could not be public rules of any social order of (co-)legislating rational beings, we deploy the concept "social" but do not give it any work to do.

should the fact that there is order of one kind when you abstract from differences imply that order of a different kind is possible when you do not? And recall that, for Kant, the *state* is a solution to the problem of order for a race of intelligent devils.[20]

The general form of the difficulty is this. If one sees the kingdom of ends as just another way of representing the moral law, then it is hard to see how it supports the idea of morality as a principle for a *social* order of rational persons (as opposed to an order of persons under law, simpliciter—each acting permissibly, violating no duty). But if one thinks of Kantian morality as inherently social, that is, if we start by thinking that the moral order must be a social order, it is hard to see what the idea of a kingdom of ends adds. What we want is an account of how the kingdom of ends—as it bears on judgment, though formally equivalent to the formula of universal law—explains what it means to think of persons as in a social union that is, as such, expressive of their rational natures.

I think we can make progress here if we develop a lead that John Rawls provides in his "Kant Lectures."[21] Wanting to understand how the kingdom of ends is supposed to bring the moral law (as an idea of reason) closer to intuition, Rawls focuses on Kant's remark that the kingdom of ends is an *ideal* (*G* 4:436). Rawls's interpretation looks to the technical notion of the *Ideal* in the *Critique of Pure Reason:* a kind of individual thing that has a special role in judgment. The first feature, that it is a kind of particular, serves Rawls's stated purpose; the second, its role in judgment, serves mine—providing a way of thinking about the nature of the order the kingdom of ends introduces.[22]

The relevant section of the first *Critique* is the "The Ideal in General"—Kant's prefatory remarks to the discussion of the Transcendental Ideal.[23] The topic is the representation in thought of the concepts (loosely speak-

---

20. Immanuel Kant, *Toward Perpetual Peace* (1795), in *Practical Philosophy* trans. and ed. Mary J. Gregor (Cambridge: Cambridge University Press, 1996), 8:366. Kant does not think that a requirement of moral social order follows from the mere possibility of order among rational beings. Attempts at world government invite "soulless despotism" (8:367).

21. Rawls, *Lectures on the History of Moral Philosophy,* pp. 208–212.

22. Rawls is also puzzled about the point of abstraction ("from personal differences between persons and from the content of their private ends") in the idea of a kingdom of ends. Further reflection on Kant's notion of the *Ideal* helps make sense of this.

23. All first *Critique* quotations in this section are from Immanuel Kant, *The Critique of Pure Reason,* trans. N. K. Smith (London: Macmillan, 1970), A567/B596–A571/B599.

ing) of reason. The general concept of the ideal is introduced this way. "No objects can be represented through pure concepts of the understanding apart from the conditions of sensibility." When applied to appearances, the pure concepts of the understanding—the categories—"can be exhibited *in concreto.*" *Ideas* are farther removed from objective reality than are categories, for "no appearance can be found in which they can be represented *in concreto.*" This is so because ideas "contain a certain completeness to which no possible empirical knowledge ever attains." The moral law is such an idea. The idea provides a conception of systematic unity that reason tries to find, if only approximately, in what is empirically possible. The *ideal* is yet further removed from objective reality. Kant says, "By the ideal I understand the idea, not merely *in concreto,* but *in individuo,* that is, as an individual thing, determinable or even determined by the idea alone."

The ideal as it figures in morality provides an example:

> Virtue, and therewith human wisdom in its complete purity, are ideas. The wise man (of the Stoics) is, however, an ideal, that is, a man existing in thought only, but in complete conformity with the idea of wisdom. As the idea gives the *rule,* so the ideal in such cases serves as the *archetype* for the complete determination of the copy; and we have no other standard for our actions than the conduct of this divine man within us, with which we compare and judge ourselves, and so reform ourselves, although we can never attain to the perfection thereby prescribed.

Kant warns that we cannot concede objective reality (existence) to the ideal. We are further warned not to try to represent the ideal in an example— as when one might depict the wise man in a story or romance. As a product of imagination and not reason, such depiction necessarily introduces arbitrary elements and limitations. Reason, rather, "thinks for itself an object which it regards as being completely determinable in accordance with principles." Although the ideal cannot exist, even in example, it is not "a figment of the brain." The ideal supplies reason with a standard of judgment. Kant compares the ideal with Platonic "ideas of the divine understanding." Ideals of reason are like Platonic ideas, insofar as they are the basis for realizing or approximating a kind of perfection. But unlike Platonic ideas, which have creative power in themselves (to bring into being copies), the ideal of reason has "practical power." As an object of reason it contains regulative principles that "form the basis of the possible perfection of certain *actions.*"

Although the idea gives complete content to the ideal, it is the ideal as individual thing that plays the role in judgment—the role one would have expected moral rules or regulative principles to play. The idea gives the rule; the ideal serves as the archetype: the rule given the form of a human life. We do not, because we cannot, use the idea in judgment. Principle (the rule of reason) is nonetheless available to judgment in the shape of an exemplary human life. Judgment, using the archetype, depends on a kind of modeling.[24]

How would it work? In what way could we use the wise man of the Stoics as an ideal: a man existing in thought only, but in complete conformity with the idea of wisdom? To think of the wise man of the Stoics is to think of a person, mature and knowledgeable, in control of his desiring, who acts on certain principles (e.g., of studied detachment from material objects, personal relationships). There is *this kind* of abstraction: we do not know what he looks like, how old he is, or what he does. We do not know how his life goes. Yet the wise man remains a standard in the sense that we can intelligibly ask: How would he behave here? But that is because *he is* a set of principles, principles that are animated in a particular way, given a certain form. The ideal is a formal *embodiment* of regulative principle. The animation is not trivial; it is necessary in order to represent the Stoic principles as ones that can be the principles of *a human life*. This is the difference between thinking of Stoic principles as such, and acting with respect to judgment based on the Stoic ideal. If we cannot instantiate Stoic principles as such (they are principles of a kind of perfection that is outside empirical possibility), we can model our actions on that of the "divine man within us." The wise man eats, marries, negotiates the obligations of citizenship, raises children, and the rest. These are the kinds of things that a human person must do; they are the settings in which virtue can be shown.[25] Though I am unable to act on a principle of forming no attachments, when

24. The analogous move is made in the *Groundwork* use of the formula of the law of nature to represent, for purposes of judgment, the formula of universal law. The explanation of this limit of judgment in using the ideas of reason is the subject of the Typic of the second *Critique* and the Schematism of the first.

25. "Remember that you ought to behave in life as you would at a banquet. As something is being passed around it comes to you; stretch out your hand and take a portion of it politely. It passes on; do not detain it. Or it has not come to you yet; do not project your desire to meet it, but wait until it comes in front of you." Epictetus, *Encheiridion* 15, in *The Discourses*, vol. 2, trans. W. A. Oldfather (Cambridge, Mass.: Harvard University Press, 1979).

faced with loss, I have a model for how to behave: a way to think about what to do.

If the kingdom of ends is an ideal in this sense, it is a representation of an idea of reason (the moral law) as an individual thing, "determinable or even determined by the idea alone." The unrepresentable perfection of the moral law *as a law* is not that of the perfection of the individual will, but of the systematic unity, or order, of rational beings under a law of autonomy. The kingdom of ends cannot then be the bare formal idea of "ends under universal law." It would not then be an individual thing. As an archetype, available in thought as a standard of judgment, it has to be an order of persons—a social order—under common law. Not persons with any particular characteristics or with any specific ends. There is that kind of abstraction. But the kingdom of ends is not persons *in abstraction* from particularity and specificity: not abstract persons. Because the ideal represents the idea of the moral law in the form of a human social order, we are to think of finite beings, in a place, with possessions, attachments, histories, and the rest. So the kingdom of ends exists, in thought only, as an *individual* order of human beings under a law of autonomy: an archetype of human order, against which we can "compare and judge ourselves, and so reform ourselves." We cannot know ahead of time just what kind of order that judgment in terms of the kingdom of ends will yield. That remains a function of the actual circumstances of living together. Though we cannot instantiate the law as a principle of order, faced with hard choices, we have a model we can interrogate about what to do.

IV

Let us suppose that the kingdom of ends is an archetype, a representation of the moral law as an individual thing. Would it make any real difference to moral judgment to have the moral law so represented? The rule of the archetype is: "act in accordance with the maxims of a member giving universal laws for a merely possible kingdom of ends" (G 4:439). It contains the "complete determination of all maxims" by the moral law, combining the idea of legislating universal law through one's maxims and the idea that one is legislating law *for* a system of ends (persons who are ends in themselves).

This representation of the moral law must be identical in its requirement to the other formulations of the categorical imperative. It can be distinct only in the *way* it represents what morality requires. However, to say that the idea of a kingdom of ends cannot be the source of a normatively distinct principle is not to say that it adds no practical content to moral judgment. *Each* formulation of the categorical imperative not only sets out a stage in the chain of conditions that must be satisfied if a categorical imperative is to be possible, it also offers what I have elsewhere called an "interpretation" of the CI's universalization requirement.[26] Moral judgment requires the interpretations that the subsequent formulations of the CI provide. If the formula of universal law tells us *that* a given maxim is impermissible, the full account of *why* it is comes only with the richer representations of the moral law provided by the subsequent formulations.

Suppose it is shown that a maxim of lying cannot be a universal law for rational agents. We still need to determine what it is about the maxim that is wrong-making in order to know, for example, whether or when we are to classify telling partial truths with deceitful lies.[27] If the wrong-making characteristic of the maxim were in the intentional falsehood, we would not. If, however, it is in the treatment of an agent's reason-giving capacity as a manipulable thing, this gives us reason to put "partial truths offered with manipulative intent or expectation" in the same category as deceitful lies. Without the formula of humanity's interpretation of maxims that fail universalization *as* maxims whose principles do not accept rational nature as a final end, this would not follow.[28]

Now if each level of interpretation of the CI further explains the wrong-making characteristics of impermissible actions and maxims, we should find ourselves able to use the idea of a kingdom-of-ends to expand the casuistical power of Kantian moral judgment. What we want is an example or class of examples where there is a maxim whose rejection by the CI procedure lacks didactic import without the kingdom-of-ends interpretation. Moral judgment, enhanced by the resources of the archetype, should expose their dependence on principles that oppose or subvert the conditions

26. This interpretation is set out in Barbara Herman, "Leaving Deontology Behind," in *The Practice of Moral Judgment* (Cambridge, Mass.: Harvard University Press, 1993).

27. *Pace* the tradition, moral judgment is not possible if we bring every maxim to judgment without a prior understanding of its morally salient features.

28. It is also the formula of humanity that directs us to regard maxims that fail the CI procedure's universalization test as containing a principle that disregards the conditions of rational agency as limits on discretionary willing. The interpretation thus also allows us to see how such diverse needs as life support, education, physical integrity, and even the social conditions of self-worth have the same ground of moral claim, based on the idea of taking the "subject who is an end in itself" as far as possible as one's own end (*G* 4:430).

of lawful union for autonomous agents, and for us in particular, the lawful union of autonomous agents with private ends.[29]

Let us consider again the status of private ends in the kingdom of ends. I earlier rejected a compossibility requirement—that only those private ends are permissible that can be jointly acted on successfully—on the grounds that a success condition for ends was not consistent with the Kantian account of permissibility. But (some) failures of compossibility look to be just the kind of thing a universalization test rejects: not everyone can win the game, the prize, the place. I believe that the kingdom-of-ends interpretation can explain why some of these failures (and not others) are morally significant. For example, maxims of unqualified competition *should* be rejected; it is when competitors have unadorned maxims of winning that competition tends to breed excess, cheating, and violence. We can say: their principles fall short of the archetype of possible laws for an order of autonomous co-legislating persons (dependent rational beings with private ends). There are other possible conceptions of a competitive end. All competitors can do their best, all can try to win, and the like. And all such maxims are compossible. But what makes this morally significant is not the possibility of joint success, but that the principle of these maxims can be understood to support a lawful social order of autonomous agents.

We can trace the significance of this sort of result in two ways. First of all it guides casuistry, allowing us to distinguish cases of agents who act on permissible maxims in circumstances where, as it happens, not all can succeed, from cases of agents with maxims whose principles are inconsistent with possible principles of an order of rational agents. Extrapolating, we could use this result to distinguish among maxims of pursuit of different categories of scarce resources. It can explain why, for example, a maxim with a "first come, first served" principle could be morally permissible for concert tickets but not for scarce medical resources. If persons have an in principle equal claim on aid, but not music, the system constraints of the kingdom of ends require (something like) the complex principles of triage for medical need, while they can permit a more laissez-faire resolution to competition for tickets.[30]

Second, the interpretation provides agents with a fuller understanding of their permissible and obligatory actions *as* moral actions. The agent who acts well, who makes the moral law her principle, acts from maxims that

29. Again, knowing *that* a maxim contains or depends on such a principle, we come to know something more about why it fails to satisfy the conditions of the CI.

30. Of course, a different view of music would challenge this permissiveness.

express the full conditions of choiceworthiness as elaborated in the interpretations of the categorical imperative. So, in the trivial case, I head off
early in the day to get tickets with an understanding that interest and willingness to queue are morally reasonable conditions of success here. Such a
conception of action would be morally inappropriate, however, where the
good in question is necessary to sustain lives. (Thus the fact that I went to a
concert yesterday need have no bearing on my going again today, whereas
among a group of starving persons, those who have eaten recently may have
less claim on remaining resources. Analogous reasoning would show the
impermissibility of hoarding.)

As an interpretation of the CI, the kingdom of ends casts as morally relevant facts those features of social life that impinge on the conditions of rational agency. It is not discretionary, then, whether such facts are reflected
in agents' maxims. Thus in circumstances of scarcity, if my action would
have an impact on vital resources, I may not consider it merely as an economic venture. One might say that in this way the kingdom of ends contributes categories of moral salience necessary for correct moral judgment.
Just as the formula of humanity informs us that to act in conformity with
the moral law we must acknowledge others in our maxims as autonomous
end-setters, so the kingdom of ends directs us to regard others as possible
co-legislators in a lawful order. By adding the *form* of the social to our conception of autonomous rational beings, the kingdom of ends both sets conditions on a social order that require consistency with autonomous rational
nature and, insofar as the kingdom of ends is a representation of the moral
law (or of willing according to the moral law), it introduces the idea of the
moral order as itself a social order. It is not an order imposed on agents, but
an order of agents whose rationality is essentially expressed as much
through social as through natural-physical means. The full deliberative
constraint derived from the kingdom of ends—of a moral order as a social
order—requires a degree and depth of adjustment to others, to their ways
of life and values, that transform the very conception of self that is the
foundation of the moral enterprise.[31]

---

31. This way of understanding the place of the social in moral judgment distinguishes the
view offered here from what has been called a "constructivist" interpretation of the kingdom
of ends. A constructivist interpretation regards the kingdom of ends as a device of representation in which the idea of a possible social union of autonomous, co-legislating agents provides a standard of moral judgment independent of the formula of universal law. Legitimate

Since individuals act from and with a complex sense of themselves, their projects, and their actions, the details of this complexity can be essential to accurate moral assessment. The adequacy of a maxim of beneficence, for example, depends not only on whether one is acting to meet a claim of need but also on the attitude of respect with which one acts: the claim of need and the aid given are to be acknowledged and expressed in a respectful way.[32] Attending to the social context of agents' actions can further complicate the moral story, disclosing a finer grain of moral requirement.

As we saw in Chapter 2, one's conception of wealth—for example, as private accumulation or as joint social product—can affect the content of maxims of providing aid. In one case there is a giving to another of what is one's own; in the other it is an exercise of trusteeship. Only the first is an act of charity; the second is a response to some kind of entitlement. In regimes of private ownership that give rise to stark inequalities, it may be hard to avoid humiliating the recipients of aid, making respectful charity difficult; by contrast, where there is entitlement, one is more straightforwardly an agent of what is due. The requirement that provision of aid be respectful (in conception *and* action) may therefore favor one conception of property over another because it supports a healthier moral climate of ownership.

It might appear to follow that if prevailing institutions of property are morally suspect because of the attitudes toward wealth and possessions they invite, then the moral failure identified by this "complete determination" of maxims could be one that the individual agent cannot remedy. This is to an extent true. Nonetheless, the uncovering of such "global" moral failure bears on how individual agents should act. Although one may not be able to transform or fully escape institutions that encourage arrogance (and servility), one can become attentive to an institution's effects and work to

principles of action are those that can be endorsed as public laws or rules of a social union through which all members can conceive of themselves and each other as ends in themselves. By contrast, what I have been exploring is the idea of the kingdom of ends as the "complete determination" of the moral law: a way of coming to see what is involved in a fully amplified (interpreted) conception of moral judgment based on the formula of universal law. The two interpretations therefore differ regarding the scope of judgment they encompass: not all actions with moral significance can be correctly represented as involving public principles of a possible social order; all actions, however, are of selves who are essentially social. A useful contrast is with the bifurcated conception of morality found in T. M. Scanlon, *What We Owe to Each Other* (Cambridge, Mass.: Harvard University Press, 1998).

32. Cf. Immanuel Kant, *The Metaphysics of Morals,* in *Practical Philosophy,* trans. and ed. Mary J. Gregor (Cambridge: Cambridge University Press, 1996), 6:453.

resist the way it shapes our responses to others. We might think about the various ways it is difficult to respond in a respectful way to homeless panhandlers—the mix of dirt and aggression, our own discomfort and moral fatigue. There can be substantial salutary effect in acknowledging the ways social institutions encourage a culture of street poverty. In addition to gaining reasons to support institutional change where that is possible, one comes to recognize the circumstances of poverty as a structural assault on the conditions of human choice and agency. Such recognition can, and should, affect one's response to "victims."[33]

This enhanced conception of judgment also alters the way we think about the general conditions of moral judgment and action. Given the complex social bases of action, there is reason to be cautious about projecting descriptions of others' actions, needs, and so on, based on an understanding of our own circumstances. Of course maxims of action must be formed on the basis of some assumptions about how others act and react. And it is reasonable to assume that others are in many significant ways like ourselves: vulnerable to interference and injury, susceptible to insult, attached to projects, to ideas, and to other persons. But because we for the most part live locally and in narratively thick settings, the way these general features are "read" tends to be parochial; in less homogeneous circumstances we may misread, or miss altogether, differences that matter.

This sort of thing is often seen when formally adequate principles are used to suppress morally significant differences. Suppose it was argued that antidiscrimination norms in hiring are no more violated in giving weight to male passengers' preferences for female flight attendants than they are when we allow female preferences for female gynecologists to matter. It is hard not to think that in so arguing there is a masking of sexual privilege behind a formal principle of equality (regarding the cases as alike) and an unwillingness to confront sexual vunerability (how could one regard the cases as alike?).[34]

---

33. The beginning of such a transformation of response can be found in the acknowledgment of the "battered wife syndrome" as part of a legitimate legal claim of self-defense. It is not a stable understanding of the problem because legal change tends to work by taking old concepts into new contexts. One can nonetheless understand the tension caused by enlarging "self-defense" as a stage toward a conceptually deeper response that, on the one hand, does not diminish the agency of the battered wife and, on the other, is open to understanding the constraint on choice as constructed by morally unacceptable social roles.

34. The issue is not (yet) about what counts as fair equality of opportunity, but the prior matter of the status or standing of preferences as such.

Because both features are uncomfortable to admit (and sometimes to see), first-order moral sincerity is not reliable. The possibility of such moral complexity enjoins moral agents to be especially careful in circumstances of social pluralism, where there are present in a society, and especially in one's normal range of activity, persons whose moral circumstances and claims reflect distinct traditions and ways of life *or* different distributions of power and privilege.

The more extreme condition also shows something about the normal one. Even ordinary moral judgment takes place within a community of judgment: a conceptual space constructed by rules of salience—typically social norms—that identify the features of our circumstances that require moral attention, as well as regulative principles that shape agents' deliberations. The most basic moral facts have a social form. A society of stoics will think about pain or anxiety in a different way from a therapeutically inclined community. It may then be that (some) content of their obligations will be different. While there are limits to the range of difference that is morally tolerable at all, and limits to what is morally possible where groups live together, the fact that there will be such differences is ineliminable and follows from the fact, recognized in the kingdom of ends, that autonomous moral agency is social. That is why failure to acknowledge the social conditions of agency—to actively identify and include them in maxims—is a moral failure.

On the other hand, the idea of a kingdom of ends instructs us that even if the social world of persons with private ends is immensely varied, moral order must be regarded as possible.[35] This does not mean that there is any unique set of ideal social relations or institutions, not for rational beings in general, and certainly not for human beings. It does mean that certain forms of disorder are morally problematic.

What kind of order is morally possible? There are different ways to picture it, connected to different views about the fit of ends in the kingdom of ends. One sort of order involves agents acting for their diverse ends, accepting full "side-constraints" of permissibility, and satisfying whatever positive moral obligations apply. It is a minimal, mostly negative ideal of order, capturing the sense of a stable, principle-based community. In this kingdom of

---

35. It is a kingdom that "would actually come into existence through maxims whose rule the categorical imperative prescribes to all rational beings *if they were universally followed*" (*G* 4:438).

ends, no one acts on maxims of deceit, no one denies a claim of need for reasons of mere self-interest, and so on.

But suppose one asked: how many languages are spoken in the kingdom of ends? how many local systems of custom and practice? We need to pay attention to the presumption of homogeneity in our picture of the kingdom of ends. There is a moral point to the first *Critique*'s injunction not to try to represent the ideal in an example (a political story or romance). Thus maxims can fail if they do not acknowledge differences that arise from specific histories that affect the ways individuals understand their lives. Consider the ease of unintended insult in socially complex circumstances, the disparities in what counts as threat or advantage. Actions thought to be harassing are often not performed from maxims of harassment, and yet one may not be wrong about what has happened. If such facts bear directly on the morality of maxims and actions, minimal order is not enough.

One source of resistance to this line of argument might be the thought that such problems are merely variants of a more general problem for Kantian ethics: its inability to move beyond an agent's conception of her action, however parochial, to a neutral conception or description suitable to action assessment. Because maxims are the objects of moral assessment, agents' subjective limitations are passed on. If I do not know that what I am saying is false, I cannot deceive; if I have forgotten an obligation, the maxim I do act on does not contain an impermissible principle; if I offer what I believe is a suitable gift, I am not insulting the recipient who, for cultural reasons, finds it offensive.

Kantian theory can deal with many normal errors through an extension of the context of assessment to maxims agents adopt before and after acting. Where the risk of advantage is high, "innocent" falsehood caused by lack of effort to acquire knowledge is a moral failure. Obligations impose requirements of preparation that allow us to condemn routine causes of omission; failures of reasonable preparation ground subsequent obligations of response. Likewise, in circumstances in which one knows or should know that divergent cultural facts affect the meaning of social gestures, one is under obligation to make one's maxims responsive to these facts. This is in part determined by the normal conditions of practical efficacy—a sincere agent wants her actions to express her volitions. I am arguing here that it is also a condition set by the deeper practical demands of the kingdom of ends.

To the extent that one assumes social homogeneity, the social bases of moral judgment remain in the background, encouraging a reasonable but mistaken expectation of uniformity in the domain of morally correct actions. But if social pluralism is deep, the set of permissible actions, taken one by one, is not likely to be well ordered. When sincere moral agents act on parochial maxims—maxims that make essential reference to a local community of judgment—that can defeat the possibility for mutual moral understanding and engagement, leaving us unable to recognize the moral content of another's action or incapable of understanding how our own sincere actions could be other than morally benign. This is a condition we are under obligation to overcome. We might say: in circumstances of social pluralism, the kingdom of ends supports an obligation to extend the community of moral judgment. Good willing is not a standard of solipsistic or parochial virtue. The obligation to act as a law-making member of a kingdom of ends thus amplifies the normative content of the categorical imperative: it is a cosmopolitan ideal.

The task of constructing a more inclusive community of moral judgment is not merely or even primarily one of finding reasonable principles for adjudicating conflict; the moral problem that comes with any deep social pluralism is prior to that in the mutual opacity of local value concepts. If we accept that there is more than one permissible way to order the social world (different institutions of property, marriage, etc.; different patterns of child-rearing, schedules of autonomy, conceptions of illness, injury, offense), then we will often not be able to tell whether someone's maxims are permissible, their practices acceptable, without undertaking the more practically freighted task of coming to moral terms with their ways of life.

The cosmopolitan ideal can reach deeply into personal and social values. Because a mutual adjustment of concepts may be necessary to secure the conditions of successful moral understanding, engagement, and colloquy, even important local values may not survive, or not in the same form. Where a community's identity depends on preserving original values, this can be a costly loss. And it is a loss that may have to be borne, even though some of the values that cannot survive exposure to "alien" ways of life were permissible in their own, once isolated, space. Might we have been a species organized in permanent autarchy? It is not likely. But it is also irrelevant, now that the extent of our interaction is manifest and irreversible.

The practical guidance provided by the kingdom of ends as an ideal is not to be found, then, in abstractions from particulars, or in the image of an ideal order, but in directions for the deliberative accommodation to particular differences. Its cosmopolitanism is a standard of deliberation—a way of getting to order from the bottom up. We do not fail to live in a kingdom of ends because we are imperfectly rational beings, our propensity to rational order interfered with by compulsions originating in our systems of desire. If that were the case, the solution would be found in coordination rules for permissible sets of ends: a political solution in the narrow sense, suitable for a race of devils. Nor is the kingdom of ends an ideal in the sense of a community of good wills; that would have no bearing on our condition. The kingdom of ends is an ideal because it is (perhaps impossibly) hard even to imagine the full import of the requirement to regard ourselves and one another as co-legislating members of a moral order: potential members, as I would put it, of a community of moral judgment. If the homogeneity of values is not a human goal, then the idea of a kingdom of ends marks a permanent practical vocation.

V

The kingdom of ends as an ideal allows us to reflect on our actions as a whole and on the institutions and practices that provide the background for action and judgment. It therefore fills two serious gaps in standard Kantian accounts of moral judgment. But must one interpret the kingdom of ends the way I have here? I think it is enough to argue that one can. The rest should be decided by the fruitfulness of the concept.

—4—

Responsibility and Moral Competence

In this and the next chapter I explore, in some preliminary ways, the circumstances of normal moral agency. Their point of departure is a familiar fact.[1] To a large extent, contingencies of upbringing determine what we are like as moral agents. Parents pass on or produce psychic deformations that have morally untoward effects. The specific moral values one grows up into are social values, some of which are decent and well-founded, while others are derived from unjust or morally limited institutions. Persons thus arrive at maturity with some virtues, but also with faults they inherit, weaknesses they may not be prepared to resist, and values that may not be adequate to the moral tasks they will come to face. The circumstances of moral agency thus open a gap between the facts of character and the requirements of moral competence and responsibility. My plan is to investigate some of the details of that gap, and to offer some conjectures about the moral-theoretic resources necessary to bridge it.

One such resource is to be found in the idea of moral literacy. Let me begin by saying some general things about what it is and why it is of interest. In speaking of moral literacy I mean to be extending the basic "reading and writing" concept of literacy as we often do. We talk of different litera*cies:* learned capabilities or skills, having to do with the acquisition and use of knowledge. Becoming literate is not an organic process, like physical growth; nor is it, like speech, the natural outcome of social life. It is a culture-dependent, intentional process. To be literate in a domain is to have the capacity to recognize and perform at some specified level of competency. One can be "barely literate" or "semi-literate." One can belong to the literati.

We do not think a person is literate in a domain if all she has possession

---

1. Versions of this chapter and chapter 5 were given as Tanner Lectures at Stanford University in April 1997.

of is a set of facts. There are things you must be able to do with or because of the facts you have access to as a literate person. You are not musically literate if you can name and date the great nineteenth-century operas but cannot hear the difference between Mozart and Verdi. Regions of learning where it makes sense to talk of literacy tend not to be closed areas of knowledge. Indeed, to be literate is typically to have a skill that is connected to the possibility of enlarged competence. The degree of competency necessary to count as literate in a domain is disputable and may not be fixed. In talking of moral literacy, I mean to draw on this conceptual background: it is a basic, learned capacity to acquire and use moral knowledge in judgment and action.

Why might such a notion be of interest? By working with a notion in which epistemic access and symbolic production (knowledge and action) are joined, we change the angle of moral inquiry; it is a way of breaking the hold of certain pictures. Questions about the substantive connections between moral knowledge and skill have not been on the table in moral philosophy for some time. Moral knowledge as a philosophical subject is for the most part owned by those who doubt there can be moral knowledge at all. The live issues about knowledge and action are often about practical failure: investigations of the fragile links between belief and action, or between the reasons there are and what we have reason to do. Absent is any very complicated story of what we are like as moral agents: of what we can do.

Equally limiting, though in a different way, have been some of the alternatives to this philosophical project. It has been suggested that the conditions for effective moral knowledge—for confident judgment and sure-footed action—require exemption from the full aspirations of critical or rational thought.[2] "Real" moral knowledge is local, rooted in tradition or practice. Reflection is not abandoned, but standards of criticism are themselves part of practice, and moral wisdom weighs against a practice in which full-voiced rational inquiry is left free to do its skeptical work. This understanding of morality can be a position of modest, tough-minded realism, or one of celebratory traditionalism.

The idea of moral literacy offers a different thread to follow. It suggests a subject matter and a standard of competency that is presumptively the same across various moral communities. It is a (nearly) universally available skill, yet one that cannot be deployed except in a local idiom. Even

2. See, for example, Bernard Williams, *Ethics and the Limits of Philosophy* (Cambridge, Mass.: Harvard University Press, 1985); or Alasdair MacIntyre, *After Virtue* (Notre Dame: University of Notre Dame Press, 1981).

more than reading literacy, it is a normative standard of adult competence. It is not necessary to decide whether moral competency is natural: it need not be evolutionarily selected. It also need not be culturally neutral. This is true for reading literacy as well: not all ways of living can survive the transition to reading-literate cultures.

Insofar as it is a capacity for knowing and doing, involving the symbolic manipulation of information as the condition for expressive action, moral literacy is a bridge notion that permits crossing from facts to reasons. Though the link between what is morally true and an agent's reasons is not simple, we should often be able to say that a competent, literate agent has reason to act as she ought, whether or not she does or can see it that way. The analytically suspect separation between motive and value will not be found in explanations of the character of the morally literate agent.

In the course of these two chapters I hope to make visible the need for a concept like moral literacy. I also plan to connect it to Kantian ideas of moral motivation, character, and autonomy. Now one might think this is a foolish idea—trying to introduce a new notion in terms of old ones that many no longer take seriously. But the abandonment of some older philosophical projects is often a function of arguments we may have good reason not to accept.

For example: One of the legacies of modern moral philosophy's Humean parentage is the derogation of motives in general, and moral motives in particular. These days, to speak in philosophical ways about action, practical judgment, or normative assessment is to speak about reasons and about the connection of reasons to desires, or as it has become customary to say, an agent's "subjective motivational set": the sorts of things that provide, or fail to provide, causal support for what we can be said to have reasons to do. Curiously, the elements of a motivational set are not motives. If there is talk about "motives," it is to use a term that is generic for "the stuff that moves us" when we act intentionally. There is a little irony here since Hume himself takes motives to be something importantly other than mere desires: motives are necessary to understand character. Humean motives provide the organization of agency; they not only support the causal chain that issues in action, they give evaluative sense to an agent's choice.[3] Somewhere in the history of a line of criticism something has been derailed.

3. That desires for sex or money are taken to be ubiquitous, presumptive motives does not show that motives are desires, but that we believe desires for sex or money can be the organizing principle of agency.

In the first of these chapters, I embark on a reconsideration of the idea of a distinctly *moral* motive and a first set of arguments for an essentially Kantian view of the matter. We will re-encounter the notion of moral literacy as part of a larger story about motivation, responsibility, contingency, and the education of moral agents. It will later frame a more wide-ranging consideration of the *external* conditions of moral character and action.

I

The idea of a distinctly moral motive is somewhat out of fashion. And certainly very few would now endorse the norm of a *singular* moral motive: the idea that all moral activity does or should arise from one motivational source, or that all moral motivation is of one kind. Two considerations weigh heavily here. The first concerns "the multiplicity of the moral." The idea is that the domain of the moral contains more variety than can be reached by any single motive. Insistence on a singular moral motive would compromise the value that the distinct regions of morality have for us: motivational commitments to beneficence, justice, and friendship *should* be different if the actions that belong to these duties are to express their distinctive concerns. The second consideration is about "indirectness": this is the idea that the *best* motives from the moral point of view may not be moral ones, or not motives that are directly concerned with the moral value of the actions they support. Some who endorse indirectness doubt the very possibility of a distinctly moral motive; others believe that the moral motive, though possible, can be less effective than other motives at producing moral action.[4]

Some facts can be marshaled on behalf of the idea of a singular motive to moral action. Morality makes claims on our lives and projects, not just about what we may do in their pursuit but also how we are to think about what we care about. It makes these claims through diverse duties and obligations, ideals and conceptions of what is good, each part claiming (nonexclusively) the special authority that is moral. If there were only distinct motives corresponding to the different claims of, say, justice, fidelity, and

---

4. Indirectness concerns are typically about motives, but they need not be; some address the content of moral beliefs. We are to accept and regulate our behavior according to *norms* that are justified, not because they express or contain moral truths, but because in acting on these norms we bring our behavior closer to moral truth than we could if we tried to realize it directly.

beneficence, it is hard to see how "the moral" could have consistent motivational authority over thought and action.

Against *indirectness* we can weigh the presumption that moral actions express some value: for example, our acknowledgment of co-membership in a community of equal persons, or, perhaps, that our moral actions exemplify human excellence. For this to be true, or authentic, actions must arise from concerns that reflect their expressive meaning.[5] Further, indirectness and other modes of moral pragmatics generally fit poorly with the reflective areas of our moral lives. The appeal of moral pragmatics is to repair an apparent lack of fit between what morality requires and our epistemic and practical abilities. But where transparency is part of what one aims to be doing—morality is one area where we have such an aim, intimacy another—strategies of indirectness introduce strain, tending to undermine the activities they are supposed to support.

Nonetheless, despite these considerations, the balance of judgment goes against the distinctly moral motive. It is thought that the considerations are not weighty enough, or their concerns can be met in other ways. While I do not think this is so, my intent here is not to re-argue their case but to shift the balance of judgment by arguing for three different, though related-things. First, that some of the rationale for endorsing indirectness and for the multiplicity of moral motives depends on an impoverished view of what a motive is and so of the role of motives in moral action and assessment. Second, that without something very much like the singular moral motive, we have striking anomalies in our judgments of responsibility. And third, that the combined responses to the first and the second point us to a different way of thinking about what a *moral* motive is supposed to do, and thereby to a defense of a distinctly moral motive.

II

One of the major routes to indirectness in ethics is the tendency in modern moral theory to make a sharp distinction between the evaluation of actions and the evaluation of motives. Actions are the primary objects of judg-

---

5. One might also argue that the roles of moral praise and blame (as opposed to reward and punishment) make better sense if their objects are a distinctive way of acting. Although we might praise a child for a successful performance, however motivated, because we believe that learning follows reinforced behavior, we do not offer moral praise to an adult without regard to her motives—not if we would address her as an adult.

ments of right and wrong; motives, the causes of intentional actions, belong to the sphere of virtue. Given the fact that most actions may be variously motivated, there is space to question any purported conceptual connection between moral motives and moral actions. It seems natural to suppose that if one sort of motive is to be accorded the status of "moral motive," the best reason for so privileging it must have to do with its efficacy in producing moral actions. And that is enough to open the door to indirectness.

Paradoxically, Kantian moral theory has been one of the chief sources for this demotion of the moral motive—at least as it has traditionally been read. If, as Kant is taken to say, an action can be right (because according to duty) regardless of motive, the moral evaluation of motives looks to be secondary to, and independent of, the moral evaluation of actions. This naturally suggests a simple efficacy view of the motive of duty. Of course, Kant also holds that acting *from* duty is the condition for the moral worth of dutiful action. The motive of duty has special status because its attachment to the categorical imperative leads to the performance of morally correct action *in a way* that no other motive can. Frequency of success is not the issue; in contrast with the motive of duty, the success of every other motive in securing morally correct action is merely contingent—an accident. What results seems to be a view that accepts the priority of action assessment *and* calls for a moral motive that resists indirectness.

However, as many have noted, it is not clear that it makes sense to prefer noncontingency over frequency of success at performing right actions. Suppose the noncontingent connection of acting from duty is rare or hard to achieve. Given the priority of action assessment, if there is a choice to be made between motivational reliability, however contingent, and conceptual connection between motive and principle (without secure efficacy), the latter might seem to be a moral luxury.[6] The point is not that we can make no sense of the Kantian view of moral worth. A dutiful action that is prompted by a concern for the fact that the action is morally required *is* a different kind of action than one prompted by a nonmoral motive. There may be good reasons to think actions done from duty are special—as, say, an expression of our capacity for autonomous willing. But that is not to explain the *moral*

---

6. A parallel argument can be made with respect to motives to moral action, such as sympathy or compassion, that express values other than connection to principle. If the motive of duty is not preferred on grounds of frequency, the exclusion of other dimensions of efficacy that a motive such as sympathy brings appears arbitrary.

value of the motive: why, if we care about morality, should we want such a motive?[7] Absent such explanation, Kantian theory seems to endorse separate assessment of action and motives, and secondary moral status for motives.

Some direct explanation of the central importance of motives in moral assessment can be drawn from Hume, the other pillar of our tradition. In discussing the origins of moral distinctions, he says: "'Tis evident, that when we praise any actions, we regard only the motives that produced them, and consider the actions as signs or indications of certain principles in the mind and temper."[8] For Hume, the primary object in the moral assessment of action is an agent's character, her disposition to be moved in certain ways. What matters is the affection of a parent for her children, the humanity of a benefactor. It is the imputed motive, the condition of character, that "bestows a merit on the actions" (*Treatise*, 478). Frequency of success in action is not an appropriate measure of moral merit, for what is of primary value with respect to a motive is the kind of concern an agent has and displays in and through her actions.[9]

And this seems right. The moral terrain between parent and child is not comprised of any set of required actions; rather, it consists in a norm for the "attention we give to our offspring" (*Treatise*, 478). Failure to provide the necessities of life can be tragic, but, depending on the circumstances, may not mark a moral failing. It is a sign, a symptom of *possible* moral failure. The relevant moral question to ask is about the underlying nature of parental attention: the *way* a parent considers a child's needs, their felt priority, the kinds of efforts made, the way failure is experienced. Is parental attention, as it ought to be, unconditional, beneficent, and specific?

Humean "moral" motives are valued neither as "good desires" nor as the efficient causes of right action. They are not valued for their objects nor because they contain a conceptual connection to moral principle. Their value

---

7. There is a further problem. Any theoretical rationale derived from considerations of autonomy or the analysis of unconditioned goodness fails to match up with our ordinary sense of the moral value of action and motives.

8. David Hume, *A Treatise of Human Nature* (1740) (hereafter abbreviated *Treatise*), ed. L. A. Selby-Bigge (Oxford: Clarendon Press, 1978), p. 477.

9. That moral distinctions are held to arise from "natural" motives does not imply that there is no category of moral motive in Hume. Moral motives are those whose presence or attribution inclines us to moral pleasure and praise. (I distinguish, as Hume does, a moral motive from a motive of duty: the latter is the default motive we make use of when our natural interests fail us.)

derives from what they naturally contain and express: facts of character. If what is important to us is the well-being of children, it is reasonable for us to be concerned about the character of parents and only derivatively about specific kinds of action. We value attentive concern because the actions that matter flow from what we care about.[10]

The attractive directness of the view does not last. If we begin with the distinct motives that mark the different regions of moral attention and concern (the domain to which Hume's "moral sense" responds), it does not follow that the cluster of motives judged to be good can co-exist in one person. We want persons to be moved by considerations of gratitude, humanity, natural affection, generosity, and industry; but there is no natural, inevitable fit, no general template, that directs their joint instantiation.[11] Even if all of the approved-of tendencies promoted the same thing, they need not promote it in a mutually consistent way. Solutions are then found in "social necessity," which, to take a Humean example, may direct a gendered division of moral labor if the virtues of good parenting conflict with those of market entrepreneurship. Such solutions are unavoidably pragmatic, not morally compelling.

Further difficulty comes with the introduction of rules and standards needed to secure stability of judgment across persons.[12] They constrain what we "should" find morally pleasing: what we praise in moral practice is not the original natural tendency as it strikes the moral sense, but a motivational descendent of an adjusted complex of dispositions and natural motives. This move to indirect justification costs more than transparency; it opens morality in the wrong way to the influence of nonmoral concerns. Suppose our moral code says that giving spare change to panhandlers does not express moral concern, but giving to the United Way does. We will not lack explanations that rationalize the distinction.[13] The problem is that some of the time such explanations will truly be rationalizations: after-the-

---

10. Outside the sphere of justice, questions of "right action" are left to custom and the practical judgment of correctly motivated agents.

11. *Treatise*, 589. Likewise, if we have an aesthetic sense, it will not necessarily pick out objects whose co-presence is aesthetically pleasing.

12. See the discussion of rules and general standards at the end of Book III of the *Treatise*. One finds here an indication of why, though the natural virtues are introduced first, their full account attends the lengthy discussion of artificial virtues. The moral *distinctions* that mark out the virtues are, indeed, natural; the actual virtues of character depend on convention.

13. A utilitarian preference for organized charity; the need to maintain the civil condition of public spaces.

fact justifications for distinctions that arise for other reasons. What counts as morality is made vulnerable to arbitrary distinctions pressed on it by interests of power, wealth, and status.[14]

If the traditional Kantian account cannot explain the moral point of a moral motive, the standard Humean account, which begins with a convincing explanation of the moral value of certain natural motives, falls prey to pragmatics and indirectness problems.

III

There is another way to think about the moral motive that can be drawn from a better reading of Kant. The actual object of primary moral assessment is not an action, but an evaluative principle (a "maxim") that represents what the agent intends to do *as* she judges it to be in some sense good.[15] The evaluative content of the maxim comes from the agent's *motive*, which gives shape to evaluative concern. The Kantian moral motive is thus not a causally effective intentional state *of* value because its object is good: *acting from duty* marks out what moral action *is*. Center stage is occupied not by the action or the action's effects, but by the agent's deliberative choice.[16] Actions that are merely "according to duty" present a defeasible

14. We should be clear about two things that are *not* the case. First, these problems of pragmatics cannot be remedied by appeal to any motive of duty. For Hume, this is an analytically dependent, second-best motive. It is what a person relies on to make good a natural deficiency (a lack of generosity, say), by bringing himself to act as he knows, by experience, a generous person would act (*Treatise*, 479). Second, we should not think that the problems creating unity of character could be resolved by appeal to the point of view of an impartial spectator. The impartial spectator is a possible, if idealized, human moral agent, who must therefore share the conditions of this difficulty. The issues that drive us to pragmatics are not defects or conditions of moral fallibility. They are rather a consequence of the nature of the Humean notion of the moral good and of its place as a component in the development of normal human agents.

15. Standard assessment schema might be: *A* proposes to do X, which will bring about E, because she thinks E is good, and sufficiently so to justify doing X; *B* proposes doing Y, which will bring about F, because she thinks Y is necessary or enjoyable to an extent that justifies doing Y, even though Y brings about F, a regrettable effect. Assessment addresses evaluative choices: for *A*, the question is whether the end justifies the means; for *B*, it concerns the grounds for discounting the moral weight of the untoward effect.

16. What distinguishes duty and honor as motives is not that they give agents different objects to achieve through action (morality vs. glory) but that they are expressed in different evaluative principles that agents so motivated take to support good reasons.

sign of right action—the action that would be performed by an agent moved by moral concern.[17] This makes better Kantian moral sense, too, for what makes an action morally wrong is the incompatibility of its maxim with the proper regard owed persons as ends-in-themselves: one fails to be *moved* in the right way by the fact that persons have a different status than things.[18]

One does not need to be a Kantian to appreciate the point of assessing actions under an agent-relative evaluative description. If this seems not to be the case, that is because many actions—and especially the actions in philosophers' examples—are of a type that seems to require no such interpretation. We normally take it to be self-evident that a punch to the nose or a racial insult is morally wrong. But we also accept the idea that actions, even these obvious actions, are only signs of moral qualities: reliable but fallible signs of deliberative choice. The punch could be an attempt to save a life, the insult an involuntary utterance of someone with Tourette's syndrome. What is significant is that when such atypical scenarios obtain, they do not *excuse* the agent for an untoward action, but defeat the attribution of moral wrongness to the action itself. This is enough to show that assumptions about deliberative choice were implicit in the self-evident examples as well.[19]

There are a few areas of morality where identification of an action-type may be sufficient for negative moral judgment: absolute prohibitions or moral taboos are examples. They represent regions with a special moral role; barriers must be thrown up so that opportunity for deliberative justification is made unavailable. *Nothing* counts as a reason for incest. As spe-

17. That is, one misreads Kant if one takes "according to duty" to mark an independent standard of right action.

18. Actions as such (regarded as events with effects) can neither be compatible nor incompatible with respect for persons. Only actions under a description that represents their deliberative origin are assessable in this way. We need to know the terms in which an agent views her action as justified treatment of a person.

19. I am not arguing that good motives are sufficient to insulate agents from charges of wrongdoing. One can, as I do, insist that motives (good and bad) determine *what* an agent does *and* hold that agents who intend to act well can be morally in error. They may be mistaken about the good they would pursue, or be deliberatively in error about the relative or justificatory value of means and ends, and so forth. There are many complex issues that cannot be addressed here about the point of view, first or third person, from which moral assessment is made.

cial or limiting cases, they do not provide counterexamples to the thesis that, in general, action assessment depends on the evaluative principle the agent employs to justify her action.[20]

Suppose one thought that, to the contrary, whether a helping action is benevolent or self-promoting, it *is* a helping action: namely, an action that meets a need. We can judge its "to-be-done-ness," and treat the rest separately as questions about the agent's virtue. But when we ask whether a helping action is X or Y, it is often its "to-be-done-ness" that is in question. We say a helping action is exploitative and so wrong, because of the way the recipient of help is regarded by the person helping (regardless of the outcome). The evaluative regard is the wrong-making feature *of the action;* it is not a case of the right action done the wrong way. And what of the self-promoting helping action? If it seems not to be wrong, that is because we often have reason to mind less being the object of advantage than being in someone's power.[21] Here Hume and Kant will agree: setting questions of justice aside, external actions are to be regarded primarily as "signs" of the way we care about things—of what we value. If the moral assessment of actions looks to motives, motives are part of the full *moral* account of what an action is.

Recall that our question was whether a distinctly moral motive would contribute anything beyond frequency of success for morally right actions. We can now see that there is something odd about the question. If it is not actions per se that are the objects of moral judgment but actions under a description that is in part determined by an agent's motive, then the very idea of "frequency of success" is misleading. Success at what? Different motives may yield the same behavior but, from the moral point of view, different actions. *Were* the contribution of the moral motive just to secure success, there would have to be *another* motive that carried the agent's de-

---

20. Some might take the fact of "rights" as evidence that I go too far: whether I have violated a right is a matter of fact, not dependent on evaluative intention. I do not think so. Whether rights are infringed, violated, or overridden depends on a congeries of considerations, some conventional, some deliberative. A right describes a specific kind of normative space around a moral concern that pre-frames possible deliberative approaches.

21. Partly this is so if we think that the benefit is an independent effect. It is clearer with omissions. The decision to withhold help because helping is not self-promoting, or the decision to withhold help when not helping is self-promoting, is much less plausibly read in terms of separate action and virtue evaluations.

liberative evaluation. The value of the success-ensuring motive would then be dependent on the value of the evaluative motive. Such a moral motive would do no independently moral work. If we are seeking a primary moral role for a moral motive, it should reside in its contribution of distinctive evaluative content.

But is there some specific moral content that it is reasonable to want all morally successful actions to have? Some one way all deliberative choice should go? We appear to have come all this way only to rejoin the problems of a singular moral motive, now sharpened by the rejection of the action–motive distinction. If the motive is central to morally relevant action-description—carrying an agent's conception of the value of her action—specific moral content would appear to introduce unacceptable monotonic value. We are not trying to do one "moral" thing when we pay a debt, lend a helping hand, thank a benefactor, or resist injustice.[22] What we *value* when we act these different ways is different. So if there is reason to bring motives into action assessment, it seems a good reason to bring in a whole set of them. But then what would make these motives *moral* would seem to have to be something external to their evaluative content. We seem to lose the idea of a motive that is both morally distinctive and morally valuable.

If this seems to exhaust the alternatives, I think it is because of the *way* we suppose a motive does its work. Philosophical discussion tends to work with a few simple models of motive: roughly, motives as desires (broadly understood); motives as complexes of belief, desire, and (possibly) intention; motives as dispositional states with objects. In all of these cases the *work* of the motive is done the same way: a motive functions as an action-generating structure, a psychological state or disposition that causes the agent to act as she believes she should. That is why it seems that if moral agents do not always act "the same way" when they are responsive to various different moral claims, there cannot be one moral motive; there must be a number of different dispositions (motivating conditions) that the morally good agent will have. The new claim—that the motive contains an agent's conception of value in acting—just folds into these accounts of how a motive works. To resist this, I want to approach the moral motive through

22. There are different marks of salience, different ranges of (morally) appropriate response and affect, and different (moral) objects of action.

a different route, taking as a point of departure its role in the development of normal moral character.

IV

The first thing to note is a truism. Moral character begins at a time prior to the possibility of reflection. It is shaped, somewhat haphazardly, by persons whose sincere efforts to bring us up well are partly undermined by ignorance, accident, and, among other things, their own moral and human failings. Most of us therefore arrive at reflection partly disabled, probably capable of secure moral performance in some areas of our lives, liable to dysfunction when challenged in others. Aspects of our own behavior may appear mysterious to us; some areas of disorder may be off-limits to examination. By the time we are able to ask questions about this, those who shape our character may not know or be able to say what they have done. Beyond the ordinary issues of self-opacity, there are barriers to acknowledgment and insight that are set up to protect the integrity or felt decency of the self. Nonetheless, most of us are expected to come to adulthood able to respond to moral considerations in a responsible way: able to measure the weight of moral reasons, act morally, and transmit moral values to our children. The nature of the background facts and the task set a developmental agenda: *something* has to be able to provide the organizing structure necessary for the formation of a stably moral character, without having to resolve the ruptures and instabilities of character even a pretty decent upbringing can leave behind. I want to suggest that an important part of this work may be done, when it is, by something it will make sense to call "the moral motive."

In looking for an account of moral motivation that is true to the perturbations of real-time character development, I do not mean to launch a psychological investigation of moral pathology. The object is to understand, from the side of morality, what moral motivation must look like, *given* a realistic picture of human character and of our routine success as moral agents. Discussion of moral education (the formation of normal moral character) was once a central part of moral philosophy. Why it is no longer central is a question worth asking. A partial answer lies in the moment that is selected as the target of philosophical inquiry. Much recent philosophical discussion starts with an adult who has some particular set of dispositions and asks, what, given just these dispositions, can a person have reason to do?[23] We do not ask: What dispositions *must* a normal adult have, if she is to do the things we expect a normal person to do? One might think this is a prior and substantive question. After all, the lexicon of possible motives that bear on morality is neither hardwired nor singular. Our capacity for acquiring moral motives is open to development in various directions, not all of them equally adequate. We lose the possibility of thinking about such issues by taking the "however-formed" adult to be the model of a normal moral agent. Driven by essentially skeptical concerns, we in effect make moral theory a passive, descriptive project. As I will argue, it is then hard to make sense of some moral judgments I think we clearly need to make.

In particular, one wants to avoid the conclusion that the actions persons can be held responsible for are limited to the range of actions they are motivationally or psychologically capable of at a time. If, for example, we believe that childhood abuse creates an adult disposition to abuse, and that the disposition to abuse works through compelling rationalizations about provocation, desertion, and the like, then we may find it harder than it should be to hold (some) abusers responsible for what they do. There is a sense in which they cannot do otherwise. Of course there is a sense in which they can. Avoiding this impasse, paying attention to the conditions that make the right judgments possible, will point us toward a different, more "active" role for moral theory in an account of moral motivation and character.

Let us examine a more familiar, lower profile kind of abuse. Imagine that neurotic and psychologically abusive parents cause a child to have a disposition to casual cruelty toward intimates. We later find an adult who gets it wrong about what is fun, what is danger, what it means to trust and be trusted; someone who seeks and betrays intimacy, who is forever at a loss about how things can go so wrong; someone who also gets unacknowledged pleasure in the distress he orchestrates. The form of cruelty, a demand for trust followed by covert betrayal, repeats the pattern of childhood abuse. Such a person is damaged or morally deformed. He is probably also a carrier: liable to pass on to his children his own difficulties with love and trust. But he is not in any deeply pathological sense an abnormal agent; he is "normal enough."

We can imagine saying to him: "Don't be cruel!"—even when we know

---

23. I ignore for now the way the dispositions a normal adult is taken to have are identified: that it is simply assumed that there is neither an objective good toward which rational agents are by nature disposed nor a conception of practical rationality whose principles give reasons for action or restraint on their own.

that his cruelty arises from aspects of his character formed in the out-of-reach early childhood nexus of distorted parental authority and love. The explanation for this is not about degrees of causality. It is that the cruel actions are in some ordinary way chosen for themselves and form part of what the casual abuser thinks good—something that is *not* the case with, for example, obsessive actions, where the causality is more direct. For the abuser, there is pleasure where there should be none. There is repetition without absence of control: the details of the abusive situation are under manipulative control; otherwise, there is no satisfaction.

The pleasure and the *pattern* of failure introduce something important. They mark the reason why, though child abuse runs in families, as may casual cruelty to intimates, agents who inherit such moral disabilities can be responsible for their actions. Where there is evidence that someone is on balance a normal moral agent, if there is enough untoward going on in his life, we blame him for not seeing it. After a certain point we expect a normal agent to recognize patterns and to take seriously the complaints of others. Morality need not tolerate obdurate blindness. Of course, no one can see everything; features of our character really do blind us from some things; it may even be necessary, in some deep practical sense, that we not attend to everything. But there are limits. And it is an important question of theory as well as practice how we identify and make sense of them.

If we see the normal enough abuser as an example of passive moral theory's "however-formed" adult, we will be tempted to a picture of him as having a character constituted by his desires and defects plus some analytically posterior connection to morality. We will see his failure as about weakness—his attachment to morality either locally absent (gappy) or insufficiently strong. If passive theory judges him responsible, it will not be because he has a defect, but because he succumbs to it. Responsibility for his action is then indirect, following only as the gap or the weakness is correctly imputed to him by an independent normative story. This is not the right case to make against the abuser. And it does not adequately distinguish the abuser from other cases of failure in a way that explains what he is responsible *for.* The scope of responsibility concerns the assignment of further moral predicates. The abuser's actions are not just faulty and imputable, they are cruel. Consider someone who behaves similarly to the abuser, but whose pain-causing failures to sustain intimate trust are caused by obsessive anxiety or fear of being engulfed. Her actions may be faulty and blameworthy; they are neither cruel nor abusive.*

Because it holds "the moral" separate from or consequent on other motivational systems, the passive story tends to focus on the just-prior-to-action state of motives, ignoring the complex etiology and structure of moral disability. This would be reasonable if moral development were a contingent and separate matter—a however-effective means to acquire an independently defined state of (good) character. All we *could* say then is that, as a result of their pasts, both agents lack something a person with morally good character has. They are incapable of practically effective evaluation: nothing in their current motives would have led them to act otherwise, if only they had noticed *X*, or reasoned more fully about *Y*. Given their defects and disabilities, they could not notice more or deliberate more effectively.

To make the case against the casually cruel abuser—to defend holding him responsible for cruel and abusive action—involves two stages of argument. First, taking in more than the agent's state just prior to action, we note that in most of his dealings with people, he is routinely moral. He is not aggressive; he probably keeps promises and tells the truth most of the time; he may even be impersonally beneficent. He knows what moral reasons are, and what response to a moral claim involves. The capacity to identify and be responsive to a wide range of moral considerations is evidence of a pattern of development that satisfies normal conditions of imputability and responsibility, extending to nonintentional wrongdoing.

Second, what makes it reasonable to accuse him of more than nonvoluntary wrongdoing, of acting cruelly—even given that he acts as he does as a result of a deformation of character—is the fact that he takes pleasure *in his agency* in the untoward outcomes. It is a sign that he acts from his own motives, not as a result of causes. This lets us see his actions flowing from his conception of the good. He is not a vehicle moved by impulses; he is no victim; his actions, and their moral predicates, are fully his.[24]

Obviously, to get it right about the full range of normal agents will require a much more complex story about moral motivation: about how motives develop and about the kind of baggage they may carry; about the ways a sense of self and a conception of the good are formed; and about the ways early trauma (in particular) can short-circuit mature practical judgment. That is not an account I can give here. But there is another part too. Moral theory must provide a *normative* account of the structure of moral motivation and character—how agents *should* develop if they are to be morally ef-

---

24. The two stages suggest a stronger conclusion. Given normal moral agency, we can distinguish among causes of action in a way that lends support to some compatibilist ambitions.

fective agents. I do want to say more about the conditions for such an account, but first, there is a last issue raised by the case of the casual abuser.

Given the form of a normal human life, and the casual abuser's particular need for intimacy, it is unlikely that he can avoid error. He is very poorly equipped to negotiate the pleasures and temptations of intimacy where there is unequal power. Some might say that even so, it is still a function of circumstances that he acts badly—a matter of moral luck—a relevant fact the preferred account ignores.[25] One wants to be wary of this move; it collapses some important distinctions, making it difficult to appreciate the evaluative role of motivating states of character.

Moral luck is about the fit of character to circumstances and conditions of action. Although we can explain the abuser's predicament in terms of lack of fit, we also have reason to think that his problem is deeper and not a matter of luck at all. The tension here is a result of two different ways we think about moral character. On the one hand, there is the passive theorist's "character is that which leads you to act well," which leaves it open whether we might not all be, at bottom, lucky abusers—like flatlanders with acrophobia. We have just looked at what this sort of account leaves out. On the other hand, we have inherited a picture from Aristotelian ethics that suggests that possession of a good character disposes one to act well across an indeterminate range of circumstances and conditions of action. This is because a person with a good character does not find reason-giving the sorts of considerations that typically lead persons to act wrongly. It is like an inoculation. One is not tempted by pleasures had at another's expense; the power in unchecked aggression isn't appealing; and so on. Much more than attachment to abstract morality is involved. There is a thoughtful detachment or disengagement from the various things that draw us into immorality. What is attractive in sources of temptation is understood and deliberately foregone. We are inclined to think that, absent catastrophe, a person with a good character in this sense is immune to moral luck. She would not have been a Nazi; she can negotiate the shoals of natural intimacy. I think that this kind of account, though appealing, makes it too easy to explain what the abuser lacks.

25. The interesting difference between this and the "X would have been a Nazi had he lived in 1942 Germany" scenario lies in the fact that the region where the casual abuser goes wrong is so centrally normal. For the casual abuser to escape wrongful action, *his* life would have to have been unusual—separate, for example, from other persons and the possibilities of intimacy and dependence.

There is, first of all, something odd about the claim made on behalf of the Aristotelian picture. It suggests a kind of fixity to the moral world that belies experience—about the kinds of actions that are right and wrong, and about the range of temptations. How could even the very best Athenian upbringing (to say nothing of the best suburban upbringing of the 1960s) prepare one to meet our end-of-the-century questions about race and gender, poverty, or the physical condition of the world?[26] There are new and difficult temptations; the pace of moral change makes it hard to imagine what it could mean to be prepared.

It is not exactly a failing of Aristotelian theory that it lacks elements that render it fit for the circumstances in which we find ourselves. It is not clear that it was intended in that sense to provide guidance to contemporary Athenians either. Aristotle's account of moral character includes a piece about the social and material setting in which the virtuous person is to live: a city of modest size with a particular kind of participatory politics, a generous level of material well-being, carefully controlled moral education, and a class within which a man of good character could experience himself as an equal among equals. In such a setting, virtuous character *is* security to moral action. As far as is humanly possible, the morally unexpected is legislated away. For the virtuous person, though success in action is still contingent, it is not really a matter of luck at all.

This idealization of the conditions of human living is part of the point of Aristotelian ethics. Aristotle's question was about the human good—about how, as a natural species, we might flourish. The solution picks out a life according to reason in circumstances in which reason *can* be an effective guide to a good life.[27] Aristotle's sensitivity to the power that chance and adversity have over success leads him to describe a human habitat in which our rational powers and pleasures could safely and fully develop. Like Plato's *Republic*, Aristotle's *Ethics* is a revolutionary theory.

---

26. Obviously, poverty, discrimination, and pollution are not new phenomena. What has changed is their moral meaning. Partly this is so because other things have changed. The degree and scope of American wealth makes the degree and effects of its absence in the South Bronx, in parts of South Central Los Angeles, in impoverished rural communities, because so clearly avoidable, unthinkable. We also have a better understanding of causes that makes the demand for change integral to moral decency.

27. We might think of the politics of Aristotle's ethics as a prescription for some of the injuries of empire.

Mostly we do not have such overtly or thoroughgoing revolutionary aspirations for moral theory. If we are to hold agents morally competent
across an extended range of conditions of action, we do better, at least at the
outset, thinking about moral character and motivation as something that
can arise through normal upbringing in quite diverse circumstances, ones
that may include some range of moral deformation, but do not, for that,
undermine our status as responsible agents or our responsibility for what
we do.

V

We might start with the idea that normal moral character is built on what I
call "moral literacy": a capacity to read and respond to the basic elements of
a moral world. It begins with the primitive and necessary acknowledgment
of the difference between persons and things and the practically effective
understanding of what it means for moral claims to be attached to persons.[28] This idea of moral status, reflected in the way moral reasons enter
agents' deliberations, is a formal requirement for something to count as a
conception of morality.[29] The requirement can be met in different ways.
Claims that rest on the status of persons can be absolute, blocking treatment of persons as "mere" means to no matter how great a good, or the
claims can be more modest, introducing a threshold that we need special
reasons to cross, a thumb on some scale of balance. Moral status is elaborated through a culturally based lexicon of basic moral wrongs and injuries

28. It may be that without the wherewithal to distinguish persons from other sorts of
things in a reason-giving way a child lacks necessary conditions for development or even survival (autistic children are sometimes thought to lack such ability). We might think, by analogy, of the necessity of acquiring concepts of causality. Whether or not the capacity to acquire
causal concepts is innate, some experiences and ways of thinking about causes have to be provided to position a child to acquire causal concepts at all. Only then can she navigate the
world in a human way. Success here, however, is no guarantee that a child could develop the
further capacity to, say, distinguish good science from magic.

29. Though some moral theories, e.g., classical utilitarianism, expand the domain of the
moral subject to include all sentient beings, I believe the distinction between persons and
nonpersons remains fundamental; it is rather that not all nonpersons are necessarily things.
It is not clear that an upbringing framed in a single calculus of value applied across all sentient beings could produce a human character at all.

that are more or less fixed and easily recognized by a morally literate person.[30]

Moral literacy as such is not a minimal conception of morality, but a minimal moral capacity. Its possession and exercise does not make one a good or even minimally decent person. That remains a function of one's substantive beliefs and practices. It is, however, what makes a person the proper subject of moral predicates. As a practical disposition that enables recognition of morally salient basic features of circumstance and action, as well as the regulatory capacity to do what is seen to be right, it is sufficient to secure agents' imputability for the effects of most of their actions and responsibility for the causal potential of their dispositions.

Not all conceptions of morality that build on a minimal moral capacity are on a par. Each sets a direction; not all directions are equally good. Because we are malleable beings, what fixity there is in our natures admits of an extraordinary diversity of expression. That is how there is room to argue on moral grounds for or against a given conception of character as a constraint on normal development. Agents whose moral concerns develop merely as an element within a mix of their overall concerns and interests will lack some capacity to recognize the nature of moral authority: they may find it unintelligible that (some) moral constraints cannot be overridden by some amount of piled up nonmoral values. Others who view morality as the interior arm of external norm-enforcement may try to get a fix on how much discomfort or guilt they can tolerate in pursuit of some contrary-to-morality project. And so on. Persons so described *are* developmentally possible *and* normatively impaired. And this is so however they may otherwise be advantaged. The question is not whether our moral theory contains an accurate description of our development, but whether we *can* develop the character that moral theory prescribes.

The manipulative abuser is someone who has much more than a minimal moral capacity; his moral deformation is limited and selective. But it is because he possesses and manifests the minimal capacity that we feel no compunction in holding him responsible for actions that he in some sense cannot help. Although he may not be able to alter the complex of habits and anxieties that dispose him to acts of casual cruelty, his actions are not be-

---

30. In circumstances of change and awkward fit between character and human habitat, the literacy metaphor is especially appropriate: it captures the idea of a fundamental mode of moral orientation that provides basic skills to interpret moral phenomena that press at the boundaries—whales and fetuses, moral claims for minority cultures, and so on.

yond his reach. He has the capability to identify them for what they are, if not the first time, then soon enough. And he is able, if he chooses, to avoid causing injury.

A minimal moral capacity functions like many other practical capacities that "license" behavior. Competence at driving a car requires some mechanical skill, recognition of salient features of road and traffic, knowledge of governing norms, *and* the capacity to resist temptations to speed or run red lights at 3 A.M. Competence does not make one a good driver, but it puts one on the road responsible for a variety of unexpected outcomes, including some that may be the product of one's own limits or incapacities. We expect that a driver with a blind spot over her right shoulder will, over time, discover the gap in her visual field, appreciate its danger, and compensate for it. She learns to turn around more completely, or she adjusts her mirrors to a different angle. That the blind spot is a fixed feature of her visual field gives her a task, not an excuse. Likewise, we may say, the abuser's guilty pleasures, the complaints and hostile reactions of his intimates, provide adequate indication of moral fault. His moral task need not be to remake his disposition. He may lack the resources to effect such change; it may not be possible. It *is* morally incumbent on him, however, to change the angle of his encounters. He is at a minimum obliged to identify and master the occasions of temptation.[31]

The abuser's disability poses special problems: personality deformations, unlike blind spots, can retain essential connections to their history and so to a person's sense of self. If he is repeating his father's pattern of abusive behavior, there may be deeply seated barriers to self-understanding and change: to see the truth about himself might require accepting unwanted truths about his father. But these are barriers to wholeness and health, not excusing conditions for blindness about the nature and effects of his actions. If he cannot mend his disability, stopping the abusive behavior may cost him things he values: spontaneity, casual confidence, at the extreme,

---

31. Of course, being a moral subject, having a minimal moral character, may not be sufficient for moral success. That is, even if the abuser comes to pay sufficient attention to the morally untoward features of his actions and dispositions, though he may resolve to do better, he may well lapse into old patterns. His character is sufficient to impute fault and in some cases to assign blame; it need not be sufficient to guarantee success. On the other hand, one doesn't want to exaggerate his difficulties. Getting it right, morally, is not equally easy for everyone; it is not unfair that this be so. Confusion about this last point has led both to excesses of excuse and to prizing as virtuous those struggles that yield success. Overcoming misfortune is indeed to be valued; it is not the same thing as virtue.

the possibility of intimate relationships.[32] At some point we revoke a license to drive.

If the conditions that give rise to moderately abusive dispositions are not so rare, the concept of ordinary moral character—the character of a moral subject—must accommodate these moral deformations of disposition and desire to which we are prone. My conjecture is that the not-so-bare idea of a minimal moral capacity does this work. It secures an ability to distinguish persons and things that is responsive to morally basic facts of injury, offense, and so on. In conjunction with the idea of basic moral literacy, it establishes common terms in which moral assertion and reasoning take place. When I am told that behavior I think of as good-natured play humiliates, I know at once that although there may be room to debate whether what I am doing really is wrong, there is no room to debate whether if it is, I can describe it as I wish or as "feels right." And if my teasing humiliates, I must stop it. The possession of a minimal moral capacity is in this way consistent with a degree of moral deformation. Such dispositions can be corrected for, even if they cannot themselves be changed. Even the obsessive who cannot control his behavior can remove himself and his behavior from harm-causing way, once he knows the moral significance of what he does.[33]

Now it doesn't take much of a stretch to recognize that the singular and distinctly moral motive is a good fit for the minimal moral capacity. It is a motive that, by itself, may not enable the agent to act well in the circumstances in which she finds herself; it may not, by itself, provide a sufficiently tooled evaluative principle to support sensitive judgment. But by itself, it is sufficient to direct the agent away from recognized harm. (That is why a repeated fault can amount to much more than multiple instances of the same thing.) Like the law's satisfaction with a defendant's knowing the difference between right and wrong for legal responsibility, the presence of the singular moral motive would be sufficient to mark one a responsible moral subject, securing some of the practical truth of "ought implies can."

32. Thus, if having been an abused child disposes one to abuse children, one may not have an unqualified right to be a parent.

33. It is clear by this point that the minimal moral capacity lies somewhere between a capacity and a disposition. As a basic structural element of character, it is like a disposition or ability; in its potential for development and increasing literacy, it is more like a capacity. For present purposes, I will treat it as sharing elements of both—as a capacity/disposition.

However, the minimal disposition with its singular moral motive cannot be the end of the moral story about motives and character. The casual abuser's moral flaw is complex: not only is he unable to act well, when he acts badly, his actions are cruel. Though sufficient to keep one out of moral trouble, the minimal moral motive does not reach into character; it does not make one a good person. What the abuser lacks, what someone had a moral obligation to provide, was an upbringing in which humanly necessary trust was not purchased at the price of a blind eye to minor cruelty. Early experience and moral teaching *ought to have* given him a disposition that responded to vulnerability as an occasion for, say, care and support, not ripe territory for abuse. And so on. This is all quite sensible. However, it appears to introduce a new kind of moral motive, or set of moral motives, whose connection to the minimal or singular moral motive is not at all clear.

Suppose we thought that the minimal moral capacity(/disposition) was something that, like language, arises in and through the activities of ordinary child-rearing, not as a primitive skill (taught with an eye to some ideal) but as an element in the repertoire of abilities that make us human (able to develop various ideals, and also deformations). It would be odd to think that there are or could be two distinct moral capacities, as though an agent first acquires a minimal moral capacity, and then, as she matures, acquires a wholly different, more complex one to replace it. There would be the same oddness in the thought that the linguistic activity of infants was "baby language"—acquired to suit the needs and abilities of infants—supplanted later on by something entirely new. Little in our development looks like that: crawling is integrally connected to walking, babble to speech, mimicry to mature social relations. It is equally implausible to imagine a normal adult with *no more than* a minimal moral capacity: someone for whom the substance of morality remains wholly external; who is indifferent to the purpose and point of moral requirements—to their value.

I would conjecture that the minimal moral motive both serves as a starting point for a more developed moral capacity *and* keeps a distinctive role in developed moral character. In the latter role, one might recall Kant's man of sympathetic temper: his capacity to act from duty alone is a resource, something he can rely on in a crisis.[34] Hume's "sense of morality or duty"

---

34. Of course the value of "acting from duty" is not exhausted in this role; the form of willing that acting from duty represents is the general form of willing of a person of good character.

works to a similar end—a disposition to be drawn on when natural motives fail. Hume's agent can condemn himself for lacking a natural motive he judges it is morally good to have. He recognizes his deficiency in the same way as he would another's: through observation of *repeated* failure to act in the ways that a person with good character would. A "sense of morality or duty" allows him to act as one ought; it is a default mode of a more developed moral capacity—a sort of *backstop* motive.[35]

We do not need Hume or Kant to appreciate the role of a backstop motive. It is a general feature of practical life. Many of the things we normally do, and even enjoy doing, go dead for us from time to time. The reasons that normally suffice to make us responsive and active fall on impassive ears. When we know that we must nevertheless act, we can. We depend on having motivational resources to pick up the slack on a bad day. We also hope our lives are not dominated by such motivationally arid moments.

But why think that the moral backstop motive is related to a motive belonging to the development of moral literacy? Might not the backstop motive be something new that emerges only as a mark of moral maturity, providing a kind of moral reliability and steadiness, responsive to the full range of an agent's moral concerns? There are such virtues of maturity, but it is not where the backstop motive resides. Some of the things we learn to do early on, that make possible later strengths and skills, continue to reside in a crisis-available form in the more mature ability. It is not necessary that this be so (here real literacy is not the right analogy), but it can be, and likely will be, if the default role is made part of the culture of the mature skill. Though fatigue and stress can render one responsively inert, most of us can still register pain-as-such as a prima facie sign of wrongdoing, and sufficient reason to desist from the action causing it until we are more confident in our judgment. Though our knowledge of what pain is will become more sophisticated, the default reaction to pain-as-such does not. The backstop or default moral motive is responsive to moral salience as such; like the early stages of the minimal moral capacity, there is direct regulation of action (that is, without deliberative involvement).

The role of the moral backstop motive is not restricted to maintaining our moral resolve (therapy for a weak will). As an evaluative element in

---

35. *Treatise,* 479. Hume's moral agent may possess a moral sense without possessing the natural motives of virtue. He can be moved by his moral judgment, then, though not in the way that a virtuous agent would be moved.

one's minimal moral character, it supports a basic capacity for recognizing and responding to moral facts. It is unlike a more developed capacity in that it does not provide sensitivity to nuance, fine-grained control, the careful integration of moral action into the fabric or ordinary life, but its function is not restricted to the familiar features of moral practice.

Access to this two-tier motivational structure can be essential in circumstances where we are faced with unexpected moral claims. In the face of demands that we respond to certain facts that we have hitherto not thought morally relevant, demands that we alter familiar and unquestioned patterns of action, our settled moral character may provide no immediate help. Sometimes *it* is the impediment. Possession of "a sense of morality or duty" might then be the only thing able to secure right action and response. Though sensitivity to basic moral facts will not provide the wherewithal for identifying what is new, *given* a new claim, the default capacity can function in morally elemental space, taking the claim-as-such as sufficient reason to change behavior. One might not know how to react well in response to new moral facts, but in the face of complaint, one often can stop behaving badly.[36] It would clearly be undesirable were this "sense of morality" alien to one's settled moral character. The right deep structural connection between the two allows that when one acts merely because one sees one must, the reasons one accepts as relevant will have access to one's developed moral character, making possible deeper, more resonant changes, as well as enlarging one's knowledge of the moral world.

If this is so, we clearly need a way to think about motives that allows for much greater structural complexity than we are accustomed to. We need to resist our proclivity to think of motives in terms of (or built out of) single end-desire pairs—having a desire for drink, wanting to promote justice. Surely this view is better explained by assumptions in action theory than by what is needed to understand moral action and character. Why not turn things around? Within the bounds of what is plausible, why not shape our view of action and motive in light of our best account of our evaluative practices?

What does one want the moral motive to be or do? I have identified three things. We want a motive, or motivational capacity, that leaves an agent

---

36. The connection between the backstop motive and the developmentally primitive minimal moral capacity helps explain this. A developmental capacity must be able to adapt to what are, from its point of view, new facts.

open to moral growth: to the increased normalization of desires to morality and to the possibility of reformation and integration of regions of moral deformity. Second, we want a motive, or motivational capacity, that, while honoring the differences in the different regions of moral concern, supports some unity for the agent acting, so that when acting morally she can be doing "one thing." This will also secure the capacity of moral action to express something *about* ourselves and *to* those we affect: that we are co-members of a community of equal persons, for example. And last, we want a motive that can perform the backstop role, yet not be outside or alien to an agent's developed moral character.

No singular moral motive, like the crude Kantian motive of duty, can play all these roles. It lacks the dynamic capacity to organize and transform other motives and interests (to be the engine, as it were, in the production of moral character), and it lacks the evaluative content to organize deliberation and regulate action. By contrast, a structurally complex and developmentally open motivational capability—a kind of educated moral literacy—seems to be of the right kind. It brings resources that can support transparency in moral action without compromising the evaluative complexity of moral requirements. Its evaluative range and backstop security meet the need for motivational efficacy that often prompts indirectness arguments, but without the costs to the evaluative coherence of moral action. Its sound function, in turn, demands that the multiplicity of the moral not go too deep: that there be a connection, material or formal, that marks diverse considerations as moral.

Is such a motivational story possible? In part this is answered by the implications of our actual evaluative practices. It is in any case not challenged by the actual motives of any "however-formed" adult. The tendency in modern moral philosophy to think about the developed system of moral motivation as if it were just a robust minimal moral capacity has made it hard to see how central moral learning is to a system of moral motives, or to appreciate the active or normative role moral theory should play in our view of moral development. The formation of motives and motivational structures is the business of morality, of what we might call its "department of education." Its clientele are not restricted to children. If we think of moral education as finished with primary skill acquisition, it can be hard to see that it is part of the nature of moral character that it remain open to change. The idea of the morally literate agent provides the outline of a view of character that takes this fact seriously.

*   *   *

In the next chapter, I continue developing this theme, but with a shift in attention from *internal* sources of character deformation to *external* ones. Just as normal moral character has to be able to accommodate some degree of psychological disorder, it also has to adjust to the possibility of moral change, perhaps even to new moral facts. By looking at normal moral character under different kinds of stress, I aim to get a clearer, and more realistic idea of what effective moral character might be.

— 5 —

Can Virtue Be Taught?
The Problem of New Moral Facts

In the previous chapter I argued against the grain of much contemporary moral thought and for the essentially Kantian idea of a distinctly moral motive, focusing mainly on its role in securing the minimal moral competence of normal moral agents. The moral motive, I argued, provides the foundation of normal moral literacy: the capacity that makes agents responsive to morally salient facts—facts about themselves, about others, and about the natural and social world. Of course, neither the distinctly moral motive nor basic moral literacy are sufficient for moral character; they are the analytical bases that make its development possible.

Part of what prompted these reflections was my puzzlement about our grounds for holding persons responsible for wrongful acts caused by psychological defects—where, for example, unhappy features of upbringing have left them disordered or in some sense deformed. I was interested in why it is, even when such agents cannot read the moral facts correctly, they are responsible for "getting it" as time goes on, or when the facts are lit for them by the claims and complaints of others. In a normal enough agent, I argued, the minimal moral motive provides the wherewithal to act as one ought when the moral facts become plain.

In this chapter, I want to examine another region where normal moral character shows gaps. When confronted with moral states of affairs of a new kind—what I shall call "new moral facts"—decent persons often act badly. They can be disoriented, resistant, defensive; they may continue with (now) wrongful actions despite the visible new moral fact, refusing or unable to take account of change. I am less interested here in questions about responsibility than in the challenges to our ideas about moral character that arise with these reactions. Resistance and defense are signs of awareness; they provide the toehold for some degree of responsibility. But they are also signs of distress, which, if it is not unreasonable, indicates something awry or incomplete in our expectations for moral agents. How can even a good upbringing prepare us for something no one yet knows? Suppose the minimal moral capacity is enough to hold agents accountable. But if, when confronted by new moral facts, normal agents cannot act well, one might well wonder what kind of moral demand could be being made. In exploring these and related questions, I also have two larger goals. One is to develop further the idea of moral literacy as a site of resources for moral learning and change. The other is to begin an investigation of the *external* circumstances of effective moral agency. Conditions for getting things right do not always reside in the character of good agents; they can depend on the kind of social institutions that shape action and character.

I

If the challenge to moral character posed by new moral facts were simply about improving its quality, there would be no special question. As with many practical skills that are interesting, it can be a permanent fact that there are various ways we will need to improve and we may not know in advance what they will be. Gaining competence in one area often opens up new possibilities of improvement elsewhere. Nor is the issue about blameless ignorance of plain facts: as when, before 1920, no one knew that the lead in paint could harm children. We know in principle and in advance that such things are possible; when we discover them, we can act appropriately. The demands on character and the claims based in new moral facts are different because new moral facts, or the ones of interest to me, upset the reasonable confidence of normal agents.

What is a new moral fact? Instead of a definition, let me point to a range of examples; the phenomenon is complex, but it is not hard to see. Setting out exactly what makes something a new moral fact is not necessary for the questions I want to ask. The things I am thinking about include claims on behalf of nonhuman entities (animals, trees, ecosystems); a cluster of gender-related injuries such as sexual harassment, spousal and date rape, violent pornography; the special harms of hate speech; identity injuries due to racism or compulsory heterosexuality. Some new facts are really new sites for moral injury of an already known sort, but not of a kind we in principle expect. They may involve the emerging visibility of a wrong that has been

masked by the confidence of entrenched practice. The discovery that medical paternalism conjoined with weak standards of informed consent violates patient autonomy is of this kind. Harder to imagine are utterly new
moral facts. There would seem to be two candidate classes: facts that were
there but were conceptually inaccessible (e.g., the moral equality of persons
as such) and things whose moral significance is *of a new kind,* brought
about by new social or material phenomena. New moral facts need not require new moral principles; they are facts that the principles we have do not
easily or directly accommodate.[1]

To explain the emergence of a new moral fact, we need not assume any
heightening of moral sensibility. Periods of moral disquiet occur from time
to time, signaled by a change in the comfort, the smoothness of surface phenomena. Moral historians might point to disruptive economic changes,
patterns of immigration, shifts in political power—any of a variety of possible causes whose effect is a challenge to the "business as usual" aspect of
morality. Whatever the cause, the effects can be deep and wide-ranging.
Once the new facts are "out," what is expected of us changes. Normal moral
attention is insufficient; dilemmas may appear in areas we thought stable;
the changes called for may disrupt established patterns of life and agents'
sense of self-worth—costs we do not normally ask individuals to bear.

A reasonable morality is well integrated into ordinary living, not something we are endlessly at war with (like a diet) or a distant goal toward
which we direct substantial amounts of our energy. As with other complex
skills we master—cooking, driving, word-processing—the abilities we have
as normal moral agents are exercised as a matter of course: they are routinely responsive to salient moral facts, comfortably engaged with our motives; they call on instrumental and not constitutive reasoning. What we are
about is not at issue. This is not to say that we never get into moral trouble:
temptation, weakness, awkward circumstances may each generate problems
we find difficult to resolve. This, too, is part of ordinary moral life. We expect to negotiate most of these difficulties; we have confidence in our level
of moral skill.

The idea of morality as a matter of course is not an endorsement of

---

1. I recognize that this way of describing the phenomenon lumps together facts whose
"newness" is sometimes epistemic, sometimes ontic. Though I spend time establishing the cre-
dentials of an instance of the latter kind of new moral fact (in part because doing so reveals a
great deal about the nature and limits of normal moral practice), the central concern of the
chapter is about *responses* to new moral facts of both kinds. This permits me to defer further
analysis of the concept of "new moral fact" to another occasion.

blandness or complacency, but an essential condition of normal living. We do not crave moral novelty; for the most part, we are not prone to moral boredom. The wish to test oneself in circumstances of moral risk belongs to a rare life-project, or to the youthful stages of development of moral character. This is not to say that morality is undemanding. Rather, its demandingness is like the demandingness of loving someone: defining the life it is part of.

If "business as usual" is integral to the place of morality in a good life, it is also a source of moral hazard. Routine practices can flatten out into habit. We may suddenly be brought up short: having become inattentive, we are involved in a moral accident. Sound routine requires executive virtues that sustain confidence and ease of action without loss of attention to a wide range of detail. It is perhaps also why it is an essential feature of morality that we ask for and give moral reasons. Where we have to justify what we do to others, especially to those affected by our actions, we have some protection against the slackness of bad habits.

New moral facts challenge moral business as usual in ways that are not so easily accommodated. This is partly because what they challenge often turns out to be embedded in ways of living we rely on, and partly because correction usually involves much more than behavioral adjustment. A good way to get a clearer idea of the complexity of all this is through an extended example. To that end, I want to discuss an argument for a kind of new moral fact that is made in some recent feminist discussions of pornography.

Pornography's historical location in moral discussion is as a matter of offense to standards of public morality. The moral question it provokes there concerns censorship: arguments are about freedom of speech and expression (its intrinsic and instrumental value), the costs and values of censorship, and maybe a bit about the special value of sexual freedom.[2] The feminist argument is about a harm to women as a class brought about by the "objectification" of women in pornography.[3] The *new* claim is not that there is something wrong in treating persons as objects or things, nor that pornography is a new site of this kind of wrongdoing. It is not objectification per se

---

2. It is not unusual that there be strong claims made on behalf of sexual freedom (Henry Miller, for example), but they have difficulty becoming integrated into the prevailing stream of moral discourse.

3. I will be interested primarily in pornography produced for heterosexual men, where the harm, whatever it is, is to or directed at women. I want to set to the side questions about "good pornography" and comparable harms to men, not because they are easy but because the discussion here is only about the *status* of a kind of moral claim.

that is the moral problem: it is what *this* objectification makes possible. We will have to take a step back to see what lies behind this distinction.

One of the central insights of Kantian ethics is that the use we make of others for our ends is inherently problematic. Whatever our intentions, to treat someone as a means is to take a moral risk, opening a door to exploitation. Most of the time routine practices and institutions provide insurance that the risk has been acknowledged and appropriate protections put in place. We can take for granted that asking for certain sorts of favors does not exceed the bounds of friendship, that the bank teller is a voluntary employee, and so on.[4] The insurance often extends to means of repair when things go awry. There are established routines of apology and restoration; there are procedures of complaint and labor protections.[5]

If the problem of objectification is a kind of moral risk, then the moral questions associated with pornography are about crossing the line: making persons vulnerable in a way that their status as persons precludes. The *new* claim is that pornography involves depiction of women (some women) that harms women as a class.

It is a difficult question whether the possession and enjoyment (sexual or otherwise) of images of others objectifies them or puts them at moral risk in any way. We do not own our images, yet considerations of privacy suggest they are not free game either.[6] More difficult still is sexual fantasy. There do seem to be circumstances and kinds of fantasy to which one might object, but how or in what terms is difficult to say. But if what is wrong with pornography is that via depiction of some it hurts others, then this must come from a different source of moral risk than pleasure in the image of another person. Arguably,

4. It can sometimes be difficult to tell when the institutions are failing to do their work. There can thus be moral injury that cannot be prevented by individual good willing; moral injury without moral wrongdoing (by anyone).

5. Even in Kantian ethics, this move from conditions of risk and wrong to *institutional* repair is essential to the conditions for normal moral action.

6. The famous V-Day kiss on the cover of *Life* magazine is a fine case in point. The picture has a plangent impact—a moment of spontaneous joy expressed in a quick and jaunty embrace. One can easily imagine someone putting it up on a wall, getting a certain sweet pleasure from looking at it. In fact, it was not such a sweet kiss; it seems to have been a small act of sexual aggression from a returning sailor on an unwilling woman, caught in a photograph. Does the woman, or the man, have a claim that the picture not be used? Has either of them somehow been injured? This is different from the more common complaint that someone has profited from one's image. In this case, the woman's complaint would be that in reproducing the picture, whatever its public meaning of joyful celebration, it repeats an injury *to her*.

it is the fact that pornography is produced for a public market—that it is an industry—that alters the nature of both the objects of pleasure and the risks in objectification. While it may be that there is no harm to anyone from some person's lurid and violent sex fantasies about all women he meets, something very different occurs if lurid and violent sex fantasies about women are a widely consumed industrial product. For the consumer, the subjects of pornography are no longer merely private objects of enjoyment.[7] Given the permeable border between industrial pornography and cultural iconography (in advertising, film, etc.), the idea of women as available for use leaves the domain of private fantasy and gains public respectability. It is this that creates, in the precise language of the Equal Employment Opportunity Commission, a "hostile environment" to the health and moral status of women.

I am not arguing that if there is a moral injury caused by industrial pornography that it warrants censorship. Nor am I suggesting that everything about the pleasures to be had in the consumption of violent pornography is bad. The issue is the credibility of the claim of injury. And that it represents a new moral fact. If to be the object of moral regard is to be someone whose use raises a moral caution, then a socially sanctioned industry depicting abuse of women qua women flouts the idea of moral caution and puts the class of persons so depicted at moral risk. Socially and publically they are not full moral subjects.[8] One need not be a Foucaultian about morals to register the significance of the social representation of moral subjects.[9] Accepting such a claim of moral injury requires a concep-

---

7. Indeed, the market demand for increased consumption requires the steady creation of new pornographic fantasy, giving the relation between sexual desire and its object a commercial life of its own.

8. This result need not be intended as such nor experienced as an injury by those affected for it to be a fact that the moral injury has occurred.

9. To the rejoinder that at most one has located a new location for these moral risks, I think we may want to say that in some cases the discovery of new contexts of harm reveals something else that counts as a new moral fact. Consider the "discovery" that victims of rape may suffer from post-traumatic stress syndrome. If so, the harm caused by rape is to be classed with the experiences of survivors of torture, war trauma, and concentrations camps. The reclassification alters the moral nature of the action. Or consider the claim that it is an essential feature of rape that it is an act against a woman qua woman, not just an assault by sexual means. On the first issue, see Judith Herman, *Trauma and Recovery* (New York: Basic Books, 1992); and Susan Brison, "Outliving Oneself," in D. Meyers, ed., *Feminists Rethink the Self* (Boulder, Colo.: Westview, 1997); on the second, see Catharine Mackinnon, *Towards a Feminist Theory of the State* (Cambridge, Mass.: Harvard University Press, 1989).

tual shift—a transformation in how we see moral injury coming about, in our awareness of the sites of vulnerability, and possibly, of the fact of gender as a relevant moral category. This is the dimension of change you would expect in the recognition of a new moral fact.

When moral concern shifts in this way, features of a practice that were visible but not seen can come into view. The feminist critique of pornography brought two cloaked facts to moral attention: that there is real violence (against women, children, animals) in the production of pornography, and that pornography is a large and enormously profitable industry. It is so common in our culture not to pay attention to the production and marketing of the things we consume that I will set the second fact to the side for now. It should be less common not to notice violence and abuse. What story does a consumer tell himself about what is happening to the actual women, men, children, and animals in violent pornography? Presumably, no story at all; nothing provokes his moral concern. In what moral terms do we describe this? Is it just hypocrisy? That would suppose a level of moral awareness that seems to be entirely absent.

There may be an explanation for this in a curious phenomenon we might describe as "taking a moral time out": *in a defined context,* an activity or kind of activity that is on its own impermissible (or problematic) is taken not to require the normal kind and degree of moral attention. Professional sports is one such area. Pornography may be another. It has something to do with the institutionalization of sources of pleasure.

From the point of view of morality, many sources of pleasure are sources of risk.[10] What we laugh at and what we find exciting or thrilling are often at the boundaries of the acceptable or permissible. Circuses, sports, comedy, pornography: certain sorts of pleasure and moral danger go together. It is a task of cultural institutions to ensure that this risk-seeking impulse is expressed in a controlled and safe way. In the spheres that exist under social license, one is permitted to take one's pleasure without the tax of normal

---

10. There is nothing "anti-pleasure" in holding that the sources of pleasure are the loci of moral danger. Were it not for the pleasures we find or anticipate (and the pains we wish to avoid or end), there would be little moral work to do; there would be little reason to do much of anything. Add to this truism another—that the risk that attends pleasures is not identifiable in any feature of the pleasurable experience—and we reach the place from which Aristotle launches his investigation of virtue: "the whole inquiry, for virtue and political science alike, must consider pleasures and pains: for if we use these well, we shall be good, and if badly, bad" (*Nicomachean Ethics,* trans. Terrance Irwin [Indianapolis: Hackett, 1985], 1105a11–13).

moral scrutiny. It is a place made safe for us. Things can be said at the Comedy Store that would be actionable in a school; people may batter each other when boxing in ways and to a degree that would gain them jail time outside the ring; and so on. Of course I do not mean to say that all of the activities so sanctioned ought to be—that there is no realm of impermissibility here. It is the phenomenon of sanction and permission that is of interest. Could one argue that pornography dwells in this space? Even violent pornography?

A moral "time out" for the expressions of the sexual imagination would depend on the presence of reliable safeguards for this kind of morally risky activity; the sexual pleasures themselves do not dictate or guarantee this, however important they are felt to be.[11] Where masculinity is associated with the eroticization of domination, men (many men) learn to achieve sexual satisfaction in connection with its assertion. Nonaccidentally, women come to eroticize submission and (many) learn to find satisfaction (including eroticized fear) in passivity and victimhood. If the risk in pornography is to women's status as full moral persons, the necessary safeguards do not seem to be in place. Indeed, the acceptance of pornography as a part of public culture would seem to undermine the very idea of safeguards.

II

At this point I want to set aside the example of pornography. It has served its purpose in detailing the potential complexity of a claim of new moral fact, especially so, given its embeddedness in sanctioned, public culture. I want now to ask more generally: where does the emergence of such a complex new moral fact leave the normal moral agent? The problem, I suggested earlier, lies in the interruption of moral "business as usual." A normal moral adult relies in equal measure on the authority of her own conscience and the authority of background cultural norms. There are rules she has been taught and internalized, and rationales for the rules that are necessary to deal with the normal range of unexpected things. Agents depend on there being substantial harmony between individual conscience and the prevailing cultural norms. It is not just that, otherwise, the exercise of indi-

---

11. This is a disturbing lacuna in Thomas Nagel's essay, "Personal Rights and Public Space," *Philosophy & Public Affairs* 24, 2 (1995): 99–107. There must be analogous concern for safeguards and viable alternatives when appealing to consent in the moral justification of prostitution.

vidual judgment is difficult to distinguish from rationalized wrongdoing; the normal (nonheroic) agent's moral confidence depends on the possibility of moving between rule and rationale, of experiencing no profound rupture between her own moral sensibility and the moral norms that govern her social world.

But what happens when the routine and the protected space for risky actions are called into question? The possibilities and conditions for detecting moral error will not be reliable. Acting well in any direct way may not be within the power, personal or social, of a sincere individual. Prevailing social norms can defeat solo efforts at change because of the presumptive weight of institutional meaning: our better intentions may not be readable as such by those who receive them. Social and internal pressures to hew to a familiar norm will likely impose distinct kinds and amounts of cost on the agent who would correct her action. And so on.

These considerations suggest that the appropriate question is a normative one: what kind of character *should* a normal agent have if she is to be acting in an environment where adherence to available practice-constitutive social norms does not guarantee right action?[12] Even if, contrary to fact, agents were not responsible for wrongful actions falling under prevailing social norms, the possibility of new moral facts would still challenge the character of the normal moral agent when the norms changed.

Ordinary virtues of character are not designed to cope with the circumstances of new moral facts. We say that complacency is a vice; some wariness about the normal is in order. And one can increase sensitivity to the likely marks of hidden moral failure: the personal and social sites of power and pleasure are almost always two of these. But one can be instructed in recognition and avoidance only for dangers that are known, and the abuses of both power and pleasure hide in the ordinary.

Even when we are warned of a danger, some of our mechanisms of recognition are counterproductive. Children who are cautioned that dogs are dangerous and dirty often display extreme aversive behavior in the face of manifestly friendly canine inquiries. Worry about dietary fat spawned a discipline of recognition and avoidance that has led to infant malnutrition in some affluent families. It is not just that those parents lack suitable knowl-

---

12. This is a way of asking, what is it reasonable to expect of a responsible moral agent? Here I am not thinking of an agent who can be blamed or held liable. In wanting to hire a responsible baby sitter, I am not seeking someone who can be blamed for dropping the baby, but a person I can be confident will care for the baby well. A *responsible agent* is one who is reliably able to avoid failure in a domain—one who can get the job done.

edge about health, though they may; the prime fuel for such dangerous behavior is an undigested mix of wariness, danger signs, and fear. If weakness
of will is a failure to follow best reasons, what we have here is a pathological
inability to make good sense out of what one knows—a paralysis of reason.

Consider a moral example: a six-year-old boy was suspended from
school because of a playground kiss. I want to set aside the debates about
whether a six year old can sexually harass (I think he can), or whether suspension from school is the right institutional response if one thinks he has
(probably it is not). I want instead to focus on the exaggerated reactions.
There was the bipolar extremity of the institutional response (either "nothing" happened, or it was a suspensible offense for a first-grader). And there
was the public reaction to the widely reported episode: the ease with which
it became an occasion to belittle the significance of sexual harassment.[13]
Both reactions were clearly off the mark. And useful.

What goes wrong in such cases is that the way of representing caution, of
marking behaviors as dangerous, facilitates a hysterical response. Now, hysteria is a response with a point: it masks something that is not bearable
to acknowledge by means of a more acceptable (if often punitive) mode
of distress. The "real" objects of anxiety are elsewhere: fear of corporeality
or mortality in the first two examples; and in the playground case, fear of
sexuality—fear of its omnipresence (of *children* as sexual beings) and fear
that male sexuality, in particular, is a site of danger. I take the playground
case to be an example of *moral* hysteria; a hysterical reaction is triggered by
an unexpected moral claim that threatens deep-seated, often quite rigid values. As in other hysterias, the thing that must be hidden must also remain
in focus; the symptom or behavior that does the hiding then deforms the
hysteric and his reactions in systematic ways. The affect of moral hysteria
need not be overt distress; it is, however, at once stubborn, confused, and
resigned to a condition of disorder that is preferable to facing the object of
fear. Evidence that opposes the manifest content of the hysterical reaction is
typically seen as tainted, misleading, the product of conspiracy. The powers
of rationalization are put to work to defeat rational judgment.

I do not think moral hysteria is merely an interesting phenomenon—a
curio from the text of moral pathology. The masking, distortion, and rigid-
ity that mark it, the disruption of sound judgment, are all too familiar in the
undomesticated areas of moral practice where convention and experience

13. Waves of letters to the *Los Angeles Times* barked: If *this* is what sexual harassment is,
only a fool would take it seriously.

have not made action ordinary and secure. It may not be the task of morality to make us safe, but moral concerns often cluster around what is dangerous and fearful—the very things we may not want to acknowledge about each other, or about ourselves. In just these places, the protective strategy of "recognition and avoidance" makes one vulnerable to hysterical response. The cure for this vulnerability, I believe, shares important features with the kind of moral character that is well suited to cope with new moral facts.

III

The circumstances that prompt moral hysteria resemble those in which moral rule-following goes awry. The wrong sort of connection to moral rules yields judgment and action that is rigid and inflexible: it blocks attention to relevant detail and encourages a tendency to act "for the sake of rules" that is blind to any underlying rationale.[14] Given the resemblance, we might try to approach the somewhat exotic concept of hysterical wariness through a more familiar question: "How do we use moral rules without subverting judgment?" Though moral hysteria is not the same as bad rule-following, the similarities are such that understanding how we avoid the one is a good beginning to understanding how we might avoid the other.

Moral activity might be like many complex practical tasks where we start with rules in order to master basic routines. Over time, we modulate our behavior as we take lessons from trial and error. One learns to cook by learning various special techniques, following recipes, discovering relevant facts about produce and spices, and so on. As time and experience accumulate, one internalizes and personalizes technique; one knows when it is all right to be less obsessive about the details of a recipe; one becomes confident in making substitutions and modifications. The early panic about mistakes (a teaspoon not a tablespoon of salt!) is replaced by confidence in one's ability to make things come out okay.

Is this an appropriate model? Children begin with moral rules. And certainly knowledge and experience matter in moral judgment as well as cooking. Increasing competence enables more sophisticated judgment and more complex activity. However, in cooking, as in art in general, beyond a certain point of competence, individual exercise of judgment is authoritative. The

14. For these reasons one sometimes suspects that those drawn to a morality of rules are fearful of real moral engagement and specific judgment.

space for idiosyncracy and so for genius, the role for taste and intuition, distinguish this region of practical activity.[15] Rules are left behind. By contrast, it is an essential feature of moral judgment and action that an agent orient herself by means of concepts or rules that support moral reasons. Moral activity is inherently interpersonal: we explain and justify our actions to one another in shared moral terms.[16] Even if circumstances press us to act in novel ways, we do not just strike out on our own, without regard to the public character of moral practice. Moral innovation is not a performance; those affected by our actions are not spectators. What makes action morally justified, what makes it the action that it is, is our having *and acting from* reasons that in principle can be offered in explanation and justification of what we do.[17]

Reasons both depend on and temper rules. In most of morality one's knowledge of reasons—the point or rationale of a rule—brings a rule into the space of deliberation.[18] Such knowledge makes rule-governed activity make sense.[19] This is not merely about comfort. Agents with access to a rule's rationale are better able to evaluate the significance of failures, and, when necessary, to break a rule with sound deliberative confidence. One needs to appreciate what will be lost, and for the sake of what sort of good or necessity. Without an understanding of a rule that reveals what it protects and enables, a rule is like a blank peg in a complex edifice: removing it may make no difference, or it could bring the whole thing down.

15. One might, as Kant did, take the possibility of genius to be an essential feature of artistic activity. Without underestimating the conservative forces within art (or cooking), the internal pressure to create something new does seem to be partly defining of the activities. If there is a role for creativity and genius in morality, its place does not seem to be in the individual extension of what is thought possible.

16. Even if one agrees with Kant that aesthetic judgment contains a claim of interpersonal validity, the success of the aesthetic claim is established through perception, or apprehension, not shared reasons. The special role of the critic is to make available the objects of artistic creativity for aesthetic appreciation.

17. Of course, one of the prerequisites for adequate interpersonal discussion is that one be willing to look at the facts: collect information, attend to nuance, and so forth. Offering justifications in terms of shared reasons is not sufficient if moral facts can be masked.

18. This is less so in the early stages of skill acquisition when one follows rules as lessons: first do this, then that. And in emergencies, rules serve in lieu of judgment; they provide guidance and security against panic. There may be regions where rules are constitutive of an activity. The rationale for these exceptions depends on the validity of the generalization.

19. This is so even when the content of a rule is arbitrary (it just directs traffic).

Absence of confidence in such situations can provoke moral panic: a reaction about fear and loss of control.[20] Excessive or blanket restrictions and penalties are reactive ways of taking a stand, or trying to, when one fears something of importance is about to be lost and feels vulnerable to blame. But what the panic-based reactive rule regulates is often not acknowledged for what it is. This is no accident. If we cannot think clearly about what is at issue, rigid rules, however destructive, can appear to be the best protection against blame.[21] But it is neither a successful nor a stable form of protection. What we are asked to do does not make sense: we lack reasons.

If reactive rules are not available, panic may be directed at the insufficiency of the rules one has. Recall the post–Anita Hill complaint that "no one knows what the rules are anymore!" For many, this was a dance around the obvious—at once revealing and suppressing it. The anxiety is palpable: focus on the rules hides what is to be protected or permitted and why. Complaints of sexual harassment *do* destabilize gender relations because they typically call into question gender-constitutive entitlements. Those distressed by thinking about the conjunction of gender, sexuality, and power will not find it easy to reflect on the problems encoded in the rules they rely on. It is worth a lot not to have to admit what might be going on.

There is no easy "fix" for such well-founded resistance. Refinements of rules and new strategies for crisis management miss the real issue. The problem never was a problem about "right rules." It is about the way one relates to moral reasons: both reasons one accepts and those one finds distressing. Agents whose moral character is hostage to rigid gender categories cannot be expected to act well, or for the right reasons, though they can be required not to act badly. Without access to relevant reasons, action and feeling are unstable.

Now, not just any kind of reason brings deliberative access to rules. Reasons can be opaque and acted for blindly; responsiveness to reasons can be shallow. Consider again the way we adopt regimens of diet or exercise. There are good, health-related reasons to do these things, but the way many

20. What must be true for it to seem reasonable or necessary to expel a junior high school student for giving a friend Midol? It is in this way that the "justs" in the injunctions to "Just say no" or "Just don't do it" take aim against thought.

21. Recall the rules against *any* teacher–student touching in the wake of the McMartin preschool abuse trials. More than fear of hysterical parents and potential litigation, the rules themselves revealed that there was something in the vulnerability of children and the sexuality of adults that was not to be thought about.

of us diet and exercise is not responsive to them, or not in the right way. Response will be shallow when, for example, our reasons are mediated by gendered norms of body shape. The effect is to block thought; it can beget dangerous behavior. To be sure, not every shallow response is inappropriate. Ordinary or routine actions do not, in normal circumstances, require more—though one needs to be wary of surface simplicity, since even simple reasons often carry complex moral and prudential provisos.

Externally imposed norms are not the only source of unacceptable shallow response. Sometimes it is forced by the limited content of the reason supporting a rule. Thus we reject both strict anti-lying imperatives and a rule of ad hoc judgment because they lack evaluative reach to what matters in truth-telling. By contrast, a deliberative presumption in favor of truth-telling *as a way* of respecting our epistemic dependence on the "word" of others may capture more precisely the relevant intuitions about why truth-telling is morally important.[22] The richer rationale would be reflected in our reasons when we told the truth (what truth we told) *and* when deliberation supported lying (when, in lying, we would not have abandoned the evaluative point of truth-telling).

Further evaluative complexity and depth arise in the course of reason-responsive action. When someone needs help, our "read" can remain on the surface (there is pain there; it should cease) or be deeper (she is a teenage mother of three, overwhelmed by responsibility and poverty). The nuance of the initial read does not determine the depth of response. A surface read may be matched with a disposition to personal involvement. Someone sees "pain there" and asks "How can I help?" She is prepared to do whatever turns out to be necessary, and cares in a way that elicits the details of abuse and neglect. A deeper read need not produce deep engagement. One may appreciate the conditions and significance of the situation and yet be unable or unwilling to respond with anything beyond occasional, somewhat grudging, charity. It may be true that we are often likely to engage more fully when we have a fuller read of the circumstances, but it does not follow, and sometimes more knowledge defeats responsive impulses. Response to need may in turn educate one's read of the situation. When I am involved, I see more, I ask new questions; considerations that I recognize as relevant

22. Utilitarian norms are evaluatively deeper, but the reasons they support also tend to be shallow in deliberative import because they reduce the moral importance of truth-telling to something else.

get more complex. At a certain point, one's read of the situation, one's developing understanding, could call for a shift in response from welfare-promoting actions to those promoting autonomy. It might equally call for less personal and more institutional response when that better meets the need personal engagement has brought one to see. And so on.

We expect a normal, or morally literate, agent to be able to take in and respond to the moral facts of her world accurately. Access to the rationale of moral rules allows for the exercise of moral intelligence, giving an agent greater control over judgment and a wider range of read and response. This is moral character working well. It may not, however, be enough to cope with new moral facts. An agent identifies features of her circumstances as reasons by interpreting them through the values she accepts. Some of her values are particular to her own life; others come from the social world in which he acts. New moral facts will throw up new values, new problems: "texts" she is not accustomed to or comfortable with reading, ones that do not fit with her values. New texts may require a different kind of appreciation, or appreciation of different things; there may be reciprocal and possibly challenging demands on one's range of moral response. It is not a straightforward matter of taking in more. There are cases where we need to read crudely and quickly, where too much information gets in the way (triage situations call for exaggerating specific saliences and silencing a range of normally relevant practical information). That is, one might have to learn to read for less; not every kind of learning increases the quantity of knowledge. Ideally, one hopes that these changes can be integrated into moral practice in a way that makes sense, perhaps even better sense, of the older practices that survive.

Moral theories that leave practices opaque do not provide accurate or full enough rationale to support literate moral intelligence. But even theories that offer transparent integration of practices and reasons may not go far enough. What gives sufficient reason to sustain activity in normal times may prove to be fertile soil for disabling stress when unexpected events destabilize a practice. The possibility of moral change needs to be integral to an agent's understanding of what morality can require. While there cannot be a requirement that agents get things right no matter what, there can be a requirement that they be appropriately responsive to the fact that even their best moral understanding can be or become unreliable. They must be prepared to recognize and acknowledge new moral facts for what they are, and with recognition, they must have resources accessible for appropriate response. Such a requirement on agents needs to be reflected in moral theory.

But is this requirement reasonable? On the one hand, we acknowledge the need for the routine, for the idea of moral "business as usual" as a necessary component of a healthy moral life, and, on the other, we require a moral intelligence that involves openness to the permanent possibility of change as an integral part of competent moral character. What is the alternative? Agents who resist change to protect their character or well-being; or others who accept change passively, experiencing morality as something that happens to them. The resulting heteronomy is no mere theoretical problem: persons who are imposed on by morality feel constrained and resentful. They may, if they are morally weak, blame those who they believe cause their distress.

IV

To take the next step, we need to go beyond the ordinary resources of good character. Just as there are structures of character that enhance an agent's ability to make her way through complexities of circumstance and the obstacles of her own psychic order, so there are *institutional* structures that enhance, or defeat, the effectiveness of moral intelligence. We have already seen that the exercise of moral intelligence depends on the availability of the right sorts of moral rationale (reasons). Now I want to argue that recognition and healthy response to new moral facts depends in part on the structure of value in the social institutions that shape an agent's moral intelligence.

Moving the argument in this direction might seem to pose a threat to the idea of deliberative autonomy. To the contrary, when looked at the right way, the actual conditions for autonomous moral agency can be seen as preparation for the problem posed by new moral facts. Let me briefly say why.

We know that moral character is the resultant of different forces: natural dispositions, active social and familial modeling, contingent matters of personal and social fortune. It is the product of a process, part passive and blind, part active yet less than fully informed, one that nonetheless is to yield a character capable of managing the later stages of its own development. It can do this if we become increasingly autonomous and self-regulating, responsible for getting things right in our actions *and* about ourselves. This work takes place in the face of an unelimable dimension of passivity in our relationship to external moral structures. One *finds* oneself in institutions with complex histories; one is *partly constituted by* values one absorbs from different parts of the social order: family values, views of gender, work, concepts of property, and so on. Whether we become deliberatively autonomous agents depends on what we do with the values we are given. To make them our own, we need to establish that the values we endorse have a legitimate supporting rationale. But whether we *can* do this is not entirely up to us: we can be defeated, we can fail to secure deliberative autonomy, if our institutions resist reason.

We carry a similar burden with new moral facts. We recognize that moral change is not a product of reasoned choice; it comes about through social and natural mechanisms. We are to accept this and yet also accept that the routes to and through moral change are in some important sense available to us as autonomous agents. What matters is the *way* change is taken into moral practice: how it is accepted, understood, and made use of, how new reasons become part of the moral order of judgment and action. We have already noted that there are two parts to this: recognizing what is new in the new moral fact and having available sound responses to new reasons. The two parts will turn out not to be so separate. And getting either of them right will turn out to depend on the background evaluative resources available to intelligent moral agents. To get a better idea of the barriers to, and so the resources needed for, recognition and response, it will be helpful to look at some other examples.

Alterations in the moral landscape sometimes just require more of us. Severe economic changes and natural disasters can introduce demands on already recognized duties of charity and mutual aid. Other kinds of change transform the basic terms of moral relations, requiring us to think and respond in unfamiliar ways.[23] Consider the increasing scope of moral presumption against causing damage to species, habitats, and ecosystems. The emergence of these claims was not a function of moral suasion or good example; their origin seems to have been in a conjunction of prosperity, a climate of welfare liberality, population increase and dispersal, better science, and the severity of late-industrial environmental damage.[24] Let the causes

---

23. Some changes do both. The moral effect of the rise of labor unions, or the movements for civil and gender rights, called for extensions of recognized duties and obligations, and also demanded new ways of looking at persons, their claims, and their circumstances.

24. The *possibility* of moral environmentalism is not new; there have been groups of persons (some Native Americans, some Nebraska farmers) who have taken themselves to stand in a relationship of moral stewardship or trusteeship to the material world that they used. But a moral possibility in this sense is neither necessary nor sufficient for introducing a new moral fact.

be what they were, the effect is that we are asked to look at the moral world in a new way.

For instance, in considering the development of riparian wetlands, we now have to ask: *How* does the loss of habitat for migrating birds matter? We need to know whether, and in what sense, the wetland or the migrating birds as a species could have interests that have independent weight against human interests.[25] Are the interests of the same kind, and so to be balanced? If they are not, and surely they are not, we need new resources for judgment. Inclusion of new claims in analogical terms disturbs the moral field less; but if the terms don't fit, or don't make good sense, not only may we fail to capture the kind of moral regard called for by the purportedly new facts, but the acknowledgment we do make may be more a sign of resistance than acceptance. If, for example, we view animal species as aggregates of living things, then we lose any distinctive claim for species. Though it would be profoundly disruptive to have to revise our concept of the moral subject, we want to avoid begging the question against the full range of possible bearers of moral value.

Some strategies of recognition include a wider range of things but do not accord them independent moral status. If the point of environmental protection is human well-being, the band of moral attention widens, though it would leave out things whose fate is indifferent to ours. Pressed to attain even wider focus, we might preach humility: things that appear not to impact human welfare may do so in ways we do not yet know. We could get to general environmental sensitivity as a tactic of wise caution. But we would not thereby secure moral attention to the thing itself for itself; the effective value of the thing itself is hostage to further balancing.[26]

Consider recommending the cessation of gender-specific attitudes that support violence toward women on the grounds that the change would be good for men; or that racial discrimination should cease in the workplace

25. An interesting treatment of this question can be found in Christopher Stone, *Should Trees Have Standing? Towards Legal Rights for Natural Objects* (Los Altos, Calif.: William Kaufmann, 1974).

26. For example, there would be no argument in place to resist the effects of discovering independent ways of securing human welfare (fancier immunizations; artificial techniques of restoration). Nor is it clear how to argue for sustaining sacrifice *for the sake of* environmental well-being when the balance of human welfare benefits does not justify it. If the only options available to us give things instrumental value, we lack resources of judgment. This can be especially hard to see when the objects of our actions are, morally speaking, silent.

because it is economically inefficient. Let both claims be true. The problem is not just that such arguments introduce treacherous contingency into moral claims; they stand in the way of seeing what is going on. This can paralyze moral thought, creating ideal conditions for hysterical response. And for the same reason, it is also grounds for angry complaint. That is why so much moral energy directed at pornography is about determining what pornography is. For if it is about pleasure, one sort of argument is appropriate; but if it is about (or also about) the sustenance of oppressive gender roles, then matters of privacy or enjoyment may be, morally speaking, irrelevant, even if true. The struggle is over the absorption of new demands, new claims of harm, into a framework that resists their full recognition. It can be hard to recognize the "what" of something new if it will call for a response one is not prepared to give.

Even if one sees the difficulty for sound judgment, it may still not be obvious why the abilities of a morally intelligent agent should be insufficient for dealing with such problems. While perception and judgment cannot function in full independence of received social content, we also have reflective capacities. We are able to think critically about the values we are given; we can modify, revise, and even reject them. Insofar as we are rational, we have a critical position "outside" our values. Surely, with care and courage, one can judge contesting claims. This line of thought misses a key point. It is not just that some values resist the efforts of reflection. The point is rather that in order for reflection to be possible, the values we have, as possible subjects of reflection, must be such that they are *evaluable.* That must be part of their *form.*

Whether values are evaluable at all and by what standards are both contingent social facts. We may not notice this because many of the standards of evaluation we use shape the development of our values. For example, it is not a necessary truth that values be mutually consistent; even as held by individuals, they often are not. But it is part of our normative practice to value consistency; we subject our values to criticism and revision when there is lack of fit between the values themselves or what they require. Children resist this; parents press for more realistic standards of value compossibility. Maturity is marked by the admission that one no longer wants to be both a ballerina and a baseball player. We can imagine moral values held in a rigid code, where the existence of practical anomalies is simply accepted as a burden to be borne (an occasion for exercise of faith or proof of frailty). It is not that way for us. We expect our values, and especially our moral values, not only to be in principle mutually instantiable but also to cohere in a meaningful way. We want our values *together* to tell a possible story: they should make sense of a life lived within their authority. If we have this sort of normative commitment, our values must be such that they can be held in a way that is open to adjustment and change, and so *authorize* reflection. That is part of their form.

One need not embrace rationalism to accept this claim about the form of values. The same logic of form is at work in David Hume when he speaks of passions and desires "yielding" or "ceasing" when we recognize mistakes of judgment or reasoning. It is part of the nature of Humean desire that it is responsive to judgment in this way. Desire does not press its case, but we go with factual judgment instead. *Desire for an object* is extinguished upon discovery that it is not what we thought it was. Indeed, for desire to be "directed by" reason, for it to be an impulse that can be given direction, the causal mechanism must be responsive to reasoning (unlike the heartbeat or a panic reflex, which operate, for the most part, independently of reasoning).[27] Hume's account of practical judgment is thus not well represented as about weighing and balancing desires; it is about the sorts considerations to which desires are open. Among them will be weighing and balancing.[28]

Of course I don't want to follow Hume too far. If Humean desires are naturally reason-responsive, they develop with respect to ends that are not themselves open to rational assessment. In this respect, I find that Kantian theory has deliberative resources more sensitive to the full range of evaluative connections. Where institutions exist that provide a moral education of the right sort, the desires and interests of a well-brought-up Kantian agent

27. See David Hume, *A Treatise of Human Nature* (1740), ed. L. A. Selby-Bigge (Oxford: Clarendon Press, 1978), pp. 413–415. To be sure, this is not full-blown practical reasoning: a desire's reason-responsiveness is not the same as a responsiveness to reasons. Even weak reason-responsiveness is unavailable on a more austere reading of Hume. To the extent that desire or passion is an original, nonrepresentational existence, Hume's picture may be that with judgment—that thing is not chocolate but a rubber toy—there is a change in the world perceived. The passion-provoking stimulus is then simply absent. The more mechanistic account would of course be less welcome to many who find the Humean position appealing.

28. Some talk of reasons carries a picture of separate values, each bringing its own weight to the scale of deliberation. Such values are not affected by the competing values they encounter. It's a picture; it can be otherwise. Of course most values, like the features of character, cannot change in will-o'-the-wisp fashion; they would not then be values: structures that organize judgment and action. But they need not be autarchic wholes either, available only for weighing and balancing. One might wonder whether balancing and weighing set valences counts as deliberation at all. Such activity seems more a matter of reckoning—there is a balance; we need to determine what it is.

will manifest a value-sensitive form, responsive to the normative (moral) principles that constitute a deliberative field.[29] Having a moral character, an agent does not deploy morality to constrain or extinguish her desires; rather, the things that she wants, those that are the basis for action and will, she wants in a particular way: wealth, if that's what she wants, *as* its accumulation is permissible and just; the well-being of friends *as* its coming about does not unfairly disadvantage others; and so forth.[30] Desires and interests that develop so as to be responsive to deliberative moral principle that reaches to ends are more amenable to adjustment and *re-founding* as change and growth prompt reconsideration of values taken as given. That is why it makes sense to reason with children about their behavior. One is not thereby mistaking them for adults, but accustoming them to justification by reasons—to being autonomous in judgment and action. There are many routes to providing children with good ends and aversions. What is gained in the Kantian story is the potential for ongoing autonomous development *within* a morally defined space.

The absence of value-sensitive desires can be costly. Suppose we find the possibility of sexual violence toward women persisting in a context of acknowledged gender equality. It may show the incompleteness of affective development. It may also show that the available routes to adult sexual and gender values created unstable and dangerous accommodations when norms of equality were introduced. If, for example, sexual desire exists in areas independent of moral contouring (because fantasy, pornography, and the like, are given a moral "time out"), it will be less value-sensitive, more entrenched. That is why it may not be possible to treat the consumption of industrial pornography as a private matter. An adult required to alter the range of what counts as normal action in sexually charged space is being asked to resist deep patterns of attraction and restraint.[31] Change brought

29. The concept of a deliberative field is developed in Barbara Herman, "Obligation and Performance" and "Agency, Attachment and Difference" in, *The Practice of Moral Judgment* (Cambridge, Mass.: Harvard University Press, 1993). The full set of principles that constitute a deliberative field are various, but their authority is dependent on the condition that entry into the field is permitted only as a value satisfies the principles of practical reason. The rite of passage often transforms the entrant.

30. The interesting kinds of moral failures will then not be about bad desires but about taking conditional reasons to be unconditional (necessary, unavoidable), either in general (a form of wickedness) or locally and episodically.

31. The necessity for long-term support, in twelve-step programs, extended psychotherapy, support groups, or medication indicates both the high degree of difficulty of some changes and our limited access to the structure of desire, once formed.

about through external pressure or conditioned resistance typically alters the cost-structure of behaviors, closing off or redirecting an avenue of desire; it may not make the behaviors unavailable or alter the desires that prompt them. It is also often a self-alienating strategy for moral self-control.

A critic of rationalist ethics might point to such phenomena as evidence that one cannot approach the affects under the direction of practical reason. I mean to be making a counterclaim: the affects sometimes resist reason because they are approached too late; they resist because they lacked the right sort of education.

Psychologists judge organisms healthy as they cope well with stress: a matter of resilience, adaptation, and repair. It is part of the normal mechanism prompting growth. In vulnerable persons, stress may instead induce anxiety, paranoia, avoidance—symptoms of resistance and protection. Health is partly a function of training. When moral upbringing is about constraint, the affects are less transformed than trained to obedience. Unexpected possibilities or new constraints can cause resistance, internal shifts of power that are sometimes difficult to understand or control. By contrast, a moral education that transforms desires, bringing them into a normatively structured deliberative field, trains agents to construct well-founded values from wants and interests, whatever their source. Accommodating new moral facts poses less of a threat to internal stability when agents' practical confidence resides in their rational abilities, not in the specific content of their values.

Since not all sets of values will support or encourage deliberative autonomy, there is a moral-theoretic demand on the evaluative foundations of educating institutions. This is not about the morality of social rules. It is possible for an institution to be just (or not unjust) but evaluatively opaque, or even encouraging of the contrary-to-autonomy dispositions of deference and passivity—just rules in a benevolent autocracy, for example, or just practices that exist as a matter of tradition. We get the wrong lessons about justice if the source of authority in ruler or tradition has evaluative precedence over the facts of justice. The facts of justice cannot then play the right role in autonomous judgment; the flexibility of sound rationale is lost in the appeal to authority.[32]

Autonomous agency is an achievement: it is possessed in degrees, acquired not only through personal but cultural effort, and so doubly contingent. The task for agents is to convert situated and time-bounded values

---

32. For a fuller discussion of the moral foundations for social institutions, see Chapter 2.

into well-founded elements of their deliberative field. The task can be made harder or easier by the *form* that socially transmitted values possess. When values have a form that resists transformation, agents who endorse them are left vulnerable in circumstances of conflict and change. Values whose form permits their location in the terms of the deliberative field have a shared ground (as when we come to see both liberty and equality expressing the conditions for human dignity). This both separates them from their heteronomous history and provides a common deliberative framework in which to work out conflict. When this work is done in productive public debate over what values mean, it is the public face of a community of moral judgment. We gain confidence in our values if we must be able to justify our actions and judgments to each other in terms of reasons we can share. Of course it would be naive to think that critical public examination of values will fully dissipate the influence of entrenched power and privilege—in institutions or in setting the terms of the deliberative field. It is rather that it is hard to see that there could be anything that could do it better.

V

What can we conclude? If autonomy is the capacity to judge and be motivated by the principles of a constructed deliberative field, its empirical realization is a function of moral education: the social and institutional provision of well-formed values and evaluative skills. Effectively autonomous agents will be morally literate; they have a developed moral intelligence that can read and respond to moral facts, incorporating their evaluative import into a shared way of life. If brought up within deliberatively open institutions, a literate agent can more readily absorb the disruption caused by *new* moral facts without losing a conception of herself as a competent agent. Her way of engaging with moral facts would *never have been* passive. Habits of interpretation and re-founding values create a character capable of moral balance and evaluative dexterity.[33]

The idea of moral literacy thus splits the difference between an individualistic conception of autonomy and a socially determined moral self. Morally speaking, we are neither wholly social nor wholly free. Moral liter-

---

33. In comments, Samuel Scheffler noted that the Kantian notions of autonomous judgment and value-sensitive desire that I have indicated are needed to cope with new moral facts will also serve agents who are taxed to resist new moral claims that are flawed and indefensible.

acy inhabits a space in between. Its role is not to fix shared moral concepts but to provide deliberative tools, modes of reasoning and reflection that we might deploy, together, with some confidence.

There is, it seems to me, a natural fit between Kantian values of rational agency and the idea of moral literacy. Agents whose fundamental moral concern is to bring their interests and projects within the evaluative space of respect for rational agency would have the kind of autonomy and effective moral literacy I have described. Even if one does not want to go that far, the idea of moral literacy itself, with its requirement of deliberatively accessible skills of recognition and response, puts pressure on accounts of moral character to accommodate some distinctively Kantian virtues.

A last thought: should we worry that acknowledgment of the fact that social institutions both shape character and constrain the range of possible moral response undermines the ambitions of normative moral theory? I don't think so. When we take seriously the social bases of moral action, judgment, and character, what we discover is the unsustainability of the division of labor between moral and social thought. The normative project is not undermined; it is just much larger than we may have imagined.

— 6 —

Training to Autonomy

Kant and the Question of Moral Education*

Kantian moral theory does not seem to provide a comfortable environment for thinking about moral education. Education is about development and change. Moral education, where it is something beyond inculcating a list of "dos and don'ts," involves the creation of a sense of self and other that makes shared moral life possible. But the Kantian moral agent, qua rational agent, is one whose capacity for morality, for good willing, comes with her autonomous nature. We *are* rational agents; insofar as we are rational, we are autonomous: able to act as morality requires—"from duty." Apart from training to make moral life easier, there does not appear to be much room to *form* or *develop* anything.

Nonetheless, Kant's interest in moral education is not peripheral to his understanding of the conditions of autonomous moral agency. The impediment to seeing this comes from interpretive confusion about the place of empirical conditions of agency in a theory that looks to a noumenal fact about rationality as the necessary *and* sufficient condition of good willing. As a way of sorting some of this out, I want to develop a very different line of thought: although autonomy is an essential property of individual rational wills, for human beings, autonomous moral agency is realized in and through a certain form of social life with others. It is this fact that sets the task for moral education, though it is a different task, taking place in a different venue, from what the orthodox view of Kant's moral theory suggests.

To show this will require several stages of argument and attention to some nonstandard texts. I will begin with a brief review of the official account of moral education. Some of its limitations will point us toward the underexplored subject of empirically conditioned practical reason. Under-

*See page 153 for an explanation of the references used in this chapter.

stood, as it often is, in an essentially Humean way, empirical practical reason[1] is the rational faculty in the service of self-love, inevitably at odds with the demands of morality: something that needs to be overcome in the moral activity of an autonomous agent. I want to argue that, to the contrary, the real problem is the *incompleteness* of empirical practical reason, exacerbated by its pretensions to be a wholly adequate determining ground of the will. Moral education is about securing the completion of empirical practical reason—a process necessary for the real possibility of pure practical reason in human agents. It is a process that turns out to be, surprisingly, a social one.

I

The official view: Kant has many sensible and interesting things to say about moral education as usually understood. He thinks that early education needs to be catechistic (*KpV* 5:151–161; *MS* 6:477–484) and that the rote lessons, given in terms of examples and stories, are chiefly directed at inculcating a feeling for action "from duty": its possibility, its motivational distinctness, and its awe-someness. After catechism comes the "erotetic method"—of question and answer—by which a young person's natural pleasure in sharpening her ability to make distinctions is deployed in the service of sorting out real from false virtue. Puzzles and hard cases, rather than fueling moral skepticism, challenge ingenuity and stretch newly acquired conceptual skills. As Kant shrewdly notes: "we finally come to like something the contemplation of which lets us feel a more extended use of our cognitive powers" (*KpV* 5:160). This knowledge is to be supplemented by vivid examples that bring the student to experience the possibility of her own powers of freedom as preparation for taking the moral law as her highest-order regulative principle of action (*KpV* 5:162).

Much of this is obvious. Children need to be taught to recognize their duties (the content of obligations) and to understand the distinctive nature of moral action. Their recognitional abilities need to be honed and their character strengthened. From his official pronouncements, we should conclude that Kant's distinctive contribution to moral education is a method for learning about acting from duty alone. Through modeling, imaginative exercises, self-criticism, and so forth, we come not only to recognize the

---

1. This locution, while familiar, is strictly speaking inaccurate. The reference is not to some separate kind of practical reason, but always to "empirically conditioned practical reason."

separateness of moral and nonmoral incentives but also to achieve a reorganization of our dispositions so that, when appropriate, we have immediate and reliable access to the moral motive. One will come to have a particular kind of strength of character, able to "refuse" the pretensions of nonmoral incentives: one learns to "exclude the principle of self-love from the highest practical principle" (*KpV* 5:74). Refusal should not be confused with renunciation. Refusal is a choice we make, supported, on the one hand, by respect for the moral law and esteem for oneself as its source and, on the other, by the reciprocal humiliation of the pretensions of the feelings to be the ultimate determining ground of the will (self-conceit). We do not thereby renounce our interest in the satisfaction of desires. However, the ability to refuse the pretensions of inclination in general also makes it easier to ignore specific contrary-to-morality inclinations, thereby enhancing the effectiveness of the moral motive.

Moral education is thus, as one would expect, propaedeutic to virtue, "the product of pure practical reason insofar as it gains ascendancy over such [opposing] inclinations with consciousness of its supremacy (based on freedom)" (*MS* 6:478). Beyond the "dos and don'ts," it provides the training needed to remedy the misfortune of our natures: that we are "finite beings" strongly and naturally motivated by concern for happiness and well-being (most often our own). For most of us, once we learn how to refuse the pretensions of self-love, it provides well-person care for a morally decent life. Should it do more?

One might think not—that there is nothing more for moral education to do. If we take one strain of his thought, Kant follows Rousseau in the idea that even the "ordinary man" exhibits the basic elements of sound moral conscience. Thus the *Groundwork* argues "from common rational cognition" (*G* 4:393). And, at a key moment in the *Critique of Practical Reason*, Kant appeals to the "order of concepts" in a man who asserts that his "lustful inclination . . . is quite irresistible to him" to show that even he is aware that in the face of the moral law, he could resist after all (*KpV* 5:30). This makes sense because we have, by nature, a "predisposition to personality": a "capacity for respect for the moral law as in itself a sufficient incentive of the will" (*R* 6:23). The predisposition reveals itself in the virtue of ordinary persons, and can be elicited from even those who are degraded or corrupt. If this is the whole story, the point of moral education is to protect us from the latter condition and provide stability and a sound foundation for the former.

However, an account of moral education as basic training for morally worthy action and stability of good character misses something fundamental. Training to virtue must include training to *value:* what value is, where in action it lies. This is not a point about purity of motive or the degree of conformity of action to morality. Failure to appreciate the connection of moral requirement to unconditioned value leads to errors in judgment; even when right action is taken, it will not be done in the right way. Actions that are only accidentally right, even if reliably so, are not responsive to moral concerns. At the extreme, moral legality—the outward conformity of action to moral principle—can be a vice. A person whose actions were governed by attention to the outward sign of dutifulness would not do what she ought. She would not correctly read the nature of moral facts even though her actions conformed to law.

The proper arena for legality is one where the task is conformity to rules. There one needs training in judgment: whether the rules apply, and if they do, about the range of freedom within a rule's domain of regulation. But Kantian moral reasoning is not in the service of rule-following. We are not in a primary moral sense required to avoid this or that *kind* of action; we are to acknowledge, in action and judgment, rational agency as a higher-order regulative value.[2] Moral judgment must thus be responsive to detail of circumstances, institutions, character: how rational nature is expressed, where it is vulnerable, how it may be made effective.

The reasons we act morally—help when there is need, refrain from harming—establish basic structures of moral connection with others, as well as our conception of ourselves as moral agents. If I see your need as a source of frustration and pain for you, which I am drawn to alleviate, then I see you as a vulnerable sentient creature, and myself as provider of a benefit. If, by contrast, I see your need as an obstacle to your effective agency, as making a claim on me that derives from the value of rational agency per se, then it is not just your need that I see differently, but you, and so myself in relation to you. Moral action expresses the sense of relation. This in turn affects how we go on: how we act when intentions go awry, or what we do if we discover, for example, that the need in question is chronic, or a source of dependency.

If this is the nature of moral action, the curriculum of moral education cannot consist of rote learning and motivational discipline. Training in

---

2. It is *reasoning* because it is deriving a particular from the universal, not judgment, strictly speaking, which is "discovering the particular as it is an instance of . . . rules" (*A* 7:199). This use of reason, also called judgment, is creative.

value requires the acquisition of a distinctive orientation toward the practical world, including the domain of possible actions and objects of action. The powers of the virtuous person not only make visible a different world (or different elements of the world), as *practical* powers, they also have as their object "to confer on [*zu erteilen*] the sensible world the form of a whole [system] of rational beings" (*KpV* 5:43). The point of moral education must then be to produce an empirical character capable of autonomous judgment and action. How empirical autonomy is possible consistent with the laws of nature is another matter, but *that it is* seems plainly to follow from the nature of the moral law and its commands. Moral pedagogy will therefore require a different kind of investigation of the empirical conditions of rational moral agency, and of nonmoral empirically conditioned practical reason, from what would be needed if its task were only the provision of rules and stability of motive or character.

II

With all this in mind, we would do well to rethink the starting place of the account of moral education. Suppose we ask: What does Kant think we are like? What is the "nature" that moral education trains? Human beings are not by nature moral agents—in the following sense. We do not see moral facts in the direct way that we perceive colors and shapes. We do not grasp the moral truths about things by being informed of their names and natures. We require certain experiences—moral experiences—and interpretations of the experiences (instruction) to become aware of and responsive to a moral world. We may have an innate predisposition to morality: a capacity to act from duty and for the sake of the moral law. But if the moral capacity is natural, its actualization in our lives is not; it must be produced (*R* 6:23).

The conjunction of interpreted experiences with the acquisition of elements of a virtuous character presents the world as a moral world and establishes in us a "second nature." It is not a *new* nature; that would be impossible. It involves a construction of a conception of self and the development of innate possibilities by which we would be able, if only ideally, to become fully moral persons. What stands in the way of this is not as clear as traditional readings of Kant would suggest.

Construction proceeds from something and is directed toward something else. Accurate accounts of both ends are essential. About nonmoral human nature, Kant is often regarded as a crude hedonist: by nature, we pursue happiness; happiness is about pleasure or the satisfaction of desires. About the goal, morality, he is taken to be a strict deontologist. Neither view is right. The mistakes about happiness need to be sorted out first, for they stand in the way of understanding the empirical (nonmoral) side of the development of practical reason.

Consider the standard picture. Whether Kant is a simple hedonist about happiness or allows for a multiplicity of ends pursued for the various reasons we pursue things, in either case, the state of happiness is some kind of contentment, and the desire for happiness is, roughly, the desire for an orderly and complete satisfaction of our desires. The role of reason in the pursuit of happiness is instrumental. We have desires; we set ends; reason points to means that we follow, insofar as we are rational. Discerning the connection between means and ends is a bit of technical or theoretical reasoning, as is the more complex task of timing and coordination that is necessary when ends are complex or of long duration. The normative grip of instrumental reasons on the will is secured through the end we desire: happiness.[3]

But this leaves a problem. The end, happiness, is indeterminate (G 4:418–419; KpV 5:25–27). It marks a practical challenge, not a discrete goal. As finite, that is, not self-sufficient beings, we have needs, and then desires for things that will meet or satisfy them (KpV 5:25). But needs are different, agent to agent, and for an agent from time to time. Not all desires can be satisfied; some we may think should not be satisfied. Part of the project of happiness for each of us is to figure out what "our" happiness amounts to. The concept or idea of happiness provides little guidance. There are various reasons for this: the limitations of our own insight; the fact about desires that the satisfaction of some brings on others; the linkage between pain and the possibility of pleasure; and so forth. The technical diagnosis of the problem is that happiness is an ideal of imagination: "an absolute whole, a maximum of well-being in my present condition and in every future condition" (G 4:418). But an ideal of imagination can provide no rule of action.

---

3. Helpful discussions of these and related issues may be found in Christine M. Korsgaard, "The Normativity of Instrumental Reason," in Garrett Cullity and Berys Gaut, eds., *Ethics and Practical Reason* (Oxford: Oxford University Press, 1997); and Andrews Reath, "Hedonism, Heteronomy and Kant's Principle of Happiness," *Pacific Philosophical Quarterly* 70, 1 (March 1989): 42–72.

We would need Leibnizian omniscience—knowledge of all the possible lives we might live—to see a clear path (*G* 4:419).[4] In addition, Kant is close enough to Stoic thought to regard the state of happiness as one in which we might approximate the condition of nonfinite rational beings: a state of *Seligkeit*—beatitude or bliss (*KpV* 5:25); a state of not wanting anything. Clearly, then, neither the idea of the end nor the state we would be in if we reached the end can be the source of determinate practical guidance.

If happiness is the region in which empirically conditioned practical reason has its own work to do, it is hard to see what work that is. There is one rational principle in the area—the hypothetical imperative—that instructs us to take sufficient means to our ends. But it applies indifferently to moral ends, trivial ends, and ends of happiness. It cannot, by itself, tell us what to do. Missing is any *non*moral rational guidance, theoretical or practical, about *ends*. Each of us is left to muddle along, to form an ordered set of ends from a happenstance stock of desires and interests plus some precepts drawn from accumulated human experience about which sorts of lives work well and which do not.[5] There is no basis in the principle of self-love to say that not just any order of ends is an adequate conception of happiness. But if one can't even say *that*, then Kant's worry that empirically determined practical reason has pretensions to advance *its* principle to be the sole determining ground of willing makes no sense: its pretensions would be empty or futile, not wrongheaded. We therefore do not seem to have a notion of the nonmoral or empirical work of practical reason in terms of which one could understand the project of moral education as the task of developing the rational faculty *from* its "natural" state of concern for one's own well-being *to* a fully moral power.[6]

---

4. To the extent that an ideal of the imagination is like an "ideal of reason," it is not a concept of a totality but a representation of it via a particular (*KrV* A567/B596–A571/B599). It gives an "archetype" of a happy life: a person of the right (ripe) age who is content with her life; someone without impossible-to-satisfy yearnings or age-inappropriate projects or health-impairing vices; a person whose life has contained a good balance of activity, rest, enjoyment, friends, work, and so forth. Practical indeterminacy comes not so much from lack of omniscience as from the ineluctable particularity of any copy of the archetype. When we imagine a happy life, we can recognize its form; we know what elements to look for. How to go about living such a life remains a problem. An ideal of imagination is unlike an ideal of reason in being "blurred" or "shadowy" and, most important, in furnishing no rule (*KrV* A570/B598).

5. These are the *Groundwork*'s "counsels of reason" (*G* 4:418).

6. This is not to say that advancing the interests of the self makes no sense. The point is about the claim that these interests have nonmoral, rational support.

In fact, Kant has a fuller view of nonmoral practical reason.[7] It is, as it ought to be, a view about *value*: the object of rational action. To discern the content of nonmoral practical reason, Kant follows Rousseau. The key pieces of his view are therefore to be found in texts where he has Rousseau on his mind. I want to look at parts of two of these: one is the *Religion,* the other is the short, lightly satiric essay "Conjectural Beginning of Human History." It may seem strange to rely on sources away from the critical philosophy for elements of Kant's view of *practical reason,* but once we have the view in sight, I think it will be evident that it is not unique to these texts.

"Conjectural Beginning" offers a philosophical "reading" of Genesis as a history of the *emergence* of reason in the human species. The conceit may be strange, but the detail is instructive. The history is presented in four stages; here, in summary, is what they are. The human animal begins as a creature of instinct, following that one sense tuned to discern in a general way the fitness or unfitness of things to be used for food, and so for survival: the sense of smell. The initial emergence of reason is provoked by the deployment of a second sense, sight, by means of which one could compare foods that are similar in look to those selected by smell, thereby extending "knowledge of sources of nourishment beyond the limits of instinct" (*CBH* 8:111). Human beings go beyond their animal nature as soon as they can ask whether a "this" that they are drawn to by one sense is comparable to a "that" that they are drawn to by another. Two things about this "moment" stand out. The awakening of reason comes from *comparison,* and the power that reason confers is to alter the order of experience—"an ability to go beyond those limits that bind all animals" (*CBH* 8:112). Even so limited a deployment of reason brings problems. With the aid of imagination, reason generates new desires—desires for things for which there is no natural urge (even a natural urge to avoid), opening us to an "abyss" of choice: an in-

---

7. What makes it seem that he does not is mainly a function of his parsimony of argument. Where Kant is concerned to argue that neither the principle of self-love nor the end of happiness can yield practical *necessity,* he needs to argue no more than to the indeterminateness of happiness as an end. Where the issue is the determining ground of volition, setting the object of the will, the only relevant fact is the passivity of the will with respect to any empirically given object (the heteronomy of its principle). Both arguments assume the contrast: that morality requires law or autonomous willing. It is not part of the argument structure of the *Groundwork* or *Critique of Practical Reason* to make anything of the fact that without morality, practical reason's ambitions to provide a complete order of ends cannot be realized. For unless morality is possible, the apparently self-defeating ambition of empirically determined practical reason would show no more than the truth of Hume's view.

finitude of possible objects of desire. But note that the first distinctive act of reason is not taking means to ends, it is a comparative, *evaluative*, judgment.

The second stage of the emergence of reason belongs to the sexual instinct. The transformative moment in this domain is the discovery that by controlling the instinct (covering the genitalia), by interjecting the imagination between desire and its object, the possibilities of enjoyment can be greatly enhanced. If in the first stage the possible *objects* of desire are extended by comparison, in the second, *instinct itself* is reshaped by "making a propensity more internal and obdurate by removing [covering] the objects of the sense" (*CBH* 8:113). This is the discovery of "refusal": "the feat whereby man passed over from mere sensual to idealistic attractions, from merely animal desires eventually to love, from the feeling for the merely pleasant to the taste for beauty" (*CBH* 8:113). Forsaking something that we immediately want, we come to want something we *imagine* would be better. Kant views this as laying the foundation for "true sociability": for moral agency and for culture. This is because, as a stage in the development of reason, it is about the redirection of the instincts, away from their natural objects and toward objects that reflect a constructed ideal. It is a first move in the construction of non-desire-based value. Not only does the redirection of instinct create new desires, the refusal of immediate sense attraction for the sake of an "idealistic attraction" establishes the possibility of *rational desires.*

The first and second stages of reason bring on a third: the capacity to think about one's life in terms of distant or possible ends. This is the fruit of knowledge. Once one can imagine an ideal and come to desire it, one is open to desires for things one does not have. This gives reason to plan and to construct an ideal of what will make life good. But the rational, constructive, and evaluative activity also reveals our limits as agents. One foresees a life of endless care, and its inevitable end, death. That is a source of despair; it is also a route to attachment to family and society, to living on through one's descendants and one's creations. In the third moment of reason, we are led to the introduction of the idea of *a human life:* the idea that different ways of living are worthwhile, not because of any amount of desire satisfaction but because they fulfill an ideal and enable us to resist despair through the extension of our lives into love and work.

"The fourth and final step that reason took in raising mankind altogether beyond the community of animals" concerns our sense of ourselves as a special kind of thing, different from and superior to animals (*CBH* 8:114).

In this moment, human beings gain a sense of entitlement of use with respect to the nonhuman world, and, correlatively, of other persons as inappropriate subjects of command and involuntary exploitation. This sense of self and others as equal members of a kind—rational being—is the condition that makes distinctly human social life possible. We may be drawn together by instinct (self-interest or love), but we have true social relations as a function of reason—reason that identifies the value of humankind by distinguishing it from the use-value of the nonhuman.[8]

It is this complex development of reason, one that alters the very nature of the natural being—giving rise to new desires, new powers, endless travail, and imagined bliss—that characterizes what we are like as rational or reasoning beings. This is the rational nature that morality at once emerges from, constrains, and completes. The contrast between pure and empirical rational nature, then, is not captured by the moral law, on the one hand, and, as we might have thought, "reason insofar as it is considered merely to be a tool for satisfying . . . many inclinations" (*CBH* 8:114), on the other.

The next piece of the account of the nonmoral development of practical reason comes from the discussion of human "predispositions" in the *Religion*. Though introduced there to help address the problem of evil, it provides key elements of the explanation of the incompleteness of the nonmoral rational will.[9]

The *Religion* divides the will into three parts, by function, "considered as elements in the fixed character and destiny of man" (*R* 6:21). Kant calls them predispositions to *animality, humanity,* and *personality.*[10] All are predispositions to *the good,* both in the sense that they do not of themselves prompt action contrary to morality and in the sense that they (together) predispose "*towards good,*" that is, "they enjoin observance of the moral law" (*R* 6:23). It

---

8. This view of other human beings is "early preparation for the limitations that reason would in the future place upon him in regard to his fellow man and which is far more necessary to establishing society than inclination and love" (*CBH* 8:114).

9. In order to represent the inaccessible ground of free choice, Kant offers a hypothesis about a "property of the will which belongs to it by nature": what he calls "the original predisposition to good in human nature" (*R* 6:21).

10. Kant indicates that we might have other predispositions, but only these have "immediate reference to the faculty of desire and the exercise of the will" (*R* 6:23). What might others be? Subvolitional physical processes, perhaps, such as digestion (patterns of hunger, satiety, and rest). Perhaps also certain aesthetic predispositions: that we will experience disinterested pleasure from certain forms. Perhaps even the systematic impulses of Reason.

is the second predisposition, to humanity, that tells us a bit more about comparative nonmoral practical reason. Again, let me give a quick summary.

The predisposition to *animality* is human physical nature; Kant describes it as "purely mechanical self-love, wherein no reason is demanded" (*R* 6:22). Its concerns are for self-preservation, for the propagation of the species (through the sexual impulse and the care of offspring), and "for community with other men, i.e., the social impulse" (*R* 6:22). Though no reason is required to explain the fact that human beings have these interests, as "original" elements of human nature, they organize the faculty of desire, giving a direction or point to desire that is independent of our will or wish.

At the other extreme is the predisposition to *personality:* "the capacity for respect for the moral law as *in itself a sufficient incentive of the will* (*R* 6:22–23). The point of calling this a predisposition is to point out that although good character needs to be acquired, it could not be acquired unless the human will had an interest in the moral law as a natural principle of its possible organization. Reason here is pure practical reason: a reason "which dictates laws unconditionally" (*R* 6:23).

In between the animal and the moral, as it were, is the predisposition to *humanity.* It involves practical reason, but a reason "subservient to other incentives" (*R* 6:23). However, it is subservient to nonrational incentives *not* because it is a deployment of instrumental reason; rather, practical reason serves nonrational incentives by making possible *comparative* assessments of happiness. The predisposition to humanity is an original (i.e., necessary) feature of human nature to "judge ourselves happy or unhappy only by making comparison with others" (*R* 6:22). We have a *physical* impulse to sociality; we come to have a *reason-supported* desire, given that we live with and among others, to make comparisons. The initial comparative impulse seeks equality with others (that no one be superior to me); but having no independent measure of worth, it is converted into an inclination to "acquire worth in the opinion of others" (*R* 6:22): no one should be in a position to judge me less worthy.

Suppose we describe the task of moral education as making the human predisposition to personality actual. On the traditional picture of our non-moral natures and of empirical practical reason, we are end-seekers who strive for the maximal satisfaction of our desires. Nonmoral rationality is about means, either directly for the object of a desire, or about strategies to maximize desire-satisfaction of different kinds over a lifetime. If this were right, a moral educator's primary task would be to teach restraint: to increase the power of refusal and to restrain the pretensions of self-love to practical priority in agents' maxims. This is the familiar lesson plan of morality versus self-interest. However, if the project of desire-satisfaction does not capture our nonmoral rational natures, the lesson plan needs to be revised.

Morality, as the expression of pure practical reason, completes and perfects what we are as rational agents.[11] This completion project must connect with the distinctive features of nonmoral rational nature. Two things have moved to center stage. One is that the evaluative principle of empirical practical reason is comparative. The other is the deeply social orientation of rational agency. The instinct to sociality ensures that we do not live our lives in isolation, while the comparative principle leads us to a sense of our own well-being that is continuously measured against the well-being of others. This suggests a different picture of the ways we are incomplete and likely to be imperfect. If reason's employment gives us a sense of the open-endedness of choice and freedom from the press of instinct, a merely comparative measure of value gives us no sense of direction; it is incomplete. But this is not the whole of the problem. In the context of our inherently social lives, the wish not to be or seem worse off than others gives way to an "arms race" for defensive superiority. Jealousy and competition become the motivational bases that give a shape to our lives. Prompting vice and wrongdoing, they are clearly an imperfect solution to the indeterminateness of our concept of happiness. Where the highest goal is to be comparatively best, the requirement that we give priority to moral over nonmoral incentives is likely to be reversed.[12]

These are the concerns that the curriculum of moral education needs to address. But there are limits on what it can include. The classical eudaimonist's move to a normative account of happiness is unavailable: for Kant, the concept of happiness *is* indeterminate. Kant also holds that the exaggerated Stoic ideal of restraint and renunciation makes human agents vulnerable to despair. We just do seek happiness; the satisfaction of desires is an ineliminable element of our practical orientation as finite rational beings with needs. Morality brings order—a final end; it creates the rational unity

---

11. The categorical imperative is the unique principle of unconditioned goodness that provides closure to the valuing activities of agents. It offers a final end—rational nature as an end in itself—that both sets a limiting condition on our ordinary pursuits and, more profoundly, gives meaning to our actions *as* the actions of a self-consciously rational agent.

12. This is argued explicitly in *R* 6:24–25.

of a system of ends (under the moral law) that the principle of self-love cannot provide. But order may not be bought at the cost of ignoring happiness. The demand for happiness is ineradicable in us, and, when made subordinate to the moral law, good. But the limited efficacy of human agency in bringing about its ends, combined with the moral indifference of nature, leaves a gap between morality and (deserved) happiness. This lack of fit between virtue and worldly reward cannot be set aside on rational grounds, since it is reason itself that disposes us to seek a whole that fully exhibits order.[13]

One response to this problem is the doctrine of moral faith (*KpV* 5:122–134). Belief in the immortality of the soul and the existence of God can give us confidence in the extension of the place and time, as well as the cause, of eventual moral order—of everything turning out for the best. There is, however, another response that Kant offers that is more directly concerned with the idea of moral education and the curricular needs of social agents whose imperfect rational natures are comparative. It looks to social or civic life of a certain sort as a kind of "finishing school" for moral development. I want to consider two elements of this—two "moments" of moral education, if you will—one drawn from the idea of interpreting history from a cosmopolitan point of view and the other an odd argument about voting. It will turn out that the instruction they give is much better suited to completing the nature of social beings whose rational nature seeks unconditioned goodness than to some Hobbesian project of restraining unbridled

---

13. If we set aside religious explanations, it is not obvious *why* reason should demand that virtue be rewarded with happiness. There is the argument from order: the combination of vice with happiness or virtue with suffering offends against one's sense of things happening for a sufficient reason. But that sense begs the question. Why should there be this connection between moral character and happiness at all? Only if the connection has been already made does it makes sense to talk about being *rewarded for* one's virtue or about having earned it. In fact, the connection is already present in the actions of both the virtuous and the vicious agent. Each, by nature, pursues happiness; not in the same way, to be sure, and not with the same substantive end (the happiness of the virtuous agent is different from the happiness of the vicious one). But only the happiness-seeking actions of the virtuous agent are, from the point of view of reason, fully justified. The happiness that a virtuous person has rational warrant to have is not some extrinsic gift of heavenly bliss, but the success of her actions and plans. That is why, if reason had control over nature, the gap between virtue and happiness would be closed. (The proportional thesis introduces complexities I cannot take up here, as does the idea that virtue should protect against unhappiness that results from external bad luck.)

self-interest. Moreover, they provide something that rational faith cannot: a means of ameliorating the competitiveness and conflict that comparative judgments provoke.[14]

III

To make room for this "public classroom" for moral education, the first thing we need to do is to dispel some myths about the aprioristic austerity and individualism of Kant's ethics. The moral life of a Kantian moral agent takes place as anyone's life does, within a specific social setting. One has various duties and obligations, invariantly, Kant thinks, concerned with norms for property and promises, truthfulness, vulnerability to needs, and some story about the development and training of the capacities we make use of in rational action. These duties and obligations to self and others have specific and local forms. We make promises this way, or in these contexts; we take care of basic human needs through private charity or the institutions of the welfare state; we have specific norms of civility and respect, and reciprocal sensitivities to insult and offense; and so on. Although the moral law underdetermines specific moral requirements, it is of course not neutral with respect to the ways things get worked out. In addition to providing the foundation for any claim of ultimate normative authority, it sets limits on the range of things that can have moral authority (or at least on the range of arguments that can be deployed to establish duties), and provides formal conditions that putative duties have to meet.

Though this way of thinking about morality is superficially at odds with the classical story of Kantian moral judgment—individual agents separately determining the permissibility of their actions through use of the categorical imperative test procedure—it is in fact necessary if the classical story is to make sense. The categorical imperative is a rule of form for maxims of action. For an agent's action to be morally justified (permissible), her maxim of action must be a real instance of a possible universal law for rational nature. Context specificity comes with the agent's maxim—a princi-

14. The passions that are aroused in comparative contest—"the manias for honor, for power, and for possession"—both require and enslave practical reason. Their insatiability makes those in their grip passive, and because they are directed to other persons, they incline judgment to consider "the mere opinion of others about the value of things as equivalent to their real value" (*A* 7:266–270).

ple that describes an action as it is taken to be choiceworthy, containing, therefore, the local descriptive and evaluative concepts an agent uses in making her choice. Further, moral judgment will have no purchase on a maxim unless it is described using morally salient concepts *prior to* any use of the categorical imperative. And these concepts, like the others an agent uses, will be social and local.[15]

This is not a sign of limit or some fault. It follows from the fact that moral life depends on a community of moral judgment. The basic features of the world that require our moral attention are identified in socially determined ways. Initially, at least, we acquire our most basic moral concepts—of harm and injury, of property and agreement—as part of a social practice. Although through experience and reflection we may extend or modify our moral lexicon, we risk loss of moral intelligibility if we set out too much on our own.

The social nature of moral concepts is not merely an external fact about them: that they are taught or acquired in social contexts. The moral concepts that agents use to describe a moral world are ones they reason with, by themselves and in colloquy with others. The terms of reasoning must be ones that can be shared. Evaluative concepts are not merely names for states of character, objects, or events of certain kinds—"vicious," "desirable," "murder." The moral rationale an agent accepts in using a moral concept alters a range of attitudes and judgments. If deceit is judged impermissible as a routine means because it subverts the conditions of respect for rational agency, then I am drawn to think about my communications with others in different ways than I would if I viewed deceit as ruled out because it causes harm. In the latter case, carefully paternalistic deceit could be justified, as might partial truths that saved feelings, to say nothing of lies that promote the greater good. None of these survive according to the former rationale. But this is not all. The different rationales alter the way we think about speech, and about those to whom we speak. In one case words have effects that need to be assessed on a calculus of benefits and harms; in the other, our words belong to a grid of connection with others like us, whose very ability to act *as rational agents* is partly dependent on what we say. Consider the different terms one would use when apologies were necessary—

15. These arguments are developed in Barbara Herman, "The Practice of Moral Judgment" and "Leaving Deontology Behind," in *The Practice of Moral Judgment* (Cambridge, Mass.: Harvard University Press, 1993), and in Chapter 2 here.

what one would be sorry for doing. So regarded, moral acts *are* social acts. It is no surprise, then, that a community of moral judgment is the condition that makes such normatively governed activity intelligible.[16]

Local moral concepts support *objective* moral judgments just in case the local concepts themselves are expressions of moral principle (i.e., if they can be shown to express the value of rational agency). Thus one of the tasks of moral education is to provide the conceptual resources through which we can construct objectively valid values. We may be brought up to respect our elders; the right kind of moral education puts us in a position to evaluate and then re-found the practice as its value is commensurate with the moral regard all are owed. Getting it right—distinguishing, say, respect for experience from deference to status-authority—is something we rarely figure out entirely on our own. This kind of developmental dependence is quite general. Consider the movement of desire from appetite to value. For any X we desire, it is (in the beginning) natural to want more of it. Natural satiety responses school us to the value of "enough" for some desirable things. For others, we may need to wait on the social lessons about acquisitiveness and greed to understand when and why more is too much. For still others, it may only be within the space of a critical public culture that we can come to see that something whose accumulation seemed to us natural and right is in fact a product of morally suspect social institutions. In all of these cases, what we require are lessons in value.

If it is in and through the creation of a community of moral judgment that practical reason develops, then the primary work of moral education is not about the repression of the errant dispositions and impulses of its trainees. That would fit a view of us as susceptible to moral imperatives, but lacking the full power of practical reason—as if we had moral ends, but only instrumental reason. But we are not like that. Moral education for us is about the creation of the right sorts of desires and ends within institutions that support and enhance them *as* the desires and ends of practically rational agents.

---

16. To be clear, the social nature of moral concepts is visible at two levels: one, as the background condition for norm-governed activity in general (conditions of acquisition) and moral activity specifically (we must in principle be able to have common judgments); second, there will inevitably be local moral practices (apology) where the moral content of the practice is socially determined.

IV

Suppose this is all reasonable. There is a practical puzzle. Moral education comes in part through social institutions. The institutions themselves are not typically based on principles that are morally well founded. They arise and change through various forces, only some of them intentionally directed. Not all change and not all institutions are good. How, morally speaking, are we to make sense of this? Moral education, though dependent on the institutions in place, must also provide tools of criticism. Bad institutions need re-formation, others need to be re-founded to give them the moral content that their "natural" histories do not provide.

In the essay "Idea for a Universal History from a Cosmopolitan Point of View," Kant provides an approach to these issues through a slightly different, but related question: How is empirical change for the better possible when most agents of change are not themselves good, nor even striving to be good? He responds this way. Social change is caused by a natural mechanism of—in Kant's terminology—"unsocial sociability." It is a background process, bringing persons into conflict with one another that they cannot resolve through social separation, but can resolve through further and more complex social connection. This would not be the case if the conflict was driven by greed (which might allow vanquishing or eliminating competitors) but is possible because the conflict is about status and excellence: something one wants more of, but wants it *from* others.[17] Agents are thus led by their deeper needs to adjust and readjust their social order, moving without intention toward more interesting moral possibilities.

On Kant's view, though the possibilities are created by the mechanism of unsocial sociability, their realization is not similarly determined. He holds that the causes of change need to be seen as, understood as, causes for some good. The idea of a progressive history provides a moral-teleological interpretation of the causal story: it makes sense of historical events. But *why* would a moral agent (an *autonomous* moral agent) need to have a progressive view of history? Suppose there were no such view? And what "good" can having such a view do for an agent? Is it just a palliative—a further requirement of moral faith—giving hope to those trying to do the right thing while all around them evil flourishes? How could agents' locating them-

---

17. Of course this only works if the others are those whose respect means something—not slaves.

selves within a historical narrative of moral progress provide a condition necessary *for* moral progress (*IUH* 8:22–24)?

From either a historical or contemporary sociological perspective, the dense complexity of social life resists any univocal empirical interpretation. Whether we take the "meaning" of history to be progressive or to reveal cycles of hegemonic oppression, we do take it to mean something: something worth contesting. Actions have intentional and social meaning (typically both, though this can come apart). Whether one is honored as "fighting the good fight" or accused of being a "running dog of capitalism" is a function of the read of the social context of action. Not every period of history can be interpreted to mean what one likes, but the inaccessibility of causes and the complexity of effects leave room for some debate about what is going on. Where a progressive interpretive narrative is possible, it can establish a social context that allows agents an expanded range of effective moral meaning for their actions and efforts, making possible further developments of institutions and of moral character.

Kant develops this idea by means of an interpretation of the rise of republican constitutionalism and the end of "wars of violent self-expansion" as a stage in the development of empirical moral character. He argues that to create a true culture of morality requires "a long internal working of each political body toward the education of its citizens" in circumstances of lawful freedom and international peace (*IUH* 8:21). Equality of citizenship and maximal liberty constrained by rights, on the one hand, and economic well-being and public education, on the other, provide the conditions in which the exercise of moral autonomy could be most fully realized in a community of persons. Given that these are multigenerational ambitions, realizable through "no one's" good intentions, and given that progress of this sort tends not to be visible through any indisputable markers (the path to stable peace and constitutional democracy was to be through war, industrial oppression, imperialism), how one looked at things from within the process would matter. It could make a difference to how events developed, and *would* make a difference to the sort of person one became as events unfolded. Belief that one's actions occur within a course of change for the better gives one access to resources of endurance, tolerance, generosity, even forgiveness. These are not merely the sort of things that make one a better person, though they do that; they also serve to promote continuing moral progress. If we believe that our actions can, over time, amount to something positive, then we may adopt ends and endorse institutions that support the direction of change, even if doing so involves some sacrifice or risk. Absent such belief, we lose important reasons to act in concert, to take risks together. There may then seem to be better reasons for risking little, for conserving whatever we have, and if we have little, conditions for nihilism or despair. A shared progressive narrative makes possible a kind of bootstrapping—a sense of the direction of history helps give history direction; it is a way of taking hold of impersonal events that brings them into the sphere of autonomous action.

There is of course no guarantee that a direction of history endorsed by an interpretation gets things right. Supporters of all sorts of millenarian ideals see their faith as creating the conditions for the "new beginning." The Kantian picture is therefore no better than its portrayal of the moral possibilities of constitutional democracy and world peace—the former for its commitment to equality of persons, the latter for the liberation of resources, material and human, for securing welfare and the public culture of reason. If that still leaves too much room for injustice, racism, or sexual oppression, or if it turns out, for reasons we cannot imagine, to be the condition for the loss and not the gain of moral culture, then Kant is wrong about the circumstances in which the rational and moral capacities of human beings can be most fully developed.

The possibility of a progressive history can make a difference even where institutions are unjust. Growing up in an unjust culture that presents itself as natural or inevitable, one might take oppressive social roles for granted and so justified; one may view gross inequalities as unfortunate, but deserved; one may see oneself as injured, but without moral standing to complain or resist. If a progressive history can include these institutions, it can support reform.[18] By providing an account of a culturally available moral ideal in a framework that represents it as a real possibility—that is, connected to an ongoing direction of historical change—the progressive history offers a transformed mode of action and expression. Victims do not need to see their injuries as deserved; the virtue of unwilling "oppressors" need not be limited to kindness, charity, or even self-sacrifice.

---

18. Of the Rousseauian emergence of social life, characterized by competition, pride, *amour propre,* Kant says: "Thus are taken the first true steps from barbarism to culture, which consists in the social worth of man; thence gradually develop all talents, and taste is refined; though continued enlightenment the beginnings are laid for a way of thought which can in time convert the coarse, natural disposition for moral discrimination into definite practical principles, and thereby change a society of men driven together by natural feelings into a moral whole" (*IUH* 8:15).

A moral culture that contains a historically progressive moral story (of itself) does not by itself turn moral persons into agents of change; nor does it (necessarily) give them revolutionary or even social reformist goals. This is for two reasons. First, the mechanism of change is not the individual moral action. The effect of individual action is limited; most of what most agents do does not reach beyond a small sphere of local interactions. It makes no moral sense to oblige agents to make attempts where they cannot succeed. Second, individual agents act within a framework of institutions that constrain what their actions can do or signify (I can give away what property I have; I cannot make it the case that what I give away is not itself property). On the other hand, recognizing the natural limitations on the possible end-related effects of individual action does not sanction a moral posture of passivity. If, for example, moral change occurs largely through change in institutions, then moral agents may be obliged to support and promote those institutions that support the possible realization of progressive moral culture. The promotion of and participation in democratic institutions would be an instance of such an obligation.

When public moral education locates us in a progressive historical narrative, we have two views of ourselves as moral agents. As individuals, our primary task is one of responsible integrity: good willing. As persons sharing the world with other persons, we try to see our activity as promoting and sustaining moral culture. In times of moral regression or catastrophe, infertile virtue may be all that is available. But if we can plausibly tell ourselves that we live in morally interesting times, concern for our own integrity is only part of the story.

Kant's view is neither strongly teleological nor at odds with rational autonomy. The mechanism of historical progress, our "unsocial sociability," is not a process akin to erosion, moving us into ever-increasing connection, until our "irritation" is resolved with the arrival of the liberal state and the end of wars of international aggression. Rather, we are constituted "by nature" to respond to certain kinds of difficulty with reason-responsive creativity and ingenuity. In similar fashion the inevitable frustrations of childhood are experienced as goads to development and learning, background features that encourage us to increase the scope of our autonomy. We are no less fully autonomous agents in the historical-social context for the fact that we might be goaded by difficulties in our "natural" interactions with others to develop and endorse increasingly effective means of living together—something we might do if we are given a sense of direction by a philosophical, morally informed sense of our history.

Participation in a political order of the right sort—a republic of equal citizens under law with a progressive public culture—thus completes the process of moral education. "By nature," human sociality is driven to competition; if not the numbing Hobbesian "power after power," still a ceaseless Rousseauian quest for public esteem. The missing element is an independent conception of the good that could give order and meaning to a human life. It can be found in a form of social life where esteem is a function of moral respect, and well-being is secured through free action under law. Republican citizenship (with peace) provides the next step in moral education, bringing empirical practical reason to completion through individual experience of an order of persons under self-given law.

V

To illustrate the way this is supposed to work, I want to take a brief look at Kant's discussion of the morally edifying role of voting. According to Kant, through participation (voting) in a constitutional republic, citizens get to experience the *form* of moral autonomy: freedom *and* constraint under law of their own making.[19] It is a kind of modeling, and, quite plausibly, a step in grasping the essence of moral agency. But suffrage is limited. Not every one who lives under the law is qualified to make it: only those who are economically independent can have the right to vote. Although Kant's argument for this is impossible to defend in all its detail, the rationale for the limit nonetheless points to, and does not undermine, the heart of the moral lesson political participation is to provide.

Kant argues that although "all men [including women and children] are free and equal *under* public law as already enacted . . . they are not equal with respect to the right to *enact* law" (*TP* 8:294). There is nothing very strange in distinguishing the class of persons under the law's protection from those who can vote; noncitizens, children, and prisoners are routinely held to lack requisite standing or qualifications. The odd feature is the particular qualification Kant uses: that a voter must be "his own master *(sui iuris)*: that he own some sort of property—among which may be counted

---

19. "In this way [entering civil society], the first true steps from barbarism to culture, in which the unique social worth of man consists, now occur, all man's talents are gradually developed, his taste is cultured, and through progressive enlightenment he begins to establish a way of thinking that can in time transform the crude natural capacity for moral discrimination into definite practical principles and thus transform a *pathologically* enforced agreement into a society and, finally, into a *moral* whole" (*IUH* 8:21).

any skill, craft, fine art, or science that supports him" (*TP* 8:295).[20] Mere laboring for a wage does not count; one is then, Kant holds, acting as a servant. Kant allows that the distinction between skilled making and mere laboring is difficult to draw. And it is hardly clear, even if we grant the distinction, why offering one's labor for hire would make one like a servant. But why should being, or being like, a servant disqualify one from voting? What in the distinction between producing and laboring, and between self-mastery and economic dependency, could be construed as vital to the moral status of voting in a constitutional republic?[21]

Perhaps one might argue this way: a servant is someone who is under the rule of another. If one's life-preserving activity (what one does to secure food and shelter) is directly dependent on the direction of others, then one's life is under their rule, and not one's own. But if, as Kant says (*MS* 6:315), dependence of this sort does not touch one's "freedom and equality as a human being," why does it disqualify one from making law? However difficult Kant thinks it is to make the maker/worker distinction, he thinks the conclusion about voting, given the distinction, is obvious.

We might consider whether Kant could think there is some relation that the skilled artisan has to the law—and so to law-making—that an unskilled laborer (in this way like a servant) does not. Kant unhelpfully suggests that the artisan, but not the laborer, has something to sell: a product whose transfer requires the law of contract (*TP* 8:295n; *MS* 6:314).[22] A better argument might point to the fact that the day-laborer needs the law primarily for protection: it secures his rights and prevents his exploitation. His *activity* does not require the environment of law; it can take place under any law that protects him. By contrast, the work of the independent artisan is facilitated and enhanced by laws that promote liberty (free contract, freedom of movement, etc.). Where there is liberty, the artisan not only can develop his distinctive kind of activity, he is encouraged by the free activity of others to do so. He is in a position to acquire a civic personality, recognized and re-

20. Women are of course disqualified before the argument gets going; they, like children, cannot be their "own master." That Kant lacks the moral imagination or will to resist this idea is hardly news.

21. It is possible that Kant is merely an apologist for traditional privilege. It does not seem to me the most interesting assumption. It is in any case not so traditional to give artisans and large landowners equal political rights (*TP* 8:296).

22. Kant seems to lack the distinction between making one's will available and selling one's labor power.

spected as such by other citizens. This, at least, is an argument of the right form.

The independent artisan can thus regard the law as an expression of his own activity and will, not merely as a source of command and protection.[23] Because of his social role, he understands what law is; and *that* is what qualifies him to vote. Moreover, since his relation to the law in voting resembles the relation of the moral agent to the moral law—the law he submits to is a law of his free activity—voting is training in autonomy. It provides the voter with an experience of himself and his co-citizens that models moral personality. By contrast, the day-laborer's relation to the law is heteronomous; the law is a means for his survival, not an expression of his freedom. He therefore lacks an understanding of what the law is that makes him unfit to make law. The training to moral personality that republican civil life can provide is unavailable, given the limits of his social circumstances.

Making law for himself and with others who are free and equal citizens, a voting citizen not only experiences autonomy, he gains insight into the form of a kingdom of ends. Voting is thereby training for moral culture. Moreover, because they understand what law signifies for autonomous agents, the laws made by such citizens will keep the possibility of ownership and independence open to all (*TP* 8:296). Free and independent citizens also support peace. War and the "never remitting preparation for war" drain resources that could be put to public education that would train all persons to be independent agents and citizens in their ways of thinking. In short, voting citizens come to respect the moral autonomy of all, and read their history in a progressive way.

This brings home the force of the claim that insofar as Kantian moral education is a training to autonomy, it is not just a lifelong task for individuals, but a task of culture. The right social institutions are the background of sound moral judgment: institutions that are just and whose rational foundations are deliberatively accessible. But beyond this, participation in a kind of civic life wherein one can see oneself as having a role in a historically progressive process is necessary for the full development of practical reason, in oneself and also, Kant thinks, in the species. This reordering of the psychic and social world is not a second-best approximation of the way things would be if only pure moral autonomy were not interfered with by the empirical morass of desire and social disorder. We can see the comple-

---

23. The feudal artisan, by contrast, must submit himself to the authority of master or guild.

tion of moral education bringing into being what Kant calls the "ectypal world"—nature transformed by reason "determining our will to confer on the sensuous world the form of a system of rational beings" (*KpV* 5:43). Training to autonomy makes autonomy empirically real.

Note

References to Kant's works in this chapter are given parenthetically in the text, using the following abbreviations, citing the page number of the relevant volume of *Kants gesammelte Schriften* (Berlin: Preussische Akademie der Wissenschaft, 1902–). Translations of works quoted are also listed.

A   *Anthropology from a Pragmatic Point of View* (1797), trans. Mary J. Gregor (The Hague: Nijhoff, 1974).

CBH   "Conjectural Beginning of Human History" (1786), in *Perpetual Peace and Other Essays*, trans. Ted Humphrey (Indianapolis: Hackett, 1983).

G   *Groundwork of the Metaphysics of Morals* (1785), trans. and ed. Mary J. Gregor, in Immanuel Kant, *Practical Philosophy* (Cambridge: Cambridge University Press, 1996).

IUH   "Idea for a Universal History from a Cosmopolitan Point of View" (1784), in *Perpetual Peace and Other Essays*, trans. Ted Humphrey (Indianapolis: Hackett, 1983).

KpV   *Critique of Practical Reason* (1788), trans. and ed. Mary J. Gregor, in Immanuel Kant, *Practical Philosophy* (Cambridge: Cambridge University Press, 1996).

KrV   *Critique of Pure Reason*, 1st ed. (A), 1781, 2nd ed. (B), 1787, trans. N. Kemp Smith (New York: St. Martin's Press, 1965).

MS   *The Metaphysics of Morals* (1797), trans. and ed. Mary J. Gregor, in Immanuel Kant, *Practical Philosophy* (Cambridge: Cambridge University Press, 1996).

R   *Religion within the Limits of Reason Alone* (1793), trans. Theodore M. Greene and Hoyt H. Hudson (New York: Harper Torchbooks, 1960).

TP   *On the Old Saw: That May be Right in Theory But It Won't Work in Practice* (1793), trans. E. B. Ashton (Philadelphia: University of Pennsylvania Press, 1974).

— 7 —

Bootstrapping

bootstrap, *v. trans.* 1. To make use of existing resources or capabilities to raise (oneself) to a new situation or state; to modify or improve by making use of what is already present.

bootstrap, *n.* A strap sewn on to a boot to help in pulling it on or looped around a boot to hold down the skirt of a lady's riding habit; a boot-lace.[1]

The attraction of bootstrapping is that you use a bit of what you already have to get some place you haven't been before, but need to go. As a strategy of argument, it is environmentally neutral. No new resources—new entities or capacities—are called for; little of what you start with is wasted. The most compelling philosophical bootstrapping arguments occur when the subject is basic—objects; the causally ordered items of experience; the choices of a perduring self—analyzed in the first instance in a theoretically plain way. The resources used in the first explanation are such ordinary items as perceptions and concepts, desires, beliefs, and the like. The bootstrapping move is prompted when further thought about what the basic subject is like reveals complexity, or some vulnerability to skeptical challenge, that outstrips the carrying capacity of the first explanation. The bootstrap is made of the same plain materials, only attached in a different place, so as to provide additional elements of argument. The idea is to provide just enough leverage in the argument to give a better account of the complexity and/or meet the skeptical challenge. Its ontological and theoretical abstemiousness make bootstrapping one of the more elegant modes of philosophical prestidigitation.

1. *The Oxford English Dictionary,* 2nd ed., electronic text.

No doubt bootstrapping is as old as philosophy, and René Descartes, the historical hero of the art. One of its recent and ambitious employments has been directed at the subject of the will—the free human will—for the purpose of showing that the work of the will, in action and choice, requires no such thing: not really. The lead practitioner in this arena is Harry Frankfurt, whose work on the will and what we care about quite reasonably dominates the discussion. Frankfurt's bootstrapping enterprise is especially powerful because he brings to his subject a rich and detailed account of the phenomena, an independent assessment of the issues marked out by philosophical tradition, and, balancing a commitment to account for the phenomena richly described with resources that demand as little theory as possible, remarkable argumentative ingenuity. In what follows, I will try to pinpoint the bootstrapping in one central theme of Frankfurt's work concerning the will, both because I think that there is much to be learned from its use and because it is important to appreciate, as Frankfurt clearly does, its limits. The issue, at the end, is about costs: of the limits, on the one hand, and of the strong assumptions needed to get past them, on the other.

The subject of the will is a natural area for the employment of bootstrapping. There seem to be things one wants to say about choice and action that call for talk about will and willing. But it remains obscure what the will is, and whether, even if we have reason to regard human agents as having wills, thinking that they do requires that we add a special item to our catalogue of mental stuff. I think we do have wills (that we must) and that the will is a distinct kind of faculty or capacity, connected in an essential way to our rationality. In this I follow Kant. Frankfurt too thinks we have wills, but the will we have is a matter of something like desire plus attitude, raised to a new state by a little bootstrapping. That's enough, he holds, for anything it is sensible to want an account of will to do, and is, moreover, the real heart of the matter about what makes human action special. Indeed, he will argue that it is just this will—desire plus attitude—that is necessary for successful reasoning, not the other way around. Since I am skeptical that one can succeed with an account of the will severed from a robust idea of practical reason, this is for me a useful place to examine the strengths and limits of the bootstrapping. After discussing Frankfurt's view, and looking briefly at what I have come to think is a very similar strategy of argument in some of Christine Korsgaard's work, I will turn (or return) to what I see as the compelling attraction of following Kant on these matters.

I

But first a little background. In most modern philosophy, it is a given that Kant's view of the will is the one to avoid. (I include among the avoiders many so-called Kantians.) There are indeed good reasons for being uneasy about any robustly Kantian view of the will. There are also, as I will try to argue, at least some good reasons for thinking it offers the more satisfactory account of rational action. Many who find Kant's notion of the will hard to take seriously do so in part because of what he says the will is, but also in part because they can't see anything sensible for it to do. As a nonnatural cause, it is metaphysically unpalatable. As the mental side of action, it seems to add nothing when we already have belief, desire, and intention. As the carrier of authoritative practical principle, bridging the gap between reason and desire, it appears to beg the question it is introduced to answer. And as practical reason itself, it either loses any distinctive identity, or if it remains essentially connected to judgment and choice, it may seem to provide evidence of a category mistake: no mode of reason can do what a faculty of choice does.

Though I am not unmoved by these worries, I do not think they survive close scrutiny. Moreover, worries, like arguments, begin in assumptions. In this case, the assumptions not only make it hard to see how there could be answers, it is not clear how there could be worries. Suppose one starts with the idea that the mental equipment relevant to action for a rational human being consists of belief, desire, and intention, and whatever faculties and capacities are necessary to arrive at beliefs, recognize desires, and form intentions. And then one looks for the place to add the will. There is then something quite natural about Hume's claim that what we call will is no more than the subjective impression of the working of the other parts as they yield up action.[2] Or that will is what Frankfurt early on called an agent's "effective desire": the "one that moves a person all the way to action."[3] That is, talk about the will is a way of talking about aspects of the work done by other things. One comes to the same conclusion even with a view of will that is more complicated. Suppose one thought, as Frankfurt

2. David Hume, *A Treatise of Human Nature* (1740), ed. L. A. Selby-Bigge (Oxford: Clarendon Press, 1978), p. 399.

3. Harry Frankfurt, "Freedom of the Will and the Concept of a Person," in *The Importance of What We Care About* (Cambridge: Cambridge University Press, 1988), p. 14.

also does, that volitions play a special role in the activity of rational agents: for example, to order and sort the material of desires in light of an agent's regulative commitments. It is not clear why such volitions have to be anything more than desires of a special sort: higher-order, endorsed, or even rationally formed desires, but just desires all the same. There would be no reason to think this matters—there are often good reasons to specially denominate some of a class if they perform special functions—unless one could show that there is something the will is supposed to do or be that is not possible for anything that was a desire. And that is not so easily made out. Then, given the premises of the worry (here's the equipment of action, why do we need the will?), there's no room for much of an answer (given the equipment, we don't).

I think we can glimpse some advantage to be had in taking the will seriously if we follow out a related dynamic that occurs in the now frozen debate about internal and external reasons for action. Kant-friendly views are thought to be at a disadvantage since they cannot explain the normative force of the considerations they claim are reasons, since nothing counts as a reason in the relevant sense that does not connect to antecedent desires or desire-like states. Attempting to reverse the argument, some on the Kantian side of things have argued that the best reason to posit a bit of responsive subjectivity is the conviction that there are reasons of a certain sort.[4] That is, if we are on solid ground in thinking that there is a certain class of reasons, then it must be that, as rational beings, we can act for them. It is in a way the right thing to say, but it is not a satisfying answer.

One source of dissatisfaction comes from the fact that the table-turning answer shares a structure of reasons and motives with the Humean critics: a theoretically concessive model of claim and response. As a result, arguments to reasons stop short because they depend on psychological states external to what the reason is. When we offer reasons, we are presenting claims whose legitimacy for an agent will depend on something else: something subjective, or receptive. *I* come to see what reasons I have by reasoning from what matters to me (construed however widely); when *you* claim I have a reason, if the claim is normative, you must consider how what the

---

4. The best examples of such arguments are in Thomas Nagel, *The Possibility of Altruism* (Oxford: Oxford University Press, 1970); and Christine M. Korsgaard, "Skepticism about Practical Reason," in *Creating the Kingdom of Ends* (Cambridge: Cambridge University Press, 1996).

reason picks out is connected to what moves me. Given this, the further claim that what it is to be rational is to be responsive to the reasons there are just puts the issue on hold.

Missing is the idea that the value a putative reason carries plays a role in the subjective condition that makes it a reason for me. My valuing X, or valuing something that leads me to value X, may connect me motivationally to X: that is, when these conditions obtain, I accept X as a reason. What it does not do is make the *value of X* my reason. Suppose one wants to say: it is the value of honesty that gives one a reason to tell the truth; or the value of human life that makes need a reason for beneficent action. And suppose we accept an argument that shows we do have a reason to speak truthfully and reason to offer help because there is something "in us" in virtue of which we directly or mediately care about truth-telling and meeting needs. If it is the former, if we just do care about truth-telling or need-meeting, then the *value* of what we care about does no work in the generation of reasons; and certainly if we don't directly care, if we care to tell the truth because we care about something else, the reasons we come to have do not express the value that honesty or persons have—in themselves. This is part of what I meant in saying that the concessive arguments *to* reasons stop short. We lack part of what makes a reason a reason—a story of its value. If we want to talk about value as something separate and reason-generating, it is not obvious that we can do this within the internalist framework of reasons and motives for action. There is no room for value, as there was no room for will.

Further, if the explanation of what gives us a motivating interest in a reason is something external to it, then there is always an extra thing, a feature of our subjectivity, that *gives* us an interest in the reason—even if this extra thing is Reason. In the end, there is some mere given—an element of passive receptivity. Now many will find in this a simple truth, not a source of worry at all. And they may do so out of the not in itself unreasonable conviction that something has to be a mere given: explanations run out. But the route to the truism leaves unexplained our relation to the given (or the givens, if there are more than one). The uncertain space left for rational reflection undermines the very idea of deliberative authority or governance.

What is wanted (or what is wanting) is a way to talk about reasons that satisfies the internalist's motivational strictures but without sacrificing the idea that reasons track values. And if part of the motivational story is to lie in the connection between reasons and values, value must make the connection without dependence on agents' independent subjective states, or without looping through them in the wrong sort of way. To get beyond the limited Humean connections, but without positing awkward new entities, a bit of a bootstrap could seem to be the right tool for the task. As I read him, in his later work Frankfurt offers just such a bootstrapping account of reasons, or of some reasons, that would establish a nonarbitrary and noncontingent connection to values (or, if not all the way to values, at least to what one cares about). Whether his account can meet the just-mentioned strictures and conditions is to be seen.

II

On Frankfurt's analytical view of a human self, rational agency consists in a system of beliefs and desires, organized hierarchically through a process—acts of reflection and identification.[5] But even before there is a self there is will. The story of will begins in desires: specifically, the set of desires one happens to have as a function of physiology and circumstance. Originally, pre-reflectively, we desire in response to our needs. Thus the first objects of desire will perforce be of a certain kind, though their local specification is adventitious. This is enough for there to be will. For Frankfurt, an agent's will is that desire which, by virtue of its effectiveness, leads her to action. So there is even will in a creature who merely has desires of different strengths, if it is so constructed that a stronger desire "wins" and issues in action. Will can be present in a creature who has no capacity to learn or to modify its desires, and a fortiori, no capacity to (in some way or other) opt for the satisfaction of one desire rather than another. Sufficient for identification of an entity's will is the manifestation of a desire-based pattern in its behavior. An entity whose will is set—so that it must act one way rather than another—is said to have a nature. In higher creatures, ones that are volitionally complex, we talk instead of having or being a self: something with a more or less stable, and more or less accessible identity.

---

5. The summary of Frankfurt's view of agency is drawn primarily from the following set of his essays: "Freedom of the Will and the Concept of the Person," "The Importance of What We Care About," and "Identification and Wholeheartedness," in *The Importance of What We Care About;* "On the Usefulness of Final Ends," "The Faintest Passion," "On the Necessity of Ideals," and the two lectures on caring, "Caring and Necessity," and "The Necessities of Love," all in *Necessity, Volition, and Love* (Cambridge: Cambridge University Press, 1999).

The exercise of a capacity for reflection—the acquisition of conscious beliefs and the capacity to employ them reflexively—can produce higher-order desires and volitions. (Can, that is, in creatures capable of being altered in these ways by the process of reflection.) Closure of the chain of desires is secured either through brute identification with some one of them or through some more reflective endorsement. We may or may not like what we find in our desires. But what we do like, and like ourselves liking, we can be said to care about. Part of our volitional complexity lies in the fact that in caring, we not only like what we like, but we make efforts to preserve as well as to satisfy our preferences. There is thus a co-development of self and will that, ideally, yields a nonaccidental coincidence between what we are—what we care about—and what we will. If our will forms as we come to care about things, our will has autonomy as we are reflectively satisfied with what we care about, and will what we will wholeheartedly. (Wholeheartedness is, by design, the practical analogue of the Cartesian norm of clear and distinct perception.)[6]

This much is enough to set (some) normative parameters for willing. On the one hand, not all of the things we might desire are, for most of us anyway, things we are able to desire wholeheartedly: not everything we desire will we find important, and many of the things we take to be important will not survive further reflection or comparison with other things we find important. On the other hand, it is important that we find things that are important to us, things that make a difference we care about, and that we succeed, as much as we can, in willing and acting for them without ambivalence. Reflection introduces a practical burden. Its normative parameters, however, have no special rational or metaphysical authority: they arise from our biological and material circumstances. We have malleable desires, reflective abilities that we cannot refrain from using, and only limited powers to shape the world (and ourselves). This gives us a task of identifying things to care about and ways of acting that minimize stress. Stochastic disrupters are ambivalence about ends, conflicts of desires, unrealizable ideals, insufficiently rich or complex ends, guilt and shame, the various forms of bad

---

6. Doubt drives further reflection and the formation of higher-order desires and volitions; wholeheartedness is achieved when one can no longer see any reason to doubt or foresee conflict. So I might begin with an ambition-driven will to promote my career, but then be uncertain when I see that so willing might yield conflict with other things I care about or might come to care about. I cannot will wholeheartedly until this is resolved. It will be resolved when I am satisfied with what I will and I do not foresee disturbing conflicts.

luck, and so on. Some of these we can manage; some are unavoidable.[7] We have a free or autonomous will just in case we have the will we want to have, and we can say we have the will we want to have when we find no further reason to question or be ambivalent about the will we do have. To be a person is to have solved this set of problems to a reasonable degree.

In case it is not obvious, the bootstrapping is this. Starting with the plain stuff of desires, beliefs, and some facts about our reflective and practical capacities and needs, a project of self-construction is described, the norms for which emerge from the building process they regulate (especially its need for stability). The end-product is a hierarchically ordered self whose volitional system is regulated by the emergent norm of wholeheartedness. Granted that this is a highly schematic presentation of a nuanced and complex view, I believe it contains sufficient detail to address my question. Can the bootstrapping in the account of normatively structured development—from desire to self and from self to person with freedom of the will—get us the connection between motivating reasons and value?[8]

Although my sketch of Frankfurt's hierarchical view of the self did not make use of any notion of value—at least not explicitly—Frankfurt avails himself of value talk, just as we should expect. Value attaches to things that can be cared about, for their own sakes or in virtue of their relation to other things we value. As we should expect, the view is abstemious. To talk of value is not to introduce any new thing. Things with value are important; and what makes something important is that its presence or absence matters: the parameters are harm, pleasure, satisfaction, and the like. Thus *our* values—the things we value—shape our actions, decisions, feelings, and deliberations in the usual way. It is an imperative of agency that we care about or value *some* things (as opposed to no thing). And if we did not have things we found or took to be ultimately important—call them final ends—that guided us in the adoption of ends for action, we would not be persons; we would lack a condition of identity.

There is a gap, however, between things that might be said to be *of value* and the things we value. One wants room to say: we may or may not value things that are of value. The bootstrapping story allows us to say: if we care

---

7. It is not clear, for example, that things we can separately embrace wholeheartedly are things that together give unity to our wills, or that this is a reasonable ideal for an individual on her own. Given what we love, loss is not something extrinsic to it.

8. Where, if values do not directly support reasons, reasons at least non-accidentally track values.

about the wrong things, we will tend to find our ends and projects unsatisfying, either because they cannot bear the weight we put on them, or because we come to believe that what we care about is in some way not important, or not as important as we thought. Though this may be true, it is not the same as saying that what we have valued is not *of value*. For recall that what we value, what we care about, begins in our desire or need, and is shaped by rational reflection. But the norms of reflection do not pick out or track truth about value. Their goal is to eliminate, as much as possible, elements in a person's values that undermine their role in securing practical identity and reflective satisfaction with life. The norms of reflection are ultimately set by the conditions of agency and identity; they guide us in gaining assurance that what we value as ends, especially as final ends, can be willed wholeheartedly. It is as if our norms of justified belief were not aimed at truth (and certainly didn't track it), but when satisfied, gave us substantial conviction that we believe what we do for the best available reasons. In similar fashion, these norms of practical reflection are a guide to confidence, not truth—that is, to confidence in ourselves as valuers, not to any truth about value.

In response, one might argue that, nonetheless, the norms are sufficient for value to play the requisite structuring role for will and action. The formal nature of what we value provides all the critical balance between value and reasons we need. Some of our values leave us a great deal of volitional discretion. Some do not. I greatly value good food and wine, but they are not so important in the scheme of things that I must drop what I'm doing when the opportunity for a good meal comes along—not if there are other more important things to attend to, and even not if I simply don't want to. Other ends and values, however, present us with imperatives; we cannot truly care about them and just ignore their reasons. And some of those imperatives, Frankfurt argues—especially ones rooted in our loves—can be unconditional, giving reasons for action that are not or no longer "up to us." We can no more abandon them, or decide we just don't care to attend to their demands, than we can cease being who we are.

Now you might think that if such ends can give unconditional reasons for action, then there is a direct connection between values and reasons to be had within the bootstrapped framework—at least for some values. It is certainly true that love for my child gives me immediate reasons to act for the sake of his needs—or at least for the more urgent ones. And as I love him, and cannot cease loving him at will or at all, his welfare gives me motivating reasons that are not "up to me." This supports the right transitivity: if when I love I value unconditionally, my reasons are unconditional as well. So surely in loving, the motivating reasons that I come to have are directly connected to value.

But are these reasons that I have when I love connected to value in the way I was looking for? I don't think so. The problem is that in loving, the support for reasons is not any value inherent in the loved person or the loving relationship. The welfare of the loved other is reason-giving for me because, and only because, I care about him. So, in a sense, the unconditioned reasons that I have are only relatively so. Given who I am, and so what I love, I do have reasons that are not up to me, that are unconditioned, and so unconditionally attached to the valued object. But the *authority* of the reasons derives from *my* caring, from my activity of valuing.

We should not go too quickly past this. What Frankfurt has shown is that the possibility of unconditioned reasons does not, as one might have thought, require external value, or anything outside the orbit of bootstrapping. They can arise from the nature of our sensitivity and capacity for love—the way we value some final ends. These unconditioned reasons are not mediated by attachment to any other end; their motivational force is secured directly with the recognition of a reason's applicability. And since the end that supports the reason is one I cannot abandon, it functions, volitionally, as unconditioned value. But there is still a condition. There is the value-to-us of unconditioned ends, paradoxically conditioned by our need for them—namely, if we are to be persons. When I do not abandon my final ends, it is not because of *their* value; it is because they have come to play a co-constitutive role in my identity as a person. The work is being done by inertia. It is inertia of a special sort, to be sure: for what I cannot abandon is myself.

So we are left with a limited result. Whether or not I love things for what I value in them, it is my loving them that makes them valuable to me. And loving is important, but not because of the value of the objects of love, but because of the value (to me) of loving. Granted, there is no third thing between my loving someone and my motivation to care about him. If I love I care. But a third thing is there, one step back, in what makes love important. This is where we reach the outer limit of the bootstrapping.

I am not at all supposing that Frankfurt would find this conclusion disturbing. Part of his project is to trace the limits of our rational powers, and to move into a more central place in our philosophical reasonings the idea that will is much more a function of where we begin as sensitive creatures than most rationalist accounts of agency allow. This shift is exhibited in his focus on the volitional structure of love (or caring), as opposed to that of morality, for he wants to show that many of the "special" features of moral reasons and value that drive rationalist accounts (their unconditional requirements, their status as final ends) are shared by the reasons of love and care. This explains, Frankfurt argues, why our loves may give us reasons that truly compete with the reasons of morality. There is an implicit claim as well. And that is that morality, too, must fit into the story of will, desire, and reflection, if it is to be important for us, and to offer us reasons we will find authoritative.

Even though this is not Frankfurt's issue, it is not unreasonable to press it. For if morality is not amenable to the same bootstrapping moves that work for love and care, both the explicit and implicit implications may need to be qualified. Frankfurt's bootstrapping is so very attractive because it succeeds in providing a robust account of volition that satisfies internalist strictures. We get an account of willing that, because it is responsive to the demands of complex ends and allows for imperatives, so situates the agent that she is normatively responsive to reasons. But this is not the same as an agent acting for reasons that track the value of what is valued. If acting from love is the best case, then although we get reasons connected to the value of what we value, that turns out not to be the same as having reasons derived from or responsive to what is of value. For Frankfurt, the value of what I value is, in the end, its value to me. This may or may not be a problem for understanding the norms of love and caring; it is an obstacle where moral norms are concerned. One fails to act morally unless the content of one's reasons is determined by nonrelative moral value.

III

This suggests an option within roughly the same space of argument that involves a more radical internalist move of a rationalist kind, one in which Reason itself is the subjective source of moral value, and so of reasons of the right sort. The option is tempting not just because subjective conditions are now given two jobs instead of just one (Frankfurt's bootstrapping had that), but because there is a rational source of values that supports reasons to which they are also motivationally responsive. What will make a consideration a reason is the connection of some fact with a Reason-derived value.

And what will make the reason effective in producing action is the same imputed feature of our rational nature. If reasons track Reason, we are awfully close to the idea that reasons track value.

The in-principle advantages of such a rationalist subjectivism are many. It rebuts the question-begging charge against the practicality of reason; it makes the right sorts of connections between value and reasons, and between reasons and motives; and, given the foundation of reasons in values that express principles of Reason, it is a subjectivism that does not require an additional elaborate story about how to secure agreement—objectivity comes with the source of moral values. However, an additional story *is* required about *who we are* that explains the priority to us of our rational, value-generating natures. That is, something has to explain *why* we will or should take the deliverances of Reason to be determinative for our choices, since we obviously need not do so. It would do no good if it turned out that Reason has been cast (or miscast) in the role of a special sort of desire, requiring something additional and itself authoritative to identify and secure the authority of Reason's reasons. This is a variant of a familiar rationalist dilemma. And familiar, if problematic, strategies of resolution are available: more bootstrapping of the "nothing offers reasons that are better than Reason's reasons" sort; identity arguments to the effects that following the dictates of Reason is the necessary condition for our being agents at all; and transcendental arguments that raise the identity arguments to a new level— that the authority of Reason's reasons is the necessary condition of one's being, practically speaking, an "I."

One finds this kind of rationalist subjectivism in some of Christine Korsgaard's work.[9] Though she uses a fuller notion of rationality than Frankfurt allows in order to forge the connection between reasons and value, the style of argument is remarkably similar: a relatively flat Humean starting point and a bootstrapping rationalism that is more Cartesian than Kantian in spirit. Korsgaard's framing idea, which she also shares with Frankfurt, is to exploit the connection between identity and autonomy to secure a

---

9. There are hints in "Skepticism about Practical Reason" and pieces of the view in "The Reasons We Can Share," both in *Creating the Kingdom of Ends,* but what I am calling the rationalist subjectivism begins to play a dominant role only in Christine M. Korsgaard with G. A. Cohen et al., *The Sources of Normativity* (Cambridge: Cambridge University Press, 1996), lecture 3; and then in Christine M. Korsgaard, "Self-Constitution in the Ethics of Plato and Kant," *Journal of Ethics* 3 (1999): 1–29.

route to rational and moral norms for willing. She would argue that actions are not, properly speaking, ours—we are not their authors but the site for forces working through us—unless the way in which we come to act is under the evaluative command of reflective reason. Like Frankfurt, she sees this as the condition for being fully a person, not a wanton. But unlike Frankfurt, she wants to get both formal and substantive rational constraints. The formal constraint is universality: reasons, to be reasons at all, may not be fully particular. The substantive constraint is that our reasons be such that through them we acknowledge the status of persons as autonomous agents—that is, as independent sources of value. The universal form of reasons is a necessary condition of agency; the norm of reciprocal relations among autonomous agents introduces morality.[10] We cannot act as agents at all unless we satisfy the formal condition. We can, however, act without the norm of reciprocity. Although as rational agents we must take something as giving us a sufficient reason to act, this could involve, at the limit, no more than the satisfaction of the Frankfurtian reflexive requirement that we have some stable final ends. Again, a third thing is required to connect morality to agency.

The Kantian argument one might expect to bring morality into an account of agency would show that there cannot be any final end that gives sufficient support for action, properly speaking, except rational nature as an end in itself. But that's an argument Korsgaard thinks cannot be made with the materials at hand. Only so much can be built on the conditions that we should be one, or whole, or unambivalent, or authors of our actions; none of these are sufficient to pick out any substantive final end.[11] Further acts of reflection (the Cartesian move) can clean up our system of ends and secure full generality of reasons. So while the normative extension to having our ends and ways of acting be ones that others can endorse or share (reciprocity) will strike some, perhaps most, as fitting with their sense of themselves as rational agents, it need not do so. And unless it is not only rational to embrace morality but also irrational to evade it, the account remains incomplete.

---

10. This is put in Kantian language—ends and ways of acting must be possible subjects of universal legislation that all can endorse or share—but its separation from the formal constraint is a sign that it is not a move in a Kantian argument.

11. Korsgaard accepts this conclusion at the end of "The Normativity of Instrumental Reason," in Garrett Cullity and Berys Gaut, eds., *Ethics and Practical Reason* (Oxford: Clarendon Press, 1997).

This may partly explain why Korsgaard is increasingly drawn to a more Platonic rationalism. Plato offers a richer story of the self or soul, where Justice, a principle of Reason (capital *R*), brings right-order to the disparate needs and wants of a human being so as to constitute her as a unified, autonomous person, one capable of being a true cause of action.[12] And, of course, Justice unifies the parts of the self in the right way, with an eye to the good of the whole.[13] The building-in of the substantive requirement, conjoined with an argument to show the inadequacy of all other principles of final ends, would of course close the gap between reasons and reason-based value.

Now in Plato, as in Kant, closing the gap calls for an additional and I believe essential portion of metaphysics. In Kant it shows up in the account of why the only possible law of an autonomous will is the moral law, and in Plato in the explanation of how the good of the person, or the state, is the good to which reason looks (or explains why a principle of unity is a principle of good for the whole). The former requires a more metaphysically contentful notion of will; the latter the teleology of the theory of Forms. Whether one can have the advantages of the Platonic story without the Forms is not clear. It is clear, and, I should add, clear to Korsgaard, that some richer metaphysics is needed. Her preference is for a robustly teleological account of action: seeing what the essence of rational action is gives the connection between the formal and the substantive norms of reason. But whichever way one goes to close the gap, bootstrapping is left behind.

What follows? To the extent that Frankfurt or Korsgaard would bootstrap their way from essentially Humean materials, plus a more complex story of the needs and identity conditions of agency, to the autonomous will, their conception of autonomy cannot outstrip the carrying capacity of the elements with which they begin. Frankfurt is not disturbed by this: having extended the notion of willing through the hierarchical ordering of desires and volitions, and making the will responsive to imperatives, he has all the autonomy or freedom of will he wants. Korsgaard is less well served by this method. Wanting more from the will, or from the concept of action, in

---

12. "The actions which are most truly a person's own are precisely those actions which most fully unify her and therefore most fully constitute her as their author." For this reason, Korsgaard considers Justice to be a principle of *self-constitution.* "Self-Constitution in the Ethics of Plato and Kant," p. 3.

13. Ibid., p. 19.

order to bridge the gap between reasons and value for the sake of a moral imperative, more has to be built into the start-up conditions. Bootstrapping is not alchemy.

When we leave bootstrapping behind, however, we appear to be caught between the twin misfortunes of moral skepticism and serious metaphysics. But before we contend with this dire prospect, I suggest we go back to the beginning of the discussion where we acceded to the elements of an essentially (and intentionally) anti-Kantian characterization of will and action. Since, after all, the problem of bridging reasons and value might be thought to be a distinctly Kantian one, a reassessment of the advantages and pitfalls of Kant's own account of the will looks like a reasonable next step. I admit that what one takes to be the worse problem matters: some might find the embrace of anything at all like Kant's account of will and action a move so fatal that, by contrast, the problems I have been pointing to are no problems at all. But I don't think so. My thought is that we have so quickly shied away from the basic elements of Kant's account of will and value, or tried to domesticate them while holding onto Kant's main conclusions, that we may not really see the force of what he tried to accomplish with his conception of practical reason. The ambition of Kant's rationalism of value can no more be cast in Cartesian or Platonic terms than his views about action fit a Humean or neo-Humean moral psychology. With this in mind, I want to spend some time looking at Kant's view, if only to indicate how dramatically different things look when one approaches action as he does. The account will perforce be sketchy; I don't think that will obscure its point.

IV

As you may recall, Kant begins the main argument of *Groundwork* II this way: "Everything in nature works in accordance with laws. Only a rational being has the capacity to act *in accordance with the representation* of laws, that is, in accordance with principles, or has a *will.* Since *reason* is required for the derivation [*Ableitung,* "drawing off"] of actions from laws, the will is nothing other than practical reason."[14] Much that is attractive and impossible in Kant's view is captured here. The attractive part is the description of our freedom to act according to *our* conception of laws, to act

---

14. Immanuel Kant, *Groundwork of the Metaphysics of Morals* (1785), in Immanuel Kant, *Practical Philosophy,* trans. and ed. Mary J. Gregor (Cambridge: Cambridge University Press, 1996), 4:412.

according to principles we represent as sufficient, or justified. The impossible part: that to have a will is to have a special causal power—the power to act from representations of law ("a kind of causality belonging to living beings insofar as they are rational").[15] And there are other problems. First Kant claims that the will is "nothing but practical reason"; just a few lines later, however, he talks about the human will as one that "does not in itself completely accord with reason." Surely he can't have it both ways: either the will *is* practical reason or it is not. If it is, then we do not easily understand how what *is* practical reason can fail to accord with reason; and if it is not, then what the will is, and how it relates to practical reason, seems up in the air. Among other things, a normative connection is missing. Now some of these problems arise from the interpretive presupposition that the Kantian concepts of volition, practical necessity, maxim, and imperative are just terminological variants of familiar notions. Others arise from the commitment, at all costs, to avoid the idea of will as a cause. The former can be corrected by more careful reading of Kant. The latter—making sense of the idea of will as cause—will take some doing.

Now you might think it crazy to try to do anything with Kant's idea of "the will's causality." And perhaps it is. But whether the very idea is insupportable is not the question I think we should ask first. First we need to understand more about what "it" is, and why it demands the commitments it does.

Things tend to go awry as soon as the discussion turns to maxims. Maxims represent actions as-they-are-willed; as such, they are the proper objects of moral (and practical) assessment. Interpretive custom is to view maxims as the means-ends principles behind actions: to do some action, in such and such circumstances, for the sake of some end. The action figures in the principle under an end-relative description (a pumping water if that's my job; a poisoning if I'm part of a terrorist group). The primary question of moral assessment is: is the principle morally justified? It is if it is universalizable; not if it is not. Nothing so far requires that we talk about will at all, or about value until we reach the final step of justification. And nothing explains how a maxim relates to any actual doing. It is natural to suppose that what brings the agent to action, given her maxim, is some desire or motive waiting in the wings, connected somehow or other to her

---

15. Ibid., 4:446.

end, that is causally sufficient to bring about the right activity. The maxim proposes, the desire disposes.

But notice that once again we are working with the tools of belief, desire, intention, plus a principle of justification and a commitment to using it (another belief-desire pair). Reason enters in judgment determining means-end fit and in assessing the universalizability of the resulting maxim. Certainly no nonrational being can conceive of its action through a principle, or employ standards of evaluation. So it must be that to have a will is to be able to do *that*. Or to be able to do that *and* care about the deliberative outcome. As before, "will" picks out nothing that cannot be captured in Humean terms. It is no surprise, then, that all the key issues remain. Whether the evaluative principle on offer is plausibly a principle of reason will be determined by independent debates about what reason's principles are. And the separate issue of motivational sufficiency is handled by the positing of a special desire or interest (the fabled "motive of duty"). Why, though, interpret Kant as if he embraced a Humean method—starting from basic, separate elements of mind brought together by iterations of simple combinatorial mechanisms to yield an account of acting on principle? As if when the agent fits together her ends, means, intentions, and desires, she acts (or tries to), and so she has a will, and a maxim. Kant is no such methodological atomist.

If we pay closer attention to Kant's exposition, we see that a maxim is not constructed from the bottom up. An agent's maxim is a principle that expresses a complex volitional judgment. The fact that maxims represent actions *as they are willed* introduces formal features beyond means-to-end fit that entail an essential evaluative component.[16] When an agent wills, and so has a maxim, she sets herself to act in a particular way, suited to promote an end, *as she judges that-way-of-acting-for-that-end-to-be good. She therein conceives of herself acting in accord with a principle or standard of value. But that's not all. The standard of value or conception of the good in terms of which we conceive our actions cannot be alien to the will. If it were, we would be back where we started, with a gap between the material of action, its subjective side, and claims we might want to make about the reasons a person has.

16. One could represent the actions of animals in terms of means-ends principles, but they would not for that be acting on maxims—not even if they were somehow conscious of so acting.

Kant avoids the gap this way. To have a will is to have a capacity to be moved to action via a conception or representation *(Vorstellung)* of law. When one wills, that is how one is moved—by means of a conception. It is easy to think this means: qua rational agent, when I set myself to act, I make use of representations or conceptions of laws to determine how to reach my ends—bits of theoretical reasoning. And certainly, as a rational being, I do that. But that is not what it is to have a *rational will*. Kant's idea is that such a will, as a capacity to be moved to action by means of an agent's conception of a law, does not move us to action by means of a conception of just *any* law. Neither a representation of the law of gravity nor of the law-like connection between arsenic and poisoning would move one to action. There would have to be, in addition, a desire not to fall or not to die. And if one were moved in that way, one wouldn't need a will. (This seems to me exactly the point that Hume presses.)

[margin annotation: RATIONAL WILL]

However, among the laws we can and do represent to ourselves is the law that is constitutive of the will's own causal power. That law can only be, Kant argues, the moral law: it is, by his argument, the principle of best (and sufficient) reasons for action (or volition). This is the idea of the moral law as a law of freedom. Now without defending either of these claims, I want to describe some of what they do to our understanding of willing. So Kant can say: in willing an action, one is moved by a perceived connection of an action to a representation of the principle of best reasons. There are not two things here that need to be matched up: the will and the principle of best reasons. The principle constitutive of the will's own activity *is* the principle of best reasons; it is what we represent to ourselves as the basis of rational choice. When we get it right—when we correctly understand what the best reasons are—we act from the moral law as the final justificatory principle of our action. Of course we do not always get it right, or choose for the best; nonrational influences can affect the representation of the will's own law (as they can our representation of any law). Thus it is true both that the will is practical reason, and that, for us, willing may not always be in accord with reason.

Suppose this is right—about Kant, I mean. The connection he makes between will and value is then not something that can be constructed from or analyzed into Humean components. A being with a will is a certain kind of cause: one capable of initiating action by deriving it from her representation of the will's own principle. An action, so derived, is what a maxim represents. That is why, if the agent misrepresents the will's law, the maxim's failure under universalization will be imputable to the agent's willing. (And also why the mark of moral failure registers as a contradiction: if we think of the categorical imperative procedure as representing the constitutive law of the will, the faulty maxim presents as a law of willing a principle that cannot be a law.) When an agent acts "from duty," the action is derived from an accurate representation of the will's law (which is then the action's subjective principle; it was always the action's objective standard). Like the classical practical syllogism, the movement from principle to judgment to action is one. There is no separate motive. (Thus, we should thankfully note, no dour "motive of duty" either.)

Is there still room to talk about faulty action as free action? Faulty action is derived from misrepresented value, from an agent's defective volitional judgment about what is best. If by free action one means, as Kant does, action derived from the will's own principle, then the action is free in that sense. (Analogously we say that mistakes in addition are mistakes *in addition*— that is, a result is derived from relevant arithmetic principles misapplied, perhaps with self-serving lack of care. Unfree action is like a child's assertion of a sum, for no arithmetic reason.) Faulty action is thus imputable to the autonomous will, since the principle of the maxim is a representation— albeit a *mis*representation—of the will's own law.[17]

Looking back to the concerns that provoked this discussion, it may be useful to summarize some of what is novel in Kant's way of thinking about will and rational action. First, the derivation of action from the constitutive principle of *volition* provides a noncontingent connection between value and reasons. Failure to be moved by a reason is a sign of a deliberative error, not a lack of subjective connection to the reason's value. Second, action requires no separate motive. Because it is derived from the will's causal principle (as a specification of it), we get the normativity of reasons without

---

17. A question remains about why one would care about getting one's willing right, since of course one can get it wrong, and indeed one will have interests that are better served if one does. Kant's answer is found in his curious discussion of the incentives of the will, where he argues that the interest in correctness of willing is *necessary* in any imperfectly rational being. This is a complicated business that I will take up elsewhere. The thing to note here, however, is the change in order of argument. When bootstrapping, absent the interest, one cannot get to reasons. Here, the connection between reasons and value is secured first. The appeal to interests comes after; it explains how one comes to care about oneself in doing what one in any case has to do. The caring is not necessary in order for us to act correctly; it is the causally necessary effect of the moral law on our sensible nature, transforming what counts as a life worth living.

having to add other motives or desires, even the special motives of rational agents.[18] Third, our rational nature is not a source of reasons in competition with anything else. No additional principle is needed to give warrant to reason's reasons. Interests we have may cause us to misrepresent what reason requires; they may cause us to be mistaken about what's best. This sets a task for practical and moral education to transform desires so that they are sensitive to reason, both by giving them appropriate objects, and by making them internally reason-responsive.[19] The good will is then the will whose willings are right—where the derivation of action gives rise to a maxim whose principle is the (correctly represented) law of a free will. (This rather neatly leaves room for empirical mistakes that do not undermine the moral worth of action.) That is why when one acts from the moral law, it is precisely the value of so acting that moves one—it is one's reason for action.

In contrast with the will of bootstrapping arguments, the Kantian will is not made up of or developed from simpler elements by identification or any kind of endorsement. The starting point is a different one. There need not have been creatures with rational wills, but there are. And insofar as there are creatures with rational wills, there is a power to produce actions that there would otherwise not be. That is, if the rational will is a causal power, if it is a distinctive way of bringing things (actions) about, then its active principle will not be the mechanical principle of cause and effect (which, of course, does not bring things about but explains their occurrence) but a principle of the kind of cause it is—a rational principle of causality. In order to talk about the will of a rational agent, then, one has to introduce conceptual elements that would not be required except for the existence of the rational will. This is metaphysics, not bootstrapping. (Indeed, if it were bootstrapping, things would go much easier for Kant: no need for the third chapter of the *Groundwork* or for the Fact of Reason.)

And finally, there is the bridge problem. On Frankfurt's view the reasons one has ultimately depend on what one values. That is why there is no direct bridge from action or agency to morality at all. This is not a difficulty

---

18. Of course, strictly speaking, what follows on the derivation from principle is a *willed* action; whether bodily movement of the appropriate sort then occurs is a question for a different story.

19. The point of moral education is not just to make us good. It responds to a demand of our freedom—to express our capacity to make reason our rule.

for Frankfurt. Morality will show up in due course as a condition (no doubt a very important condition) of various things that make human life go well. For Kant, the bridge is present in the idea that the law of the rational will's causal power is the moral law. The law of the Kantian rational will is, simply (!), the condition of free action, and thus is, *eo ipso*, the moral law. So it really is metaphysics all the way.

That leaves us with the elephant in the living room: the will as a kind of causality and all that. We need to be careful about what we take the problem to be. If we are worried about the will's causality because we do not countenance any mental causes, then I would hazard that the worry is not about Kant, and in any case depends on views about explanation and materialism or science that are not themselves compelling. I think we should argue that we have reason to accept the will as a cause because it provides the best explanation of what we do when we act morally, and, perhaps, whenever we act in a way that is directly responsive to value. I have tried to indicate why one might want such an explanation, and some of the costs of doing without it. If the worry is about the will as *noumenon*, we want to be sure we understand what Kant wants from this idea. It is one thing if he is committed to some higher or other reality beyond or behind ours. But it is doubtful he has any such idea (or that, consistent with his views, he could). Certainly, the idea of mental cause does not by itself require noumenal causality. That is why I take the will not to violate but to extend our "one world" account of what there is.[20] Some have argued that all this is easier if we adopt a "two standpoints" view of action. This leaves me uneasy. Either volitional judgment is sufficient for action or it is not. Of course much depends on what it means to think of ourselves as free causes "from a practical point of view." But unless the will's own law *is* the principle of rational action—not how we think of it, but what it is—then there is room for skeptical challenge to the authority of reason's reasons.

The point I would press is really one about methodological priority. I don't know whether there can be a metaphysically acceptable account of the kind of cause Kant thinks the will is. On the other hand, we don't understand much about this kind of cause apart from what we can say about the will. So trying to see what motivates Kant's idea of will and willing seems to me some kind of plain good sense. And I have tried to suggest that some

20. It may be that the Kantian will is not an object of sense, and so not a possible object of experience. It would not be the only thing about ourselves we had a priori warrant to believe.

things we want to say about reasons and value are available to us if we take Kant's account of the will seriously. It would be unfortunate to lose these insights because of premature metaphysical squeamishness. In arguing that what we want cannot be had with beliefs and desires and truly virtuoso bootstrapping, I hope to have offered some pragmatic reasons to be more open-minded about the will itself.

— 8 —

Rethinking Kant's Hedonism

> . . . advise him of his happy state—
> Happiness in his power left free to will,
> Left to his own free will, his will though free
> Yet mutable.
>
> —JOHN MILTON, *PARADISE LOST*

At the very center of the argument in the *Critique of Practical Reason* Kant makes a pair of claims that have been hard to live with (or live down). In his terms they are: (1) that all empirical practical principles are of "one and the same kind," falling under "the principle of self-love or one's own happiness" (*KpV* 5:22),[1] and (2) that in acting on such principles, the determining ground of action is in every case pleasure.[2] When we add the rule of deliberation that is supposed to follow from (1) and (2)—that when choosing among nonmoral options of action, a *quantitative* measure of expected pleasure is the only possible principle of choice (*KpV* 5:23)—we get the full flower of Kant's hedonism. Nonmoral action is about pleasure; the rule of choice is to maximize it. In marked contrast to his transformative approach to moral action and choice, Kant's embrace of hedonism seems poorly thought out, something of an embarrassment, better ignored than taken seriously.

To be sure, friendly interpretations of the relevant texts have been offered

---

1. Immanuel Kant, *Critique of Practical Reason* (1788), in *Practical Philosophy*, trans. and ed. Mary J. Gregor (Cambridge: Cambridge University Press, 1996). Immanuel Kant, *Groundwork of the Metaphysics of Morals* (1785), in *Practical Philosophy*. Immanuel Kant, *Religion within the Boundaries of Mere Reason* (1793), in *Religion and Rational Theology*, trans. and ed. George di Giovanni and Allen W. Wood (Cambridge: Cambridge University Press, 1996).

2. Considerations about pleasure are meant to include displeasures and pains. Kant seems to hold the standard view that pleasures and pains are of the same kind (modifications of some single sensibility) and therefore can straightforwardly be compared.

that would save Kant from the infelicity of hedonism.[3] I no longer think that is the right strategy, primarily because the reading of the texts that tags Kant with a hedonist account of nonmoral action and choice is so clearly correct. Since I have no desire to interpret Kant as embracing a foolish view, in dealing with Kant's hedonism, I take a different tack: namely, to suggest that his reasons for putting forward the view, when and as he does, *are* worth taking seriously.

In the discussion that follows I have two aims. One I have just mentioned—to make some sense out of Kant's employment of hedonism. The other is larger, and will run in the background of the discussion. Kant's hedonism, as I see it, plays a methodological role. It sets the terms for an exploration of the limits of subjective theories of value. Whether they derive from the cruder forms of psychological hedonism or from the sophisticated endorsements of complex valuing, Kant argues that *all* subjective theories are really single-valued. They give rise to views of happiness that are all formally the same as hedonism. And because hedonism can support a remarkably sophisticated account of action and choice, it cannot be dismissed out of hand. The threat is that in the absence of access to objective values, or values derived from some other authoritative source, hedonism is the *true* theory of motivation and choice. Kant's argument in the *Critique of Practical Reason* is that escape from hedonism—theoretically *and* practically—is to be had only through a correct appreciation of the value inherent in the moral law. Trying to figure out how he could think this and also retain a clear distinction between the concerns of morality and those of happiness will be the subject of the last part of this chapter.

3. The best of these try to salvage the initial pair of claims by relegating the ubiquitous role of pleasure to the causal history of our desires and interests, not their objects—we value our ends for various reasons—and then account for the hedonism of choice by treating happiness as the idea of the maximal sum of expected satisfactions to which the various activities and projects contribute different amounts. (Cf., for example, Andrews Reath, "Hedonism, Heteronomy and Kant's Principle of Happiness," *Pacific Philosophical Quarterly* 70 [1989]: 42–72.) This separation of value in a deliberative principle from the value of ends is not always benign. It's not that we can't separate them; we often have to make choices on grounds that don't reflect the values that make alternatives options for us. When this happens, deliberation is not so much about adjudicating between the options or their values as about the introduction of a third value that for one reason or another has greater "say" in determining what we should do. Then the saving strategy would give us this: what makes X of interest to me may be its feature α, but what makes me choose X over Y is the *satisfaction* I get from engagement with an α-featured object or activity. So if a summative pleasure or satisfaction conception of happiness plays the role of the third value, the saving strategy does not take Kant very much off the hook.

I will start off by examining each of the elements that set up the hedonism: the claim that all empirical practical principles are of the same kind; that the determining ground of nonmoral action is a feeling of pleasure; and last, the quantitative principle of choice. About the first I will argue that even if it is not a successful view, it is not altogether implausible. The second will require some further thoughts about the place of pleasure in Kant's theory of mind and action. And about the third, I want to look closely at the examples Kant uses to illustrate the deliberative principle—what I call the hedonism of choice. They indicate the place where we can begin to see the larger issues that hedonism raises for him.

I. Happiness and the Principle of Self-Love

Hedonism enters early in the second *Critique* as part of an argument to show that because the principle of happiness is a material principle, and therefore empirical, it cannot be the basis of any practical law, and so, a fortiori, cannot be the basis of the moral law. The first two theorems and their arguments set the stage (*KpV* 5:21–22):

> *Theorem I:* All practical principles that presuppose an *object* (matter) of the faculty of desire as the determining ground of the will are, without exception, empirical and can furnish no practical laws.

Kant argues: a material practical principle determines the will by virtue of a subject's pleasure in the possible reality of some object, and since there is no necessary connection between any object and a rational agent's capacity to feel pleasure or displeasure, no material principle can be a law. He then advances a twofold claim:

> *Theorem II:* All material practical principles as such are, without exception, of one and the same kind and come under the general principle of self-love or one's own happiness.

The argument for Theorem I introduces a psychological basis for hedonism; Theorem II and its argument connect the hedonism to a theory of happiness. There is much that is puzzling in these texts; some of the puzzles turn out to be superficial, some not. Since the most accessible point of entry is through the connection between self-love and happiness in Theorem II, I will start there. So, first off, we need to ask why Kant would hold that all material practical principles are of the same kind.

If one thought that by self-love Kant just means concern for one's interests, whatever they are, then in saying that all material practical principles are of the same kind Kant could be making no more than a formal point. To say that one acts on a principle of self-love would just be to say: whatever one's object of action, it is an object of action because, and only because, one has a subjective interest in its existence as an effect of action. Kant would then be a kind of motivational internalist about actions on material principles. There is at least nothing puzzling about that.

But if this were right, Kant should not go on to identify self-love and happiness. All of the actions that fall under self-love, so understood, would outstrip any reasonable conception of human happiness. In fact, Kant does *not* identify self-love and happiness, but the *principle* of self-love and the *principle* of one's own happiness. He says that someone acts on a principle of self-love when the source of her action is feeling (receptivity), not understanding or rational concepts of value. The claim that the *principle* of happiness is the principle of self-love is therefore trivially true. How so? Happiness, Kant says, is "a rational being's consciousness of the agreeableness of life uninterruptedly accompanying his whole existence" (*KpV* 5:22)—it is a state or condition we necessarily desire. The idea of my life going well—however I understand that—is necessarily pleasing or agreeable to me. But then if happiness itself is a material object of desire, someone acting on a *principle* of making happiness the object of her will acts on the *principle* of self-love: feeling or receptivity—pleasure felt in the representation of the reality of an object—is the condition of desire and so of choice.[4] This looks like no more than an elaboration of Kantian internalism.

If there is no immediate textual problem with the identification of the principles of happiness and self-love, the account highlights other features of the argument that call for explanation. One is the role played by pleasure in explaining the connection between self-love and happiness; another is the rather odd conception of happiness.

Now the mere fact that pleasure has entered the story does not by itself signify much. Considered most generally, pleasure is an element in the

---

4. Here is the full remark about happiness and self-love: "Now, a rational being's consciousness of the agreeableness of life uninterruptedly accompanying his whole existence is *happiness,* and the principle of making this the supreme determining ground of choice is the principle of self-love. Thus all material principles, which place the determining ground of choice in the pleasure or displeasure to be felt in the reality of some object, are wholly *of the same kind* insofar as they belong without exception to the principle of self-love or one's own happiness" (*KpV* 5:23).

Kantian account of mind as it bears on action, signifying a subjective relation between agent and object: a relation of fit.[5] It can precede active desire or it can be an effect of the determination of the faculty of desire by something else. As Kant sees it, for *all* determinations of the will and *all* action there is pleasure in the representation of the *agreement* of an object or action and the faculty of desire or choice. Pleasure is the empirical mark of caring about something. Without it—that is, unless there is a "representation of agreement of an object or action with the subjective conditions of life"—there is no action.[6] (*Mutatis mutandis* for aversion.)[7] This is true whether we are talking about animals or beings with a rational will, or about nonmoral or moral action. In its primary role, pleasure is not a piece of an hedonic theory of value but an element in the metaphysics of action.

5. Consider the long footnote in the Preface of the second *Critique* where Kant offers what he calls a "neutral" account of the faculty of desire: neutral because it leaves it "undecided at the beginning" whether the supreme principle of practical philosophy can be empirical. It gives the pieces of the practical psychology in their sparest form. Separating out the sentences, we get the following formulations:

Life is the faculty of a being to act in accordance with laws of the faculty of desire.

The *faculty of desire* is a being's *faculty to be by means of its representations the cause of the reality of these representations.*

Pleasure is the *representation of the agreement of an object or of an action with the subjective conditions of life,* i.e., with the faculty of the *causality of a representation with respect to the reality of its object* (or with respect to the determination of the powers of the subject to action in order to produce the object). (*KpV* 5:11n)

So, suppose an active being (person or animal) is thirsty. Seeing water nearby, and other things being equal, it is able, by means of its representation of the water as thirst-relevant (as the result of an habitual or conceptual association of drinking water and the relief of thirst), to be moved to drink. For this to happen, a being need only be a thing possessed of "life"—that is, capable of acting from representations and as a cause of the object it represents. A moral being recognizes a duty-invoking need. She is able, other things equal, by means of her (suitable) representation of the need, to help. We will not know until later in the argument whether the principles/laws of these two types of action are of the same kind. At this point, as Kant says, the account is neutral. But then what is also neutral is the place of pleasure in the operation of the faculty of desire. In both cases, pleasure comes from the representation of the fit between object and active powers. What is left undecided is "the question whether pleasure must always be put at the basis of the faculty of desire or whether under certain conditions pleasure only follows upon its determination."

6. Here I am intimating a distinction between determination of the will and empirical conditions of action that will be developed a bit later.

7. In the sense at issue, aversion is a special case of pleasure, not a distinct mode of feeling. The pleasure is in the avoidance of the object of aversion.

The nature and purpose of pleasure, of feeling, belongs to the account of all action of all things possessed of what Kant calls "life."

Therefore, when Kant assumes psychological hedonism as the truth about nonmoral actions, it is *not* because pleasure is part of the causal history of nonmoral action, but because he holds that in action on a material principle, pleasure always precedes and *determines* the activity of the faculty of desire. Material practical principles determine the will with respect to an object as a function of "the agreeableness . . . expected from the object, which impels activity to produce it" (*KpV* 5:23). This is a further specification of why all such principles are of the same kind. That is, if, in our nonmoral actions, we always act in anticipation of pleasure, and pleasure in what we do (as we go along) is the measure of happiness, then it makes sense to think of actions on all material principles as coming under the general principle of self-love or the principle of happiness.

Let us turn now to the conception of happiness. There are various ways in which Kant's talk about happiness is odd. Sometimes Kant describes happiness as an end, indeed as a *necessary* end for human beings; sometimes he describes it as a state. I will suppose he means it is (somehow) both. It is an unusual state, more like a tone or quality: "a rational being's consciousness of the agreeableness of life uninterruptedly accompanying his whole existence." That is, whatever happiness is materially, in thinking of one's life as happy, one thinks of it as being and feeling agreeable as it goes along. (The source of this notion seems to be the Stoic ideal of self-sufficiency—a state of never wanting anything, and in that negative sense, feeling satisfied [*KpV* 5:25].) For us, the idea of happiness as a state of satisfaction is "a problem imposed on [every rational but finite being] by his finite nature itself, because he is needy" (*KpV* 5:25). We cannot avoid having desires; we don't get to satisfaction without work. So given an original set of desires, and the tastes and interests I develop, I will be moved to plan and live so that as much as possible things go well for me, and I get (or feel) satisfaction from what I do. But if this is what happiness involves, how is it an end? It is not an end in a strongly directive sense, given that there is no predetermined set or order of desires that will yield satisfaction, no necessary objects. We do seek satisfaction; given our desires, the task may be complex. It fits with this that Kant says the concept or idea of happiness is *indeterminate:* as an end, it sets a task that is in significant ways open-ended.[8]

---

8. That happiness is an idea of the imagination, and not of reason, partly explains this.

But if happiness is any kind of end, in what sense can it be necessary? Were the necessity natural, then it would be a physical or psychological tendency (a purpose) and not an end. The very idea of a naturally necessary end conflicts with Kant's idea of an elective will. So the necessity must be rational. Yet if reason is to make happiness an end, and so necessary, it must do so in virtue of what we are like as natural beings: as finite rational beings with desires.[9] But what sort of *natural* fact would be the basis for *reason* setting us an end of happiness? Why should reason care whether we are happy, or with respect to our desires, satisfied?[10]

Here is a possible story. Given the organization of our faculty of desire, we cannot help but be interested in our welfare, because we cannot be indifferent to our state of agreeableness. But what puts happiness on the table for us is something more than this. Because we are rational *and* possess imagination, we not only can conceive of doing and feeling otherwise than we do, we recognize that we have a future whose shape we are able to affect. We come to have the concept of our life, something that we foresee will go along and be pleasurable, or not, depending (partly) on the wisdom of our choices. Happiness is a problem imposed on us, in that each of us has to decide how to live *a life,* even if our choice is to do no more than satisfy this or that presenting desire. Given our natures as rational and sensible beings with the concept of a life, we have the end of happiness. It is a (quasi-)constitutive feature of the way in which we conceive of our material ends, and in that sense a necessity of our human nature.

Beginning with a variety of needs, desires, and interests, work needs to be done with and among them: develop some, defer others, sublimate, repress—the whole battery of techniques, conscious and unconscious, by which we come to be the specific individuals we are. In this way the demand for satisfaction with one's existence drives a process of individuation.[11] And

---

9. In the *Groundwork* Kant says that the purpose of happiness is one that "can be presupposed a priori and with certainty as being present in everyone because it belongs to his essence" (G 4:416)—which is to say, is true of us, as finite rational beings, by necessity.

10. Of course, if reason's demands typically gave us a life of pain, or permitted few satisfactions, we would find its object difficult to love. But these are second-order considerations—as are those that depend on the fact that morality requires that we be concerned with the happiness of others. Happiness already has to be in the orbit of reason's concerns for duties of beneficence to make sense.

11. Choice involves giving structure to the material of maxims via a conception of the good.

reciprocally, in and through becoming a particular person, we partially resolve the indeterminacy of our conception of happiness. (Only the *idea* of happiness is indeterminate; each of us perforce works out a more determinate conception.) This is part of the explanation why our happiness is a "commission from the side of sensibility" that reason cannot refuse (*KpV* 5:61). It is only through a finite rational being's formation of a relatively determinate conception of happiness as an end she pursues in her actions that she becomes an agent: namely, a person with reasonably stable and mutually adjusted interests, second-order desires, executive capacities, and the rest.[12] But if we are in the business of "person construction," it will matter a great deal what tools we have. If we are restricted to a hedonism of choice, there will be questions about the shape, or the kind of unity of self, we could hope to achieve.

II. The Hedonism of Choice

Kant's full-blown hedonism consists in the view that, for all nonmoral action, we act according to a principle that represents possible objects of choice in terms of their expected pleasure or agreeableness.[13] The range of the hedonism is wide, applying not only to the usual material choices but also to the satisfactions we find "in the mere exercise of our powers, in the consciousness of our strength of soul in overcoming obstacles opposed to our plans," and on to any conception of virtue as a discipline promising a higher kind of satisfaction (*KpV* 5:23–25). As we have seen, even our happiness is an object of interest only because we represent it as a state of agreeable feeling.

Hedonism is usually taken to be implausible because it conflicts with important claims we make about value and choice. We want to say: some objects are worth choosing because of what they are: beautiful, expressive of some

12. Moreover, if there is a reciprocal relation between the pursuit of happiness and self-individuation, and if self-individuation is a necessary condition for rational agency in finite rational beings with needs, then the *actual* satisfaction of (some) desires and inclinations that are part of an agent's conception of happiness is also necessary. That is why the right relation of morality to happiness is rational self-love. For its own reasons, reason cannot ignore our desires. So, contrary to what one might have thought, the problem sensibility poses for morality is not that desires tempt us away from virtue. The problem arises from a feature of our *rational* natures, from self-conceit—a flawed rational principle of desire-satisfaction.

13. It is not qua representation that it pleases, though that might be true too. It is expected satisfaction that is doing the work.

truth, or in some other way of intrinsic value. We might in fact choose such objects as we thought they would give us greater overall satisfaction or make our lives worthwhile, but we think we *ought* to choose them (and ought to be able to choose them) because of what they are—beautiful, or true. Kant seems to hold that we *cannot* do that, not just that we sometimes do not.

In coming to terms with Kant's view, I want first to push the hedonism as far as it can go. It is important for the larger argument that the hedonism not fail prematurely. What we need to find is the place where it becomes inescapably implausible, since, if I am right, it is Kant's own location of this limit that sets the stage for his more complete view of the relationship between happiness and the moral law. For awhile, then, I will try to defend a sophisticated hedonism that might well be Kant's.

Consider the truisms of friendship. We say: we should care about friends because they are our friends, and not because the activities that caring involves promise pleasure. And we should care about friendship because it is one of the goods of human life. Life without others we care about is defective, even when isolation is something we don't mind. When we spend time with a friend it is not because we expect more pleasure than we would get from a visit to the local multiplex. We spend time with friends because that is what friends do.

But a sophisticated hedonism does not imply that every *action* is performed for the sake of the pleasure it separately provides. We can only be moved by the sense that a proposed action or end is agreeable, but we can just as well be responsive to the agreeableness of complex ends as to simple ends or immediate satisfactions. Where ends are rich and complex, they dictate complex courses of action to be taken for their sake. In having a friend one has a range of commitments and interests structured by the kind of thing friendship is. My deciding to spend time talking with a friend rather than going to the movies need not be explained by the pleasure I expect from the time talking. Of course sometimes a choice to spend time with people is best explained by an interest in the pleasure of their company—and sometimes we spend time with friends for that reason. One of the values of friendship is that it increases our opportunities for these and other pleasures. A hedonism can be sensible in these ways. And it can be sensible because the agent's representation of his proposed action is *as* friendship-promoting, which he finds pleasurable.

What of the election of friendship as an end? If our idea of happiness is caught by the thought of "consciousness of the agreeableness of life uninterruptedly accompanying [one's] whole existence," and if we choose friendship for the sake of happiness, then we would choose to have friends because we thought having them would make our life better, in the sense of containing more enjoyable, more satisfying experiences. Surely this makes *some* sense, partly because of the special pleasures of friendship, but also because with good friends, some of the hardships of life are more bearable. And with the best friends, one has access, it is said, to some of the higher forms of feeling that we are capable of having.[14] If this is not the right view of happiness, or of friendship, it is neither foolish nor self-evidently false.

Abstracting, we can say that once we allow for complex ends, we create room *within the hedonism of choice* for the idea of acting for the sake of something other than our pleasure in the immediate object of that action. I take my dog to the vet not for the pleasure of the trip but because I care about her health and well-being. Kant will say my interest in her well-being is explained by my feelings for her; but then I often say that, too. *Why* we have the ends we do is left unexplained. Some things move me; others don't. Individual characteristics, education, and cultural variations can explain some of the variation in our ends, but explanations of ends in these terms don't get us beyond the causes of differences in receptivity.

What we cannot do on this account is have friends for nonmoral reasons other than that having them gives us pleasure, or read instructive books not for the pleasure of it (immediate or instrumental) but for the sake of the truth to be gained. Given Kant's insistence that the division between material and formal determining grounds of the will is exhaustive—that everything that is a possible principle or object of action belongs either to the sphere of autonomy or to self-love—it would appear that we (necessarily) care for everything that is not a part of morality as an element or way of securing a hedonically satisfying life. Lost, then, one wants to say, are the values of things for their own sakes as a basis of choice—painting, playing music, friendship, learning, the beauties of nature. Is the thought, though, that it is good to have and value these things whether or not they make our lives (*any* lives?) go better? But couldn't one dispute this? The question is about the experience of, say, beautiful things—why we should choose to have such experiences. And then it is certainly not the most foolish thing to say that we should bring the experience of beauty into our lives because a

---

14. It is not just piety to the ancients that has Kant pointing repeatedly to Epicurus.

life lived with beauty is a more fully enjoyable one. Aesthetic pleasure may be disinterested, but our interest in having such pleasures is not. They give us, directly or indirectly, satisfactions that contribute to an agreeable life, and, moral considerations aside, that is why we seek to have them.

If we can in these terms understand how we could have and pursue distinct ends as contributing to an overall satisfying life, they give little sense of where these ends come from for us, or why they have the weight they do prior to our grasp of their fit in our lives. Since we cannot appeal to the intrinsic value of ends, we might be left with no more than the instrumental connection of ends to the various biological and psychological elements of our constitution. The form of explanation would be Humean: investigating why we care about what we do, we would regress to some finite list of things that just do matter to us.

Kant has some additional resources for a principle of end-adoption that fits with this sort of hedonism. As part of the account of our psychological nature as dependent rational beings in *Religion within the Boundaries of Mere Reason,* he introduces a capacity that he calls our "predisposition to humanity": an original feature of human nature that leads us to "judge ourselves happy or unhappy only by making comparison with others" (*R* 6:22).[15] Following Rousseau, Kant assumes that the initial comparative impulse seeks equality (that no one be superior to me); but since we have no independent measures of value or of our own worth, it turns into a desire to "acquire worth in the opinion of others" (*R* 6:22) no one should be in a position to judge me her inferior. Since this is a judgment best secured by each striving to be better than the others, and in terms that each will recognize, we gain a social source for ends. Of course, it is a problematic source of things to be valued. The ends one takes on may or may not fit with what one needs; one will come to prefer ends that satisfy a "more is better" rule; and, having a comparative basis of self-worth, one will be drawn into a futile race for competitive superiority.[16] Worse still, it is a basis of self-

---

15. The three practical predispositions are for animality, humanity, and personality. The first presses us toward procreation and living with others; the last is the pre-disposition to make the moral law the fundamental maxim of our will. They are all said to be in some sense good. A fuller discussion of the practical predispositions is in section 2 of Chapter 6.

16. An interesting upshot of this is that extreme individualism in the pursuit of happiness is tempered by the fact that the happiness we pursue must be coordinate in kind. Since by nature we live together, and by nature we care about how we stand in the regard of others, we must live in ways that are mutually intelligible. (This is a condition of having a culture.) The facts of difference we prize tend to be in style or mode, or in features of life that do not directly

value that encourages feelings of jealousy and envy, which prompt vice and wrongdoing.[17] But at this stage of the story, that is beside the point. What matters here is that, consistent with the hedonic story, our predisposition to humanity gives us reason to accept ends as our own because they are valued by those whose judgment of our worth matters to us. By itself, this social source of ends does not add a great deal. However, as we will see later on, it plays a key role in the argument that makes dignity, rather than pleasure, a source of value for (some) nonmoral actions. Let us return now to the main discussion. There is more to be said in defense of a sophisticated hedonism.

It is often argued that the inadequacy of any hedonism is easily shown by its inability to countenance actions for ends the agent knows she will not experience (effects at a distance, posthumous effects, etc.). Now, it is quite normal for us to act when success is uncertain. The representation of the value of an end along with the degree of uncertainty of its occurring is part of the calculation of choiceworthiness of actions. So either I am able to choose in conditions of uncertainty or I can never act for an effect that is not immediate. In cases of effects at a distance and posthumous effects, there is of course no uncertainty about the effect of the end on the agent. But the issue is in important ways the same. In Kant's terms, we act when we judge there is an appropriate relation of fit between the representation of an end and our active powers (that is, the reality of an end coming about by means of our agency as its cause). Suppose that on my deathbed I create a bequest that will in ten years' time provide scholarship funds for some group of deserving students. What gives me satisfaction—all the satisfaction I need to act—is the setting in motion of the train of events that will make real an effect ten years hence. The setting-in-motion is something I can do now; its trajectory pleases.

Kantian theory of action is in an important way holistic: motive, action, and end are connected in the agent's principle, or maxim. To act under uncertainty is to judge the probability of making an end real worth some expenditure; it is the whole—action, end, uncertainty—that strikes the agent as agreeable. Likewise, where we act for a distant end, it is the whole—the

challenge defining cultural norms. But such convergence of direction does not produce a determinate concept, and, of course, does its work at the very high cost of arbitrary cultural oppression. The lack of a value-norm for happiness is not exclusively a philosopher's problem.

17. Where the highest goal is to be comparatively best, morality is an obstacle. It prompts not just immoral actions, but a tendency to reverse the priority of moral and nonmoral incentives. See *R* 6:24–25.

action and its eventual effect—that pleases.[18] Kant's theory is in this way able to accommodate a general feature of action: the frame of an action *outstrips* our activity and willing.

There are various modes of outstripping. My actions initiate sequences of effects that outstrip my intentions (sometimes extending my responsibility beyond my intentions as well). My plans often outstrip anything I can do here and now. And likewise my intentions can outstrip my life, extending my agency past my death. Sophisticated hedonism can include all this. However I make determinate the content of happiness, I make choices that I believe will together make my life an agreeable one. My activity is directed at giving a shape to the world that I find pleasing.[19] Thus we are brought to view our lives in different ways: we do think of our lives in terms of moments or passages of time, but we also think of our living as a creative force, something that makes things happen. That is why one can have satisfaction in acting for ends one won't live to see. The story of a life—its effect on the world—can have more extended temporal boundaries than the life itself. So along with fame and monuments, courses of action that carry our agency beyond our life-span allow us to be present in, by giving shape to, the future. Such actions contribute as much to the sense of a life going well as do actions for ends that one expects to see realized. The representation of a world where my action has this creative effect pleases—not as a wish, but as an end engaging my agency and activity. For this reason, faced with the devil's choice between helping her child but believing she has not, and leaving her child to suffer but believing she has helped, the sophisticated hedonist can make the right choice. When she represents the future her actions will bring about, she will represent the relevant concerns correctly.

What she cannot do, of course, is take the needs of her child as a per se reason for action. But since what the hedonist theory entails is that there cannot be such a basis for choice, its absence in the account is hardly an ob-

18. Although the thing I would produce is not yet here, it is the reality of the end to be produced that pleases, though "from here" my access to that reality is by way of a representation. It is rather like hearing the whistle of a train as it approaches the station: one is pleased that the train is near, though all one has is the whistle that represents it.

19. Although the work of articulating a conception of happiness takes place as life goes along, the point of view that anchors the conception is not similarly ongoing. We do not regard each moment in life as having the same weight; there are factors of aging and reflection, but also features of the kinds of experiences we have that provide abiding points of reference (not all of which are as sustaining as we may at the time think they will be).

jection. There would be a problem if the theory could not countenance acting for ends that outstrip expected experience; but since it can, the basic theoretical commitment of hedonism is not, so far, challenged.

The remaining issue is the hedonism of choice as a principle of deliberation. This is the view that, in choosing between options for action, the only thing that concerns an agent "if the determination of his will rests on the feeling of agreeableness or disagreeableness that he expects from some cause . . . in order to decide upon a choice, is how intense, how long, how easily acquired, and how often repeated this agreeableness is" (*KpV* 5:23).[20] Kant has almost always been read as simply accepting this further feature of the hedonism of choice. I now think he may have had something else in mind, at least at this point in the argument of the *Critique of Practical Reason* where he announces it: namely, to use the unpalatable consequences of a hedonism of choice to show the limits of empirical practical reason (i.e., the principle of self-love) as a fundamental principle of will, even in its own domain of nonmoral choice.

The hedonic principle of choice is introduced to make sense of cases where we trade what is, in our own considered opinion, a "better" for a "worse" option. Here are Kant's examples.

> The same human being can return unread an instructive book that he cannot again obtain, in order not to miss a hunt; he can leave in the middle of a fine speech in order not to be late for a meal; he can leave an intellectual conversation, such as he otherwise values highly, in order to take his place at the gaming table; he can even repulse a poor man who at other times it is a joy for him to benefit because he now has only enough money in his pocket to pay for his admission to the theater. (*KpV* 5:23)

And why do people do such things? It is usually assumed that Kant reasons this way. To so choose among courses of action, we must be using a calculus of pleasure. Then all that must matter to us about books, speeches, charity, or the theater is the amount of pleasure to be gained from each. The proof is in what we do. However, there are warning signs that things are not so simple. The list of paired choices are ones that Kant, and presumably we,

20. Essential to the hedonism of choice is the claim that all pleasure is of one kind, "not only insofar as it can always be cognized only empirically but also insofar as it affects one and the same vital force that is manifested in the faculty of desire, and in this respect can differ only in degree from any other determining ground" (*KpV* 5:23).

disapprove of. But on what grounds could he disapprove of them if hedonic fungibility is true? And what is the point of its being "the same human being" who makes these choices? The pairs are also familiar examples of practical irrationality: weakness of will or some other misvaluing of goods. It seems strange that Kant is silent about all this.

Suppose one did find the pairs disturbing, and wanted to explain them. People *do* make such choices, and they do not always on reflection regret them. Kant's question could be: how could this make sense? Perhaps the idea is this: *if* someone reads instructive books for the enjoyment of them, then other kinds of enjoyment will sometimes be more pleasurable, and when they are, preferable. And *if* someone has friends because spending time with them makes him feel good, then at those times when other things would make him feel better, he will ignore a friend for the sake of the more agreeable activity. Choosing the worse over the better in these cases is not an instance of weakness of will. It is explained by the principle of choice underlying the agent's more specific maxims, a principle that he takes on in his adoption of ends for their contribution to his happiness. More generally: if all of my ends are embedded in maxims that have the same material form (if, that is, they are valued in the same terms), then it may at times be difficult for me to see why I should stay with a pursuit that is arduous when another is immediately available and easy. It may be *ir*rational to choose otherwise. So if we find such choices disturbing, as Kant clearly does, perhaps he has identified the source of concern.

Of course, such choices are not always wrong. Contingent circumstances and the nature of one's character may warrant acting with an eye to satisfactions. One cannot be a friend at all if one does not give friendship a certain prominence in one's choices. But for someone for whom friendship comes hard, or who lives among thieves, choosing to balance the satisfactions to be had from other ends with that of friendship as an end might even be best. The problem is that in the normal course of things we cannot appeal to the hedonic principle to distinguish cases like these from cases we want to say exhibit practical irrationality. Taking only the perspective of empirical practical reason, our wills look like animal wills. So if empirical practical reason were all there was, we would lack the resources to *achieve* weakness of will—or strength of will, either.

The absence of an account of weakness, or strength, of will is a symptom of a larger problem. Under the rule of self-love, there is no principle that could show the choices in Kant's examples to be irrational or imprudent. We may have complex plans of life that usually direct our choices, but we can have no *reason* to prefer them in the face of stronger inclination or momentary change of heart. Neither the principle nor the end of happiness can play a regulative role; the principle is just another material practical principle, and the end is indeterminate in content. The importance of happiness to us, as the importance of any end, is a function of our receptivity—of whether and how much we find the idea of its realization pleasing. If our desires happen to be calm and the environment friendly to them, we will act in stable ways, and feel our lives accumulating meaning and satisfaction. But this will be an accident, a function of good fortune. The principle of self-love, with its hedonic principle of choice, lacks the practical resources to give us more.[21] This, finally, is the place where hedonism runs out.

III. Happiness and the Moral Law

We are left with what I shall call "the problem of natural happiness." We have an idea of happiness; the desire that things go well for us moves us to make this idea determinate. But the guidance provided by any such determinate idea or end is always defeasible, since the only principle of construction is hedonic and idiosyncratic. Neither one's own settled ends nor any wisdom drawn from the lives of others can provide a rational counterweight to strong attractions. The comparative measure of value offers some structure, but no well-founded direction—or much freedom, if envy, jealousy, and competition are the motivational bases that shape our lives. So while we can, in a sense, imagine life going well, we gain no rational purchase on our choices based on that idea. What we can imagine outstrips the resources of practical deliberation.

In the absence of any independent domain of nonmoral value, the remaining possibility for a solution to the problem of natural happiness is that the structure of nonmoral choice can somehow be affected by the moral law, or by what happens when we acknowledge the law as the fundamental determining ground of our will. If we rule out the moralization of all choice as a possible solution, what's left is the idea that the moral law can somehow alter our character with respect to the content of *non*moral action and choice. To do this, it would have to make possible the rational transformation of (some) desires, and the enabling of (some) distinctly human modes of valuation so that we no longer had to regard all nonmoral ends as

21. This will be a problem with any theory that tries to get normative purchase out of hierarchically structured desires.

hedonically fungible. New resources of rational structure would be necessary to support ends that we had nonhedonic reasons to adopt and sustain. These are ends that might, in turn, provide release from the strains of comparative self-valuation.

The moral law may not look like much of a resource because we tend to mischaracterize its charge. Especially given Kant's philosophical preoccupations, it is natural to think that the sole effect of the moral law on our character is to enable action from duty. But its effect is much more wide-ranging. For example: moral agents require a wide range of rational capacities, of planning and organization, deferral and recall, responsiveness to change, and so forth, in order to do what morality requires of them. Under the aegis of the moral law we will develop general capacities of agency that we otherwise might not. I say "might not," for all sorts of higher-order capacities may develop if one happens to be so inclined that what one cares about most demands them. But we can imagine environments so friendly (or so hostile) to our natures that it does not make sense that we would be motivated to develop a wide range of complex practical abilities.[22] By contrast, the moral law gives us noncontingent and authoritative reasons to develop practical capacities and to be mindful of the effect of generic and idiosyncratic weaknesses.[23]

As with most acquired practical abilities, exercise is required to maintain use. So if I am to be capable of effective planning, I must plan. And since to plan I must have longer term projects, there are, odd as this may seem, moral reasons to live a life of greater rather than lesser complexity. Of course this seems backward. There is a seamlessness to ordinary develop-

---

22. This is the point of Kant's South Sea Islanders example (*G* 4:423): the demands of instrumental rationality are contingent.

23. It's not that we must develop all the powers that we could possibly have; rather, we may not neglect specifically moral abilities, or those general executive capacities that enable us to initiate and carry out complex projects. The injunction not to neglect amounts to a requirement that we be mindful of the conditions and circumstances of our agency. There are faults and weaknesses to which all of us are prone to some degree (a tendency to exaggerate the importance of our own interests, for example), and there are idiosyncratic deficiencies and shortcomings—ways we are prone to be lax in our actions or inattentive to certain sorts of morally salient facts. These may not be matters of indifference to us, and we are obliged to resist or overcome those flaws of character we detect. Further, we need to acquire and maintain some flexibility and openness to change: we cannot be rule-bound, nor can we assume that practices in whose terms we learned morality are impervious to criticism and change.

ment that usually makes attention to reasons of this sort unnecessary. But the reasons are there, and they have priority. (We can see this in worries about children who for too long remain dependent on their parents. It is not just their welfare and dignity that are at issue. We think they need to do things to prepare themselves to take their place as members of a public moral culture.) That our psychology is such that we typically enjoy the exercise of higher-order rational capacities is a further feature of the seamlessness. The idea is not, of course, to go for practical complexity *tout court*. But we can see why Kant maintains that, other things equal, for most of us there is moral value to living in social settings that are intellectually and practically demanding.[24]

Having the ability to pursue complex projects does not by itself resolve the problem of natural happiness. We still have no noninstrumental reason to prefer one kind of activity over another, or reason to stay with the discipline of a complex end when another appealing activity is available. So even though the practical impact of the moral law is not cabined off from the structure of our rational agency generally, we do not yet see how the law could alter the reasons we have, or are capable of having, in the pursuit of happiness. To get to this, we need to look at two often neglected features of Kantian rational psychology. The first is that rationality is not an "add-on" to an independent, nonrational course of development. The fact that we are rational alters the desires we come to have: not just which objects we pursue, but the content and structure of the desires we act on. The second feature builds on the first: there is a connection between the development of higher-order rational capacities, *reason*-based pleasures, and our *dignity* as rational agents. It supports something like a Kantian version of John Stuart Mill's doctrine of the "quality of pleasures," and is for Kant, as it was for Mill, the pivotal element in a solution to the problem hedonism poses for a theory of happiness.

About the first feature: we allow into our story notice of the fact that desires do not lie outside the sphere of normal development. New desires are created, and old ones are (at least partially) transformed as we mature. The thirst of a newborn and that of an adult are likely connected, but they are hardly the same thing. Much of our developing system of desires is both

24. See, for example, Immanuel Kant, "A Conjectural Beginning of Human History" and "Idea for a Universal History from a Cosmopolitan Point of View," in *Perpetual Peace and Other Essays,* trans. Ted Humphreys (Indianapolis: Hackett, 1983).

fact- and reason-responsive. We may cease desiring what we see is impossible; a general desire becomes a desire for some specific object; we desire some things only as our acting for or having their object does not violate this or that constraint (that is, sensitivity to constraint can be internal to the desire itself).[25] Because the object and internal structure of desires change as we mature, we get some pre-reflective yet rational organization, and the elimination of some sources of potential conflict, in the course of normal development of the system of desires.

Although all of this may happen to us, it does not follow that we have reason to prefer more complex desires, or reason to *value* ones we might happen to have. In just this regard, Kant praises Epicurus for his honesty in recognizing that even if the source of an activity were in the representation of a "higher cognitive faculty," so long as our principle of action appeals to the satisfaction we expect, the action (and its reasons) remain of the same kind "as those of the coarsest senses" (*KpV* 5:24–25)[26] Neither fancy liking, nor endorsement, nor reflective commitment to ends gets us beyond one mode or another of our passive receptivity. But it does make us open to changes in desire that might be prompted from another source of value, were there one.

This brings us to the second feature—the idea that the moral notion of *dignity* might provide the link to happiness. I mentioned Mill a moment ago because he, like Kant, thinks the route of escape from crude hedonism is via an account of higher pleasures supported by a notion of the dignity of rational persons. The difference between them on this is instructive. Mill introduces a "sense of dignity" to explain the preference for activities and ways of life that involve the exercise of rational capacities: not only do they provide access to a broader palette of more durable satisfactions—interesting work and enjoyments in the usual sense—we also came to value ourselves in exercising powers commensurate with our dignity.[27] Indeed, Mill notes, a sense of dignity is "so essential a part of the happiness of those in whom

25. For more on this view of desires, see Chapter 1.

26. This is the occasion for one of Kant's rare philosophical jokes. He compares those who take "more refined" pleasures to be "different ways of determining the will" to "ignorant people who would like to dabble in metaphysics [and] think of matter so refined, so super-refined, that they make themselves giddy with it and then believe that in this way they have devised a *spiritual* and yet extended being."

27. And since one can have a sense of dignity to the extent that one has access to one's higher faculties (some mix of capabilities and developed abilities), the claim is not specific to any one way of life or mode of culture.

it is strong that nothing that conflicts with it could be otherwise than momentarily an object of desire to them."[28]

Mill's "sense of dignity" explains why it is not *hedonically* irrational to prefer a way of life that engages the mind, for it names a special source of self-referential pleasure. This is enough if you think, as Mill does, that "next to selfishness, the principal cause which makes life unsatisfactory is want of mental cultivation."[29] But because Millian dignity merely extends the domain of satisfactions, it provides no solution for the problem Kant has with natural happiness (Mill does not disagree).[30] By contrast, because Kant can provide a separate and nonhedonic foundation for the value of (or inherent in) dignity, if there is a way to connect dignity with nonmoral choices, then it is a possible candidate for the solution.

The problem from the Kantian side is getting the notion of dignity—which has its basis in the moral law as a law of our will—first, to have application in the domain of happiness, and second, to provide some form for the happiness we seek. The Kantian notion of dignity is a status concept: it expresses the fact that rational nature as an end-in-itself constrains, both negatively and positively, what may be willed. But once I satisfy the moral law, what difference can it make whether I spend my leisure time constructively or sybaritically, have solid friendships or a host of casual acquaintances, have work that productively engages my rational capacities or instead just spend my time filling out forms?

Certainly it makes some difference that our nonmoral activities have causal consequences for our moral character. If my work (or my play) deadens my powers of judgment, or creates in me a dependence on the wills of others, then I have moral reasons to alter my situation or in other ways resist these effects.[31] But if this were the extent of the penetration of the moral

---

28. J. S. Mill, *Utilitarianism* (1861), ed. and introd. George Sher (Indianapolis: Hackett, 1979), p. 9. Other things equal, work that engages understanding is better—that is, preferred—to work that is mindless. To participate in decisions is preferable to merely following orders. We find it better, other things equal, to be able to discriminate among a variety of tastes than simply to eat to satiety. And so on.

29. Ibid., p. 13.

30. This will be so whether the source value is hedonic or the more neutral post-Humean hierarchical commitments.

31. And so for our commitment to morality, too. Thus Kant argues for the indirect duty to promote our own happiness: "for discontent with one's condition under many pressing cares and amid unsatisfied wants might easily become a great temptation to transgress one's duties" (*G* 4:399).

law into the domain of happiness, after satisfying constraints of permissibility, obligatory ends, and concerns for the health of our moral character, it would leave the hedonic principle of choice, constrained by the effects of social competition, as the final arbiter of the content of happiness.

Dignity can affect the content of happiness first and most directly through the effect of the recognition of the authority of the moral law on feelings. To a happiness-pursuer, the encounter with the moral law involves a shock of self-recognition.[32] We see that what we had taken to be first in the order of value—our satisfaction—is not. We are also revealed to ourselves to be persons of moral standing or dignity: our own rational nature as a source of value that has authority over all action and choice. This confrontation with "the sublimity of our own nature" gives rise to a strong, positive feeling—a kind of self-approbation, whose source is not in desire or our passive receptivity, but in the moral law itself. Not because of its strength, but because of its source, this feeling in turn affects the structure of material incentives: by altering our sense of who we are, it changes what we count as our well-being.

Although happiness and morality remain distinct, we gain a decisive interest from the side of happiness in keeping them correctly aligned. For one thing, I can get pleasure from a dignity-based conception of myself only if I live up to it. There are various ways I can fail to sustain a commitment to the priority of the moral, but there is no way that is rationally defensible. And if out of weakness or self-hatred I reverse the order of value of morality and self-love, I cannot rationally value myself for doing so. It would be as if I allowed a self-serving mistake to persist in an argument and for that reason claimed pride in my philosophical powers.

The second way that dignity enters the account of happiness is by providing closure to the comparative impulse. We gain an autonomous and not merely comparative measure of self-worth. Given an idea of happiness that now includes the moral powers as defining who I am, how could that not matter to the way I live? To think of myself as in any way important gives rise to a desire to express that value—to make it real through my actions. In addition, the self-conception and sense of worth that comes with recogniz-

---

32. This recognition is the empirical side of the Fact of Reason. For more on the effect of the moral law on our feelings, see Barbara Herman, "Transforming Incentives," in Åsa Carlson, ed., *Philosophical Aspects of the Emotions* (Stockholm: Thales, 2005). The account is drawn from Book 1, Chapter III of the second *Critique*: "On the Incentives of Pure Practical Reason."

ing that I am a being with dignity will change the terms of recognition I want from others. From the perspective of morality, our equality as persons with dignity is a nondiscretionary and prior demand. That is, morality requires each to accord all others their status as persons, and we must likewise insist on it for ourselves. We are, and are essentially, equal. But from the perspective of happiness, where in desiring not to be or seem to be less worthy than others one was drawn into an open-ended and escalating pursuit of tokens of public esteem (wealth, power, etc.), once dignity is in the picture, there is a different value I will want recognized, and it will be satisfied by the respect to which I am entitled.

However, even if the moral law in this way provides conceptual closure for the comparative impulse, it does not thereby fully solve the problem of natural happiness. The new source of self-valuation is independent of the judgment of others, but it is also ours without regard to how we live.[33] Even living a morally good life, in the duty-attending sense, is not the answer. On the one hand, if we will want our life activity to be and be seen as expressive of our dignity, the opacity of virtue, as well as the contingency of the occasions for its visibility—some lives are morally pretty quiet—can render even a deep moral commitment invisible. And on the other, as a happiness-seeking creature whose practical identity is formed in the interplay of abilities, dispositions, circumstances, and the ordering work of the hedonic principle of choice, living a good life leaves most of what I do and care about separate from the dignity-based sense of my value. If in large portions of my life I am indifferent to the exercise, expression, and development of my moral, or reason-related, powers, my life will express some other value. The Kantian "two natures" problem will have moved from philosophy into the life of the individual agent.[34]

If, analytically, there are separate principles that regulate the volitional activity of human beings, we should not be surprised if what is analytically the case is empirically realized. That is, we may in fact live our lives divided, responsive to the strictures of morality, but for the rest, under the sway of an at best sensible hedonism. The ambition of Kant's argument cannot be to show that dignity *necessarily* solves the problem of natural happiness, but

33. We do not lose dignity in acting immorally.

34. The "two natures" view of human agency and the problem of natural happiness are at bottom the same; when we understand how we can be "one," we will have solved the problem of natural happiness.

that it *can*. In the last part of the chapter, I want to take a brief look at how this might be made to happen. One striking feature of the account is that, in the normal course of things, the solution to the problem of natural happiness is a developmental achievement, and one that is dependent on the availability of the right kind of external, social support.[35]

IV. Kantian Paideia

We start with the recognition that the solution to the problem of natural happiness does not follow from the moral law. It is not knowable a priori; it is not part of the concept of dignity. The solution belongs to the domain of what can be made or constructed—that is, within the purview of moral education. Now, moral education can, indeed it should, aim at more than sensitization to standards of moral correctness. Children can be brought up *to* the idea that their value as persons lies in their dignity. And if they are confident that their social world is an arena for its expression, they will, as they can, make choices that reflect and express their sense of their value. In this way they will come to understand what the value of dignity is. Knowing that persons are to be treated as ends-in-themselves sets children a task, but the knowledge genuinely informs their moral understanding only as they can safely experience and work through the temptations and vulnerabilities of different sorts of relationships. They thereby gain a concrete sense of who they are, making their dignity real.[36]

Such experiences will give shape to a person's idea of happiness. If we imagine an upbringing that attuned children to the ways persons who recognize one another's dignity act together, it is reasonable to suppose that in the normal course of things they would be drawn to relationships that offer the opportunity to explore and enjoy a life in which respect and intimacy are mutually enhancing. Likewise, we might think, forms of work, struc-

---

35. This would be consistent with the view we have of those whose nonmoral activities and ends are formed "naturally": we do not see how the recognition of the moral law could have any effect, beyond constraint, on the shape of a person's conception of happiness.

36. Friendship is a particularly significant relationship for this sort of learning. The intimacy and mutual regard in some sorts of friendships lets us go further in exploring what our dignity amounts to. I can act respectfully toward a stranger. But outside the sphere of negative duties and necessary kindness or beneficence, we are constrained. The boundaries of another's dignity are not always clear; and the possibilities for reciprocal acknowledgment extremely limited.

tures of family life, and relations to art and culture that are respectful of dignity would be sought out by persons whose idea of happiness was given shape by their sense of themselves as persons with dignity.[37] Of course, not everything should be valued in the same way. Some of what we do properly belongs to the sphere of the hedonic principle—it would be perverse to make every choice and preference an occasion for the display of refined taste. On the other hand, not everything we enjoy is good for us—and one sense in which there are attractive relationships, kinds of work, and kinds of leisure that we should nonetheless forgo is in this way explained.

It is a chronic error in moral psychology to investigate the limits of what is possible from the perspective of the "however formed" adult. Not a great deal follows from the fact that many are indifferent to some set of concerns—choose abusive friends or relationships that flatter. The best explanation may be, as Mill argues it often is, the want of a certain sort of education, or the early and stable provision of opportunity. Kant differs from Mill in the foundation he offers for the value of dignity, but they are one in their view of the profound difference there is for human life when the value of dignity is given room to be central to persons' conceptions of their happiness.

To come to value friendship as an occasion to explore the ways mutual dignity can play out in ordinary life is not to regard such relationships as a stage for specifically moral action. Brought up within morality, we become a different sort of person. We care about different things from those we would have cared about if differently educated, and we also may care about some of the same things in a different way. The picture is not that the person of good upbringing has special access to a class of nonhedonic, objective reasons. (As if, like an expert, she could report to the rest of humankind on the truth about the good life.) What she has is a self-conception that becomes an aspect of the content of activities and relationships she values. This is part of the reason why an agent whose choices are shaped by dignity-based concerns can have reason to resist the blandishments of immediate pleasures. She has such reasons because (some of) her nonmoral choices

---

37. Though it may be next to impossible to explain to one's adolescent child that what he does now will look different to him later, and that it is the point of view that he now lacks that ought to determine his choices, one might hope that a child brought up to value his dignity *because* he has been so valued can resist some bits of fashion, or some exploitative relationships, for the sake of what is valuable to him now.

now express her own objective value. (It is the presence of such reasons that also creates the possibility of ordinary weakness of will. Both analytically and phenomenologically, weakness of will requires more than one value or principle of choice, and a standard of correctness that goes beyond subjective commitment to ends.)

I don't think there is anything psychologically extravagant here. The recognition that one is a person with dignity gives rise to a desire to organize wants and aspirations *as* the wants and aspirations of that kind of a self. This then carries outward. Discovering that some forms of work or friendship or even leisure fail to underwrite our self-regard, we prefer others. There is nothing strange in this. The man whose pride is based in his physical prowess will choose activities that give him opportunities for its development and expression. Someone who values her musical gifts will not ignore them, not if she is normal and otherwise well-circumstanced. We can have abilities and talents that mean nothing to us, and which it is not unreasonable to ignore. But we cannot (normally) value ourselves for having some capacity or ability and live without the desire to involve it in our activities, if we have a choice.[38] And unlike features of ourselves that we value or not as we will, someone brought up to an awareness of her dignity, cannot, with good reason, ignore it. So we say: dignity is not of value because a subject values it; it is to be valued for its value. But that's not the whole story. When valued for its value, dignity transforms subjectivity. There are activities, kinds of work, and kinds of relationships that, when freely chosen, express either lack of self-regard or self-contempt. These are different faults. At the extreme, both may lead agents to impermissible activities, especially to the violation of duties to oneself. But only someone who knows her value can have self-contempt.

Two things direct this account of dignity-shaped happiness beyond the individual and outward to social institutions. Respect for ourselves and for others *as pursuers of happiness* gives us reason to create and support social arrangements in which the relevant rational capacities of persons are developed and have wide opportunity for expression. Second, the fact that we are affected in our self-regard by the judgment of others gives us reason to seek a social order of value in which the equal status of persons is publicly ac-

---

38. Self-valuation based on unexpressed gifts—what I could do or be if I wished—is, other things equal, more like magical thinking than normal choice. It can be a mark of regret—what I could have done, if I'd had the chance; it is more likely a sign of disorder.

knowledged and secure. Taking both together, we should not be surprised to find that Kant argues for a form of public institutions in which social esteem is related to the conditions of equal, autonomous agency. Indeed, in his full political view, Kant embraces a modernized version of the classical ideal: participation in a political order of the right sort—a republic of equal citizens under law with a progressive public culture—will complete the process of human development, and provide the best conditions for human happiness.

Kant's ideal is that through active citizenship in a republican form of government, persons can express their free, legislating personality in a context of equal regard. The voting citizen of a republic can regard the law as an expression of her own activity and will, not merely as a source of command and protection. Making law for herself and with others who are free and equal citizens, she both gains insight into her own autonomy and she sees herself as a co-producer of a rational order. Seeing herself and others in this light, the citizen gains reasons to support public education and welfare, and to seek peace—as the empirical conditions appropriate to the pursuit of happiness informed by a sense of dignity.[39]

Though Kant's conception of politics is not ours, in his embrace of the moral possibilities in republican citizenship we at least gain a concrete idea of what might be involved in seeing rational agency expressed through institutional forms, and a sense of why it matters. We may find Kant's view of politics naive, and think about the social circumstances for the self-expression of our rational agency in more modest terms. There are many activities and institutions rich in opportunity for the development, exercise, and display of our rational powers. Work, art, social relationships—all may provide avenues for expression and mutual recognition of our fundamental value as rational agents. But because there is a fair amount of chance in the "fit" between a person's talents and the social world she happens to inhabit, the loss of confidence in public or civic life as an avenue of self-expression is not just a loss of one possibility among others. Where political life is a real possibility, we can act together as equals, making law for ourselves that brings into being what Kant calls the "ectypal world"—nature transformed by reason "determining our will to confer on the sensuous

---

39. These views are presented in the second essay of Kant's "Theory and Practice" and in the *Rechslehre*, part 1 of the *Metaphysics of Morals*. I discuss their connection with canonical Kantian moral theory in Chapter 6.

world the form of a system of rational beings" (*KpV* 5:43). One of the deeply appealing motivations of John Rawls's political vision is the formulation of terms for a scheme of social cooperation that returns this possibility to the political world. It is, of course, a moral ideal. But it is not just that. According to the Kantian arguments I have been examining, it may be a necessary goal if we are to bring reason to our pursuit of happiness.

— 9 —

The Scope of Moral Requirement

The subject of this chapter is the duty of beneficence: the obligation we have to promote one another's good. It is generally agreed that there is a duty of easy rescue; we are required to provide aid when that will prevent or relieve dire conditions for someone, when the cost to us is slight or moderate. And also that there is a companion duty of consideration or helpfulness, a requirement that we "lend a hand" to persons whose permissible activities or projects would founder without some small help we might easily provide. What is less clear is the nature and scope of the moral requirement in other cases. It is difficult to be sure about the sorts of need that fall under beneficence, how much can be required of us, and toward whom.

In moral theories that take the promotion of well-being as their core value, beneficence comes naturally. The philosophical and practical challenge is to bring it under control.[1] Once the claim of need is acknowledged, it is not easy to see what, morally, can constrain its demand. In theories whose core value does not refer to well-being, while it may be obvious that there is a duty of beneficence, its source is often not so clear. Typically, something about the value of persons is said to support a concern for well-being directly, or as a weighty derivative value. Here, too, it has not been easy to specify the duty's scope and a level of reasonable response.

In many accounts of beneficence, a great deal of work tends to be done by the intuition that the duty cannot be very demanding: it can neither absorb large amounts of our resources nor require a great deal of practical attention. But a slippery slope threatens. If it is allowed that the duty might be

---

1. The *locus classicus* of the modern challenge is Peter Singer's "Famine, Affluence, and Morality" *Philosophy & Public Affairs* 1, 3 (1972): 229–243. Singer, of course, was not seeking to bring the duty under control.

even somewhat demanding, might impose real costs on our activities and plans, then given any reasonable account of the need that might trigger beneficence, there is no well-founded stopping point on the demand up to the point of reducing the aid-provider to comparable neediness. Even with the introduction of a lateral requirement, for example, that we cannot be called on to assume more than our fair share of the burden of meeting need, it remains an open empirical question whether that share might not be large.[2]

The issues here reflect two independent currents in our moral understanding. One is the relation of fit between morality and ordinary life: that whatever morality requires of us, it should not make our lives unlivable, or too severe. The other is the conviction that we must negotiate a decent response to the irrefutable facts of need—of hunger, disease, and poverty. The tension between them plays out in many ways: it can, for example, seem reasonable to think that we have different and perhaps special obligations to persons in need who are in one sense or another local to us—to friends, family, or co-workers—than we do to those at a distance; we also recognize a continuum of need to which we seem obligated to respond impartially, regardless of relation or locale. If we regard these currents as reflecting independent values, of human well-being and the moderation of moral demand, or of the local and the global, the resources for resolving the tensions between them seem limited to some sort of balancing. But it is hard to imagine striking a balance that will not seem or be arbitrary.

My own view is that neither the intuitions about cases, nor the tensions within morality they point to, make available sufficient resources of argument to take us past this point. Whether the problems associated with beneficence are intractable, or turn out to be expressions of parochial sentiment, or something else, will depend on how things look when they are located in a more comprehensive moral view. We should not, for example, just assume that questions about the limits of obligation, about the fit of obligations in a decent life, are to be negotiated by appeal to extra-moral value, as if it were obvious that morality cannot get it right about what reasonably matters to us. Nor should we just assume that there is (or is not) some natural division in obligation that tracks group affiliations or relationships.

What I propose to do here, after a brief canvass of some of the intuitions that generate the tensions, is to introduce a theoretical framework for

---

2. For the best recent account of these issues, see Liam B. Murphy, *Moral Demands in Non-ideal Theory* (Oxford: Oxford University Press, 2000).

thinking about them that is drawn from a comprehensive moral view: specifically, Kant's account of obligatory ends and the imperfect duties they support. It is an avenue not much tried, and there are some obvious advantages to be hoped for in reframing scope questions in the terms of an agency-sensitive theory such as Kant's. Obligatory ends turn out to be a useful axis of inquiry because they present beneficence, the duty to take others' happiness as one's end, within a unified account of duties to self and others. Somewhat unexpectedly, their way of carving up moral space makes some sense of our bias toward the local in beneficence, as well as offering a very different perspective on the demandingness of the duty.

I will treat as a separate question how such an agency-based account of beneficence fits with the different obligation to need we have in justice. Though both justice and beneficence can have the same object—human welfare—they negotiate distinct domains of concern. What I hope to show is that in a variety of interesting ways justice and beneficence both limit and complete one another.

In any discussion of need, questions of injustice, both rectificatory and distributive, can swamp other issues. But the moral tensions the facts of need introduce are not necessarily the product of injustice, though injustice can surely make them more complicated. Philosophically, there is a prior, independent issue concerning our moral relations to one another: a question about the moral standing of one's own life, and how one is to think about this in a decent way.

I. The Primacy of the Local

If one thought there were a single, general duty of beneficence, the equal moral standing of persons would bring all who had need within its scope, and the most needy, wherever they are, would have the largest prima facie claim. The current combined resources of technology and the capacity for large-scale projects make global beneficence practicable. People can be fed, medicine delivered, technology and expertise exported.

A competing perspective on beneficence arises from the ways everyday morality is inherently local.[3] Two parameters structure this perspective: the

3. The beginnings of a more general account of the importance of the social and so local bases of morality can be found in Barbara Herman, "Morality and Everyday Life," *Proceedings and Addresses of the American Philosophical Association* 74, 2 (2000): 29–45.

fact that ordinary beneficence has the form of a duty of mutual aid, and, something more fundamental, the ideal fit of morality in everyday activity. Mutual aid is not the idea that in helping one thereby banks some good will or gratitude that can be called on for one's own need, like insurance. It is a conception of a moral relationship we are in when we live among others. The fact that *we* stand ready to help makes it an intelligible, normal act to ask for aid. The obligation is no doubt felt most strongly where we are closest to each other, and it follows out lines of connection and affiliation.

The place of morality in everyday life is ideally marked by a certain seamlessness, an absence of conflict between morality and interest. It is not just that we have internalized norms and so no longer notice them; we depend on the stability and structure of a morally configured world for the possibility of normal action. As a matter of course, we count on each other not only not to harm or deceive but also for help. This is not to say that no conflicts occur between what morality requires and goals we may pursue. However, morality is hardly unique in posing challenges to our efforts to integrate diverse principles and ends. The normal agent develops skills to manage potential conflicts, and to recuperate when there is loss. Some ends and values are not negotiable, and for the normal agent, moral values are chief among these.

The seamlessness of everyday morality, however we account for it, partly explains why the encounter with need at a distance will seem to have a different moral character than that with local need.[4] We are connected in more complex ways to those around us: personal interactions, shared institutions, claims of social justice introduce overlapping reasons to attend to the needs of local others that do not apply at a distance. There are also various internal features of beneficence, of the relation of providing aid or help, that push toward the weightiness or priority of the local. To be responsive to need requires that one know what it looks like. Some aspects of need are universal: the integrity of life and limb; disease and disability; the necessities of human sustenance. But once we go beyond urgent need, the nature and status of different needs become increasingly local and context de-

---

4. I do not mean to suggest that these metaphors mark a single, uniform metric. I am in many ways closer to my son across the country than to a neighbor down the street. On the other hand, distance matters. An important argument for the significance of spatial distance is to be found in F. M. Kamm, "Does Distance Matter Morally to the Duty to Rescue?" *Law and Philosophy* 19 (2000): 655–681.

pendent. Think of the range of things a person might require to be an effective member of her community: from literacy to clean and presentable clothes.[5] Locally, for the most part, need—or the need that counts—is a well-recognized part of everyday life. If we are attentive, we often can act directly and with confidence. We divide a task; make a call; offer a loan. In more specific settings of family or work or voluntary association, other needs will present themselves, and we have more nuanced resources to offer.

In responding to need at a distance, providing appropriately tailored help is difficult: there are special burdens of investigation and on creativity of response. The line between beneficence and paternalism may be harder to draw, conditions of dependence harder to see. Often we just contribute money. Need at-a-distance can also be less visible. This is not to say that salience is the condition of obligation; rather, what is differently salient, *if* we are not at fault for not seeing, will have a different place in the configuration of obligations.[6]

There also appear to be differences in the extent of our obligation. Normally, in providing aid, we take on new responsibilities. You have a headache; I offer aspirin, but by mistake give you antacid. Even if it is now harder to give you the aspirin you need than it would have been, because I started helping, I now have to do more. If the aspirin I give you makes you suddenly ill, I am at the front of the line of those who should get you help.[7] While just such extensions of responsibility often make people hesitate to help in the first place, they also mark out the contours of what it means to be members of a community. We see this easily in the context of family relationships. But even with strangers: if I have dialed 911 for help and no one comes, I have taken on a further reason to see things through.

That we do not seem open to comparable extensions when we aid at a distance may be a function of the fact that we most often meet these obligations through contributions to charitable and public institutions. To be sure, using an intermediary gives rise to *other* responsibilities. We ought to investigate the helping institutions we support: ask about their expense-to-donation ratio, about their decision-making process, or even about how responsible

5. Amartya Sen develops this idea (which he associates with Adam Smith's notion of "necessaries") in *Development as Freedom* (New York: Random House, 1999), chap. 3.

6. A very different sort of problem of salience is introduced by the televised cause *du jour.*

7. It is a mistake, I think, to treat such cases as about fault or negligence. In some contexts, responsibility can be extended simply by embarking on a course of action.

they are in the way they provide aid. However, if the aid they deliver on our behalf is not right, or not enough, we do not seem responsible for more *because* we contributed to the failed effort. That this may also be the case wherever there is large-scale aid suggests that the metric of local-global may not provide an independent basis for getting a clear picture of the obligation.

In both spheres, taxation and institutional tithing make the demanding more ordinary by making it less intrusive; but, as we well know, that something can be made ordinary does not show we have an adequate moral account of it.

I do not mean to insist on any of these intuitions about cases. They can be disputed; different accounts can be given of their conclusions. I do think that collectively these and other such reports indicate the presence of a subject matter: something to be explained, or explained away. This is a good enough reason to turn to a more comprehensive moral theory.

II. The Familiar Kantian Account

Kant's account of beneficence is found in two places: the last of the examples illustrating the formulations of the categorical imperative in the *Groundwork of the Metaphysics of Morals,* and the doctrine of obligatory ends in the second part of the *Metaphysics of Morals.* For present purposes, I will be less concerned with reconstructing the details of Kant's arguments than with describing the shape and structure of the duty of beneficence they advance.

The *Groundwork* pattern of argument tells us that we may not act in ways (on maxims) that cannot be universally or rationally willed. In the example about beneficence, Kant argues that we may not adopt, because we cannot rationally will, a maxim of never helping anyone.[8] However, the duty that follows, that we must adopt a maxim of sometimes helping, is by itself too minimal to give guidance about when we are to act.

We can derive a bit more content for the duty from an assumption needed to make the argument work. General facts about human vulnerability and limited efficacy indicate that our very agency can be threatened or undermined in ways we may not, on our own, be able to resist. Such facts

---

8. The argument is found at *Groundwork* 4:423. Translations from the *Groundwork* (hereafter abbreviated *G*), the *Critique of Practical Reason,* and the *Metaphysics of Morals* (hereafter abbreviated *MS*) are, with some modifications, from Immanuel Kant, *Practical Philosophy,* trans. and ed. Mary J. Gregor (Cambridge: Cambridge University Press, 1996).

are used to explain why no one could rationally will or assent to a universal principle of nonbeneficence. Suppose they do explain it. Then, if it is because of the ineliminability of agency vulnerability that we have a duty of beneficence, it is reasonable to think that threats to agency are the needs to which the duty of beneficence requires us to respond. This is enough to shift the burden of justification in such cases to reasons for not helping. But it is not clear how it secures more than easy rescue when life is in danger. We get no guidance about the range of agency needs that might trigger beneficence, or about how much we must sacrifice when such needs are threatened.

The best explanation for this indeterminacy is that the point of the first *Groundwork* argument is directed elsewhere. Rather than setting parameters for the casuistry of beneficence, the purpose of the argument is to show that and also why need, or a category of need, is morally salient. It cannot just be assumed that the needs of others must be our moral concern. This is not a quirk of Kantian rationalism. Even for Hume, while sympathy brings need to our attention, something else is necessary to show that attending to need (or to some kinds of need) is a moral virtue, not a fact we may, if we will, develop strategies to ignore.

The *Groundwork*'s formula of humanity has more to say about beneficence (*G* 4:429–430). In explicating the injunction to treat humanity (rational nature) as an end, Kant concludes that we must take the fact that happiness is the natural end of human beings as a reason to strive, as much as we can, to further the ends of others. This is because "[t]he ends of a subject who is an end in himself must as far as possible be my ends also." The implications for a duty of beneficence could be clearer. Taken literally, these terms for the duty would render it incoherent. For everyone to strive to make all ends of all others their ends also would not leave enough of ends that are truly a person's own to form a conception of the happiness others are to promote.

So we might ask: what could it sensibly mean for the ends of others to be ends for me—to be, as much as possible, my ends also? There is a continuum of ways to connect with the ends of another: noninterference, joint action for the end, support of your action for your end, support for your action for your reasons. Ends and reasons may also have a place within a conception of a life, and be (partly) valued as they do. Most ends we pursue we value conditionally: vacations matter, but less (or more) if we are supporting an aged parent, or have just finished a major piece of work. What we can make of another's ends will vary with our situation and our relationship. So Kant's "as much as we can" might be relative in its practical import. We can take on very little of a stranger's end; in such cases, a limited yet stringent duty of easy rescue makes sense. With regard to our child or partner, the situation is quite different; indeed, we easily err in the other direction, making their ends too much our own. So *if* we must attend to the happiness of others by "making their ends our own," a relationship-sensitive account of the obligation eliminates some of the conceptual difficulty. It would also give beneficence something like a point of view.

Elaborating the idea of beneficence in this way suggests the shape casuistical principles might take. My being part of complex cooperative or affiliative relations connects me in many different ways to needs as they bear on ends or a way of life that I can share. It might explain why needs of those close to us have priority, or why, when our helping causes harm locally, our responsibility for the harm is typically much greater, and the fault more likely to shade toward negligence than inadvertence. Moreover, if intimacy and dependence articulate beneficence, our obligations will more easily fit in everyday life. They can come to be among the things we just do: as we look both ways before crossing the street, we hold a door for someone burdened with packages, or leave work to take a friend to the hospital, or attend a school play.

If a relationally specified duty helps make sense of the requirement that we make others' ends our own, it leaves many questions unanswered. What moral grounds are there for accepting this specification? It is not that our capacity to help is limited in this way. Since even relationally specified beneficence cannot reasonably require response to all needs that arise from the pursuit of ends, what sets the limit? We seem to have left behind the thought that the needs at issue connect to the vulnerabilities of rational agency. And just as we have reason to worry that open-ended beneficence abroad would constrain the kinds of caring we could permissibly allow ourselves, unfettered beneficence at home would surely introduce its own disruptive demands.

Once again the best explanation for the limited result lies in what Kant was trying to do. As I read it, the formula-of-humanity argument is designed to show only that obligations to others are conceptually connected to the fact of our pursuit of ends generally, and so to our end of happiness. How this result fits with the earlier argument about the vulnerability of rational agency, and what significance it has, if any, for limiting the duty of beneficence, remains to be worked out. To take on this task we must first address a more fundamental question: how to think about the moral standing of our own ends—our happiness—in the mix of ends we are to make our own. Providing tools to answer this question is one of the signal accomplishments of Kant's doctrine of obligatory ends.

III. Obligatory Ends

Let me begin this section with a few general remarks about the *Metaphysics of Morals,* since its purpose and method are less familiar than that of the *Groundwork.* In the *Metaphysics of Morals* the kinds of duties and obligations that apply to us are arrived at as "specifications" of the moral law. The structure of argument is not one of direct derivation; instead, the moral law, as the constitutive principle of practical rationality, determines specific conditions on rational willing for our kind of rational being (finite, limited), in the particular circumstances in which we act (a shared material world of moderate scarcity). The specification proceeds in stages. It begins with the facts that human agents do not naturally coordinate their use of things (or each other) and yet require coordinated conditions of use to act effectively. To meet this need, the first principle of right secures the moral idea of positive law: that a part of morality (the conditions and norms of externally free action) is to be worked out in terms of civic order and legal sanction. These conditions make the institutions of property and contract morally possible, and provide a framework for institutional rules that dictates their consistency with the (external) freedom of all. One striking consequence of Kant's argument is that ownership is not (morally) more fundamental than citizenship. Conditions for the latter may therefore constrain the permissions that come with the former (e.g., making morally mandatory taxation for public education and welfare).

A second sequence of specification is drawn from the first principle of virtue, which sets possibility conditions for good willing. For human rational agents, a condition for *internal* freedom, for good willing, is that there be ends it is obligatory to have. Otherwise, Kant argues, morality cannot unconditionally direct agents' action. The first principle of virtue sets two obligatory ends: our own perfection and the happiness of others.[9] They neither replace

---

9. Perfection concerns the cultivation of an agent's natural and moral capacities, those needed for the furthering of ends in general, and whatever is necessary for virtue. Cf. *MS* 6:391–393. Happiness, for Kant, names the set of objects, whatever they are, the realization of which matches our idea of a life that will please us. Cf. *G* 4:417–419; *Critique of Practical Reason,* 5:22–26.

our natural interest in our own happiness nor compete with it as independent goals. As ends we must have, they are to give form to the way we conceive of our happiness. If the first principles of right create a normative social world fit for human activity (a world of right, not merely force), so, analogously, we can say that obligatory ends make the natural end of happiness an end fit for autonomous human agents: an end of rational choice, not merely desire. They are the beginning of an account of why and how "own-happiness" (for want of a better term) has weight in our moral deliberations.

We do not normally think of Kantian theory as having morally positive things to say about own-happiness. This should strike us as paradoxical, in Kant, or in any nonconsequentialist theory that extends beneficence beyond rescue. Why would we have moral concern for each others' happiness when our own happiness lacks moral significance for each of us, except insofar as it is the object of restriction and constraint, a cause of temptation, and the like? Rights and perfect duties protect our liberty, not our happiness. This may be part of the reason why, beyond rescue, negative tasks and small efforts tend to be the focus of attention in many nonconsequentialist discussions of aid, and why any more substantial engagement with the happiness of others is frequently located in the space of supererogatory actions, though even that makes little sense in a moral theory that does not give own-happiness a place. Impartial morality seems to be indifferent to the success or failure of our projects as such because, from the moral point of view, there is no loss if we wind up doing one permissible thing rather than another. Of course *we* most often don't have that view of what we do.

One familiar way to fix this is through special relations and obligations: to fellow citizen, family member, co-worker, friend. They place us in distinctive settings of cooperative activity or coordinate concern that give us moral interest in the success of the ordinary projects of some specific others, and they in ours. However, the logic of the fix is strange. Of course it matters to us that we have special relations, and our having them gives us reasons. But if mattering to us is sufficient to secure moral standing, then one wouldn't need to be talking about *special* relations and obligations. It would be odd to think that if morality is indifferent to what I care about, it gains an interest in what I care about because I stand in some relation to someone else.[10] This lack of argument makes itself felt in a disturbing adhocery in the as-

---

10. It is only odd (or empty) if it is the mere fact of the relationship that makes it matter; it is circular if it matters morally because it is a relation to others that I care about.

signment of relative weights among special obligations, and between them and impartial beneficence.[11]

There are obvious and sound reasons to resist the partitioning of value between own-happiness and morality. Even if, analytically, morality and happiness are separate, the way a normal adult functions does not keep them so. If happiness is the province of own-interest, it is not populated merely by natural desire. Part of the social effect of a moral culture is to transform our desires and so our idea of own-happiness. We teach honesty, and expect normal agents not to covet what belongs to others. We restrain a child's impulse to strike out when angry or hurt, and expect adults in distress to desire sustained connection rather than violent resolutions.

It is in just this moral space that obligatory ends do their work. They introduce *positive* moral conditions into the pursuit of happiness, requiring that the activities and ends we choose for the sake of happiness must also, in the ways that they can, be valued as they promote our perfection (natural and moral) and the happiness of others. And, as I will argue, because the moral work of obligatory ends is done through shaping the pursuit of happiness from the inside, they draw own-happiness into the space of moral reasons.

Before going on, I should note that it has been customary to interpret Kant's doctrine of obligatory ends differently. They tend to be regarded as the source of positive duties, though duties that are defeasible if in conflict with our interests. Kant's idea that obligatory ends leave a "playroom [*latitudo*] for free choice in following . . . the [moral] law" (*MS* 6:390) is seen as an attractive invitation to the agent to decide for herself when and to what extent she will act for an obligatory end. Less attention is paid to the more rigorous claim that the latitude of duty is "not to be taken as permission to make exception to the [prescribed] maxim of actions but only as permission to limit one maxim of duty by another (e.g., love of one's neighbor in general by love of one's parents)" (*MS* 6:390).[12] One can see why it is tempt-

---

11. One might suppose that it is not merely the fact that others are related to us that gives rise to special obligations, but the additional fact that closeness creates special vulnerabilities. Where there is vulnerability we must be concerned not to harm, but not helping will count as a harm in these contexts only if it is independently the case that happiness matters.

12. An exception is Onora O'Neill, "Instituting Principles: Between Duty and Action," *Southern Journal of Philosophy* 36 (1997): 79–96; see also Onora O'Neill, *Towards Justice and Virtue* (Cambridge: Cambridge University Press, 1996), chap. 7. For other accounts of obligatory ends, see Thomas E. Hill, Jr., "Kant on Imperfect Duty and Supererogation," in *Dignity and Practical Reason* (Ithaca, N.Y.: Cornell University Press, 1992); and Marcia Baron, *Kantian Ethics Almost without Apology* (Ithaca, N.Y.: Cornell University Press, 1995), chaps. 4 and 5.

ing to downplay this aspect of the latitude. By emphasizing free choice, interpreters credit Kant with seeking a sensible way to fit positive duties into a plausible moral schema without swamping out our own concerns. I satisfy the obligatory end of the happiness of others by committing myself to provide help sometimes.[13]

However, the idea of an obligatory end that gives us a "do something sometimes" duty cannot be right. If the needs of others support moral reasons, it is not credible that just *any* interest of ours is sufficient to set them aside (so long as we sometimes help someone, or even plan to). A more promising idea is to take seriously Kant's striking claim about the latitude of obligatory ends: that it is only a permission to limit one maxim of duty by another, the effect of which, he says, is to *widen* the field for moral action, and not to create room to decline to act.

To understand this claim, a good place to start is with some formal features of obligatory ends. If an end is obligatory, and as such a source of duties, it is one that in some way we must always have. As Kant presents them, it is clear that obligatory ends not only establish moral conditions for the pursuit of happiness, they also jointly constitute the material final end of human action: that is, they are ends for the sake of which we are to act *and* in light of which other ends are to be chosen. (It is in this role that they answer to the possibility condition of unconditionally good action: absent obligatory ends, all actions would be chosen for the sake of contingent ends, and no action could be unconditionally good [*MS* 6:382].) As to why the obligatory ends are just the two (our own perfection and the happiness of others) Kant's answer is, if not simple, direct: "What, in the relation of a human being to himself and others, *can* be an end [for pure practical reason] *is* an end for pure practical reason" (*MS* 6:395). Of the four candidate kinds of to-be-promoted ends (our own and others' happiness, our own and others' perfection), it makes no sense to have a duty to adopt an end we necessarily have (the end of our own happiness)[14] or an end we can only indirectly promote (correctness in end-adoption by others: their perfection);[15] what remains is our own perfection and the happiness of others.

13. However, since on such a view there is no act of helping that must be performed (setting aside easy rescue), and since it is likely that every act of helping that one does perform one was free not to do, all or almost all such acts turn out to be supererogatory.

14. Happiness seems to be a naturally necessary end for us because we not only have desires, we also have desires about our desires (singly, and over our whole life).

15. One might think we must also have the end of developing the moral character of others: providing them with moral instruction and with training for their natural faculties, such

We can think of the two obligatory ends as the complete material specification of rational nature as an end in itself for human rational agents. They are permanent and ubiquitous: permanent because obligatory, ubiquitous because jointly final and materially exhaustive. It follows that a condition on my acting for my own happiness (being beneficent to myself) is taking the happiness of others as an end, and also that a condition of my acting for the sake of the happiness of others is some attention to myself (*MS* 6:451).

It does *not* follow that everything I do must be in the service of promoting one or another obligatory end. To have an obligatory end is to be committed to a set of considerations as always deliberatively salient; they will not always direct one to action. It is in this sense that obligatory ends give rise to imperfect duties: there can be no rule specifying "precisely in what way one is to act and how much one is to do by the action for an end that is also a duty" (*MS* 6:390). The "latitude" for choice that comes with an imperfect duty is not about frequency of acting for the end, but a space for judgment as to how (and how much), in appropriate circumstances, the end might be promoted.

As an imperfect duty, beneficence will have its content determined by judgment directed at the value its supporting obligatory end expresses. The object of beneficence, human well-being, is not the value that sets the duty. Neither the satisfaction of desire per se nor the promotion of any arbitrary conception of happiness could obligate us. If well-being matters, it will be because of its connection with the core value of rational agency. The appeal to that value in the *Groundwork* yields (at least) a duty to aid when agency is threatened. What remains to be explained is how less urgent projects could matter in a way that allows us to claim from others some of the cost of pursuing them, or, correlatively, to resist the claims of others on resources we want for our purposes. At issue is why, in the face of need, a human life is not to be regarded as a warehouse of potentially distributable skills and possessions.

The resistance to this use of persons should come from the same features of human agency and happiness that make beneficence beyond rescue a

---

as memory, imagination, judgment, and understanding. We will have concern for the character of others, but it falls under the end of their happiness. To act from the obligatory end of others' happiness is not just a matter of helping them get a lot of what they want. We should want that they get things right (e.g., that they not crave what they ought not have, that they be able to act for their ends effectively, that they not use others merely as a means) and so be concerned with the elements of their natural and moral perfection. Cf. *MS* 6:394.

duty. A likely account of what they might be goes this way. It takes some doing to become an effective agent, and some more to sustain agency. Our agency arises in ordered stages; it is the result of a process shaped by natural and social resources, completed by our own choices. Within a range of normal variation, there are general conditions for effective agency. Many of the resources that support successful or developing agents cannot be made available for use by others without undermining the agency from which they would be withdrawn. Think of what a parent gives a child, or education, or the stuff of physical and cultural identity. I could have shifted my parenting activities to a child needier than my son. But (let us assume) because I could not have done that without damaging him, it is not the sort of thing I could have sensibly been required to do (or him to forgo) for the sake of benefiting others, regardless of how well off my son was on many measures. Compare this with an *n*th year of recreational dance lessons, or a summer hiking in the mountains; these are important goods for those who have them, but it is less shocking to imagine that they (in the form of the resources that support them) are in principle available for transfer. Because effective agency is not like getting one's adult teeth, it will not just happen with time and food, a moral theory that prizes the value of rational agency has to be especially sensitive to its social and material conditions as it goes about the business of parceling out goods.

Now, the vehicle that drives the development of human rational agency is the natural interest we have in our own happiness.[16] To be a creature with happiness as an end is to have a practical interest in one's life going well. But this bare interest gives no object of action; it rather sets a practical task of working out an idea of how one's life is to go, which in turn is the basis for developing specific projects and objects of action. In doing the work of articulating a conception of own-happiness, we become a particular agent: we develop needs (and interests), executive skills, special vulnerabilities and strengths. Clearly, then, whatever is involved in making the happiness of others my end, it cannot much resemble what is involved for me in having my own happiness as an end.

For these and related reasons, the adjustment negotiated between own-happiness and morality is complex. It is not just that in the pursuit of happiness we cannot violate moral requirements. If we do not care enough

---

16. I give a fuller account of the developmental role of happiness in Chapter 8.

about ourselves, we may become less able agents: we can lose the courage to act well or the strength to resist temptation. We may also undervalue our happiness by exaggerating the nature and extent of moral requirement. The vices of moral fanaticism and avarice, Kant argues, violate a duty to oneself insofar as they are assaults on the healthy pursuit of our interests, and prevent us from enjoying life (*MS* 6:408, 433–434). But why should denying oneself enjoyment be a vice—I mean, a Kantian vice? Enjoyment is not a kind of minimum wage to keep moral workers happy so that they won't go on strike. The thought is rather that unless one is willing and to some degree able to enjoy life, one cannot appreciate and so correctly evaluate the range of human concerns. One will not make wise judgments about either one's own needs as an agent, or about the happiness of others.

In thinking about the conditions for sound judgment, it is perhaps less difficult to grasp how impairment of the capacity to suffer, or to feel pain, might disable someone's ability to discern what matters morally. Kant's point here is that a healthy capacity for enjoyment is the positive side of this same practical ability. The instrumental role of enjoyment does not make enjoyment instrumental. It rather explains why morality takes it seriously.[17]

The role of own-happiness in the moral story is in this way extended. If the drive to happiness prompts the development necessary for rational agency, and so for moral action, the positive experiences of free enjoyment enable moral judgment. Time and cultural space are therefore part of the conditions of effective moral agency. We require safety and stability, material well-being sufficient to support the pursuit of an idea of happiness, freedom to learn through repetition and mistakes, the opportunity to acquire the evaluative skills for assessing complex arrays of greater and lesser goods. (Kant adds the need to be acquainted with beauty: to apprehend, through aesthetic enjoyment, pleasure that is not the pleasure of satisfied desire.)[18] Confidence in one's abilities as a moral agent is not gained through

17. There is an inevitable question here about high-end enjoyments: surfing in exotic locales, expensive pleasures, and the like. There are several things to say. Introducing enjoyments into an account of moral agency is not about raising the baseline for what we get to keep for ourselves, but about introducing a different set of reasons for having access to resources and, with them, an additional moral burden in acquiring preferences. On the other hand, one need not be simplistic about how enjoyments fit into lives. Some high-end activities are more sustaining, even if infrequently pursued.

18. Immanuel Kant, *Critique of the Power of Judgment,* (1790), trans. Paul Guyer and Eric Matthews, ed. Paul Guyer (Cambridge: Cambridge University Press, 2000), 5:353–354.

moral action alone; it comes through the myriad small things we experience and do, projects we take on, long-term goals that we care about and enjoy. In an environment in which we cannot enjoy what we do, we do not flourish as agents. The conditions for effective moral agency are not, then, to be regarded as luxuries. Although to an extent contextually specific, and very often resource-demanding, the cultural conditions of moral agency are matters of moral necessity.[19]

This pattern of argument not only permits but can require agency-based concerns for oneself to have priority over needs-claims of others. But because the needs on which agency depends are situationally specific, we may not be able to say in advance or in the abstract where the line is to be drawn between what we require for ourselves and what can permissibly be made available for others. Resolving this indeterminacy calls for judgment that attends to particulars, not merely the balancing of competing values. So someone's judgment that she should continue her education rather than send money to Oxfam can be a moral judgment, not a limitation on the reach of moral requirements. In such a case, the obligatory end of one's own perfection limits action for the end of others' happiness.

To get this result it might seem as though one must resort to some sort of balancing after all. But such an objection misses the point. It is true that different considerations are in play: one person's education, others' needs. But the argument does not ask for their relative weights. *If* education is a necessity in some context for effective agency, then it (or the wherewithal to support it) is not available for distribution to others. Whether one may sacrifice such a resource for the sake of others is not, then, entirely discretionary.

In moving elements of own-happiness into the space of moral reasons for each agent, happiness is not subsumed by morality, as if the determination of what makes my life go best is to be made impersonally. What is absorbed into morality is the *status* of the pursuit of happiness. This is not just about finding moral space for our own happiness; without the status argument, we would lack an account of why the happiness of others matters morally—how it *could* matter—in a theory that does not accord satisfaction of desire intrinsic moral value. The happiness of others matters

---

19. There are those who are "by nature" well-suited to morality. Instinctual demands may be modest; sympathetic attunement with others high. From the fact that in the most dire circumstances such persons may act well, it does not follow that the normal conditions for the development of moral agency are not to be regarded as necessities.

morally for the same reasons that my happiness matters: the pursuit of happiness is the organizing principle of our kind of agency.[20]

One of the dangers in treating emergencies as central cases of beneficence is that they distort the picture of what the duty of beneficence is about. Emergency cases make vivid the scale of human suffering as if it required no argument to show that relief of suffering is a first-order moral obligation. In the Kantian account of beneficence, the point of the help we may be required to give, in both emergency and normal cases, is not to alleviate suffering per se but to alleviate suffering because of what suffering signifies for beings like us. In the face of unnecessary suffering one naturally thinks: how could it not be better that it cease? And if someone can easily make it stop, what good reason can one have not to do so? There is no reason to deny that. Nor to deny that relief of suffering per se is the proper object of our kindness and compassion. Even if suffering per se is not the object of beneficence, responsiveness to suffering comes with it. Bringing a sphere of human concern into the space of moral attention changes the way we look at things intimately related to it. Given that we have moral reason to be concerned with the happiness of others, we will have reason to be concerned with their pain and suffering. What is at issue is the *order* of concern.

IV. The Latitude of Beneficence

Having brought own-happiness into the space of moral reasons, we are in a better position to consider what the latitude of beneficence, as an imperfect duty, amounts to. As we shall see, the salutary effect of locating the argument for beneficence under an obligatory end is to transform the way concern for self is connected to concern for others so that judgment need not be about adjudicating between own- and others'-happiness by means of the weighing and balancing of kinds of interests and numbers of persons.

It is a consequence of the developmental role of own-happiness that we are open to the shaping effect of ends. Given ends of importance and presence, the reasons they provide become salient across a wide range of a person's practical concerns, becoming part of what makes one this person rather than that one. The combined facts of the ubiquity and requiredness

---

20. That is why Kant locates duties of *respect* among the duties concerned with happiness. MS 6:462–468. It bears saying that giving happiness moral status does not supplant the more familiar ways that happiness of self and others matters to us.

of obligatory ends place them among the central shaping norms for a human life. Whether or not we must act frequently for their sake, they will be strongly directive. To take on as obligatory the end of the happiness of others calls for the development and deployment of skills of interpersonal awareness: perceptiveness about other lives; judgment about the fit of one's abilities and resources with the needs of others; the acquisition of dispositions of appropriate helpfulness (attitudes of humility and respect; wariness about paternalism and dependence, and so forth). It is not as though we have a duty to become social beings, as if that were contrary to our nature; as with the more familiar duties of respect, our social connections are to be formed and framed by these (among other) moral attitudes. However, as we develop more beneficence-related skills, our opportunities to act for the sake of others' happiness will increase. This need not be a burden, for the development of the skills that reveal need typically involves enhanced capacities of attachment, care, and concern.

The obligations of parents provide a useful intuitive guide in thinking about the shape of duties under obligatory ends. For example: once responsibility for a child is taken on, one gains ends whose standing in deliberation is not discretionary. They may be onerous or not. It is unlike a job one may not find fulfilling and so leave, or even a friendship, which though it gives nondiscretionary ends, if outgrown, can, with care, be eased away from. And because the occasions to act on parenting ends are pervasive and the ends nondiscretionary, being a parent often becomes central to who one conceives oneself to be. When the role is welcomed, the concerns that belong to the obligation enter the space of reasons of own-happiness, effecting a link between morality and the actions of everyday life. Of course it need not be so; and when it is not, the obligations can exact a heavy toll, not just on time and energy but also, sometimes, as a cause of shame.

The point of the analogy is to suggest that we get it wrong about obligatory ends if we think of them as setting a parallel and competing agenda to our own. Obligatory ends provide positive norms for how one should treat oneself and others while going about the business of one's life. When all works well, moral deliberation can be coincident with the contours of reasonable ambition, attachment, and interest, while such ends, in turn, can routinely support our moral well-being. And just as it is not always wrong to let a child cry, since the interests of children, important as they are, are not the only interests that should matter to those who care for them, simply doing more for an obligatory end is no sure sign of virtue. Self-sacrifice will be a vice if it leads to the neglect of activities and attachments that keep us effectively engaged with the world. How this will work out in a life is not easy to say. Given our different abilities and tolerances, where the line is drawn is neither fixed nor certain. Though one can state the rule, it remains a task of judgment to assess the relevant particulars.

If we stopped here, it might look as though all that has happened is a shift in the balance point between own and other interests: more for own-happiness because, morally, we require it. Indeed the balance has shifted, but not in that way. Facts about us, personal as well as social, may call for more (or less) attention to own-happiness, but also, the degree and kind of our moral involvement with the happiness of others will partly be a function of how we live with them. As relationships become closer, the field for the practice of beneficence typically widens. Those with extensive families and dependencies, wide networks of friends and associates, will bring into their lives, via these relationships, extensive areas of concern. Those with more solitary lives will not be free of moral concern for others, but the interests of others will be less pervasive because others are less important in the way such a life is lived. Indeed, having made certain decisions about how to live one's life, say, ones that require the focused development of special talents, one may have closed off, morally speaking, certain ways of living with others. That is, such decisions affect not just obligations but permissions as well. We can now understand why it is that how often and how much I might offer help could in a sense be up to me and it still be the case that "I don't feel like it" is not a reason for not helping.

If, as you run frantically down the path, I could easily step aside to let you through and I think that I need not because I am as entitled as you are to be there, I simply fail to understand how the needs of others provide reasons for me. Where I am more involved with others, I have greater opportunity to have an impact on their happiness. We know a lot more about the conditions of happiness or well-being of those with whom we live or work, and those to whom we are closest are often those we can most easily harm by our neglect. When I do not help a stranger with his project, I am not neglecting him. But when a co-worker or friend is similarly needful, the threshold of neglect is much lower.

It follows that, independently of the relationships we are in, we cannot say what the full content of our imperfect duty toward others will be. Whether we take on greater relational burdens is up to us; it belongs to the space of decisions about our lives over which we have authority. Some of the goods of a human life will increase the shared terrain of morality and happiness. It works both ways. In making adjustments for one's own concerns and the needs of one's friends, one works out what kind of friendship one has. If we extend ourselves into relations with others, our moral involvement with their happiness and well-being widens.[21] Among the reasons why general charity or welfare can be taken care of by public institutions is that, though we each stand to the need of strangers under the duty of beneficence, they require help, not our help.

V. Strangers, Inherited Obligations, and Moral Triage

Once strangers appear on the scene, we are immediately faced with other complicating factors. Not all strangers are related to us in the same way; not all their claims of need point to beneficence. Some strangers are our fellow citizens; some are not. Some needs ought to be met as a matter of justice. The task of elaborating and keeping track of these sometimes conflicting currents of claim and relation is considerable, and not something one should expect from the resources of an argument for beneficence. There is, however, a more limited question in the arena of these issues that we are in a position to examine, and that is whether the general structure of obligation to self and other based on obligatory ends has any bearing on the scope of moral requirement once we leave the space of relationships. This is a question about the connections between the argument for beneficence and justice. In discussing this, I consider only an approximately Kantian or liberal account of social justice, based in something like a nation or state. Both assumptions are controversial. I make them because of their fit with Kant's own arguments about these matters, but also because the conclusions have some bearing on the circumstances in which we currently live.

Let me start with claims of justice for fellow citizens. In any complex social order, it is not always possible to tease apart the sources of need. Sometimes it arises directly from the distribution of benefits and burdens: the n percent unemployment that is supposedly necessary to a healthy economy; sometimes there are those whose abilities and skills simply do not fit

---

21. To be sure, not every element of every conception of happiness is one that has to be realized. Because I very much want something, have hung my hat on it, it does not follow that you or anyone has reason to help me get it. Setbacks are normal. We are or should be capable of adjusting our ends in the face of reversals; a healthy agent has significant recuperative powers.

the available forms of productive life. A just system of social rules ought, morally, to include some program of public support for those in need to remedy the imperfections of human-designed institutions and to extend the benefits of social cooperation to those whom misfortune hinders from making their own way. Most of what is required of us individually in this way of helping strangers falls under the general obligation to support just institutions. The demand on our resources may or may not be considerable, but in modestly decent social circumstances it is neither unfair nor undermining of the possibility of one's having a whole and healthy life.

However a community works this out, there will be residual individual obligations to aid that belong to beneficence. One has direct responsibilities for pressing needs that arise outside of or in the crevices of the institutional framework of support. Someone falls and is hurt; an elderly neighbor suddenly needs help getting to the doctor. Locating individual responsibility for the needs of others in the places institutions cannot reach, the residual obligation is respectful of the life intruded on, and if demanding, it is only so as circumstances are in some way unusual. If, living in a just society, one happens to be the person in front of whom large numbers of people trip and fall, then one is unlucky, and large demands are indeed made on one's time and resources. There can be no moral guarantee that one will get to live the life one wants.

What, then, is the status of those outside our framework of relationships and political institutions? Typically, those not in our own community to whose need we might attend are members of other societies: some, perhaps, lacking resources and unable to meet their citizens' needs, others, perhaps, unjust and unwilling to do so. One natural thought is that such local failures give rise to or trigger global or general obligations. That is, legitimate needs that fail to be met within a society might be the basis of claims against all of us who might help: a secondary claim of beneficence. If they were, there would be a moral connection to need at-a-distance, though we could not straightaway conclude that we simply inherit all of the moral work. Not every moral failure that calls for remedy warrants a response of the same kind. Failures of the educational system in our own community don't burden us to teach, or repair classrooms, though they do burden us with some responsibility for the unmet need. Sometimes *how* a failure comes about affects the obligations others inherit.

Inherited obligations belong to a rather interesting if not much examined class: obligations that are satisfied by persons other than those who originally bear them. Some obligations can be contracted out. Other obligations move on to others in less sharply defined ways: they can be passed on or down; they can be individually obligating, and yet be shared; they can (literally) be inherited. One can act as an obligation-surrogate (grandparents raising their children's children) or substitute (child-care workers); one can be a relief worker (taking a neighbor's children to school on a hectic morning). In many cases, the derived obligation will not be the same as the primary obligation. One may take on only an aspect of another's more general obligation (if the child I am driving to school has a fever, I am not thereby obligated to take him to the doctor); it may not be appropriate in some circumstances for the holder of the derived obligation to act; in some cases, the derived obligation is only to forestall some bad effect that would occur were the original obligation to be unmet. Some cases might generate a derived obligation to help restore the primary obligation holder to full functioning. One can imagine cases in which the obligation (or what it can require) weakens as it descends; in other cases (easy rescue, for example) it may be the same at all declined positions.

What is the bearing of this on the duty to aid? If a class of need first imposes moral obligations on local social institutions (claims of justice), and general obligations to meet distant need are inherited from them (secondary beneficence), it is not likely that the inherited obligation will have the shape of open-ended, universal beneficence. The shape of the secondary duty of beneficence will depend on, among other things, whether inheritance here preserves the scope and stringency of the primary obligation in justice, and whether it makes any difference if the failure that triggers the inherited obligation is moral (injustice, corruption) or merely practical (resource insufficiency, earthquake). However, if our obligations to need at a distance are inherited, one thing we do know is that the delivery of aid should not interfere with sound local institutions; and where those do not exist, we should not act in ways that make their development less likely. Otherwise we do not adequately respect the priority of the local, primary obligation. We now recognize that in some disaster situations, direct palliative aid addressed to individual need can be hazardous. Heroic food aid creates refugee camps, encourages abandonment of the land, and promotes dependency and corruption. Many conclude that we must therefore adopt alternative models of aid such as training in new farming techniques, establishing local markets, promoting female literacy, which, while not directed at immediate suffering, do more, over time, to diminish overall need and to create the possibility of effective local responsibility.

Suppose this is right. Would those whose current needs are not met have grounds for complaint against us when resources are diverted from aid to the project of institution building? If we had a direct obligation to meet their needs, then a rationale of balancing present suffering against future benefits to possible future persons would fail to address the claims on help that present persons make. But if our moral relation to need at-a-distance is inherited, what is inherited is not individual obligations to meet need but a society's failed welfare obligation. We inherit a complex set of derived obligations that require us to respond to a situation in which there is both institutional failure and unmet welfare needs. We are obliged to attend to both.

Inherited obligations serve two masters. They respect the content of the primary obligations they take over, and they reflect the conditions that engage inheritance (consent, in some cases; beneficence in the case at hand). This can make specifying the inherited obligation a complex business. With respect to need, the primary obligation of a society consists in the use of its resources to ensure, first, that food, shelter, and basic health care are available to all citizens. It is reasonable to think that the primary obligation extends beyond that, to those things necessary for adequate social and economic functioning, as these are understood locally. The values of agency that Kantian beneficence is responsive to suggest that the line for the inherited obligation should also be drawn at this higher level of functioning. The derived general obligation will therefore reflect the social conditions in the locale of the primary obligation. It should in any case be no more extensive than the extended primary social obligation, but it may be less. A society can generate "needs" for very high levels of well-being, but it is not likely that meeting such needs is a part of secondary beneficence, any more than contributing to the pet projects of this or that person is among the things we must do if we have their happiness as our end.

A few caveats. Nothing in this account speaks to the issue of equality (within and between societies) or to claims of global justice. So to say that we might have only a limited secondary obligation under beneficence to provide aid to strangers at-a-distance is not to deny that we might be otherwise obligated to take steps to reduce global inequality, or to rectify instances of global injustice. Moreover, I have been talking mainly about individual obligations to aid, which, obviously, are not the only obligations to aid or to ameliorate states of need (or inequality) there may be. If the primary obligation for social welfare is one of justice, it belongs to members of a society collectively, as the bearers of benefits and burdens of social cooperation. As individuals, we have a duty to support just institutions and to supply backstop aid. Obligations toward need at-a-distance are often met through institutions (to take advantage of economies of scale, and the like), but I do not think these derived obligations are institutional or held by us collectively: there does not seem to be a natural collectivity to receive the obligation short of all of us—that is, all who are capable of assuming the inherited obligation.

If our individual obligation to persons in need at-a-distance were an inherited secondary obligation, that would provide some explanation of otherwise puzzling moral facts, especially the limitedness of the obligation, and the special sensitivity that seems warranted to social and institutional effects. I have not argued directly for the inherited individual obligation, and the moral facts, if they are facts, might be explained some other way. But apart from exploitation or other injustice, it is hard to see how a society, whose raison d'être and authority derive from its role in securing the fair distribution of the burdens and benefits of social cooperation for its members, would inherit failures of obligation from other cooperative schemes and so warrant to tax its own members on their behalf.[22] A secondary (inherited) obligation to aid *can* devolve on us as individuals because, given the obligatory end of the happiness of others, we already have an indeterminate obligation to all persons that bears on their need. The secondary obligation is not one we would have but for failure elsewhere to meet an obligation of justice. Such failures partly specify the content of our otherwise indeterminate obligation.

Difficult questions remain. Even if it were only failures of primary obligations that oblige us to provide aid at-a-distance, and even if only at a subsistence level, when we consider both episodic and chronic global emergency conditions, the demand on our resources could be considerable. The empirical claims here are not uncontroversial. But for purposes of this discussion, I want to assume a high level of demand, for this puts the most pressure on the argument.

It is sometimes suggested that we may limit our response because it is not possible to live a life where we may be drawn this way and that by moral de-

---

22. There are many issues to be sorted about injustice and its effects on group-to-group obligations. A society that is not an exploiter might incur obligations if some of its members are or have been. Exploitation (or other injustice) as a cause of need might alter the status of one society's claim on others, regardless of causal responsibility. And so on. Given this complexity, I have tried to restrict my remarks as much as possible to the circumstances of individuals who could provide help and their moral relation to those who need it.

mands. This isn't quite right. Where we have strong bonds of relationship, or are members of a cooperative endeavor, prolonged emergencies may dramatically alter the shape of our lives, limiting, by demands on our resources and time, much that we would like to do. It is not unreasonable that unchosen events shape our ends and lives, or that relationships and social connections extend our vulnerability (they also offer protection). Most of us organize our ends and activities knowing this, minimizing or eliminating activities that cannot survive interruption. Because we have strong reason to avoid conditions where the intrusion of repeated and different demands can cumulatively undermine normal goals and projects, some of our positive obligations are best met through the mediation of political and nonpolitical institutions. The more finite burdens of paying for insurance, or paying taxes, can free us from the costs of having to weigh our needs against the lives and needs of others, but only to a limited extent.

If, however, our duties to others at-a-distance fall under beneficence as an inheritance of defaulted social obligations, the inherited obligations must fit with the structure of relational duties we already have, and also with our morally required concern for ourselves. For this reason, not only will the general duty to others be limited, in order to meet our primary duties of beneficence, we may also be required to expend resources on higher-function needs close to us rather than on more basic needs at a distance.

One might straightaway object that morality always requires equal concern. But equal concern does not require equal action. Parents have equal obligations to their children to help them develop and flourish, though what they are required to do for each depends on the needs and interests each has. Teachers make extra efforts to improve the work of weaker students, or provide special assignments for those who would benefit from additional challenges. This is all familiar, and easily resides within the space of equal concern.

The issue seems much more difficult in cases of chronic and extensive need. Consider, by way of analogy, a family with two children, where one child has such enormous physical and psychological needs (for health care, special training, and the like) that there are no nonsubsistence resources in the family that could not be absorbed in bringing the first child toward normal self-sufficiency. Beyond some baseline of reasonable care, it is not obviously impermissible to expend resources on some of the higher-order needs of the second child (piano lessons, college). And this may be done without having to balance overall costs and benefits. If this intuition can be generalized, it would suggest that something like moral triage may have a role to play in adjudicating claims of need.[23]

Triage is a way of sorting needs to be met according to values other than urgency. In medicine, triage protocols direct that some needs not be addressed because a person cannot be made well; others because resources can be used elsewhere to better effect; lesser needs go unmet because they can be borne. The Kantian duty of beneficence, though derived from the obligatory end of others' happiness, neither directs us to bring about the greatest good nor to meet only the most urgent needs. It directs us to attend to the well-being of persons as we can, because and insofar as it is in and through the pursuit of happiness that persons create and sustain themselves as agents. If agency-related needs are the object of aid, then triage may well be an appropriate model for judgment.

One of the attractions of thinking in terms of triage is that its rules trim at both ends. So if a principle of triage permits agency-sensitive direction of resources on the one side, it should also require something analogous to need that can be borne. And it can. There are levels of luxury that are morally gratuitous, however much coveted, and the felt need for such things does not enter the space of beneficence. To be sure, the line between culture, high culture, and mere luxury is not easy to draw. But from the point of view of morality, culture is not just another preference; it is a morally protected good, even though it creates new needs, and transforms some of the new needs into necessities. The culture of luxury is another matter. This does not seem to be an impossibly difficult judgment to make.

VI. Conclusion

Kantian obligations of beneficence are not additive; we are not always obliged (or permitted) to help the greatest number; some robust level of concern for oneself is obligatory. Indeed, for each of us, coming to recognize what is possible *sub specie* beneficence is a moral demand on self-

---

23. Although the example supports the intuition about triage, it is doubtful that triage is the best way to think about extreme burdens on families. They more plausibly generate a secondary obligation going in the other direction, from the individual or family to the community or state. If there are good reasons for families to take primary responsibility for some kinds of needs, there are equally good reasons for the community to be responsible for extreme conditions of individuals.

knowledge: of understanding the conditions and limits of our own moral agency. When Kant asks, "How far should one expend one's resources in practicing beneficence?" and answers, not to the point of needing help oneself, he is not arguing that you ought to go that far, but that you may *not* go farther (*MS* 6:454). Or at least may not on grounds of beneficence.

What we *must* do to meet the needs of others is to be worked out primarily through the relational specifications of beneficence, but also local institutions of justice, and secondary obligations to strangers at-a-distance. Whether the duties of aid singly or in sum turn out to be demanding, and if demanding, intrusive, is in part up to us and how we manage our lives, but in any case not anything that is or ought to be determinable in advance. The upshot of locating beneficence in the space of obligatory ends is not tidy answers about what to do but a wide-ranging deliberative resource. This is the kind of result one should hope for if moral theory is to cohere with real-world moral complexity.

A last point. Kant remarks that, as a matter of fact, most of the burdens of poverty are the result of injustice. Much of what we do to meet need only repairs injustice—not our law-breaking, but our being party to and beneficiaries of unjust laws and unfair practices, past and present.[24] Such reparative action does not belong to beneficence, and so does not fall under the rules of moral triage. To the extent that this is so, the argument for the space of own-happiness within beneficence may provide more of an ideal than a sufficient guide to what we are obligated to do now for need we could meet.

24. See *MS* 6:454; and Immanuel Kant, *Lectures on Ethics,* ed. Peter Heath and Jerome Schneewind, trans. Peter Heath (Cambridge: Cambridge University Press, 1997), 27:416.

— 10 —

The Will and Its Objects

Anyone who spends time with Kant's practical philosophy has some kind of painful encounter with Kant's notion of will. And no wonder. It is the locus of unconditioned value; it lies at the crossroads between reason and desire; it *is* practical reason; it is the faculty of choice, and also the causal instrument by means of which reason would shape the world to its form. Add to this the will's cohabitation with things noumenal and you get a very strange notion. The question is whether it's worth trying to come to terms with it. Kant thinks he needs the will to account for free rational action: that no combination of belief, desire, intention, planning, or critical reflection can explain it. It is a bold claim, and if plausible, perhaps worth some pain. But even to begin thinking about whether he could be right, we need to have a clearer idea of what sort of work the will is supposed to do.

What I will present here is something of a halfway station, still more burdened with Kant jargon than I would like, and a little schizophrenic, bouncing back and forth between interpreting Kant's gnomic remarks and trying to say in a plain way what I think he means. Overall, I argue for two theses, and try to make a little sense of one surprising consequence. The theses are that desire is not a primitive in Kant's considered view of things, and that the rational will is a *kind* of faculty of desire expressed in a norm-constituted ability. The consequence is that there is and has to be *one* end for a rational will in all of its willings.

The texts I will mainly be relying on for an account of the rational will are in the Introduction to Kant's *Metaphysics of Morals.* They came to the forefront of my thinking about the will in a roundabout way—while I was trying to make sense of something else. Since it is the "something else" that provided a kind of key, I propose to re-enter the texts on the will from that same place.

I

In his discussion of the strains of beneficence in the *Tugendlehre,* Kant makes the odd claim that unlike benevolence, which can be unlimited because it does not require anything to be done, acts of beneficence—doing good from duty—are difficult because they are "at the cost of forgoing the satisfaction of concupiscence and of active injury to it in many cases".[1] The first odd thing is that the cost worth marking is to concupiscence and not to happiness. The second is: Why *concupiscence* at all? It is hard to fathom why beneficence should conflict in some special way with sexual lust, or even with, what concupiscence also means, avidity of desire or craving in general.

Although Kant doesn't make explicit the contrast with happiness, we can still ask: is it possible that acts of beneficence don't (or don't have to) threaten happiness? Some might argue that we avoid that threat because beneficent acts are supererogatory, so it's in our control to pick the acts we want to do, or at least ones that don't threaten our happiness. I doubt this is a plausible picture of supererogation, but that doesn't matter here, for if the threat to happiness were removed by its being up to us when we help, it would only make it more puzzling that beneficence does threaten concupiscence. I think a more plausible account of beneficence directs us to take the happiness of others into account when we act—indeed, whenever we act—*in the way that* we are to take the conditions of respect for persons into account whenever we act.[2] That is to say, the concerns of beneficence do not oppose our pursuit of happiness, but rather are to inflect and shape our idea of what happiness is. We might think, by analogy, of friendship, where acting for another's sake isn't separate from a concern for one's own happiness. Friendship and beneficence as well also require concern for self.

Let us suppose that there is no inevitable threat to happiness from beneficence; why, then, are there costs of forgoing the satisfaction of concupiscence when acting beneficently? And why is it helping *from duty* that imposes the cost? If the issue is the possible conflict between what I want for myself and what I am obliged to do for you, the cost should arise regardless

---

1. "Benevolence can be unlimited, since nothing need be done with it. But it is more difficult to *do good,* especially if it is to be done not from affection (love) for others but from duty, at the cost of forgoing the satisfaction of concupiscence [*Konkupiszenz*] and of active injury to it in many cases" Immanuel Kant, *Metaphysics of Morals* (1797) (hereafter abbreviated *MS*), in *Practical Philosophy,* trans and ed. Mary J. Gregor (Cambridge: Cambridge University Press, 1996), 6:393.

2. For more on these issues see see Chapters 8 and 11.

of motive. It may indeed be harder to do good from duty than from love, but why is the currency of the hardness so specific and so peculiar?

A hint of an answer comes in an earlier mention of concupiscence in the Introduction to the *Metaphysics of Morals* (at 6:213). Kant says: "Concupiscence (lusting after something) must . . . be distinguished from desire itself, as a stimulus to determining desire." This, too, is a surprising remark. If concupiscence is a *stimulus to desire,* then to say that acts of beneficence are at odds with concupiscence is not to say that they interfere with what we desire, but rather with something we *might* desire. But how would forgoing what we might desire explain why it can be difficult to do good? Here is a possible reason. If we are to take a certain sort of interest in the happiness of others, we may need to exercise restraint not just on our desire-satisfaction, but on which desires we allow ourselves to have. Some desires are strictly incompatible with concern for another's well-being. So resisting something *as a desire*—forgoing opportunities *to* desire—could be what forgoing the satisfaction of concupiscence amounts to, or even its "active injury." Because concupiscence operates prior to desire, forgoing its satisfaction does not as such weigh in the scales of happiness. And further, if we come to our beneficent acts from an acknowledged obligatory end—that is, from duty in its full sense—we would forgo in advance the expression of concupiscence in any desire not fitting with our end (and given the unruly nature of lust, this is not a trivial constraint). So the in-principle conflict is not between happiness or desire and morality, but between morality and a source of desire. It may look like a small difference, but I think it is not, and that in the difference—between desire and source of desire—there is a key to making sense of Kant's notion of the will.

Many of the familiar interpretations of the will follow a *Groundwork* metaphor that locates the will at a crossroads between two incentives for action. On the sensible side, we have desires for objects that arise directly from pleasure in our representation of them. On the moral side, we have an interest of reason that provides its own kind of incentive. Any pleasure or feeling associated with the rational incentive is consequent to its will-determining effect.[3] One might characterize this as a sort of structural Humeanism about the springs of action, with the Kantian addition of a special, nonsensible incentive.

What then does the will do? One might equally ask: given these materials, what *could* the will do? The activity available to the will seems to be ei-

3. We get interests of inclination when we understand that certain *kinds* of desired objects will please us. Pleasure, either antecedent or consequent to the determination of the faculty of desire, always precedes action.

ther as a "deciding faculty," given competing desires, or as the faculty by means of which the agent chooses to act to realize an object of desire *or* for a rational interest. In making a choice, if the will identifies with sensible desire, it (or its act) is heteronomous; if it commits to rational or moral interests, it (or its act) is autonomous. How it does one or the other is a mystery, and one not much helped by the claim that the moral law is in some way internal to the will—its law—making *all* of choice dependent on its exercise and yet *autonomy* the unique form of volitional *self*-identification.

For the standard view, the paragraph about concupiscence in the Introduction strikes a discordant note. It occurs just after Kant has distinguished interests of reason from interests of desire in the narrow sense (or sensible desire); he then says we must *also* distinguish concupiscence from desire, "as a stimulus determining desire." Kant continues: "Concupiscence is . . . a sensible modification of the mind . . . that has not yet become an act of the faculty of desire" (*MS* 6:213). That is, *along with the interests of reason,* concupiscence is to be distinguished from desire, and is prior to desire (strictly, to an act of the faculty of desire). It is no doubt distinctive among the sources of desire in its orientation to sensible pleasure, and may therefore be, like passion, a threat to rational agency. But it is not a state of desiring something intensely, or for pleasure; it is not, as Kant thinks of it, a desire at all.[4] Its role is to offer something—an intense orientation toward pleasure—*to* the faculty of desire, the upshot of which may be one or another desire.

If in being antecedent to a determination of the faculty of desire, concupiscence *is* like an interest of reason, that raises the question about the transition from a "modification of mind" to "an act of the faculty of desire" in *both* cases. And since what immediately follows the remarks on concupiscence is an account of choice and will, one might suppose that they explain what this transition amounts to—*in both cases.*[5]

---

4. Compare with "inducements of the senses"; Immanual Kant, *Lectures on Ethics,* ed. Peter Heath and Jerome Schneewind, trans. Peter Heath (Cambridge: Cambridge University Press, 1997), 27:395.

5. A word about the structure of the discussion in this section of the Introduction. The section is about the "faculties of the human mind" as they relate to the moral law. It begins with a generic account of the faculty of desire—something common to all things that can be said to have "life"—beings who are moved by means of their representations to be the cause of the objects of these representations (*MS* 6:211). Two paragraphs are devoted to the general account of a faculty of desire; then there is one about the difference in the order of the role of pleasure in the determinations of the faculty of desire, distinguishing interests of inclination and reason; and then there is the paragraph about concupiscence. At this point, the discussion shifts from talking about the elements of the faculty of desire in general and introduces

Now given that both choice and will are introduced as part of an account of "the faculty of desire in accordance with concepts," it seems prudent to back up a step to get a sense of what, in a general way, a faculty of desire is supposed to do.

II

Kant attributes a faculty of desire to all things that have "life"—beings who by means of their representations act to cause the objects of these representations (*MS* 6:211). To be so moved to action is to have desires and aversions, states that are essentially connected with pleasure or displeasure in a representation. Although there is always pleasure where there is desire, pleasure need not precede desire: it may either arise from desire (as it does in the case of interests of reason) or play a role in its generation (as in the case of sensible appetites).

In an animal's faculty of desire, instinctual organization is keyed to perceptual representations in such a way that, for example, seeing something as food or as dangerous, the animal feels a pleasure or a displeasure, and, by a consequent determination of its faculty of desire as an effect, is moved to act (to eat or flee). Kant holds that the connection between the systems of representation and action, made by way of the faculty of desire, need not make use of materials suitable for the cognition of objects (*MS* 6:212). The pleasure and displeasure essential to the generation of desire are simply functional states of an organism. Beyond the fact of the relation of some object and a subject, pleasure and displeasure, he says, "cannot be explained more clearly in themselves; instead one can only specify what results they have in certain circumstances, so as to make them recognizable in practice" (*MS* 6:212).[6]

In a being who acts to bring things about by means of its representations, we might think of the pleasure as a "toward-relation" of the active being to the represented object of action. (English once also had the word "froward," but alas, we have it no more.) *We* can come to be in such a relation by a state or

the idea of a "faculty of desire according to concepts," which leads to the introduction of "will." So it is not a far stretch to conclude that the reason for introducing the faculty of desire according to concepts is precisely to explain how our faculty of desire is determined (comes to desire) by the sources in appetite and reason.

6. In particular, they indicate or express nothing at all about the object, but "simply a relation to the subject." This is one way pleasure and displeasure are unlike sensation: Kant says that a sensation *of* red or sweet makes reference to an object; the pleasure *in* what is red or sweet does not. These are definitional claims.

condition, such as concupiscence, that serves as a stimulus-cause to desire, or, at the other extreme, by a representation of a rational principle. Imagine the state one is in, when hungry, catching the smell of newly baked bread. It puts one in a toward-relation to an object, which gives rise to a desire for it—and then, perhaps, action. Or imagine seeing someone in need whom one recognizes one ought to help. The recognition is sufficient to make providing help one's object. One feels "right" about acting, shame or guilt if one turns away.

This gets us to the first interpretive thesis. The Kantian faculty of desire is not a faculty of *desires*. In a simple living thing, given a toward-relation, it will desire; if unimpeded, it will go on to act to get or bring about the object of its desire. It will have been oriented toward its object by pleasure in a representation *prior to* having a desire for it. Kant calls the determination of the faculty of desire *in us* caused by prior sensible pleasure at a possible object of action "desire in the narrow sense." These are the states we think of as "desires"—for food or sex or sleep. But these desires *for* food, and so on, are not primitive elements of the desire-system; like rational desires or interests, they are determinations *of* a desiderative faculty. About rational desire, we will need to understand how it is possible to determine (the faculty of) desire some other way than via pleasure in an object. Why such a determination, were it possible, necessarily has pleasure as its effect is an a priori claim for Kant: pleasure *is* the toward-relation to possible objects of action, so if the faculty of desire is determined in some way, then there is a toward relation. But *this* toward-relation is not a cause of desire.[7]

Note that in associating pleasure with desire, there is no conflation or confusion about the pleasure that can be the end of action with the pleasure that accompanies activity. What Kant does is move desire away from feeling and closer to activity, and offer a separate state, the toward-relation, which will occur either before or after desire, depending upon whether it or something else determines the faculty of desire to desire.[8] One could think of the

7. So Kant's sympathetic man, by virtue of his sympathetic temperament, is in a toward-relation to what will bring someone relief. He is not caused by his sympathy to act; his sympathy causes a desire to help. In the contrasting morally worthy action, the faculty of desire is determined directly by the recognition of a need-that-morally-ought-to-be-met; only then is the agent in a toward-relation to what will bring relief. As we might say, his recognition of need provides sufficient reason for helping. The effect of this kind of toward-relation shows in the typical affect associated with either being unable to act (frustration and distress), or with a choice not to act (guilt or shame).

8. Given a determination of desire, nothing further, causally, need come between desire and activity, though activity will be directed toward its object under the control of some guiding mechanism, which may include rational deliberation and choice.

toward-relation as a primitive kind of pro-attitude. Among the different kinds of beings able to bring things about through their coordinated systems of representation and activity, we will find different kinds of pro-attitude, individuated by the source of the determination of their faculties of desire.

If a living thing has a faculty of desire just in case it is capable of being the cause of the object of its representations by means of those representations, it then makes sense that active agents with different kinds of representational and practical capacities—of imagination, cognition, and reason—will have differently constituted faculties of desire. The bee's desire for pollen is instinctual, expressed in the activation of its flight and navigation systems. The rational agent's desire to help is, or can be, derived from a moral conception, and expressed in rationally self-governed activity. Developed interests of *both* sensibility and reason can be sufficient in us for action: just knowing it is time for lunch is enough to make me head for the refrigerator.

III

I want to focus now on *our kind* of faculty of desire: a faculty of desire in accordance with concepts, one that *includes* will and choice. In light of the preceding discussion, we should be hesitant to regard will and choice as directed at desire already given. If we get to desire only through a determination of the faculty of desire, and our kind of faculty of desire can be determined by a rational principle, then will and choice may be seen as partly producing desire, not just engaging with it. I'll begin with the passage that introduces will and choice—the one that directly follows the paragraph about concupiscence.

> The faculty of desire in accordance with concepts, insofar as the ground determining it to action lies within itself and not in its object, is called a faculty *to do or refrain from doing as one pleases.* Insofar as it is joined with one's consciousness of the ability to bring about its object by one's action it is called *choice* [*Willkür*]; if it is not joined with this consciousness it is called *wish.* The faculty of desire whose inner determining ground, hence even what pleases it, lies within the subject's reason is called the *will* [*Wille*]. The will is therefore the faculty of desire considered not so much in relation to action (as choice is) but rather in relation to the ground determining choice to action. The will itself, strictly speaking, has no determining

ground; insofar as it can determine choice, it is instead practical reason it-self. (*MS* 6:213)

Here is a rough gloss of this very dense text. Some living things have a faculty of desire in accordance with concepts; some do not. Living things with a faculty of desire in accordance with concepts are further distinguished by whether the ground determining the faculty of desire to action lies in its object or in the faculty of desire itself; they are further distinguished if the determination of desire lies in the subject's reason. (We need not assume that all stages mark real possibilities.)[9] Agents with a reason-determined faculty of desire are thus *self-determining,* or capable of self-determination. Their self-determination has two faces: we see one as the faculty of desire leads to action, the other when we consider the faculty of desire in relation to its determining ground—that is, to the source of desire itself. The former is called choice *(Willkür)* "insofar as it is joined with one's consciousness of the ability to bring about its object by one's action"; the latter is will *(Wille).*

To begin unpacking this, we might start with the role concepts play in generating desire. Concepts are a particular way of representing. Since concepts can be used in the representation of objects, one natural role for them in the determination of the faculty of desire is in the recognition of some object as a "this"—that is, *as* food, or *as* a love object, or *as* someone in pain—something which, represented as "this," triggers the toward-relation that determines the faculty of desire (or just: gives rise to a desire). But the contrast Kant is interested in does not seem to be between agents who represent via concepts and those who don't (concept-users might in principle include some animals; animals can represent things as a "this" or "that");[10]

9. The method of the *Metaphysics of Morals* account of will is constructive. Suppose you were trying to understand human locomotion. You might begin with the most general idea of self-moving things—animate beings whose principle of motion is internal (unlike a rock, which can move, but cannot move itself). Or in trying to get at speech, you began with the idea of an animal for whom conspecific communication was a natural function. Then you would add pieces that were necessary until you got to the capacity. There might or might not be a kind of creature that inhabits (or could inhabit?) every stage. Each piece added is necessary; it yields an analytically distinct stage that may or may not correspond to one that is, or is naturally, possible.

10. Certainly, very small children and many nonhuman animals have informationally rich and specific perceptual representations. The slender textual evidence about animal minds suggests that Kant might accept this point, not the in principle claim. I use the stronger since it seems to me that Kant's presentation of the faculty of desire allows it.

but between those in whom the concepts that figure in the ground determining a faculty of desire to action lie "within itself, and not in its object." Only then do we have "a faculty to do or refrain from doing as one pleases."[11]

Where we put the emphasis matters. If it is a faculty to do or refrain as one *pleases,* why need concepts? The faculty of desire of the lowest sort of living thing leads to action according to its state of pleasure. So perhaps the phrase should be read "to do or refrain as *one* pleases": that is, at one's discretion. The latter emphasis points to a self-conscious agent, not just a system of representation and activity. Where there are merely coordinated systems of representation and activity, some activity may arise through representations generated by aspects or elements of the agent, some by what the agent as a whole is responsive to. A locus of agency that can act or not as *it* pleases has something of its own to add to the generation of activity—a determining ground of activity that does not lie in objects external to the faculty of desire. But an exercise of discretion is not an arbitrary preference; it is for a reason. And if the reason is not in the objects (because it lies within the faculty of desire itself), then the most natural Kantian thought is that it is from reason: principles of practical reason or rational concepts of the good. What else could come from the faculty of desire *of* a rational agent? So, while some animals might and most human agents can come to desire using concepts, only the faculty of desire of a rational agent brings to the generation of activity something of its own, the representation of which produces, or is a condition of, its desire. It is in this way that the faculty of desire of a rational being is self-determining. One's rational nature is a source of what pleases, and it somehow gives one the power to act or refrain from acting *as* one pleases.

The faculty to do or refrain from doing as one pleases is called *choice* when combined with consciousness of the ability to bring about its object by action, and *wish* when it is not.[12] So in the case of rational beings, it fol-

11. *Belieben:* in the sense of at one's will, pleasure, or discretion.

12. Choice and wish are the two modes of the faculty of desire in accordance with concepts, insofar as the ground determining it to action lies within itself. Wish is directed at possible ends (we can construe wish with possible negative as well as positive sense, as in: "I wish I hadn't done that"). It is not clear what the full domain of wish is. Weakly, it can be "I wish I were in Paris now"—having as its object something that pertains to me as a possible effect action, but not something I can bring about (not because it is, e.g., too costly, but because I cannot be in Paris if I am in Los Angeles). But then, what of "I wish *you* hadn't done that"? Or "I wish I were ten years younger." Does wish encompass all that we care about happening but are not in a position to effect by our own action?—for example, that our children arrive safely at

lows that *no* exercise of choice is object-determined. This resembles but is not quite the same as what has come to be called "the incorporation thesis," according to which rational agents act on their desires or inclinations only as they incorporate them into their maxims of action. What I am suggesting here is that *prior* to choice the desiderative state of an agent is *already* partly constructed by an inner and rational determining ground of our kind of faculty of desire. Choice is responsive to reasons already there.

The idea is familiar. When we choose, we do so for a reason; and when we act for a reason we do not merely act on brute desire. We say that something is sweet is a reason to eat it; that someone is in need is a reason to provide help. But in the context of action and choice, our so saying carries *ceteris paribus* clauses that point both to further external conditions (that the sweet thing is not a poison; that the person in need is not already being helped) and to standards of rationality (that the reason fits with my scheme of ends—I am not on a diet, or allergic to chocolate; or that the need in question is one we may permissibly support). Once we are in the space of reasons, there are norms of correctness that apply. And they apply not merely to choice but to wish also—a result that is not uninteresting, given how much closer to one's heart wish can be.

There is also the issue of the voluntary status of an act—the conditions that make choices and actions our own, a matter of *our* discretion. Kant remarks: "We call it a natural cause, or inclination, when, for example, a person is brought by hunger and physical hardship to obey his parents, or to be diligent. Even among animals, these *causa determinantes* operate to possible ends, for taming them, and man is like them in that respect."[13] When hunger and physical hardship—two sources of pain—bring us in this way to obedient and diligent actions, the principle of action is external to the agent's discretion or will. That we can know what we are doing, even why, does not make the action or the choice in such circumstances any more our own; no more does the fact that our "taming" proceeds by way of *our* feelings: what is tamed—that is, brought to respond as another wills—is our

their destination, that flood waters recede before they do more damage, that time heal some wounds. Are these just things I would act to effect if I could? (Can't I wish for something and be unwilling to act for it? Something I want to happen, but not by my agency?) Wish is only possible in a rational being. Clearly there are other modalities of wanting that nonrational animals may have: a sense of loss, yearning, hope. Because wish also involves ends, it sorts with choice.

    13. *Lectures on Ethics*, 27:494.

feelings. For any way of determining the will to count as an agent's acting or not as she pleases, for there to be something that counts as her discretion, there has to be a way to connect choice to a principle that belongs to the agent. We cannot say straightaway what the principle is, only that there must be one.[14]

I used to think that we got to Kant's view of voluntary action through the notion of an elective will. Choice *(Willkür)*, the vehicle of election, as part of a whole, *Wille*, which contains a rational principle that choice can, but need not, use. As part of its free spontaneity, choice could make it its principle to act on the strongest presenting desire, or for the greatest good for the greatest number, or for the moral law. But, as I have already indicated, choice does not seem to be in the business of electing principles, but of using or doing its work by way of them. So we are left with a puzzle about where in the analytic history of a determination of the rational faculty of desire principles of choice or reasons enter.

It seems clear in the passage quoted earlier (*MS* 6:213) that the object of choice is action, not ends or principles. The activity of choice shows in the agent's consciousness of herself as an "acting cause" for the sake of something that is either the effect of action, or is the action itself conceived of as something "to be done." Actions are chosen when we are not compelled by external forces—passions, other persons, and so on—and when the determining ground of action lies within the faculty-of-desire-in-accordance-with-concepts. We can choose to reach some desired state by this means or by that. But our reasons for choosing, our ends, cannot themselves be the object of choice, at least not directly.[15]

So we say: having the end of climbing Mount Whitney, I have reason to buy new boots. Reasons of this kind triangulate between the way the world is and the ends we have. Given my end and a shopping opportunity, other things equal, I will buy boots. But what of *reasons for ends?* Ends, for Kant, are connected to what pleases, and what pleases is a function either of the toward-relation we are in with objects or the toward-relation we have given rational practical interests. But ends are not given by the toward-relation. Given a representation of that stuff as water, if I am thirsty, I am inclined toward it. I may or may not be in a position to do something to get it. Given

---

14. Such "taming" would not affect our freedom, just the self-directedness of our wants and preferences.

15. We can put ourselves in a position where we will come to have reasons we want to have; but the reasons we have, given the maneuver, are not then objects of choice.

a representation of A's need as "to be taken care of," whether or not I am in a position to act, I will want to. In neither case do I yet have an end.

In sensible beings with needs and interests, the faculty of desire secures the transition from representation to action. It can do this via nonrational systems (providing efficient causes of action) or via rational concepts that govern choice of action for a goal judged to be good (a final cause). When rational concepts secure the transition from representation to action, they do so by casting a possible object of action as an end. The difference is in the representation of the object—not merely as pleasing, but *as good*. How Kant gets to this is the next thing to consider.

IV

If a rational being can represent its own agency to itself, it can ask "What shall I do?" And if the structure of its faculty of desire gives it even limited power to constrain its activity to wait on an answer, and then to act in conformity with the answer it gives, this would be one way of understanding what it means to have the capacity to act or not as one pleases. We associate this capacity of choice with Kant's "negative idea of freedom": the freedom from compulsion or constraint by external, chiefly sensible, causes. We are in this sense free even if we take direction from authority, or decide to act on our strongest presenting desire.[16] We encounter this sense of freedom in any and every deliberative engagement. However, Kant's contention, here and elsewhere, is that the negative idea of freedom cannot account for freedom of choice or will: something positive is necessary as its condition. A faculty-of-desire-according-to-concepts cannot be self-determining with respect to choice if it is not also self-determining with respect to reasons (or ends)—that is, what pleases—*and*, Kant holds, it can only be self-determining with respect to reasons if its determining ground is *in reason*.

Kant's startling claim is that the ground in question is, more specifically, the moral law. That is, if there were no moral law, there could not be free choice at all. There are two ways to take this. One is that given the moral law as its metaphysical condition, choice is both possible and unconstrained; the other is that the exercise of choice, *any* choice, depends in some way on the moral law as *its* determining ground (or final end). I think the latter is

16. It is a power of choice "so long as the opposite of my desire is still in my control"; Immanuel Kant, *Lectures on Metaphysics*, trans. and ed. Karl Ameriks and Steve Navagon (Cambridge: Cambridge University Press, 1997), 28:677. Note that it is the opposite of desire that must remain in my control, not any action.

Kant's view; indeed, that it has to be. The harder task is to show that it makes some sense. In any case, here is what Kant says:

> That choice which can be determined by *pure reason* is called free choice. That which can be determined only by *inclination* (sensible impulse, *stimulus*) would be animal choice *(arbitrium brutum)*. Human choice, however, is a choice that can indeed be *affected* but not *determined* by impulses, and is therefore of itself (apart from an acquired proficiency of reason) not pure but can still be determined to actions by pure will. *Freedom* of choice is this independence from being *determined* by sensible impulses; this is the negative concept of freedom. The positive concept of freedom is that of the ability of pure reason to be of itself practical. But this is not possible except by the subjection of the maxim of every action to the condition its qualifying as universal law. (*MS* 6:213–214)[17]

The most obvious reason to balk at this is the implausibility of having morality as the basis or final end of all action and choice. But morality and the moral law are not the same thing, so we should wait to see what the claim amounts to before digging in. The other worry is that if human choice is only free when maxims of action are subjected to the condition of "qualifying as universal law," contramoral choice is unfree. Some have tried to save the positive idea of freedom by arguing that "qualifying as universal law" is not a moral criterion, but only the reflective requirement of the generality of reasons, necessary for something to count as a proper action at all.[18] This is partly right; but it is wrong about the point of the positive requirement, and, more curiously, about Kant's understanding of moral error.

So why does Kant deny the possibility of free choice without the strong condition of the positive idea of freedom? The contrary possibility amounts

---

17. Note two things. Neither here nor in the *Groundwork* does Kant talk about negative freedom. There is no such property of the will; there is only a negative *concept* of the will's freedom—a concept "unfruitful for insight into its essence" (Immanuel Kant, *Groundwork of the Metaphysics of Morals* (1785), in *Practical Philosophy,* trans. and ed. Mary J. Gregor (Cambridge: Cambridge University Press, 1996), 4:446). Second, "animal choice" is not the same as human choice minus the practicality of pure reason. "Choice" names that aspect of a faculty of desire in its relation to action; in the case of animals, this relation is by way of efficient causality between systems of representation and activity (whether or not the animal can make use of concepts); in the case of human beings, the determining ground of choice lies within the faculty-of-desire-according-to-concepts.

18. I am thinking here of Christine Korsgaard's position in *Sources of Normativity* (Cambridge: Cambridge University Press, 1996).

to the confinement of rational action and choice to the principle of happiness, broadly understood, and the end of happiness, though it depends on reason, is not sufficient to support freedom.

The argument goes this way.[19] Our consciousness of ourselves as a locus of activity allows us to take aspects of ourselves as objects of desire or aversion. Given our ability to understand causal connections and to imagine things otherwise, we come to have desires directed at our desires, and construct an idea of our happiness as a scheme of preferences. We also can figure out and then act on practical principles for maximizing their satisfaction. But, Kant claims, neither ability gives us freedom of choice or will. This is because as an object of desire, the idea of happiness supports no more than a toward-relation to a subset of our preferences. It is a more complex toward-relation than, say, being moved by the idea of the taste of an apple, but in both cases the faculty of desire is dependent on a represented object that we find pleasing. Nonmoral principles of satisfaction-maximization provide sound strategies, but they can give no *reason* for acting if our simple and complex desires do not.

It is true that in developing our idea of happiness, we become managers of our desires: we learn to encourage, redirect, or even suppress desires as fits our emerging scheme of what we overall want. We will likely discover that we need to coordinate what we do for our happiness with what others do for theirs. It would be surprising if there were not convergence between principles of coordination that arise among relative equals and principles of moral obligation. But the one can't stand in for the other, Kant claims, because morality does, and happiness does not get us beyond a complex toward-relation *to* a *reason* for action. I don't mean that we cannot figure out *why* we desire happiness—why, that is, the idea of a coherent scheme of ends the overall satisfaction of which we judge possible is pleasing; rather, the claim is that unless a rational agent comes to choice and action by way of a representation that is different in kind from mere desire or preference—a representation that could possibly be of something *as objectively good*—she remains determined by sensible impulses, however fancy they may be.[20] Kant remarks that what animals cannot do is "make the representation of a

19. Here I follow in a loose fashion the argument of the first six sections of Book One, Chapter I of the *Critique of Practical Reason*.

20. Both elective principles and empirical concepts of the good—things that are good for you, or good for doing this or that—are, like objects of sensibility, external to the will.

thing that they desire, much less of an end, why they want or do not want something."[21] It is this "why" that is at issue in the claimed unintelligibility of any free-standing idea of negative freedom.

In thinking about this, we might equally well ask where *value* or good enters in the history of rational action. When the system of desire of a lower organism is working as it is supposed to, it will desire what is functionally good for it. But this sort of value plays no role in the operation of the system of desire: it cannot guide or regulate its activity; the system works or not. Preferences are action-guiding: they provide a functional notion of *valuing:* supporting principles or goals around which an agent purposefully organizes her action and projects so that she has a sense of accomplishment when she is successful—she has done something that matters to her—disappointment if she fails. But while preferences can express what an agent values, they have no internal connection to what is *of value,* no matter how ramified they are. There is something missing from the self-direction the agent attributes to herself.

What can be misleading is that the capacity for negotiating value, that is, for organizing one's activity with respect to a final end, is exercised when we act from higher-order preferences. This general capacity is identified in the *Groundwork* as a rational agent's ability "to act in accordance with the representation of laws . . . [or] . . . in accordance with principles."[22] It is in virtue of this capacity that an agent has a will. And having this capacity, she can act in accordance with *all sorts of* principles. The issue about value that lives between the negative and positive concepts of freedom can then be put this way: is the capacity to act in accordance with principles fully independent of the nature or content of principles, or is it a capacity whose exercise depends on some good-related principle or law that nonetheless leaves us able to act on other principles? If the role of the rational faculty of desire is to bring us from whatever sources of desire there are to the possibility of choice, the view has to be the second. Some concept of value has to play a role to translate (Kant would say "synthesize") the material of desire into a form that can be addressed by judgment and deliberation, and so choice. The difficulty is not that choice must negotiate heterogeneous possibilities; what I have been arguing on Kant's behalf is that the raw stuff of desire cannot even make an appearance as part of the subject-matter of deliberation (or on, what I elsewhere call, an agent's deliberative field).

---

21. *Lectures on Metaphysics,* 28:589.

22. Immanuel Kant, *Groundwork of the Metaphysics of Morals* (1785), in *Practical Philosophy,* trans. and ed. Mary J. Gregor (Cambridge: Cambridge University Press, 1996), 4:412.

Interestingly, the same point can be made in developmental terms. An infant's first urges have no object—they are not desires *for* anything; they are states of feeling that can be affected by what they meet. States that "cathect" with an object become individuated by it—they become desires for that thing (or later, for that kind of thing).[23] But there is yet nothing for choice to work on, nothing to deliberate about; there are just facts of need or desire. These facts are like other facts—a wall, parental love, a stop sign— things that, engaged with one way or another, will have a subjective effect. For there to be deliberation and choice, we require additional conceptualization, not just as a this or a that, but in terms that render states and objects deliberatively salient. A wall is an obstacle or a potential climbing adventure; parental love, the balm that heals or a suffocating embrace; a stop sign, an inconvenience or a signal of danger. Only if one already knows that they are one or the other, or both, can one deliberate and choose. And when one chooses, the idea is to get something right.

So for there to be rational action, there has to be a synthesis of the stuff of desire to bring it under concepts, and something must determine the concepts that direct the synthesis so that correct deliberation and choice are possible. It is a bit like doing taxes. There is the file of receipts and canceled checks, then the categories one sorts them into as determined by the rules one will later use to figure out what one owes or can get away with not paying. Temporally one starts with the clutter; formally, the first thing is the rule or principle.

Now for the possibility of *free* action, it is not enough to say that deliberation and choice depend on concepts to synthesize the manifold of feeling; the concepts must also be rational concepts. Specifically, Kant claims, every determination of free choice depends on reason's own principle—the moral law. Of course, even if we can now understand *why* Kant might think there has to be such a principle, we still need to see *how* the moral law might possibly play this role. Here is how I think Kant thinks it works.[24]

If the will is the capacity of a rational agent to be moved to action by her representation of reasons or principles, it is a power of a certain sort. Every power is constituted by a law, or inner principle, that is responsible for producing its characteristic effects. So among the laws we can represent to our-

23. Some states are keyed to pick up some objects, and will do so if the environment is normal. The configuration of light and dark that maps the features of the human face for a newborn; the shape of nipple and breast; etc. Other states are less coded, and often less tractable. Adults are familiar with diffuse anxiety states that resist object-interpretation.

24. What follows offers a somewhat sharper version of an idea I sketched in Chapter 7.

selves is the law constitutive of the will's own power. Let us assume, for the sake of argument, that the law of the power that is the will is, or is equivalent to, the moral law.[25] Now for a rational agent to will something she must have a conception of herself as willing (e.g., of herself as an acting cause for her ends). Then, in willing an action—any action—an agent is moved by a perceived connection of the action to her representation of herself willing an end, which is to say, according to a representation of the will's constitutive principle (as a power to produce effects). If the principle constitutive of the will's own activity were the moral law, then *it* would be what we (always and necessarily) represent to ourselves in and as a condition of rational choice. When we represent it accurately, we in fact see the moral law as the ultimate justificatory or good-constituting principle of our action. When we *mis*represent it, as we may when nonrational influences affect or interfere with our representation of the will's own law (as they can our representation of any law), then we may or may not act permissibly, but our willing will not exhibit the form of the law. Still, whether or not an agent's specific volition is in conformity with the moral law (whether it accurately represents it), the moral law always is the condition of a possible willing, and so is, in that sense, its principle. We thus explain how it can both be the case that the will *is* practical reason and our willings not necessarily be good—they do not necessarily follow reason's principle.

This is still not to say that the moral law does or can play this role—that it could be the principle of the will's distinctive causal power—only that Kant thinks it does. Showing this is a large project, and for another occasion. What we can do here is provide some elaboration of the idea of the will as a power that has a norm as its law or principle. Its usefulness in thinking about both will and moral action is at least some evidence that the idea is on the right track.

V

Let us go back to the general idea that a rational agent acts by way of a representation of a law or principle. Suppose I would fire an arrow at a distant target. However I think of it, my activity falls under the laws of gravity: if the target is distant, I will not succeed unless I aim high. If I am aware of the

25. Recall that assuming just this much is consistent with the moral law being the metaphysical condition of fully unconstrained choice.

laws governing this activity, and have the end of hitting the target, then I consciously make the law that anyway governs what I am doing my principle, and use it to calibrate my release-point. When I act well, I represent a law that informs a standard of correctness for my action, given my end. The essential difference in the claim about willing is that the law in question is the law of the will's own power.

One exhibits freedom of the will in having a practically effective conception of oneself as acting for reasons: one has some consideration in mind that one judges to provide justification for what one would do, whether or not one is correct that it does provide justification. But, I take Kant to argue, this is only because there *are* reasons or objective standards of justification for action that one's mistaken (or correct) judgment purports to represent. If our sense of acting freely, which seems only to require the negative concept of freedom, is to be more than an illusion, it depends on our power to act for reasons; if there are no reasons, no objective standards, then there is no such power, and we are not free.

Consider on just this point the striking conclusion of a discussion about freedom of choice. In rejecting the claim that a person can come to know freedom from his experience of being "able to choose in opposition to his (law-giving) reason," Kant says: "Only freedom in relation to the internal lawgiving of reason is a *capacity*[26] [*Vermögen*]; the possibility of deviating from it is an *incapacity* [*Unvermögen*]" (MS 6:227).[27] This is an idea worth exploring.

26. Gregor translates *Vermögen* as "ability"; it is variously Kant's term for power and sometimes for a faculty. I take "capacity" to be more fundamental than "ability" (capacities are the conditions of abilities) and therefore in this context the more apt term. But the governing concept is about powers.

27. Here is the full text: "But we can see indeed that, although experience shows that the human being as a *sensible being* is able to choose in opposition to *as well as* in conformity with the law, his freedom as an *intelligible being* cannot be defined by this, since appearances cannot make any supersensible object (such as free choice [*Willkür*]) understandable. We can also see that freedom can never be located in a rational subject's being able to choose in opposition to his (lawgiving) reason, even though experience proves often enough that this happens (though we still cannot comprehend how this is possible). —For it is one thing to accept a proposition (on the basis of experience) and another to make in the *expository principle* (of the concept of free choice [*Willkür*]) and the universal principle for distinguishing it (from *arbitrio bruto s. servo*); for the first does not maintain that the feature belongs *necessarily* to the concept, but the second requires this. —Only freedom in relation to the internal lawgiving of reason is really an ability [*Vermögen*]; the possibility of deviating from it is an inability

Now, not every absence of a capacity is an incapacity. An incapacity is not just a lack of ability to do something. Our lacking the capacity and the ability to leap tall buildings at a single bound is not an incapacity. Absence of song in a bird is an incapacity only if what it *is* doing—trying to mate—is a failure that cannot be described without reference to song.[28] In the case of the will, there is something we *are* able to do: choose contrary to the "internal lawgiving of reason"; it is an *incapacity* only if it can be shown to be a deviant or defective mode of an ability we have in virtue of a conceptually prior capacity. And this is just what Kant thinks. Looking at the will this way directly eliminates the permissive interpretation, according to which we have a general power to act according to a conception of law or principle that allows us to act for the moral law *or* against it: a power to pick our rule. We then do not need a separate argument to show that in acting against the moral law we make a mistake or misuse our power.[29] On the strict reading, in virtue of the capacity or *power* to do the right thing we have the *ability* to do wrong, so wrongful action is directly a misuse of the power (an act of a free will, though not an expression of freedom in action).

But this may seem too quick. Suppose I use a fancy hand-tool as a doorstop. In the way that I use it, it seems better to say that I ignore its powers than that I misuse it—the tool's powers are irrelevant to my use. So not every anomalous use of a power implies misuse. Sometimes the real capacities of things are used counter to their natural or designed purpose and for something else. Consider the separation of pleasure from the reproductive use of our sexual powers; the use of a peach-basket to play a new kind of

[*Un-vermögen*]. How can the former be defined by the latter? It would be a definition that added to the practical concept the *exercise* of it, as this is taught by experience, a *hybrid definition* . . . that puts the concept in a false light" (*MS* 6:226–227) (unless otherwise indicated, "choice" in this passage is not *Willkür* but *das Vermögen der Wahl*).

28. In a species, one can imagine a mating ritual that is punctuated with intervals for a performance that is never forthcoming. Perhaps here we would speak of the loss of a capacity. Straight-ahead empirical investigation may be inadequate to say whether an absence or lack is an incapacity. One might need to know some history of a species, or have a comparison species of the right sort at hand to see which of its actions are ineffectual tryings, failed attempts, or just unhappy omissions. Biological cases are difficult since species adapt to changes, and old "incapacities" can come to be or be part of new powers.

29. As best as I can tell, this is Henry Allison's interpretation. It is also implicit in Christine Korsgaard's revisionary Kantianism. See Henry Allison, *Kant's Theory of Freedom* (Cambridge: Cambridge University Press, 1990); Korsgaard, *The Sources of Normativity*.

ball game. Many artifacts and powers fit variously into our intentions; sometimes subsystems are retooled for the emerging needs of the whole. They are also not because of that cases of misuse or incapacity.

Closer to the kind of *Vermögen* that Kant could have in mind are what we might call "norm-constituted powers." As a teacher, I have the power to assign grades. More precisely, I have the power to assign grades according to judgments of merit. (A baseball umpire's power is to call balls and strikes based on judgments about the location of pitches in the strike zone.) We know what the power is because it is granted in specific terms. Having this power, I can misuse it. But compare my putting grades down according to some aesthetic feel for the pattern of As, Bs, and Cs on the grade sheet and assigning grades according to favoritism or bribes. It's not clear that the former is a use of the power at all, whereas the latter clearly is a use that is a misuse. (Or compare an umpire who calls the game according to some astrological algorithm with one who takes money to fix a game.) The power that I have as a teacher is not the power to assign grades by merit *or* by personal preference, though having the power to assign grades by merit I am able to assign them by preference. In misusing the power in this way, I exercise it. I may think I have the power to do whichever I want, but I am mistaken—what I then exhibit is an incapacity, an *Unvermögen*.[30]

So if the will as a faculty-of-desire-in-accordance-with-concepts is this kind of power to act and refrain from acting as we please, then to explain the power, there must be a principle of choice—of value—internal to the faculty that constitutes it. For if not, the principle of the will that constituted its power would not provide a principle of justification for choice, and such a will would be heteronomous, not free. But if the principle of value in question is constitutive of the power of choice, it is involved in all willed action: that is, all rational action necessarily depends on a single principle of choice.[31]

30. Note a further Kantian point: we cannot tell what powers someone has merely from observing what she does or knowing what powers she thinks she has. Authorizing someone to act on my behalf, I give him certain powers. I thereby (often) put him in a position to abuse them. We might think of the power as an ability plus a set of permissions. If I loan my car to you, I give you the ability and the permission to drive it. You do not thereby have the power to loan it to someone else, though you are able to do that.

31. Lest one think this is just too much to take on, consider the obvious, less Kantian alternative to the norm-constituted view: the will as a wholly executive faculty, making deci-

Note that in saying this, no claim is being made that all values, or all valid claims of value, reduce to a single kind of value. Kant's argument is about the metaphysics of value, not about what is of value. The single principle of value defines a power: the capacity to act for reasons. Although the kinds of value may be many, the principle of a power has to be one.[32]

As a heuristic, consider another, slightly exaggerated, norm-constituted power whose principles function somewhat like the moral law. The principles of accountancy define a power that enables accountants to evaluate the financial condition of persons and corporations. Although the power can be used to defraud, the power does not stand equally toward assessing *and* defrauding. One is a straightforward exercise; the other a misuse that hides its intentions behind a deceptive appearance of straightforward exercise. Fraud thus depends on the standards of correctness. (One should begin to see the shape of the categorical imperative procedure in this.) As a standard of correctness in bookkeeping, the principles of accountancy are principles of value. They set an end that accountants ought to realize in their assess-

sions and setting the agent to action (perhaps also belief) on the basis of reasons it receives either from an independent faculty of intuition or from judgment about the reasons that bear. The will then either is a bridge from judgment to intention, or it mobilizes our forces to carry out intention (if we think that intention is already implicated in the last step of practical deliberation). We do use "weakness of will" to describe failures to act on our judgment of what is best, and "strong-willed" as a term of criticism (sometimes admiration) when we do not allow countervailing reasons to affect an already set course of action. Together they suggest a faculty that ought to be but isn't always or necessarily responsive to the balance of reasons, both in the formation of an intention and in support of a continuing course or plan of action. It seems to me that we have here an account of will in a theory of coming to act that either contains one faculty too many or one too few. If one is drawn to the thought that what it is to be a creature capable of responding to considerations as reasons is to be moved by judgment to action or belief, as the case may be, then the will looks as though it is adding something extra (if it is not just the generic name of being so moved). This is the one too many. If, on the other hand, one thinks that there has to be an extra step—there is judgment, whose verdict is about the balance of reasons, and then there is a separate deciding or executive faculty that initiates (and perhaps controls) action—then unless the will is just a passive mechanism that receives judgment and executes it (takes orders, as it were), there needs to be something else that establishes the will's relation to reasons judgments. So here we have one too few.

32. It really is a principle of *value* because it gives the will its formal object. Think of the analogous claim we might make about belief: that a principle of the norm-constituted power of belief-formation gives belief its formal object, truth.

ments. One can engage in accountancy or not; but if one does, one has the end of doing it correctly: one does not elect it. Of course, some accountants serve other ends as well.

To describe the will as a norm-constituted power, we can draw on this form. It will be a power defined by a principle; the principle—a principle of correctness (and so of value) for a kind of activity—giving an end of pursuing activity of that kind according to its standard.[33] The power of the will, of our kind of faculty of desire—enables actions for reasons. This is not merely action accompanied by the thought of justification, but action from reasons that are beholden to a standard of correctness for reasons. The principle thus gives rational agents the end of pursuing their activity according to the standard of good reasons, and warrants understanding the activity of others in the same normative light.[34] But unlike accountancy, which one can engage in or not, the employment in choice and action of the power of the rational will is not up to us. Whenever we act we are subject to the standard of correctness in willing: it is our end if anything is. Since the principle that is the standard of correctness in willing is constitutive of the will's power, it cannot be elected (or rejected), though it bears on the election of other ends and the choice of action for ends as the condition of their possibility. In short: the will as a power to act freely gives rational agents the end of conforming their activity to the norm of free willing.[35]

Now the end of rational willing as such has to be a formal end, since the will itself has no "material," no object of interest beyond itself. On the other hand, since the principle of the will has no condition to limit it, its end is always in play. As an end that is not an end in the to-be-produced sense (as a state of affairs that could be the effect of action), it can serve as a limiting condition on action or as a standard for elective ends. Limiting conditions are eliminative, directing agents not to act in ways that conflict with them. Standards of end-election direct agents to objects of concern—giving them positive reasons to do something. Though a formal end does not provide

33. In the case of the will the principle is in addition a law of rational nature's causality.

34. One acknowledges this whenever one asks for a justification for action.

35. The argument for this is the argument for autonomy. If the rational will does not have an end given by its inner principle, then its ends would be given in some other way—by nature, or by some other principle (e.g., the principle of happiness). Such a will would be subject to external determination, and not free.

the material content of ends, it can require that we conceive of our material ends in its terms, and choose them for its reasons.[36]

Drawing on some Kantian moral theory, we should suppose that the formal end in question has to be rational nature as an end-in-itself. It functions as a limiting condition on all of an agent's willings—agents are to refrain from acting on any maxims that fail to be consistent with rational nature as an end-in-itself[37]—and so in that sense it is always one's end whatever else one does or aims to do. But we are also looking for a positive standard for elective ends that is not a directive to adopt a to-be-produced end. Consider the difference between accepting as a condition on my acting for an end that its pursuit will not harm you, and having your interests be part of what I attend to in determining and pursuing my ends. Your interests figure in both, but not in the same way. Rational nature as an end-in-itself constrains end-adoption in this second way, requiring that we make concern for the happiness of others and our own rational and moral well-being a standard for end-adoption for all our ends. In giving us these obligatory ends, we are directed to connect the value to us of our ordinary ends with the value of (our own and others') rational nature as an end-in-itself. It is when our own and others' happiness are understood in relation to the development and health of rational agency that they are properly sources of reasons. This doesn't mean that in acting for our happiness we act for morality or the good of rational nature. Rather we understand something about why happiness matters beyond the fact that we desire it (not everything we desire is, after all, something we have reason to have). Further, in seeing the value of our own happiness in terms other than those of our own desire, we make use of a reason that is equally a reason to be attentive to the happiness of others.

Working out how obligatory ends shape our other ends, and what imperfect duties they support, is the topic of Chapter 11. Here, I would briefly note three things. If this is the way the formal end affects our material ends, it is not directing us to discrete, independent goals; the formal end does not moralize everything it touches; nor does it force us to value the multiplicity

36. Not every material end can be so conceived; when not, we may not act for it. One might think of this as a permissibility condition for ends.

37. In terms closer to the formula of universal law we might say that a maxim is to be rejected whose principle could not be the principle of a rational will: namely, when it has the form of an *Unvermögen*: the form of willing both a principle of correctness *and* its misuse.

of things we care about only in moral terms. The standard of correctness for willing directs us to care about and care for the dignity and rational well-being of persons as we go about our business with and among them. If this is right, the seemingly implausible requirement that there be one end, one principle, for all of our choices and willings may not be so implausible after all. It is just the requirement that we act morally when we act.

—11—

Obligatory Ends

In this and the next chapter I aim to offer something like a brief in support
of reinstating positive duties to a central place in moral theory, and certainly in Kantian moral theory.[1] General positive duties—duties to relieve
suffering and to meet need, duties of self-development, perhaps duties to
promote justice—are not always welcome in modern moral theories. (This
is in contrast to other, more limited, positive duties: tightly restricted requirements; duties that arise from voluntary and special obligations; duties
associated with certain roles and offices.) The general duties have infelici-
tous features. They tend to involve open-ended requirements to promote
some good. Then, depending on the theory of value that generates them, or
the theory of the person with which they must cohere, they are either very
demanding or they allow the agent extensive discretion in satisfying them.
It is hard to be friendly to a moral category that allows us either great freedom in deciding when and how to act or virtually no freedom at all.

Consider the positive duty to help the needy (the starving, the homeless . . .). There is a value—something that would be good to bring about—
and it is incumbent on those who can to act for that end. Since there is a
great deal of need, and much that can be done, it is hard to see how in our
present circumstances we could be justified in doing less than quite a lot.
Over against this we put our nice lives and families, the pleasures of a rich
culture, and want to say that these give us reasons not to have to do very
much to end hunger, AIDS, illiteracy. Striking a balance this way is not credible. A more reasonable thought is that the problem arises from the way we

1. Versions of these two chapters were delivered as Whitehead Lectures at Harvard University in May 2003.

are looking at the issues: once the open-ended positive duty to help is on the table, the difficulty is inevitable. Perhaps, then, we should not think in terms of general positive duties. It does not follow that we will be indifferent to hunger, AIDS, and the like; but if, for example, these are needs that must be met as a matter of justice, or there is a restricted duty of beneficence (delimited by the idea of a fair share), then we can negotiate such moral matters with fewer theoretical and practical discomforts.

My reason for wanting to look again at the idea of positive duties does not arise from skepticism about the viability of such solutions, though I do think they miss something (I will say more about this later). I am interested in positive duties as they belong to an element of moral requirement that applies first of all to *ends,* and only secondarily to actions. Now some might hold that the idea of morality dictating ends—what we are to care about—is implausible on its face. They see the requirements of morality setting constraints on what we may do (or may not omit) for the sake of what we care about. (And although we should care about morality—have "acting morally" as an end—it cannot be a moral requirement that we do so.) To the contrary, I think there are many good reasons to hold that morality *is* directed at ends; the ones I want to focus on make the connection by way of principles of rational willing. The positive duties that follow are end-supported rather than value-directed; and, as I will argue, because this does not require that we maximize or even promote anything, they avoid the in-felicities associated with general positive duties.

The plan is to develop this idea along two fronts. In this chapter I will trace out an idea of obligatory ends that is introduced in the second part of Kant's *Metaphysics of Morals* as a condition of free, rational action. In a somewhat surprising way, the positive duties obligatory ends generate—especially the duties to the self—are needed to complete an account of individual rational agency. In Chapter 12 I will be looking at how this set of ends and duties provides us with essential deliberative resources to be morally responsive to the complex, and historically specific social world in which we have to act. Along the way, I will touch on a set of related topics that obligatory ends illuminate: the idea of rational ends; a deliberative basis for the unity of persons; the effects of social institutions and the history of immoralities on individual obligation; something about the impartiality that morality requires of us; and last, an idea of moral improvisation—that there are places in impartial moral space where moral creativity is both needed and allowed. Overall, obligatory ends make possible a holism of practical reason that enables morality to function seamlessly in everyday life. At the same time, they support positive duties that make us attentive to the dangers of that seamlessness—complacency, injustice—and responsible for resisting those forms of wrongdoing that result.

Although the view of obligatory ends and positive duties I offer emerges from an interpretation of Kant's moral theory, it is my hope that by the time we are done, their value will be obvious on its own, independent of this source. And to the extent that Kant-inspired intuitions are often the ones most resistant to the idea of positive duties, revealing this face of Kantian moral theory should help in recalibrating them.

Kant argues that unless there are obligatory ends there are no free actions.[2] He also holds that there are only two obligatory ends: one's own (rational) perfection and the happiness of others, each of which is a source of positive duties. It follows that the two ends must somehow be ends of *all* rational action.[3] To see how one might arrive at this view, we will begin with a set of somewhat technical arguments about the role of the will in free action and choice. They will set the stage for a more wide-ranging discussion of the obligatory ends and their duties.

I

From a contemporary perspective, probably the most important claim that Kant makes is that *value*, and not just valu*ing*, is a condition of free rational action, and so of morality. It is a variant of the *Euthyphro* argument. Valuing is an attitude that may be responsive to facts about the agent, to facts about objects, or to some standard of value that identifies an object as appropriate to treat in a special way. Valuing, which need be no more than a fancy form of pro-attitude, requires some rational abilities, but not full-blown rational agency. Value is, by contrast, a standard of correctness for a sphere of activity. If there are rational standards for action—a way or ways it is correct to act—there is value. The Kantian thesis of volitional autonomy is that there is a general standard of correctness for action derived from (or representing) the constitutive principle of the power of rational

2. Immanuel Kant, *Metaphysics of Morals* (1797), in *Practical Philosophy,* trans. and ed. Mary J. Gregor (Cambridge: Cambridge University Press, 1996), 6:385.

3. In Chapter 9 I describe the two ends as "the complete material specification of rational nature as an end in itself for human rational agents." Part of my purpose in this chapter is to more fully understand how that could be so.

action itself—that is, the will. If this were not the case, the will would stand
in some to-be-determined relation to a standard or standards external to
it—standards not necessary to its function as a rational will—satisfaction
of which would determine when its willings were correct (even rational).
And this, Kant claims, is not possible, if the will is free. Since a free will is
neither a merely executive nor a fully elective power, if it does not in some
sense supply its own standards for action and choice, then it is not a rational
will—that is, a power to affect the world according to reason.

The most unsettling claim that Kant makes about the general standard of
correctness for action is that it is supplied by the moral law as the constitutive principle of the rational will—of free choice. It is unsettling both because it is hard to understand how *that* principle could be a necessary part
or condition of willing generally, and hard to accept that the principle of
morality is necessary for freedom of choice—hard if for no other reason
than the difficulty in then explaining "bad" choices. The problem is that
Kant's view is not just that the moral law is somehow the metaphysical condition of freedom of the will, making free choice both possible and unconstrained. Rather, the full strangeness of the view is that the exercise of even
bad choice depends in some way on the moral law as *its* determining ground.

One might have thought that to have a rational will is to have a will able
to come to action for reasons, not causes, that is, able to act in accordance
with principles: *all sorts* of principles. This is true, but misleading. There
are, in effect, two options: either the capacity to act in accordance with principles is fully independent of the content of the principles, or it is a capacity whose exercise depends on some principle that makes us able to act on
other principles, even defective ones.[4] Kant affirms the second option, and
it commits him to two things: first, free choice is rational choice, and
rational choice is only possible if there are objective reasons—correct
standards for choosing; and second, the thesis of volitional autonomy,
according to which correct standards for action have to be (or be derived
from) the principle of the power of the rational will itself. *And,* since choice
of action is with respect to ends, free choice requires standards of correctness for ends.

Now the idea of a power whose constitutive principle makes possible
both its correct and its incorrect employment is actually not so strange.

---

4. In Kant's terms, this is the question whether there can be a negative idea of freedom
without a positive one.

There is a class of familiar powers that we have that work this way: I call them "norm-constituted powers." I discuss this notion at some length in Chapter 10 and argue there for interpreting the rational will as such a power. Here I will do no more than briefly sketch the way powers of this sort work, and what the rational will would be like if it were one.

In the ordinary cases, persons come to have norm-constituted powers by inhabiting a social role. Some social roles give powers that are permissions (to inspect, investigate, direct); other roles confer powers that are partly constituted by a norm that sets a rule or standard of correct performance. Examples of the latter are teachers who assign grades, referees of games, tax assessors who determine property values. Only someone in the role can exercise the power;[5] and those in the role not only can, but should, in virtue of what the role is, act according to its standards (as set by law, or rule books, or common practices). The standards are guides for judging (and then acting) in accordance with principles of value, in the sense that they are connected to ends for the agent to realize in role-guided activity.[6] It is a further feature of such roles that in conveying the power to act according to a standard, they also give the agent an ability to subvert it. An agent in the role can let her judgment be affected by bribes, whims, or astrological signs, though (usually) not openly. This is not to say that the power is neutral with respect to which kind of thing is done: one is a use, the other a misuse of the power. The power that I have as a teacher is not the power to assign grades by merit *or* by personal preference, though having the power to assign grades by merit I am able to assign them by preference. But to misuse the power in this way, I must exercise it.

It is fairly straightforward to apply this model to the rational will. If the rational will is a norm-constituted power, it is a power defined by a principle, a principle of correctness (and so of value) for a kind of activity, that gives rational agents the end of pursuing that kind of activity according to its standard. Now add this to the way we also think of the power of the will: as enabling actions for reasons. This is not just action accompanied by thoughts of justification, but action that *comes from* judgments about reasons that are beholden to a standard of correctness. If the will itself is a

5. Others can pretend or imitate, though they are not for that free of the standards (it must at least appear that they follow them, if their pretense is to be successful), even if their reasons for adhering to them are not the same.

6. Ends that may or may not be distinct from the instantiated standards.

norm-constituted power, the standard that the principle of the will's power introduces is a standard for reasons for action. We, who have wills, then have the end of acting for good reasons. But unlike teaching or refereeing, which one can engage in or not, the employment in choice and action of the power of the rational will is not up to us. *Whenever* we act purposively, we are subject to the standard of correctness in willing. Insofar as the principle that is the standard of correctness in willing is constitutive of the will's power, it is not a principle that is to be elected (or refused), though it bears on the election of all ends and on the choice of actions for ends as the condition of their possibility. Even bad choices must then be explained in terms that it sets.

Here is a more canonically Kantian way of describing the same idea. The will is a faculty of desire, a way of bringing things about, whose principle of choice-determination is rational: an internal standard of goodness for choice (and so action) for rational beings of our kind (living, finite, etc.). The will attends to, but is not determined to action by, natural and acquired desires or interests. The principle of the will as a rational cause determines choice of action in two related ways: as a norm for what we ought to do, and as the principle that enables us to choose and do what we ought—for its own sake. This power of choice and decision is free in the double senses of *not* being determined by external (alien causes) and of being determined by the principle of its own nature—a principle of value. There is no independent good to which the will is responsive.[7] Kant refers to this as the "Paradox of Method":[8] a rational will acts for the good, but the good is not prior to the moral law, and the moral law is the constitutive principle of (all) rational willing (the principle of the will's causal power).

We make bad choices because we are not perfectly rational. The imperfection of our rational nature is not, however, about deficiencies of knowledge or attention or self-mastery. Our willing is imperfectly rational because the way the principle of the will determines choice is by means of our representation of that principle, and our representations can be *mis*representations: partial, incomplete, historically limited, even idiosyncratic. Thus, although we may describe the power of the will as a responsiveness to the good (choice determined by the will's constitutive principle), the same

---

7. This is *not* to say that there is nothing independent of the will to which it is responsive; if the principle of the will gives guidance for decision and action, it does so in light of some will-independent (subject)-matter.

8. Immanuel Kant, *Critique of Practical Reason,* (1788), in *Practical Philosophy,* trans. and ed. Mary J. Gregor (Cambridge: Cambridge University Press, 1996), 5:63.

power is exercised when an agent acts well or badly, so long as she takes herself to have reason to act as she does.[9]

II

Not surprisingly, having given elements of a philosophical or metaphysical account of rational willing, the challenge is to say something substantive about what the will's principle is. We have it that the will is a norm-constituted power and a principle or law of rational causality. The first normative element of a rational principle of any sort is universality: a formal standard. We can think of it as a variant of the generality of reasons condition, a defeasible standard in the sense that departures from strict universality are allowed if the domain is properly narrowed, so that the principle is exceptionless where it applies. Kant's version of the requirement is, roughly, that an agent's principle, or maxim, is not valid if a condition of its success as a principle of action is that it not be one (similarly situated) others act on. This picks out *moral* failures in Kantian ethics because violations of that standard fail to respect the rational power they depend on—that is, they are subversive misuses of the power of the will in the sense that *were* they, as the agent represents, valid principles of action, they could not be principles of a rational power.[10] Disrespect for that in virtue of which rational agency is possible is what marks the domain of morality.[11] If no valid principle of action can have a form that is inconsistent with the will's principle qua rational cause, then we have a first piece of an account of how the rational will as an autonomous, norm-constituted power can be practically directive.

However, satisfaction of the universality requirement is only a necessary condition of rational action. An action is not rational (the effect of a possible rational cause) unless it can be "derived from" rational principles or ends. So something more is needed. We sometimes say we have a reason for action, or a *pro tanto* reason, when a consideration of a certain sort obtains—

9. One might say that in these ways authority and content can separate. This turns a metaphysical feature into an epistemological problem.

10. Thus, although agents take themselves to have reasons for action once they represent a means-end connection of interest to them, they have no reason at all unless the principle they would act on satisfies the formal standard of correctness. It then follows that, in Kantian theory, the so-called hypothetical imperative is not an independent standard of rational action.

11. Why this mode of disrespect is especially important can be described in various ways: the condition of our freedom, that in virtue of which our actions are truly our own, etc.

hunger gives a reason to get food or to eat. If there turn out to be more pressing considerations around, or no permissible action is available, we say our reason was not sufficient, or not sufficient in this case. The Kantian version of this is more restrictive. Given a consideration that inclines me to act, I may or may not have a reason at all. I cannot have a reason if the way I would act fails the universality requirement. But I also have no reason if all there is to say for the action is that I desire or want its object, whether or not there is anything to be said against the way of acting for it. The object of my interest must be of value; it too must have rational support. But if it is the principle of rational willing that provides a standard for action (a source of value), it has to be a source of value for ends as well, *if* an agent acts for reasons or makes a (rational) choice.[12] We might say: the will has to give itself at least one end for all its willings, if we ever act for reasons.

What could this end be? Here is one possibility. Since human agents do not automatically will correctly, one end we must have, insofar as we have a rational will, is: "will correctly." According to the universality requirement, willings are not correct unless well-formed. Then agents with the end of willing correctly are enjoined to take whatever means are necessary to that end. In this way, a necessary condition for rational willing generates a sufficient one. This looks like a trick, but it's not.

The argument works this way. Given the imperfection of our rational nature, there are many causes of our failure to meet the universality condition. We may think our maxim has universal scope, not noticing background assumptions to the contrary; we may mistakenly regard ourselves or our circumstances as unique. Correct exercise of a power often requires tools and preparation. If we are prone to error, in order to satisfy the end of willing correctly we must take preventive and anticipatory means. But since the maxims at issue are all of our maxims, the errors at issue will likely arise in all the areas in which we act. The necessary means will then be of two sorts: first, general abilities required for rational action—for getting things right—involving information acquisition, imagination, deliberation, self-governance; and second, activities and ways of living that support, or do not

---

12. In the end one may want to abandon the project of translating Kantian ideas about rational action into our way of talking about reasons. We speak of good reasons and bad ones, *pro tanto* reasons and reasons all things considered. A person who wants to cause another pain has *a* reason to hit him. On Kant's account, such an action is simply not rational, not justified: one cannot have reason to do it.

undermine, rational activity generally, and that police regions of activity where contra-rational temptation comes easily. Securing the conditions for rational willing is the purpose of duties to the self.

But there is an obvious problem. Although there will be much that we need to do to secure conformity with the universality requirement, it is not enough that we have *an* end that requires the development and sustenance of those skills and abilities to ensure satisfaction of a necessary condition of rational action. The will's standard of correctness was to be for all willing, a source of value for reasons for a wide array of choices. So we appear to have reached a predictable stalemate. Either rational choice and action in general somehow do stand under the value set by the will's principle, or we can have no reasons for action in the usual sense at all. But how *could* the will be the value source of ends or reasons generally? It looks as though the end of correct willing and *its* material conditions are the only possible objects that the will gives itself.

The way out of the stalemate involves a shift in the way we look at its elements. Suppose we took reasons to be the upshot of courses of *reasoning,* and reasoning to be a sequence of thoughts connected by principles, then we have a reason to do X (eat, keep a promise, have a child) just in case there is a course of reasoning from justified or true premises to X. But what counts as a valid course of reasoning is a function of rational principles. So if, as Kant would say, the will just is practical reason, then through reasoning we must be able to "derive" actions from the will's principle. Our desires and interests give us material to reason about.

Now, principles of reasoning fit their subject-matter. It's not that there are special logics for physics and for ethics, but that the fundamental category concepts for a kind of subject determine how we ought to think about it. To reason about how something works, or whether A causes B, we use rules of thought suited to the material world. Notions of cause and of power, of substance and motion, are, in the sense I have in mind, rules of reasoning. Because calling something a cause entails that it temporally precede its effects, satisfy some counterfactuals, be consistent with other known causal connections, and so on, causal claims enter our reasoning about the material world in determinate ways. In the same manner, reasons-claims reflect determinate rules of thought about choice and action. That we conceive of ourselves as initiating action for ends implies that reasoning about our activity will have instrumental form. That we represent our lives as temporally extended and are at least not indifferent to how things go for

our future selves implies that some idea of happiness will influence our reasoning about what to do. And then because in reasoning about what to do
we necessarily conceive of ourselves as free rational agents—that is, able to
choose for reasons—our reasoning is further subject to whatever follows
from that conception.

However, sound reasoning requires true or justified premises. Although
an object of desire may be the target of action chosen for a reason, it is not
as such an acceptable premise for a course of reasoning to action—it is not
a premise at all. Objects of desire only appear to give us reasons because we
take it to be in some sense good to satisfy a desire by realizing its object. But
then that's a different matter. When we choose to act in a way that will realize an object of desire, the choice is governed by a standard of correct willing. This is the point where obligatory ends enter. We get correct premises
of practical reasoning when the objects for which we would act are objects
for which we should or may act under the authority of an obligatory end.

The idea is this. In virtue of having the end "will correctly," we have the
subordinate (though obligatory) end of promoting and preserving our
rational abilities. The scope of this end is not limited to any specific set of
rationality-producing activities: possible ends are to be judged good (or
bad) as their promotion tends to affect the ability to will and judge correctly. As we make choices, a condition of their value—what makes an object of interest an end—is that it be of a kind suitable to an agent with the
end of "willing correctly."

III

One of the reasonable worries to have when a moral theory introduces a
ubiquitous, positive end is that it thereby makes the content of that end the
object of all action the end governs. It would be unacceptable, even silly, to
think that in choosing to meet a friend for lunch, or to go to the movies instead of working an extra hour on this year's taxes, we had to choose for the
sake of enhancing our rational abilities. We reject such dominant end views
because, as Rawls put it, "the self is disfigured and put in the service of one
of its ends for the sake of system."[13] But ends can relate to activity in ways
that don't generate this problem, even when the scope of the end is global.

13. John Rawls, *A Theory of Justice* (Cambridge, Mass.: Harvard University Press, 1971),
p. 554.

Think of the end of not violating rights (a side-constraint); or not acting foolishly or destructively (both regulative ends). Of course we can success-fully *not* do all kinds of things while meeting a friend for lunch or going to the movies. If I am going here, I am not going there. If I meet you for lunch, I am not sending an armored brigade into Baghdad. If, however, I go here because I think I should not go there, or meet you for lunch on con-dition that I am not committed elsewhere, then the condition enters, as an end, into the story of my action, directing what I do, but not as what I do it for.

Obligatory ends play a similar but slightly different role. When I honor them, I do not go to a movie or have lunch with a friend because or on con-dition that these acts will benefit my rational nature. I act because I expect to have an enjoyable or stimulating time. The obligatory end's role is to ex-plain why or how these considerations can *justify* acting (what makes the object—enjoyment—an end). The answer they provide is that enjoyments and spending time with friends are *kinds* of thing it is good for us to do.[14] Putting it a bit baldly: it is important for people to enjoy themselves because a life without pleasures makes us less able to sustain higher rational func-tion. (It is no accident that depression is both a state without pleasure and one in which it is hard to think clearly.) Some enjoyments may themselves be thought good (aesthetic ones, perhaps), but even then, it is not as enjoy-ment, simply. It is of course not a condition on this or that trip to the movies or the museum that it provide rational benefit. Nor is there some amount of enjoyment, like the RDA for a vitamin, that is enough. When our lives work well, we get pleasure from many of the things we do, and it is im-portant, not just nice for us, that this happen.[15] Obviously, pleasures and enjoyments can also be bad for us. Some few are simply hazardous. But most pleasures that cause trouble do so when they become the focus of large stretches of our life—we become dull, insensitive, rationally inert.[16]

14. If we let ourselves go, we might enjoy all sorts of things. The world of the bad person or the wanton is larger than the ordinary person's: there are all kinds of things that they can do that most of us cannot. But, we say, not everything we might enjoy is good for us.

15. We should expect that, given our rational natures, many of the things we naturally care about will be of the kind that we ought to care about. We might think in these terms of Rawls's Aristotelian Principle.

16. Whatever the cause of addictions, just their ability to cancel out judgment makes them morally dangerous.

Overall, obligatory ends explain why the way pleasure and enjoyment enter our lives requires our moral attention. They function as final ends, setting the terms for correct premises of practical reasoning, but without negating the heterogeneity of our interests.

There is no fixed set of activities that fulfill the conditions set by an obligatory end. Different societies (in the large and the small) will provide different opportunities. The role of the obligatory end is not to partition the space of possible actions, but to give agents a standard for their end-setting. This does not mean that we need always to be on the lookout for opportunities for rational development. Our ordinary choices take place against a background of knowledge about what is and isn't good for us. On the other hand, since we are responsible for getting things right, we need to be aware of and attentive to how things can go wrong. Being a teacher or a doctor can involve kinds of activity that are friendly to our rational functioning, or stultifying and damaging. (Profit-driven managed care is not bad only for patients.) With decent institutions, and an interest in doing an activity well, we support our rational abilities as a matter of course. But work that involves callous treatment of others, or hours of boring and repetitive action, ought to be avoided: not chosen, but more importantly, not offered. Some conditions affect us all, others are person-specific—stress tolerance; the ability to make difficult decisions quickly; negotiating complex lines of authority. Having certain vulnerabilities, or just lacking skills, can make someone susceptible to injuries to her rational abilities. One can become hasty in judgment or with others, or deferential, or prejudiced, or someone who just follows orders.[17]

The significance of having an obligatory end depends on very general facts about us. We are active beings: we respond to stimuli; we initiate courses of action. We consciously act to make a difference—on ourselves, on the material world, and on others. How we go about this is a project of self-making, or rational planning, or simply, the pursuit of happiness. Its upshot, not at all our intention, is that we acquire rational abilities. We learn to adjust desire to the world as we find it; we explore the limits of what we can change. We acquire skills to trim, modify, even abandon things we care about for the sake of what we care about more. One of the roles of

17. The control of access to ability-enhancing work is one of the avenues of construction of a status-stratified society.

obligatory ends is to provide a shape for this development; in a sense, they turn a natural process into a moral one, and, even when only weakly acknowledged, transform a being with rational abilities into a person.[18] The effect is intimate. Since obligatory ends do not directly regulate action, but constrain us to attend to the contours of our life as a rational agent, they partly determine who we are, what we love.[19]

Although the authority of the mandates derived from obligatory ends is the principle of autonomous willing, the practical concepts an agent acquires will come from interaction with those who are responsible for her education and development. Partly this is because the process begins early, in the shaping of attitudes toward correctness in thought and action, partly it is because the actual concepts will tend to have social form. Children, and not only children, cannot be instructed: "Go out and have a rationality enhancing life." We learn about good and evil through tales of heroes and heroines, saints and martyrs; we learn about the shapes of lives a bit later, through story and example, biography and popular culture.

Whether we acquire the concepts and abilities we need for full moral agency is not, then, entirely up to us. Lacking adequate evaluative concepts, our reasoning will make less sense. At the extreme, if the social world makes the effects of action unpredictable, if good intentions are not likely to produce good results, skepticism about agency is a natural result. Kafka's Joseph K. is the anti-hero of this story.

Mostly, however, when a person's character is not morally well formed, she will either act badly, or if not, because some other source of motivation is sufficient to keep her actions in line, the relationship she will have to morality is likely to be harder, more conflictual. The space for temptation is variable, a function of when one thinks that acting morally is a sacrifice, something hard to justify from within one's life, unconnected to what one most cares about. Some regard this as the start of a philosophical problem—how to prove that any normal person has sufficient reason to act morally; I think there is much to be said for treating it as a practical task—something to fix or prevent.

18. As with other norms of rationality, they affect cognition and judgment independently of self-conscious moral awareness.

19. They thereby introduce an idea of correctness into a region one might have thought was at most constrained by and not constituted by moral norms.

IV

To this point, I have discussed obligatory ends by way of just one end, the
obligatory end of one's own perfection, which, I have argued, arises
straightaway from the norm of correctness in willing. There is a second
obligatory end—that of the happiness of others—and it is time to bring
it forward. About each obligatory end, we need to address two questions.
One is about how to argue *to* the obligatory end, the other about the end's
content—what it requires of us.

So why should attending to the happiness of *others* belong to or be a
specification of the principle of rational willing? The question is not, how
do we show that morality requires that we attend to others? That, we may
assume, is asked and answered long before we get to obligatory ends. What
we need to know is why others' *happiness* should matter in the way that an
obligatory end would require. As a start we might notice that it is by means
of our effect on the happiness of others that we tend to affect their rational
condition and abilities. We teach things someone wants to know, or we refuse to; we provide support and sustenance that allows them to pursue useful projects; we go to the movies and have lunch together. (Our reasons for
promoting an element of another's happiness need not be the same as their
own.)[20] But that doesn't explain why the welfare of the rational nature of
others is an obligatory end for us. The connection is (and has to be)
through the conditions of our own rational willing.[21] In the full sense of rational abilities that fall under obligatory ends as so far laid out—rational
and moral abilities generally—we have very strong reasons to want those
we interact with to have them. (Even moral skeptics argue that we have a
strong interest in the moral character of others.) Our own rational abilities
are in many ways dependent on those of others; indeed, the coherence to us

20. This is familiar with children: their idea that learning to play the guitar would impress
their friends is not what we promote in arranging lessons. Issues are more complex with
adults, where, for the sake of their happiness, we are more likely to omit support for things we
judge harmful than to support beneficial things they value for inappropriate reasons.

21. Why don't I take what would be the easier route and argue that in virtue of our having
the end "will correctly" we have an end of securing correctness in willing where and as we
can—namely, by selective engagement with the happiness of others? Recall: I do not have the
end of willing correctly because I value willing correctly (that would make it hard not to care
about correct willing other places). I have the end "will correctly" because I have a will of a
certain sort. What needs to be argued is that in virtue of this, I have reason to value the correct exercise of the rational powers of others (and so have their happiness as an end).

of the human world depends on assuming that others act for reasons, that they care about doing things correctly. So, even if we might benefit in some way from the rational disability of others, we may not think it in general good that we do so. In having the end of the happiness of others, understood in this way, we express the value of giving, as much as we are able, rational and moral form to the world.

There is a further reason to have the happiness of others as an obligatory end. We are, from the beginning of our lives, involved with others as a way of becoming who we are. And if we do not get this connection right, our rational agency is impaired. This is a familiar theme in many accounts of infant development. They describe the infant as caught in a process that she neither initiates nor controls, but which is necessary for her to come to have the self-consciousness of a person with rational powers of action. Movement takes place from an initial sense of being one with another, through separation and anxiety, to new terms of connection. If the beginning is the feeling of identity, it is no surprise that even preconceptually separation is experienced as a threat of annihilation. In order to negotiate the project of becoming a human self, both dependency and aggression have to be domesticated by an infant who lacks all the strategies of rationalization and self-protection that adults routinely deploy. Not surprisingly, we remain sensitive to regression in both domains.

The upshot of this process is to establish a connection to others in which sorting this out is essential to being oneself—a self. The hard-won terms of healthy connection depend on the recognition not just that the happiness of others—what they care about—can occasionally be directed away from us without our being endangered, but also that their well-being is a source of pleasure to us, something that makes our lives go well. (Finding pleasure in giving presents is an accomplishment.) If in making the separation, a child is cold or ruthless about the well-being of the other, then she may be unable to love, and so fail to become a complete human self. On the other hand, the child's agency can also be compromised if the happiness she comes to value is not good for her—if it is hostile to her well-being. What we have is a natural developmental process that is not *for* morality but that, when reasonably successful, makes morality possible and that morality completes.[22]

A healthy person cares about some others; morality directs her to be con-

22. We might think of this as the interpersonal variant of Kant's unsocial sociability.

cerned for persons generally, and focuses her attention on their rational well-being.[23] Guilt, regret, and the desire to repair are part of the normal trajectory of intimate relations. Morality re-forms these basic patterns so that they reflect objective values. It is not just the lineaments of connection that need to be reformed, but the idea of happiness they carry as well. At the extremes, natural greed and the fantasy of making things whole again (wanting too much, doing too much), get replaced by a rational plan of life and a greater realism about the value of attachment (not everything can or should be "made better") and the nature of the goods we should provide.

Morality, on this account, does not compete with our loves and attachments, but transforms them. One product of this process is a healthy, separate self, able to act for objective reasons. But things need not go well. Development can yield a defective self if the separation is made on different terms. Others may be seen as objects of manipulation (it may be useful to learn to pretend otherwise) or open exploitation. A form of self-conceit—to use Kant's term—can block the apprehension of the source of one's own value. Such an agent need not be less able to make her way in the world of things, but she will be incapable of some sorts of relationships, and so impaired in the world of persons and attachments.[24]

If we think about a formed life, some things will typically function for a person as core values, anchors of meaning for the rest. They can be other persons: a child, a lover, a hero; but also an institution, such as a state or church, or a calling. There may be much or little that one can do for the sake of some of these basic goods; they can be outside one's practical reach. Which sorts of things can anchor a life is a historically contingent matter. Institutions may be corrupt and so unworthy of commitment; child mortality has to be relatively low for it to be intelligible to organize one's life around having only one or two children; one has to be lucky in the match of one's talents with socially available forms of activity.

How one loves and how one negotiates the loss of what or who is loved implicate each other. Bernard Williams talks of the loss of "ground projects" leaving a person with no reason to go on living.[25] And surely that can

23. Not the well-being of their reasoning per se, but on those elements of happiness that are part of a rational agent's, or *this* rational agent's, life going well.

24. There may even be collateral benefits. Charismatic leaders, self-absorbed artists, may have powers that result from their flaws. The natural world is not a moral order.

25. Bernard Williams, "Persons, Character and Morality," in *Moral Luck* (Cambridge: Cambridge University Press, 1981), pp. 12–14.

be so: without *this*—my son, my work, my country—life is not worth living. But it does not follow from the fact that things can be that way that it is normal or healthy. Such losses are the topic of Freud's extraordinary essay "Mourning and Melancholia," where the obvious pathology in *some* responses to loss led him to suggest a pathology of attachment as part of its explanation.[26] Freud's suggestion bears on the importance to our psychic health of having objective value as a source of reasons or attachments rather than having our reasons arise from what we find ourselves valuing. (This is not about choosing one way or the other, but about the kinds of basic attachments one is able to make.)

It is normal for persons to suffer grave losses, and, after a period of mourning (or, as Freud says, "when the work of mourning is completed" [245]) for them to recover and resume their lives, and to form new attachments. A different and abnormal pattern arises in some cases where a loss leads to damage of a person's self-regard. Life, Freud observes, cannot resume for the melancholic because in his own eyes he has been shown not worthy of it. The puzzle is why "[a]n object loss is transformed into an ego loss and the conflict between the ego and the loved person into a cleavage between the critical activity of the ego and the ego altered by identification" (249). Freud's tentative thesis is that for this to happen it must already have been the case that there was an identification of the self with the loved object. The original object choice "had been effected on a narcissistic basis." Thus the loss to be negotiated is a loss of self as well as a loss for the self, and to the extent that the loss occasions anger, self-reproach is one of its dimensions. Why this happens, why there would be this catastrophic mislocation of self-love, is, Freud argues, difficult to explain. But the features of depression—of melancholia—that he points to make sense together.

If an essential element of the history of my love for X is that *my* attraction to X was part of what made X attractive, then my love for X is in a sense about me. And if my love for X is important, a ground project, narcissistic identification would explain why it may not seem possible to forgo the object in the face of practical or moral obstacles; why its absence might seem to undermine all reasons for living. If I am narcissistically identified with this love, or that ideal, failure or harms to them will be experienced as attacks on my ego, and my impotence to avert the loss makes myself an object of my own anger.

Where, by contrast, one's love is based in the objective value of some-

---

26. *The Standard Edition of the Complete Psychological Works of Sigmund Freud,* vol. 14, ed. James Strachey (London: Hogarth Press, 1966), pp. 243–258.

thing—value secured not by one's loving but by its worth—a loss is a severe blow, but it is a loss of something in the world, not, however it may feel, a loss of oneself. The world remains, and what is of value in it can, over time, reassert itself; new attachments can form. But where the ground projects we identify with endow our lives with meaning, make a world of value for us, their loss cannot be repaired in the normal ways: it is we who are lost. So it is an interesting question whether the remedy to Williams's challenge to the authority of morality—how can we have reason to act morally if so acting would undermine a ground project?—is philosophical or psychological.

A psychological story about the role of objective value in healthy attachment, and of the costs of narcissistic identification, does not show that there *is* objective value, or if there is, what it is like. It is meant mainly as an anti-skeptical caution. What may seem to be mere philosophical possibilities are sometimes real ones, and if they are real possibilities, they might sometimes be a sign of disorder.

It is hardly surprising that we are prone to evaluative pathologies. We are the center of what we care about, or at least we begin that way, and most of us continue to find the path of narcissistic identification easy. The pathologies (or our vulnerability to them) can also be greatly enhanced by institutions and groups that gain allegiance through the mechanisms of identification. They meet needs, but the satisfactions of regressive attachment also impose costs. One gets solidarity, perhaps visibility and voice, the possibility of shared anger; one risks hyper-sensitivity, tendencies to moral exaggeration and paranoia, ego-exposure. Institutions or allegiances that have this profile encourage attachments for the wrong reasons, creating unhealthy conditions of agency.

V

The morality of obligatory ends leads to an expansive conception of morality—governing all action that affects persons. But obligatory ends also frame a holistic account of practical reason—of norms governing willing. One might think this is not possible, for there are spheres of activity that do not impact rational beings. But, as Kant pointed out, even activities that are directed at animals or the environment are still matters of dutiful concern insofar as they also have an effect on our moral sensibilities.[27] Rather than

---

27. *Metaphysics of Morals*, 6:442–443.

seeing this as a back-end way to get something said about animals and the environment, I take it as a remark about how obligatory ends work at the limit. Kant's point is that we can only have "duties to" those agents who can put us under obligation, agents whose ends we can promote by our action. This leaves out animals and things, neither of which have ends; it also leaves out God, whose ends we can neither know nor affect. But from the fact that we cannot have "duties to" something, it does not follow that we are morally free to act toward it in any way we wish. Being indifferent to pain, wasteful, insensitive to the beauties of nature are not ways of acting that can be included in sound courses of reasoning. They are not kinds of activity (as aims or as means) that are, in the obligatory end sense, good for us. This is not because if we are insensitive to animals we will be insensitive to persons (though that may be so) but because indifference and insensitivity are hostile to reason, to getting things right, and therefore not part of justified ways of acting. Animals do suffer; old-growth forests are beautiful. This doesn't settle questions about the use of animals or things; it is possible that for this or that purpose we must steel ourselves against the pain we must cause, or the loss of a forest. It brings these considerations into our reasoning about what we may do.

VI

I have so far discussed two roles for obligatory ends: as the value conditions for premises of reasoning to action, and as categories that direct our affective and conceptual practical development. They have a third role, the first one we tend to notice, in setting positive duties to act. In this last section, I want to look at how the form of these duties is shaped by the values that come from the obligatory ends.

With regard to our positive duties to others, it is customary to focus on beneficence alone: the duty to provide aid, as one is able, to others in need. But there is a long tradition, shared by Kant, that locates beneficence within a framework of other positive duties, both narrow and wide, that concern our response to the perceived differential between our own and others' states of well-being. So we are to resist temptations of disrespect when we feel superior: that we not expect others to think less of themselves in comparison to us; that we not expose others' faults for no reason, or make them the object of amusement. There are conditions of need that we must become sensitive to and may not ignore, but also directives that we not demean those we help. And then there is the duty of gratitude, strictly owed a genuine bene-

factor, and also psychologically necessary to maintain the principle of beneficence: an inability to be freely grateful as a recipient tends to undermine
one's will to provide unselfish help. The rationale for each of these duties fits
the agenda of the obligatory end—that in our relations with others, that aspect of their happiness that affects their rational well-being must be our end.

Most of these positive duties, while difficult to get right, are not demanding in an intrusive way, though some are ubiquitous and some are stringent.
Requiring that a person's idea of happiness have room for gratitude (acknowledging that one is not self-sufficient) or that well-being not depend on
humiliating others does not limit our liberty in unreasonable ways.

It is only the duty of beneficence, and elements of the duty of self-
perfection, that, because of their open-endedness (more can always be done)
might exhaust our abilities and resources, intruding to an unacceptable degree on what we care about. One response is to emphasize the fact that these
are imperfect duties that leave agents leeway about fulfilling them. But this
is hardly a satisfying answer. The idea of obligatory ends suggests a different
line of thought.

We will, under beneficence, have some general duty to help others, but
we will have much more demanding duties to help those whose happiness
is enmeshed with our own. This is not because we need to honor our personal attachments, but because our understanding of the lives of those we
are close to is often better (or ought to be better), and because what we are
able to do can be more finely tuned to the actual needs we take on. Both my
son and the checkout clerk at the supermarket have needs. But there is little
I can provide the clerk besides fungible resources. I am in no position to
give him money on condition that he take a class that will get him out of
this dead-end job, whereas I can (sometimes) advise and support my son in
ways that will shape his life. The genies and anonymous benefactors of popular fables either give wealth or wishes; more engaged benefaction depends
on the development of a relationship in which there is understanding and
trust. In mature relationships, we have reason to accept the judgment of
others about what they need, though that does not diminish our responsibility for what we do. *If* the reason we are to be concerned with the happiness of others is that it is our point of access to their rational well-being,
these are the results we should expect. Viewing beneficence in this way does
not diminish our concern for their happiness in the usual sense; it rather introduces shared or shareable terms of judgment. When we are not in a position to exercise judgment, because need is at a distance, or the needy are

strangers to us, or private charity is inappropriate, public institutions can do the work of beneficence for us, and that part of our general duty is met by contributing a fair share of support.

The full content of our duty toward others will therefore depend on the relationships we are in. Whether we form a family or have a wide circle of friends is up to us; but if we do extend ourselves into relations with others, we become implicated in their happiness and well-being. Of course, many of the goods of a human life come to us this way as well. Although more extensive relations may give us more to do by way of providing help, sometimes more than we expected or planned for, it is not the kind of sacrifice that those who are concerned with open-ended beneficence worry about.[28]

A word about the demandingness of the duties of self-perfection. For the most part, our rational abilities and skills develop as we pursue a variety of activities. Unless an environment is terribly impoverished or culturally degraded, what the duty requires is taken care of as a matter of course. Work and play, relationships, group activities are or can be demanding in ways that are both enjoyable and good for us. However, since it is often institutions, of education and law, that train abilities and provide useful opportunities, some failures are not primarily imputable to the individuals who remain deficient. But when things work well, there is no special burden, no set of exercises we must perform, no endless sequence of self-improvement classes.

Where the pursuit of happiness and the needs of our rational agency may come apart is in ways of living that are absorbed in self-destructive pleasures (self-destructive to our rational abilities as a result of quantity or kind). Still, although it may be a nuisance to eat healthily, drink alcohol mainly in moderation, and attend to the needs of one's recalcitrant body, these also are not the sorts of burdens that give rise to worries about the demandingness of positive duties. Having to forgo some pleasure, or a kind of activity to which we are attracted, involves some discipline, but no unreasonable sacrifice.

Things are much more complicated concerning our moral personality or character. Here I think we do have extensive and demanding duties, some provoked by the way in which it is easy to be selfish (the convenience of ly-

---

28. The hardest cases—emergencies, extreme poverty—do not, I believe, fall under obligatory ends. Emergencies are directly governed by moral requirements on action; the circumstances of extreme poverty by complex considerations of justice. I discuss these issues more fully in Chapter 9.

ing as a means, the attachment to wealth that leads to avarice, the servile willingness to trade status for benefits), others by our having ultimate moral responsibility for what we do (we require a competent conscience, and sufficient knowledge of our moral condition to make accurate and effective moral assessments). Some of this can be taken care of by the background structure of ordinary moral life: those who are decently brought up avoid a fair amount of moral difficulty as a matter of course. (A culture that values privacy probably has curtains; and inhibitions.) But moral environments are inevitably incomplete and faulty, and each seems to put some forms of wrongdoing within easy reach. Moreover, if we do not live in morally transparent times, if our institutions mask forms of wrongful activity, then we will need to be wary of unintended complicity with wrongdoing. And if, as I believe, we can be responsible even in these situations for getting things right, then our duties of *moral* self-perfection, our duties to be and become effective moral agents, may turn out to be ones that are genuinely demanding.

So it is true, the requirements of morality regulated by obligatory ends and positive duties may be demanding, but not in the ways that call forth familiar objections. The demandingness is not quantitative—there is not some large amount of good we are to do—nor is it fully directive—picking out our actions at every step. That sort of demandingness prompts arguments to limit the scope of morality for the sake of private ends—our freedom to do what we will. But obligatory ends do not in those ways determine what we are to do; they rather set conditions for having a life we can have reason to value. That is how they contribute to Kant's claim that morality is the condition of our freedom.

—12—

Moral Improvisation

In the most general terms, Kantian ethics is about the rules and standards necessary for free rational action and choice. It provides guidance, first of all, through the rule of permissibility associated with the categorical imperative, but also by way of two obligatory ends—of one's own perfection and the happiness of others—whose role in the theory is rarely taken seriously enough. When it is, they transform the way we should think about Kantian ethics. In the previous chapter, I sketched out a picture of Kantian moral theory that gives a central place to obligatory ends. Here I want to explore some of the far-reaching effects obligatory ends may have on our understanding of what morality can require of us.

Obligatory ends lead us to think about the way morality becomes situated in a life. They identify the kinds of things it is objectively good for a person to do, and so provide the categories, or basic value concepts, for the premises of sound practical reasoning. Unlike standards of justice, or negative duties, which provide rules for action (we should not deceive or take others' possessions), obligatory ends place demands on our intentions and motives, our reasons for acting. They require that we choose activities as they are friendly to our own and others' rational natures; they give reason to reject ways of living and even social structures that are detrimental to good reasoning (lives of excess, avarice, rigidly authoritarian social organization). They are to be our ends, directive and regulative, whatever other ends we may have. *That* I enjoy something does not explain why or whether it is good to do. We do not need to explain the *liking*, but how enjoyment should figure in a life that requires a significant level of rational functioning (morality calls on rational abilities that we neither have nor sustain as a matter of course). Since our actions affect others in all sorts of ways (we help, harm, support, and interfere with them), we are required to regulate these interactions with an eye to the development and sustenance of their rational abilities, not just our own. The two obligatory ends also generate positive duties that more closely regulate regions of activity where we are tempted to act in ways that are inconsistent with the value of rational agency: duties of beneficence, gratitude, and respect; duties to avoid servility and avarice; and most especially, duties concerning our own moral agency. Since we have ultimate responsibility for acting correctly, for most of us, the duty to be and to become an effective moral agents is both complex and likely quite demanding.

To explore the effect of obligatory ends on the commitments of agency, and, especially, the scope of moral responsibility, will require some idealized imagining of what we would be like if our moral abilities were fully realized in the way that obligatory ends direct. Moral theory is not merely a descriptive enterprise about what our duties are, given what we are like as agents. The however-formed person may not appreciate reasons that the well-formed person can. On the other hand, morality cannot require truly exotic dispositions or a nearly perfect social setting as a condition for our acting well. It *can*, however, require that we develop sensitivities that we may lack, that we be able to act well in unexpected and difficult situations, and that social and political institutions be responsive to moral needs— taking on some of our moral burdens, enabling effective moral criticism. It is a rather practical and realistic notion of the ideal.

My approach to this large set of issues will be in terms of four more limited topics: the kind of unity obligatory ends give the lives they shape; the ways they require moral and political creativity; the importance, therefore, of moral history; and last, the significance of the idea that the positive duties they set are imperfect.

I

In an obvious sense, obligatory ends do their work by shaping an agent's pursuit of happiness. They manage tendencies to activity that are natural for us. Persons *will* pursue the satisfaction of their desires; they need to learn when the way they are inclined to act is bad for them, when to take the interests of others into account, and to conceive of what they do in terms of value, not merely desire. Morality, broadly conceived, has this educative task. In coming to see the conditions of rational agency as the first element in claims of value, in learning what to do and what to attend to, and what counts as sound reasoning, we are made and make ourselves into effective moral agents. The distinctive feature of this route to moral agency, and so for our sense of ourselves as moral agents, is the emphasis on our deliberative and critical abilities.

Although the work of obligatory ends is a discipline for the pursuit of happiness, it is not hostile to the sorts of things we care about. Indeed, a morality that did not see the need for enjoyments or strong attachments, or that was uncomfortable with parents giving special time and attention to their children, would not be credible. However, morality need not be equally sanguine about what we care about *as* we are inclined to care about it. It asks whether some of the things we feel we must do—taking special care of our friends and children—are kinds of things that are good for them, and for us, as rational agents, and it requires that we give priority to the answer, whatever else we may value in acting.[1]

If we should take on the obligations of parenting or friendship in these terms, it does not mean that we should love our friends or children because it is a moral thing to do, or act for their sake out of a sense of obligation. The idea is rather that, in loving our friends and children, morality is one of the norms that shapes what that love amounts to. The obligatory ends that regulate our loves require that we be attentive to, because we may be responsible for, the development or rational health of those we love, and of ourselves. So it may be required that we sometimes say no because to do more would tilt us toward self-neglect, or that we should check a tendency to indulge our children's escalating desires, because too much stuff is foolish and can affect a person's sense of what is important. These homilies of good parenting partly explain why this activity is a kind that morality has to take into account.

Obligatory ends not only discipline the pursuit of happiness, they introduce a kind of deliberative unity by way of their governance of an agent's active desires and interests. This occurs, first, because they are *obligatory,* and so always of deliberative import, and second, because their value content is derived from a single source that has general application—the principle that sets the standard for correct willing. It is natural when we think of ends to think of means and of instrumental reasons. But ends are not just states of affairs with targets drawn on them, and means are not merely arrows aimed

---

1. Special obligations are thus not needed to justify such partiality, for the purposes of *impartial* morality are served this way.

at the target. It is better to think of an end as providing guidance for reasoning. Sometimes it is a matter of indifference how we get what we want—I can buy it, find it, you can give it to me. Sometimes a way of getting what we want can ruin it. When I find out that my success came at your expense, I may not take myself to have succeeded after all. We explain this by saying it was not simply a state of affairs that I wanted, but a state of affairs that satisfied a set of conditions (including, to be sure, that I get what I want). The agent's end is evaluatively complex. Obligatory ends add a noncontingent element to that evaluative complexity. That makes even our instrumental reasoning no longer merely a matter of causal efficiency, because instrumental reasoning is responsive to the structure and substance of our ends.

The importance of deliberative unity can be missed if we oversimplify practical reasoning by working with isolated examples. In a normal agent, even the simple decision to stay home and read a book rather than have a night on the town operates in a complex deliberative framework of wants and interests, preferences and conditions on action. Some, but hardly all of the elements of complexity are moral. When things are working well, little is at issue in my deliberative activity apart from determining which thing I prefer to do. But that is because I take myself to know without further thought that my options are permissible: I rely on my memory (that I have no outstanding obligations that require me to do one of these things, or something else entirely), I count on the everydayness of things (there are no life-endangering wires attached to the ordinary objects I might use), and I assume that obligations with a larger, impersonal scope (world hunger, the needy elderly, victims of war) are being managed well enough in the background. Of course I may be wrong about any of these things. And although it matters that I get things right, the way that it matters does not impinge on normal decision-making. There is a certain seamlessness to ordinary thought and action. We are warranted in taking a great deal for granted in the background of our deliberations, and the warrant is both reasonable (normally) and necessary, else we would be unable to function as normal persons.[2]

2. That an ordinary agent in ordinary circumstances needs to be able to act confidently and directly, to go about her business without a sense of pitfalls and snares, is not special to morality. One of the reasons so many people resent a certain large software company is that it both inserted its products into ordinary life *and* they are unreliable. Activities of any degree of complexity—skiing, musical composition, cooking—rely on a background of learned skills and assumptions. This does not mean that they are fixed, or immune to innovation. But reconsideration of fundamentals is unsettling and cannot be taken on too frequently without undermining a region of our activity.

For the most part, then, we deliberate neither about ends nor about means. We come to decisions with ends in hand and a library of practical knowledge at our disposal. This is not because we are all too busy, or overly programmed, or lacking in spontaneity. Those may be problems, but their solution hardly requires that we come to each choice as if born anew. If we did not know our ends, or most of them, and if we did not have a catalogue of means at hand, there would be little of any complexity we could undertake. So the truism of our form of agency, one that builds on competencies and seeks increasingly complex activity, is that when we decide what to do now, we must already know a great deal about what we are already doing.

II

For normal action to be possible, the restrictions and positive requirements of morality have to become part of common knowledge, and to some extent, part of the way we come to desire. There is, at least in principle, a moment when it is open to reflection whether there is good reason to be honest or fair in one's dealings with others. But the question is not permanently open, and for many of us it never gets asked. One is brought up so that values of fairness and honesty become constitutive of our relations, or at least of the central ones. It's not that we don't think about them. We affirm these values in our judgments, teach them, refine their scope or stringency, inflect them with style; but their primary function is as background premises in our practical reasoning. A great deal of practical and moral knowledge must be integrated into an agent's deliberative field if she is to be able to act smoothly and with normative confidence, or, when circumstances require it, to deliberate about what to do. When this background is not stable, when values or basic factual assumptions are in question, we may not be immobilized, but there is often a sense of having to guess at or rethink familiar things. Acting in the dark, morally, is a situation to be avoided. There are areas of life where novelty and risk-taking can be fun; morality is not one of them.

The structure of the deliberative field is determined objectively by the norms of rational deliberation, and subjectively by the agent's grasp of factual and evaluative connections. Moral error comes from mistaken representation either of formal elements of the field, or of the facts judged to be salient. Ideally, when an agent gets it right, the deliberative field is unified: the principles of practical reasoning, including the moral principle, can be co-instantiated. Because obligatory ends introduce lines of reasoning from fundamental moral values to the concerns we normally think of as belonging to happiness,[3] finding the pursuit of some interest blocked by a moral prohibition is not a sign of a conflicting value. However, since the way obligatory ends construct a bridge between morality and happiness is by bringing considerations of rational well-being into the forefront of judgments of value, they alter the terms of our attachments, creating some critical distance from the fluency of the ordinary. We become alert to the possibility that our feelings of fit can be misleading. Examples of this are not hard to find.

In many adult relationships, routines develop whose rationale is mutual benefit. Even if that's how they start, we know they can evolve into structures of deference and domination. In a complex work environment, one need not know much to know that a task that is a matter of course for one person can be a source of enormous anxiety for another. We are aware that it isn't easy to negotiate the obstacle course of gratitude, the giving and accepting of favors, the beneficial use of one's good fortune. However we come to help, we are committed to a certain degree of critical vigilance. Paternalism lurks in the provision of all sorts of goods; one takes oneself simply to be concerned with the happiness of another, but, it turns out, only conditionally so. In most of these cases what is required is not deliberation *de novo*, but an increase of attention, and a degree of flexibility in response to what one encounters.

How we understand relations with friends or marital partners is not usually up to us. There is a social division of labor that has an impact on our private lives—who takes care of the needy, the children, the elderly. It may be harder to see wrongdoing if inappropriate actions are embedded in an accepted routine endorsed by background social institutions. But just because this is so ordinary and inevitable, acting under obligatory ends we are required to be alert to such possibilities, develop means of increased sensitivity to the way institutions hide injuries, and be prepared to remedy them, as we can. Even in matters of social justice, where one might hope the background social order will do the heavy lifting, we are not free to let things be

---

3. That our actions not be of a kind that are bad for us as rational agents makes the justificatory standards of all of our choices more complex: "that I want to" is not ever the full story, even if it turns out that here, and for this choice, "that you want to" is sufficient justification. (Going to see *Dumb and Dumber* doesn't make you stupid; celebrating a culture that cynically encourages permanent adolescence might.)

as we find them. The domain of obligatory ends is continuous with many of the concerns of justice, and intimately engaged with the effects of injustice. So we may have to seek out and take on justice-related burdens whether or not we have acted wrongfully. And this should not be surprising, since in contrast to claims *of* justice, for what one is due, the demand *for* just institutions follows from the nature of our *moral* interest in happiness.

Some of the critical work can be done by means of incorporating a kind of activity within the deliberative field. For example: We think friendship is a good thing in that it offers a sphere of intimacy in which activities and feelings can be experienced and shared, it is a locus of special pleasures, it can extend the base of mutual reliance, mitigating isolation, and so on. Some of the goods of friendship are instrumental, some are good in themselves. This conception of friendship is quite comfortable with morality. But not every conception of friendship is so accommodating (one for all and all for one; clan ideals of brotherhood). So either we will have to argue for the priority of the moral over other, independent values, or argue for the place of morality in the formation of other values, challenging their independence.

Since each and every moral consideration is not likely always to outweigh everything else—we cannot say in advance how important all the demands of friendship might be, or in which circumstances some moral requirement ought to be set aside, or taken care of later—it does not make much sense to argue for the priority of the moral in a general way. Even if we argued for the priority of some moral values, or for the conditional priority of, for example, rules of moral permissibility, we would still need to explain why some cost to friendship provides a condition that justifies our doing or omitting something that would otherwise be wrong to do or omit.

Instead of trying to fit together the autonomous spheres of morality and friendship—and why not also art, sport, and work—we might consider how these things that we care about stand with respect to the value introduced by obligatory ends. It is not hard to see that persons who care about others as intimate equals, who have special commitments to each other's well-being, and so on, will be in relationships that enhance their practical abilities, connect them with reasons that do not start in their own needs, and give them access to pleasures that make them more engaged in living. The benefits of that kind of friendship are valued by the person who has them, but they are also, in the wide sense in which I am using the term, moral goods. Friendship, so valued, is then part of morality—as are, in different ways, art and sport and work. They are set into a deliberative framework that gives them an importance that transcends our caring about them, though they would not have that importance unless we cared.

If obligatory ends set basic values for choice, what gives an activity standing in the deliberative field is its being of a kind that is supportive of our rational abilities. That won't be the basis on which we choose friends or work, but it is a necessary condition for our choice being a good one. Where the needs of friendship conflict with what would be required by some duty, instead of making cross-value judgments, we can ask whether an exception of this kind to the duty makes the duty itself cohere better with the values of the deliberative field. Note that the question that has to be answered is not, may I lie if it would advance the rational interests of my friend? but, is lying in order to advance the rational interests of friends a possible rational principle?[4] The incompatibility of lying in general with rational activity suggests a negative deliberative conclusion. Would it be different if the purpose of the deception was to save lives? One might want to distinguish lies that block coercive aggression from lies that promote some good: stopping a mugger or a tank and getting someone into a better college. Producing a unified deliberative field does not eliminate hard cases; it rather allows us to think about our interests and our obligations as they are differently seated in our lives, and as valuable, if they are, because objectively good.

III

In imagining the construction of a deliberative field, we are imagining the construction of a unified agent. The unity is formal, not substantive (there is no ideal unified set of desires, for example). It is a unity in many ways of the agent's own making, but in other and equally important ways, it is not. The external sources seem to be fourfold. There are objective principles of correctness for action and obligatory ends that reconfigure desires and interests as possible objects of rational choice. There are projects derived from positive duties that will fit with other things we value, but may impinge on specific preferences (to say that they fit is not to say that both can be acted on as we might wish; it is to say that both kinds can belong to a well-formed

4. This also eliminates a worry about perverse agents—ones whose rational abilities are somehow dependent on their performing immoral acts. Justification tracks kinds; it is then both logically and psychologically possible that there be persons who cannot flourish within the framework of objective value.

life). And last, there are the constraining facts of the world in which one acts. We cannot choose anything we want, nor can we be whatever we wish to be. The roles and institutions present in our social world preconfigure our possibilities, some in ways that are hospitable to what moral value allows, some not.[5] So, even ideally, in becoming ourselves we work within norms, some rational and moral, some social, with ultimate responsibility for being right about what we choose.

Deliberative unity does not give the agent every kind of unity she might want. It might, for example, preclude wholeheartedness, if by that is meant reflective satisfaction with one's affective and volitional condition.[6] Knowing the complexity of my circumstances, of the limits to the knowledge that lies behind my ends and choices, I need not be ambivalent or skeptical, but a little cautious and a lot humble about my aims and actions. One needs to be on the lookout for unintended consequences, not because of fear of a hidden moral quagmire, but because in forming one's intentions, however carefully, one may not have seen far or wide enough; even a careful agent may not fully understand what she does.[7] I say: "I'm just having a little fun." You respond: "No, that's cruel." The edge often goes to the response because cruelty so often occurs precisely because one is not attending to something, or attending, but not under the right description.

We certainly have reasons for wanting to avoid ambivalence. It impedes activity; our deliberations lack closure; choice is forced. It can lead to various forms of damaging double-mindedness. Those one loves cannot be confident in being loved. Work that requires effort and concentration may be tarnished, even inhibited, if one is still tracking a forgone option. But if these are the kinds of costs that come with ambivalence, there are ways to avoid them that do not require anything like wholeheartedness. One can learn to let go of the options not taken, however attractive, especially when they do not provide reasons against what one has chosen.[8] There are strategies of focus and attention, engagement with the pleasures of the option

---

5. Some attractive activities likewise have acceptable forms in some social worlds, some not.

6. One might think here of Harry Frankfurt's claim in his essay "The Faintest Passion" that it is "a necessary truth about us that we wholeheartedly desire to be wholehearted." See Harry Frankfurt, *Necessity, Volition, and Love* (Cambridge: Cambridge University Press, 1999), p. 106.

7. Insofar as I act because I judge that X is to be done, I intend to X. But whether what I do is correctly described as X-ing is not in the same way under my control.

8. And when they do, their continued presence may help keep one honest, or decent.

taken that can make a decision made in the face of ambivalence one that one comes to have no reason to regret. There is an important difference between having made a hard decision, aware of some good forgone (it would not otherwise have been a hard decision), and feeling the pull of what is set aside as a kind of tax on one's choice.

Confidence and absorption are two other forms of volitional unity. Normally we seek absorption only for a time, and usually in special activities (an athlete's "zone," the heightened attention of the musician practicing, the immersion of self in play or sex). We know that these states are not normal, and that, however appealing, even tempting, they offer neither a practical ideal nor any guarantee that we are not at the same time overlooking important things. Absorption may be necessary for certain sorts of creative activity, and if so, these activities may involve practical risks. Confidence is different. One can be confident in what one is doing while remaining open to correction, to the need for adjustment. There can be false confidence, but not false absorption. We are confident when we believe our abilities and judgment are up to the task. I need to know who I am and what I can do, but I need not be some one thing, or unaware that my arrival at this place has had costs, or indifferent to the possibility that the bases that I appeal to for justification may not all be sound, or within my control.

Morality introduces other kinds of unity, some of which we might not like. It is a requirement of moral agency that we recognize that our activity is morally hostage in ways that we may not now see. The circle of effects of most of our acts dissipates quickly, and we can easily see to the end of the chain. But it is not always so, and the fact that one could not reasonably have expected a bad outcome does not leave one off the hook, though one may well not be to blame. Something I do as it happens puts you in harm's way; I am not free to ignore what unfolds. This is in some ways strange. We have a duty not to harm. We cannot have a duty not to be an unwitting part of a harmful causal sequence. How do we get a duty to pick up the pieces of an action that is not morally imputable to us? One way could be via the connection to others that is the basis of all positive duties based in our obligatory ends. The obligatory end of others' happiness requires that we regard our actions, whatever our intent, as they bear on the well-being of others. So intended and unintended effects, as well as omissions, get factored in. And as we must be mindful of what we do, we are responsible for what we effect. In general, our duty to take care of others is stronger as our relationship is closer, and the relationship of being a proximate cause of harm is very close, if unchosen. Choice is not in any case the necessary metric of relationship. There are relationships we are born into, others in which we simply find ourselves. I have greater concern for my neighbor than yours for no more reason than I happened to land next to mine. What I do or refrain from doing, intentionally and not, can make a considerable difference to her well-being. Similarly, if I have negatively, though faultlessly, had a direct impact on the well-being of another, that can be enough of a connection to put me at or near the front of those who might help. To be sure, others may have greater responsibility; my relation to the harm may be more distant or indirect. What is to be explained is why even in the absence of either causal or moral responsibility (in the usual sense), the obligation to fix things might be mine.

There is a similar extension of responsibility that comes with the incompleteness of our knowledge. Even if those who designed the Tacoma Narrows Bridge—a state-of-the-art suspension bridge that collapsed in unanticipated winds—built to the limit of prevailing engineering standards, the fact that there were likely to be significant things they did not know makes them responsible for the bridge's failure. Not that they owe damages and the like, but that the failure belongs to them. This is because one of their ends—building safely—always demanded more than the available means. Reasoning does not always go from the end to the means at hand. The end of building a safe bridge puts pressure on the builders to expand their knowledge and their skills. Because of the riskiness of the activity, their responsibility is open-ended, though the same is not true of blame, if they acted responsibly.

The phenomenon occurs equally when the unexpected effect is on oneself. When my home improvement project turns into an obsession, even if I manage to fulfill all my specific duties and obligations, or trim them back so that I can spend yet more time with my contractor, there is a failure here, and I think it is a kind of moral failure, of not preparing well for managing a psychologically demanding project. Why not be consumed, if that's how it goes, so long as the taxes get paid, the children are fed, and classes taught? Because the extreme and unnecessary devotion of attention and energy to such a project is the kind of thing that makes one generally less able to respond and act well, given what may come one's way. It is not an enormous moral failure, but it is one, at the least of a duty to oneself.[9]

9. For related reasons, we speak of obsessions as life-depriving, though they obviously give those subject to them reason to live.

Because obligatory ends require heightened attention to the effects of what we do on the rational well-being of ourselves and others, they give us positive duties to give our life a moral shape. In a sense, moral training that was originally among the obligations of those who raised us becomes the subject matter of duties to self. The responsibility we have is then that we be or become a certain kind of agent. There is no paradox here. If we are moral subjects, we have the capacity to act morally. Theoretically there may be kinds of rational agents in whom the capacity entails the ability. We are not like that. For us, the capacity is given, the ability is acquired. And each of us has final responsibility for developing the abilities necessary for moral reasoning and action.

IV

If there are moral norms that constrain self-making, it is also the case that in the course of becoming a deliberatively unified self, an agent shapes morality. As she fills out her projects and relationships, she may extend herself in ways that generate new duties, or discover obligations with respect to things not thought to be within morality's scope; she may come to be critical of morality as she finds it and perhaps need to discover a way to make repairs or a new way to act well. There is no ideal moral system, no set of perfect rules that we approximate. Some parts of morality involve practices, and then we cannot just set off on our own. However, in other areas we may need to be creative. If morality is about the conditions necessary for rational persons to live well, living together, and if it includes obligatory ends of the kind I have been discussing, then the content of extensive regions of what we ought to do will be in important ways up to us.

I do not mean to say that we create morality—as if we invented it at a conference or on a playing field. It is more like our contribution to the norms for a physically healthy life. Broken bones, cancer, organ failures are objectively bad. We should avoid them if we can. But the prescription for a healthy life is in principle open: fact-sensitive, revisable, to some extent relative to other choices we make, risks we are willing to take. (Does the standard of health for a woman include child-bearing even though it involves risks to health?) We cannot simply create the norms that apply to us; we can and do shape them. And if we shape them, we will need reflective and critical abilities to do the work well. The ability to act creatively and correctively will obviously depend on the evaluative richness of our moral knowledge. This puts a burden on the providers of moral instruction to ensure that the value content of requirements is accessible, and in terms that suit our needs as moral agents.

A mature moral agent should thereby have some ability to negotiate complex or changing circumstances. Procedures of deliberation anchored in (the right kinds of) moral concepts give her resources to respond to unexpected or unfamiliar events; she can challenge or even set aside familiar moral practices in order to accommodate a new situation. In doing this, she engages in a kind of moral improvisation. It does not mark an abandonment of moral values, but is a way of extending them that remains subject to the same standards of justification that were directed at suspect actions set aside. Not every region of morality permits improvisation, but many do. And not every improvisation marks out a way the rest of us should act. The situation that warranted the move may be unusual; our circumstances may be less hospitable to the change; the new way of acting may depend on talents and abilities of the improvising agent not widely available (an easy reach for you can be supererogatory for me).[10] We might think of the many different adjustments couples make in their living arrangements as they became increasingly sensitive to the moral import of choices about career and family.

The umbrella of protection from constant deliberation that is necessary for ordinary life depends on trust in the background institutions that support these activities: that our ways of doing things are all right, and that we have an adequate system of warnings that will flag unanticipated moral danger. But the very seamlessness of ordinary morality that is necessary for everyday judgment and action also poses a danger; it can easily mask injustice, prejudice, and other forms of moral blindness. Ordinary morality is wary of moral conflicts, but we need not be. The rules of ordinary morality are middle-level principles that structure deliberation. They need to be consistent—it cannot be the case that they could never be co-instantiable— but they need not co-determine what is to be done without the active intervention of a moral reasoner.

When wrongful conditions are systematically embedded in our institutions, in formal and casual practices, it can be difficult to see what to do even when it is easy to see that something is wrong. It is not just that the solutions are hard to find; the very identification of a claim of injustice or ex-

---

10. Is there room for moral genius? Would it be a form of leadership by example? Can it be exemplary? Whatever our answers, there is value in making room for these questions.

clusion often provokes campaigns of resistance and denial. The moral history of environmental hazards, of racial and sexual discrimination, of basic welfare rights, traces the tension between discovery and resistance. Some resistance is attributable to vice: greed, selfishness, racism; some simply belongs to morality as a structuring element of everyday life, one of whose roles is to provide stable assurance about the moral adequacy of normal action.

Sometimes the history of a wrong is essential to, and so ought not be divorced from, what the wrong means, or, in some cases, from its remedy. A good example is the current debate in the United States about affirmative action; it is complicated by the presence of two different strands of argument, one about justice in access, the other about a just remedy for past wrongs (discrimination, slavery). Procedures that might well be benign in an egalitarian setting, or thought to be fair in current circumstances, are challenged on two different fronts. It is a very different question whether one may use identity-based preferences to remedy inequality, or to adjust the conditions of access to gateway institutions and jobs in response to a continuing history of social discrimination. The answers may be the same, but the way one understands what one does is different, as are the categories in terms of which we acknowledge legitimate complaint. One argument is based on statistics, under-representation, the values of diversity. The problem to be addressed might or might not be the result of moral failure (as opposed to error or even accident). The other argument is on a different moral plane, condemning the application of ideals of formal equality as masking a continuation of institutional racism. The wrongs picked out are different, and failure to express the difference in both argument and remedy can cast suspicion on the moral adequacy of a response.

One sign that suspicion could be warranted is found in the treatment of shared history. The willful erasure of difficult parts of the history coupled with a conviction that "the past is in the past" casts doubt on the moral neutrality of appeals to formally correct arrangements. In this case, it is the legacy of chattel slavery. Americans accept that slavery was a moral stain on their history through the middle of the nineteenth century. But since the spirit and the effects of an institution do not necessarily cease when the institution is dismantled, its legacy has to be traced with unusual honesty before it can be said that, morally speaking, it is in a now morally irrelevant, distant past. If it turns out that there is a failure to acknowledge or teach uncomfortable large chunks of this history, it is not paranoid to read the silence as a sign that the past that is repressed remains morally active.

Does this mean that moral agents need to be historians? In a sense, yes. We are all consumers of history, of the stories that describe how things come to be. If the stories we believe are suspect, then we fail as moral agents if we do not seek out different ones. In this light we ought to ask: What does it mean for American history and moral culture that lynching, particularly of African Americans, has a place in it? Suppose one thought: here is a dark piece of the past that is, fortunately, in the past. It is an item in the catalogue of moral horrors, but it has no current moral bearing: the practice and the effects of lynching are long over. There are some compelling reasons to think this is wrong. Precisely because it has been an effaced piece of twentieth-century history, lynching bears on the questions of whether and to what extent the legacy of chattel slavery has continuing moral effects.[11]

Making a case for such a claim of course depends on the evidence for the effacement. Such details matter in another way as well, since the larger the thing that is absent from "history," the more interesting the moral questions we should ask. So I want to pause for the moment to look at the record. The example may be parochial; the general point I would make with it is not.

The Tuskegee Institute archives record 3,417 lynchings of blacks in the United States between 1882 and 1944; considered estimates of the actual numbers are much higher. Prior to World War II, thousands of blacks migrated to northern states in part to escape a climate of violence, where being black could be sufficient cause to be summarily tortured and killed. Federal anti-lynching legislation, repeatedly proposed, never became law.[12] 1952 was the first year without a single recorded lynching, though 1952 was not the year of the last recorded lynching.

Up through the late 1930s, many lynchings were public spectacles. On some occasions, thousands gathered for a lynching—men, women, and their children. People sometimes do things together that they cannot imagine doing in isolation, but these collective and often festive events speak of something else. The popularity of photographic postcards of lynchings, the practice of collecting and displaying body parts of the murdered victims,

---

11. The information that informs this discussion is from Phillip Dray, *At the Hands of Persons Unknown* (New York: Random House, 2002), and James Allen, *Without Sanctuary*, an exhibition of photographs and postcards of lynchings that can be viewed at www.withoutsanctuary.org.

12. One of the earliest petitions to the United Nations Commission on Human Rights called for international condemnation of U.S. racial policy for, among other things, its unwillingness to outlaw lynching.

indicate that lynchings were occasions people wanted to remember, to make part of their family life. There was collective pride in being there, in witnessing the event. It is impossibly hard to understand, but people were eager to claim the acts as their own, and to make them part of their children's memories and moral education.

How far in the past does something like this need to be in order to lack present moral force? What is remembered and spoken, or hidden and suppressed, shapes the ideas in terms of which moral and practical possibilities of the future are understood. It is difficult to imagine how one would trace the moral consequences of either the active memory or the silence in this case. But if we remember that a teenager in the 1930s is someone's grandparent in the 1970s or 1980s, then the moral history of many black and white families is unlikely to be the official one, and it is surely a history, whether of silence or speech, that affects the character of our current moral culture.

Different kinds of past injustice place different demands on memory. The South African Truth and Reconciliation Act was concerned with the necessity of turning an unspeakable recent past into an acknowledged collective past so that there would be some usable moral thread in the history of the new state. The pressure on moral history that came from the experience of Nazi mass murder in central Europe was not the same. Here the demand on memory is not in the service of finding a way for oppressor and oppressed to live together, but in making continuously present the fact that an unthinkable human limit was transgressed, in the hope that knowledge of the possibility is a barrier to its happening again. The efforts made to move lynching into the active public history of American race relations is a similar piece of moral historiography; it offers some evidence that it is not yet possible to make ahistorical moral arguments about equality and race.

How would a moral history that included the facts of lynching matter? Here is a conjecture. One reason that affirmative action policies are resisted is that they seem unfair. In an effort to shape the future, it can seem that some are asked to bear burdens they do not choose for ideals they may not value. Knowing little about history increases the room for resentment. Knowing a lot more history, more of us might welcome an opportunity to be the ones to include those who were wrongfully excluded. The moral imagination is labile—subject to enthusiams of reform and anxieties of loss—and its management is among our most pressing obligations. If we do not attend to moral history, or look beneath the public face of institutions, we fail not just a duty to others but also the duty we have to ourselves to deliberate rationally.

V

Because cultures can hide or efface their histories, or their current unjust policies, we cannot be confident that a moral practice that would satisfy criteria of moral adequacy were it evaluated on its own, or as part of some other, more just social order, is in fact permissible. It follows that an agent's moral circumstances may not be the ones she sincerely takes them to be. (Not every aspect of a moral order is suspect: promises are to be kept, acts of kindness performed, truth and trust preserved. But what counts as kindness, or who counts as trustworthy, may not be unaffected.) If this is a real possibility, then one should be prepared to accept that some familiar ways of acting may need to be changed, even if an activity is one that is in its own terms defensible. Moral history makes connections that can alter one's obligations.

The importance of history and context to correct moral judgment reveals that morality is in important ways a local institution.[13] (It is not the only reason for thinking that it is.) There can be universal human rights, principles of international justice, moral rules that no decent society can be without, and it still be the case that the concepts and competencies that make up our moral abilities tend to be firmly anchored in a place. I don't think this feature of moral practice is a bad thing; it certainly doesn't imply anything like moral relativism. There are objective standards for what will count as a response to problems that require moral solutions. But if morality is in these ways local, it may make some forms of moral traveling difficult.[14] Some regions of local morality—those that shape intimate relations,

13. The local is not an absolute notion. Different elements of our lives can be local in different ways. There are things one does in one's family that don't fit outside it; we may choose communities of one sort to live in but of quite another sort for our work, or our vacations. How much variation persons can tolerate or negotiate is hard to say; it may be like the ability to think in several languages—only some can do it. Whether one's moral self has to have a home depends on what we understand the obligations of agency to be. If the gap becomes too wide, the values instantiated too different, the agent's integrity comes into question.

14. There are other positions one can occupy: a visitor or a child can certainly act in accordance with the rules of the social moral world in which she finds herself without being able to act fully in their terms: a "when in Rome" morality. What may matter to the visitor, but not to the child, is not understanding why the moral world she finds has this or that particu-

or the conditions of fit for moral criticism and reform—may not translate. There may also be related constraints on how or even whether some groups can live together and continue to maintain their separate identities.

That what any one of us can do in response to large or systematic wrongs is very limited is no reason to think the moral assignments are not ours. The source of a wrong can create a collective burden; but the bearers of the burden are individuals, even when they act collectively in fashioning a remedy. The space between seeing that something is wrong and making it right is filled by a mix of individual and public action. Individuals can be the agents of change, through their own immediate behavior, but also by way of their institutional roles. By choosing to live in racially integrated communities, or by being in a position to alter the gender conditions of one's workplace, one can take steps to change a moral environment. This is a place where the flow between morality and politics is natural. We can protest, join groups, initiate lawsuits, "work from within." Moral change that requires new categories, or abandonment of central older ones, is hard; without some level of social agreement, the risk of unintelligibility and unintended harm can be great. One of the dimensions of moral creativity and improvisation will then be social—something we have to do together. If one of the positive duties we have is to promote just institutions, to ensure that injustices are not ignored, then it is a moral constraint on the institutions we have to permit and promote the kinds of activity that make this possible. The freedoms of speech and assembly are therefore freedoms that morality requires.

More than a modest degree of improvisation cannot be required since people vary significantly in their abilities to imagine and carry out alternative ways of acting. And grand improvisations are very hard to pull off. If those affected by an action cannot read it correctly, cannot respond in its spirit, then the improvisation is a failure—though not all causes of such a failure are innocent. There is not a lot of room for moral genius, though some for virtuosity.

---

lar feature; what *will* matter is any serious conflict she finds between the recognized moral rules of the locale visited and the moral actions she understands as required, whose values she acts "from" or honors in acting morally. It may be that she discovers the local rules are possible instances of values that are familiar to her; then she can deliberate, awkwardly perhaps, as with any new language. But it may also be that they are not, or that though she can connect the actions and systems of actions with values that are familiar to her, those for whom the actions are local hold other values—that is, that the commonality of morally sanctioned action is in some sense accidental.

VI

So how much can we be required to do? Most moral theories have difficulty answering this sort of question across their domain. Typically, if how much one is to do in some moral region is not fixed, there will be a minimal standard: *this* much everyone has to do. In certain areas, the minimal standard then comes to be regarded as an independent duty. We see something like this with the strict duties of easy rescue and small kindnesses, a standard of providing help that one may not fall below, and then with the more open duty of beneficence, that allows the agent to determine for herself how much to do, and under what circumstances, and at what cost. However, since bearing costs is something morality can require, it may seem puzzling why there should be two obligations with the same content, one strict and one open to choice.

One familiar resolution of the puzzle is in terms of imperfect duties—duties whose concept implies room for agents' discretion about how and when to satisfy them. Our duty to make charitable contributions allows us to say yes to Oxfam and no to the United Way, so long as we sometimes give. The strictness of easy rescue is then explained as a limiting case on the imperfect one: one could not consistently acknowledge a duty to aid and refrain from helping when the need is great and helping is easy. But even easy rescue is an unstable notion—one easy rescue is easy, but if there are four of the same kind in a row, is it now not easy? If a duty allows for discretion, why can't it be exercised here? and if here, why not in the first place?[15] There does not seem much guidance to be drawn from thinking about a moral requirement this way.

One source of the difficulty with imperfect duties comes from interpreting an agent's discretion as a "count" notion: so long as one does something for an imperfect duty, one is free not to do more. If there are positive duties—of beneficence, to promote justice, of moral improvement—they make little sense as part of an annual "to do" list, something the morally efficient take care of early, and the rest of us race around in December trying to get done. Nor is the discretion like tithing. Tithing is a budgeting device—M percent for clothes, N percent for housing, 10 percent for charity. It assumes a whole of which charity is to be a part. Income is a recurring whole

15. One impulse for moving easy rescue out of the sphere of imperfect duties is to remove discretion—its natural extension is good samaritan laws.

used for various purposes; past a certain point, anyone can live without 10 percent of it. We can budget other resources, too—our time and energy, our bodies, our relationships—but it is a perverse way to give a life shape. And unlike charity, the needs that beneficence responds to don't come in the form of an annual appeal.

Another way of looking at the puzzle is in terms of the supererogatory. Here an agent does more than is required, but the role of discretion seems different. The central cases are exceptional moral actions, that either because of what they are, or because of their costs, are not required. They are moral actions because the considerations that move these agents belong to morality, and absent the conditions that make the actions exceptional, they are what one ought to do.[16] Moreover, persons who perform supererogatory actions have not merely chosen to do more than they must for *whatever* reason. The reasons for which they act have to be continuous with the moral reasons that apply to all of us. This is perhaps why it would be "off" for the hero or the sacrificer—falling on the grenade, giving up a kidney—to think of what they do *as* supererogatory.[17] She may recognize that the circumstances do not strictly obligate—she would not criticize others for not acting—but if she sees the action as one *she* could or could not perform, genuinely just a matter of choosing, then the action, though praiseworthy, is a different moral animal. Partly, this is because one must correctly value what one gives up.[18] Partly it is because the hero and the sacrificer regard themselves as doing something they have to do. The recognition that the action is supererogatory, and as such praiseworthy, comes third-personally.

When, out of kindness or concern, a person does more than she must— stays later, runs the extra errand, shares a task to make things easier—are her actions supererogatory? Is there anything gained in thinking they are? I don't think so. Actions of this sort are ordinary, and often provoke a familiar colloquy. The recipient says, "You didn't have to do that"; "You shouldn't

---

16. There is nothing exceptional in Superman covering a grenade; he ought to do it.

17. Compare this with the person who, feeling flush, makes an especially generous charitable contribution.

18. It is not praiseworthy to save another's life in order to hasten one's own demise, or to give what one doesn't care about having. The pleasure of the saintly in their "way" is not a mark against their sincerity, or a sign that the choices they have made have not been difficult. It seems an indication or expression that they have found what they find to be a good way to live.

have"; or "However can I thank you"; and the reply is "It was really nothing"; "I am happy to help"; "Don't be silly, you'd have done the same for me." Both movements are instructive. The first step in the exchange acknowledges something; the second does not rebut what is acknowledged, but asks that it be taken a certain way. When sincere, the deflection of the thanks or the praise is a way of describing how this person sees their relationship.[19] For just this reason, we may sometimes want our gratitude to be accepted as a way of limiting a relationship.

But now imagine the following pattern of action. Presented with a dozen episodes of need of the same kind, A helps every other person whose need presents (let other things be equal). In each case in which A acts, he does more than he is required to do; in no case is there any great sacrifice. In some cases he acts, in some he doesn't. Something here is not praiseworthy, and not because A does less than he must, for he does more than he must every time he acts. The peculiarity of the omissions raises a question about the positive actions. If the difference is explained by how A feels at the moment of choice, given that A recognizes that he is not required to act in any of the cases, then he cannot be taking the need as a reason for action, but the need-when-I-feel-like-responding-to-it. So although the every-other-time helper does more than he must, the way he comes to act, rather than making his actions (or himself) praiseworthy, shows him to be morally capricious. So the puzzle remains.

I think what distinguishes imperfect duties from perfect ones, and what is misrepresented by the count interpretation of discretion, is in the reasons agents may put forward to justify their *not* acting. Perfect duties—not to lie or harm or trespass—can be overridden in the presence of *other* moral consid-

---

19. Thus the oddness, and source of hurt, when someone who has sincerely spoken this way, looks at the next situation of the same sort as if it were an open matter of choice. Not that having helped once gives you a commitment to help again; but having taken the need to be a reason, and having indicated that you regarded your action as having no special merit, you have said something about the kind of person you are, or about how you see your relationship with me, and that has to be acknowledged when the need comes around again. There may be no fault: you were just being polite; I heard the remarks as indication of the way you saw things—the kind of person you are; how you took yourself to stand in relation to me. You may have been a bit insincere; I may be overeager to see relationship where there really is no more than kindness. But the opportunity for the misunderstanding can reflect something about the meaning of the exchange. That is when the exchange has the tinge of insincerity—an exchange of politenesses.

erations. Imperfect duties, by contrast, allow an agent some say about how the duty will figure in her life. One may decide to have nothing to do with large public charities; or commit to working in one's neighborhood; or volunteer for an international relief organization. Right now one may be able to do little: one's work is demanding, or one's children are. As these things change, the role of the positive duty in one's life should change too. As Kant put it: one duty limits another, extending rather than limiting the field of moral action.[20] Because the morally relevant reasons arise from the shape of a particular life, what must be done will not be the same for everyone.

This might explain why agents who lead morally exceptional lives often see themselves as having to live as they do. Their sense of connection with others, their response to human need, in part defines them.[21] That does not make what they do less praiseworthy—though it is the whole and not each action that is exemplary. It is like joining the fire brigade: you do not have to do it, though you may feel you must; but once you are there, the rest is straight obligation. What may be of further interest is the issue of exit. Leaving to the side issues of reliance that may arise as a result of past choices— how to think about them is not obvious—the fact that a way of life was not required makes it permissible to stop, even though while engaged in it, one is under obligation to act.[22]

Characterizing the sphere of discretion this way comports well with the account of obligatory ends. There is space for creative action—even of a whole life—by way of the structure of obligations of impartial morality. A person with many friends has much wider moral exposure than a person with few or none, and not just because requirements are a function of numbers, but because friendship is a relationship that is partly constituted by mutual dependencies. It is not a violation of impartial morality that one person has to negotiate heavy demands from aging parents while another does not. It may, however, be a violation of *justice* if, for example, nursing costs for elderly parents fall on their children. In such cases, the positive,

20. Immanuel Kant, *The Metaphysics of Morals* (1797), in *Practical Philosophy*, trans. and ed. Mary J. Gregor (Cambridge: Cambridge University Press, 1996), 6:390.

21. I am inclined to understand the single heroic act in the same way, though if the person survives it, less an expression of a life than defining it *post factum*. This may be why the heroic act can become a burden, something the hero has to live up to.

22. Obligations to parents and children, to one's country, have a similar structure, though different terms of entry and exit. The burdens of special obligations give an agent reasons that can rebut the claim of a more general duty.

imperfect duties we get from obligatory ends make us vulnerable to the effects of institutional failures of responsibility.[23]

However, like public education, which is a general entitlement that all children have to start life with adequate equipment, it is hard to see why a decent end of life is not also something we are due.[24] Were there no public schools, individuals would have more extensive obligations than they do to provide children with the skills and resources for a successful and moral life. The fact that this would outstrip the abilities of many possible providers is itself part of the argument for public education. Likewise for provision for the end of life. Indeed, one of the roles the state should play is to equalize provision of resources in regions of normal need that individuals cannot reasonably be expected to manage on their own.[25] This is why many of our *non*relational positive duties are best taken care of through social institutions. More generally, there is a moral burden on institutions, beyond those of justice, to do their work in ways that maintain an environment in which we can reasonably deliberate and effectively act.

Still, most of our positive duties involve specific relations—friend, family member, fellow citizen—and if these relations are both socially formed and idiosyncratically inflected, no determinate account of positive duties is possible. Part of what I do in satisfying imperfect duties is shape the relationships that make claims on me, and in so doing, shape myself. In most instances it is ensemble work, where some things are made possible for me by what others do, on their own and in response to me. Thus the metaphor of improvisation.

So how much *are* we to do? There is no amount, no set of obligations we can fully discharge, nor should we expect there to be. Rather, there is an in-

---

23. This problem is particularly acute in the United States. When we consider the way the very old and infirm are cared for, there should be no surprise that the socially confirmed mix of values we have cannot all be satisfied: longevity as a good in itself; technology-intensive medical care; ultimate family responsibility; very limited state support. Perhaps no element is per se wrong or per se necessary; the acute moral problem arises from having them all at once.

24. It is morally irrelevant that the history of public education legislation involved a need to produce factory workers and to assimilate immigrants, and that no such need is present for negotiating life's exit. Sometimes practical exigencies prompt changes that then allow us to realize moral entitlements.

25. Where the state acts as my surrogate, the way needs are met often does not and sometimes should not reflect the structure of the primary relationship (it is not the job of the state or its institutions to replace me; it is just to do some of my moral work).

junction to extend the domain of what we are responsible for and to make an expansive notion of due diligence a part of ordinary and intimate actions.

Given this, we should ask a natural last question. Do we need such an ambitious conception of morality, one with obligatory ends and complexly structured, open-ended positive duties? The answer begins with the sort of conjecture I have entertained here: that those subject only to more modest minimal moral requirements on action are not well positioned to negotiate the historically specific social world in which they find themselves. A morality of positive duties under the authority of obligatory ends, rather than assuming that each agent is a complete and competent deliberator, the autonomous author of actions, gives the individual agent responsibility for becoming such an agent, to the extent that she can do this on her own, and for supporting the social and political conditions that improve the chances for rational agency generally. This way of thinking about morality enlarges the scope of our responsibility; it also discloses some of the extensive resources we have for managing it.

— 13 —

Contingency in Obligation

This chapter begins with an exploration of a set of tensions that arise between some ambitions of moral theory and the role of morality in the regulation and construction of ordinary life. It ends with a conjecture about moral justification in a moment of radical social and constitutional transition, and a challenge to the view that when such moments are politically necessary they may be normatively discontinuous with morality. The route from beginning to end is by way of an account of various kinds of contingent obligations. The idea is that in coming to terms with contingency in obligation within morality we acquire resources to extend the reach of moral justification across the putative gap between morality and political necessity.

An important strand of modern moral theory aspires to capture the connected standards of universality of rule or principle and the unconditional nature of obligation. This can come to be regarded as the source of an ideal of sorts: that there be universality in the content of obligation as well.[1] Our moral lives, by contrast, are run through with obligations that are contingent, in form as well as content, specific to here and now. We are answerable to moral demands that arise from evolving institutions as well as from the vagaries of human life. One response from the side of theory might find our moral lives to that degree imperfect. I doubt that could be right. A different response would take the measure of the contingency as a challenge to the

---

1. One might wonder whether there is the thought here that all good persons should act in the same way—recognizable as such to one another.

300

ambitions of moral theory.[2] Once we appreciate the many different ways that obligations are contingent, where things genuinely could have been otherwise, it might be wondered how we could support the claim of objectivity that is thought to be necessary for the unconditionality of obligation. In some cases the answer is easy, but not in all. My plan is to approach the topic of contingency in obligation in the spirit of this challenge, examining contested claims from the bottom up. I regard the ways we engage with morality in both ordinary and unusual circumstances as providing data, and adopt the working hypothesis that some of the difficulties we encounter may have their source in the ambitions of moral theory, or in the way we interpret them, rather than in the facts of moral life. Reversing the angle of inquiry can often reveal occluded aspects of things; in this case, one hoped-for effect of the shift is some increased insight into the conditions that can give rise to moral obligations.

Some of the questions I will consider may appear more empirical than philosophical. This oddity of method is appropriate to the subject: ethics is a boundary discipline, beholden both to its internal standards (of correctness in judgment and action) and to the conditions of the practical world it orders. This can leave it open, in particular cases, to contest which sort of question we ought to be asking.

Consider, in this light, an initial piece of data and the consequences that flow from it for moral theory. Knowing in advance where our obligations lie, what claims of duty we may encounter, is not just practically useful for planning, but essential—arguably necessary—for living a coherent life.[3] If compelling moral demands, personal or impersonal, may be lying in wait for us around any corner, we would have to set ourselves to anticipate and manage them; and if we cannot know in advance what they are, it is reasonable to think that even the best of us would be rendered less able to invest ourselves, our energy and attention, in the projects and relationships

2. Or as a challenge to conceiving of morality in these terms. One might, for example, use the Hegelian distinction between *Moralität* and *Sittlichkeit* to traverse this domain, the first marking a set of timeless obligations and rights, the other the obligations that belong to historically specific forms of life. While sensitive to many of the moral phenomena I describe, this kind of division tends to miss the contingency that occurs at all levels of obligation.

3. This piece of data shows up in different moments of philosophical discussion: in arguments about integrity and the need for space free of positive moral demands; as a background condition in accounts of flourishing; as a limit on the scope of our responsibility.

that make life worthwhile. A great deal of practical uncertainty of any sort tends to be bad for us; moral uncertainty is especially problematic because moral demands, when they do show up, can override other concerns. This fact, on its own, pushes moral life to be conservative, resistant to change. And because most of us live locally, embedded in complex social and institutional networks, the conservative content of morality that we encounter will also often be local: promises are to be made *this* way, help to be offered like *that*.

These features of moral life—that it resists change and has a local face—have other sources as well. Morality is important in and to our lives: it is to be maintained against strong passions, and it can require the sacrifice of valued interests. Such importance would be belied if morality were inconstant or readily changed.[4] And since it is part of morality's work to mold and direct institutions and relationships, it must appear in a form that fits with what they are locally like, else it would not be able to provide the constancy of direction that is among the conditions of flourishing for both institutions and individuals.

But the story of what we want from morality—the kind of thing we want it to be—contains elements that suggest that the constancy or stability of morality and its local face may not be in total harmony. We might want the stability of morality to arise not from its pragmatic encounter with local mores or our psychological needs, but to reflect the fact that it tracks or expresses some objective truth about the way things ought to be. The local aspect of lived morality suggests, if not full-blown relativism, something other than the universality of moral principle that is often regarded as the telltale of objectivity.

There is also the matter of moral correction and moral change (they are not the same). One might think: The more local the shape of our moral understanding, the more likely it is to be wrong, in large ways and small. This would create problems at different levels. There is the potential challenge the occurrence of local error sets for moral stability (assuming errors discovered are things to be corrected). But also, the very unavoidability of local error might make one think that the project of looking at "lived morality" cannot belong to philosophical inquiry. At best, perhaps, it belongs to its less formal department of engineering or office of pragmatics—

4. See, for example, H. L. A. Hart, *The Concept of Law* (Oxford: Clarendon Press, 1961), pp. 169–171.

applied ethics in a literal sense. But is this right? Inquiry directed at determining correct moral principles and standards is certainly sharply different from a project of understanding the conditions needed for agents in actual social settings to absorb morality and negotiate moral requirements. But why think it follows that the latter kind of inquiry is normatively, and so philosophically, limited?

Suppose that the Doctrine of the Double Effect is a true principle of permissibility (harms that arise as unintended but foreseen effects of overall beneficial action count less than they would if intended). The lesson of double-effect would be lost in a moral space that was dependent on strict performance standards (imagine a society in which traditional forms of action play a central and extensive role in social life). Where trust depends on external signs, claiming that one's intention was not directly engaged with a harm caused may not be a credible way to mark a moral difference.[5] But even if this were a social or psychological fact, it would not challenge the correctness of the doctrine's standard. What is left to ask is whether it is necessarily a good thing to have (or bad to lack) the doctrine playing a significant role in moral practice. How could that be a philosophical question? One might equally ask: how could it be anything else? It is certainly not an empirical or sociological question ("a good thing" in what sense?). It is a question about the contingency of moral content and its significance for claims of obligation. I don't see how we can understand what morality is about without answering it.

If one of the projects of morality is to make the world different, more habitable, more ordered, shaped by our understanding of what is right and good, then the situated agent, living in some specific social space, has to be in the forefront of philosophical reflection. Against an assumed background of objective moral principle, we will ask agent-centered epistemological questions: how should we decide what to do, how to be, given where we now find ourselves? There is precedent for asking the question this way in Kant: morality as a philosophical subject must have its pure or rational part, where we investigate the nature of its authority and the objective principles that lie at its foundation, *and* it must have an empirical part, where we come to grasp what we are to be like and what we are to do—here and

---

5. This is not all arcane. Taboos can be a moral form of strict liability (sexual activity with minors). And sometimes, where temptation to abuse is high, we may want to rescind individual authority (military interrogations offer an instructive example).

now, and toward the future.[6] But then we do need to make philosophical (as well as practical) space for thinking about moral correction and change, and so find a way to manage the contingency in obligation that results.

As we shall see, not all contingency in obligation raises problems. Sometimes the contingency is in secondary principles or meta-rules of response to moral failure, but there is unconditional obligation at the ground level for agents acting. Less easy to accommodate would be ground-level obligations that impose significant burdens but that arise in ways that cannot be anticipated: where the kind of thing we may be required to do is not in or implied by our lexicon of duties.[7]

I think there are difficult obligations of this kind, and that they come about chiefly in conditions where creative solutions to moral difficulties are needed or attempted, often in the space between individual morality and politics. At the limit, there are occasions where the morally innovative or improvisatory acts of some can obligate all. Such a class of obligations would raise questions at many levels: about the closure of moral theory, about the stability conditions for coherent moral action and character, about the conditions of legitimacy for the creation of new obligations, and about their justification.

In what follows, I start out by describing some of the relevant data about our moral lives and circumstances that include the easier to tolerate aspects of contingency in obligation. After canvassing a range of harder cases and the resources morality requires to manage them, I take up the more radical idea of allowing for moral improvisation in moral theory and deliberative reflection. This will in turn provide a framework for examining the very different kind of contingency where political necessity can seem to override or supplant the authority of moral justification. I approach this topic by way of a real case: the obligations that arose with the creation of the South African Truth and Reconciliation Commission. Although the context is political—the establishment of a new constitutional community in post-apartheid South Africa—and with the creation of the Commission came abrogations of fundamental rights and the imposition of new obligations, I aim to show that jus-

6. Immanuel Kant, *Groundwork of the Metaphysics of Morals* (1785), in *Practical Philosophy*, trans. and ed. Mary J. Gregor (Cambridge: Cambridge University Press, 1996), 4:388–389. On one side we get ethics, the subject matter of the *Sittenlehre*, the second part of Kant's *Metaphysics of Morals*; on the other side we get psychology or sociology, what Kant calls "practical anthropology."

7. The sense of "implied" here is deliberative: even if after the fact one might show something to follow as a consequence, if the reasoning was not available—not just difficult, but practically beyond reckoning—then the consequence is not deliberatively implied by what we know.

tifying what was done by appeal to "political necessity" is not necessary, and that by using resources drawn from other forms of contingent obligations, the contested actions can be located within the extended scope of morality, and that the new obligations, though radically contingent, are morally justified.

I

Resistance to contingency in obligation, or to any moral novelty, runs deep, and has its source in the way morality figures in our everyday life. The normal moral agent—someone well brought up, with no errant psychological spikes or troughs—will have integrated determinate moral concerns and moral limits into the content and structure of her projects, even into the possible objects of her desires.[8] In ordinary circumstances, she will move seamlessly in the space of pragmatic and moral reasons. For the most part, moral questions will not and need not arise because her actions and choices are already responsive to the moral norms that apply. Politeness, offering a helping hand, queuing, honesty, respect, and the like, are not separate from what a decent person wants to do.

Some of this just belongs to practical competence. We make judgments and valid inferences without overtly thinking about them, either because we just "see" connections, or because we have acquired some appropriate habits of response—the way an experienced driver responds to a skid, or a competent chess player engages a defense. Although we might say that someone who responds in this way does so "without thinking," we also take her reasons to be accessible, or reconstructable: we know a lot about what we are doing, and why we do this rather than that. There is nothing peculiar to morality in this, though morality may require that we be able to look at things in a finer grain, or with more focused attention, depending, for example, on the kinds of responsibility we have for things going wrong.[9] A

---

8. I use "normal moral agent" as a term of art. She is the subject addressed by the non-heroic elements of a moral theory, or, what amounts to the same thing, the object of good parenting. The elements of character of a normal moral agent will not be the same across times and places, but the feature of fit is constant: hers is the character that is at home in her social world. In some severe circumstances, there may be no place for a "normal" agent; in others, what is normal will hardly be moral. Although morality ideally provides guidance in all circumstances, it would produce an order—a moral order—in which most of us can most of the time be at home.

9. There may also be differences in the extent to which we can recover our reasons in the moment, a matter of deliberative agility, even creativity, at the limit.

little lack of attention to what we are doing in wandering through a market is of negligible significance, a benign absent-mindedness or fugue; we can't be so easy on ourselves where what is at stake is important to what we care about, or where our attention is under moral direction.

A different source of moral seamlessness, one most intimately related to our agency, runs even more quietly in the way we approach choice and decision. There are reasons not to careen into people as one passes through a crowded lobby, and there are reasons to express gratitude for a favor done. If you ask me why I said "thanks," or avoided collision with the someone in my path, the reason I retrieve does not explain why I did "this rather than that," for there was no *that* for me in the space of possibilities. This restriction of the space of possibilities (of actions as well as objects of action) partly constitutes our moral character and is a necessary condition of virtue. Decision in such cases is not a result of choice or calculation. In accounting for this, we are drawn less to analogies with skills and more to field features of perception. From where I stand, there is no path through the space now occupied by someone else, just as there is no question about whether to express gratitude—though some, to be sure, about how best to do it. However we account for this field feature, the plain fact is that the world of the normal moral agent has a moral shape.

Though morality aims to shape the world of human action, parts of it are made to order. Whatever the account of fundamental principles, morality is responsive in certain obvious ways to the basic needs of human existence. But while it is neither arbitrary nor contingent that pain and suffering figure centrally in moral thought, how they count, and whose pain and suffering counts, may be, to some extent, an open question. I do not mean that we just decide these matters—that there are no standards here—but rather that there may be some indeterminacy, something we must fill out. Between the blue-blood's hangnail and the loss of a species of toad there is a lot of space for working out costs and harms and responsibility. But even if the standard of obligation we arrive at is in some sense negotiable, because we are in better (or worse) circumstances, or understand and are able to do more, it is a standard nonetheless—not an arbitrary rule—as there is justification for the lines being drawn where they are. The fact that even core morality has to be filled out in these ways does not render it less objective, or less fixed from the point of view of the acting agent.[10]

10. Some might dispute this, pointing to elements of morality—respect for persons, for example—that are immutable. But what respect for persons amounts to is not always the

Another locus of moral contingency has a different explanation. When land, or the means of production, are owned privately, we are in a specific space of rights and permissions that shapes much of what the world looks like to us. But while property must be stably organized in some way to establish rightful possession, there is no unique way of doing this: things could have been—still can be—otherwise. This kind of contingency of obligation is well accommodated by a two-level theory: abstract principles reflecting fundamental needs, interests, and values, which offer direction for the construction of more determinate rules and practices. Although which rule or standard is adopted is contingent, again, for the normal agent acting, the obligations and duties are set.

However, the same features that morality must have if we are to be able to live in its terms—that it can figure in the acquisition of basic practical skills, organize perception, and set the background conditions for everyday life—are, when internalized for these purposes, sources of tension and resistance if the content of our duties ought to change, or if we are presented with a region of moral concern with which we have little experience. Our practical skills, our sense of salience and confident response are most at home in set practices. Yet, somewhat paradoxically, it is just these abilities that must be called on if we are to be appropriately responsive to new reasons in unfamiliar circumstances: to absorb significant change without harm we require the stability of character and moral self-confidence that normal moral life provides. So there is something a bit perplexing here in the terms of fit between good or normal moral character and developing demands of obligation.

It strikes me as doubtful that there is *an* ideal type of character fit both for negotiating normal action and conditions demanding change. Indeed, there are as likely to be many ideal types as there are to be any. We require certain abilities, but neither the route to them nor the psychological configuration in which they reside need be of one kind. One reason for this is that normal character development is not cost free. We each come to adult agency with a mix of tendencies: some beneficial, some inclining us to cause harm.[11] If we are lucky in life—in choices and circumstances—our flaws

---

same; what is immutable is that respect play a central role in justifications of the ways we may treat each other.

11. We have regions of high sensitivity and of likely negligence; we tend to replicate past injuries. So we may harm without intention to cause harm; yet when we do, we should not say it is accidental.

may not tarnish our record. If we are not lucky, the very tendencies that give us confidence in action may turn out to be ones we ought not to rely on.

One kind of bad luck can occur when social circumstances evolve in morally unexpected ways. Patterns of behavior that were normal and inoffensive may be revealed to be sites of injury; something once thought charming comes to be regarded as demeaning, even an expression of aggression or dominance. Reasonable claims of innocence are no protection against fault.[12] When this happens, reactions are often defensive, and sometimes hysterical; the world can come to be an alien and hostile place, and acting well can seem out of reach. The comfortable fit of seamless requirements and confidence is replaced by a moral demand that we not only acknowledge uncomfortable truths, but also remake ourselves in their light.

If a significant degree of self-knowledge and self-reform is morally required, the recognition that much of our self-knowledge only comes through trial and error, while self-reform is, at best, an uneven process, ought to bear on how we frame notions of responsibility, blame, and obligations of self-improvement. We do not expect people to know themselves *ab initio*, but we do expect them to learn from their mistakes. Likewise, though we cannot expect people to develop independently of their upbringing, we do expect them to move beyond the limitations of what they are taught. Our account of character and obligation will then have to have a view about how to make responsible moral agents—what sort of upbringing, in what conditions, produces agents who are able to generate and respond to new knowledge about themselves and their environment. The processes are interdependent: the content of known morality is reflected in our moral training; moral training includes abilities for self-shaping; these abilities make us responsible for creating and sustaining our moral character in the face of new knowledge; and so we must become trainers of ourselves. If ever there were a virtuous circle, this is one.

Of course, more than increased self-knowledge is involved. If the world in which the normal agent acts throws up new questions, unanticipated relationships, and human-made circumstances, we should expect to have obligations to initiate moral inquiries, to expand the base of relevant knowledge, to engage with and excavate morally relevant history. This too will put pressure on our moral understanding, on the type and content of the obligations we take ourselves to have, as well as what we need to be like in order to meet them.

---

12. We may then have good reason to respond differently to first offenses than to repeated ones, especially when repetition occurs in the face of what has become obvious.

II

Details aside, many of these points are obvious. Normal moral agents are made out of messy stuff; the contexts of action are to some degree opaque; ways in which we change the world (including ourselves) will often turn around and change morality. A natural response might be a reminder that the lived morality of actual agents is not the morality of philosophical or moral theory. And perhaps we might say this in the same spirit with which we say that our ordinary experience of and beliefs about the world are not science. But hard science is not an ideal of ordinary belief, whereas many regard the content of moral theory—at least its principles and procedures of deliberation—as something to be purposefully realized in our actions and practices. This is perhaps why some think that the facts of unavoidable failure and limits of our practical abilities and our moral knowledge, when coupled with the contingencies the world (and other people) may throw at us, point to a different kind of two-level moral theory, not now abstract principle and rules of application, but a moral analogue of what, in the case of political institutions, Rawls called "nonideal theory."[13] There's a lot to be said about nonideal moral theory. I want to say only a little.

Parallel to the political case, nonideal moral theory negotiates two regions of difficulty. First, there is a moral analogue of institutional noncompliance. Without assuming anything very bad about people, there is an expectable degree of moral failure: promises will be broken, lies told; anger will erupt into violence. Second, parallel to the problem of unjust institutions, there are the seriously immoral actions of some that pose practical and moral threats to others—where, for example, violence or coercion compel people into situations in which impermissible actions or ends are (rationally or morally) unavoidable. Nonideal theory will then introduce strategies for managing propensities to failure within the normal (norms of apology, blame, and repair), and principles for permissible resistance and response to wrongful actions, including, especially, resistance and response to those kinds of actions that make persons of moral integrity vulnerable to the purposes of wrongdoers.

13. For useful discussion on this topic, see Christine M. Korsgaard, "The Right to Lie: Kant on Dealing with Evil," *Philosophy & Public Affairs,* 15:4 (Fall 1986): 325–429; Liam B. Murphy, *Moral Demands in Nonideal Theory* (New York: Oxford University Press, 2000); Seana Shiffrin, "Paternalism, Unconscionability Doctrine, and Accommodation," *Philosophy & Public Affairs,* 29:3 (Summer 2000): 205–250; and Tamar Schapiro, "Complaince, Complicity, and the Nature of Nonideal Conditions," *The Journal of Philosophy,* 100:7 (July 2003): 329–355.

Morality could also be nonideal in a more ordinary sense. Failures of agents might show lived-morality to be in some way deficient if they arose because attempting to follow moral rules or ideals imposed large psychological and material burdens, or routinely involved one in moral conflicts, or because the circumstances or the moral rules made it too hard or too time-consuming to determine what to do. Or it might be nonideal because of the uneasy fit between morality and the social institutions in which moral action takes place: for example, economic institutions that produce severe inequalities can make the unadjusted individual burdens of care too high. Considerations of this sort are sometimes brought forward to favor "common sense" and rule conceptions of morality, so that the interface between agent and principle is made simpler, or burdens are shifted from individual to group.[14]

Of course not all moral failures are at the level of individual moral action. We might have available to us a set of principles that would get us closer now to a better state, but that, over time, would do less well than some other set whose flaws have more immediate untoward effects.[15] Or we might have a region that calls for procedural regulation and no fully adequate procedure is available. We might have practices that in one case or another fail to realize their defining purpose, but overall guide well. Though a moral practice is constituted by its rules, it is justified by its purpose. Given unavoidable imperfections or shifting demands of circumstances, the practice is in principle open to change, adjustment, or fine-tuning of the rules (different metaphors will suit different occasions). Most practices can survive such changes; they are organic in that way. But practices must also be somewhat resistant to change and challenge: if they were not, their rules would lack authority.

In the political case, nonideal theory presupposes as an ideal an objective to be achieved (for Rawls, the "well-ordered society"). In the moral case, it is hard to say whether we should be looking toward a moral order of things (a kingdom of ends) or perfect virtue, if they are different, or even if there is a sense in which the ideal in morality is something we are to promote. (I doubt that it is. If what made one think that lived morality calls for nonideal theory is that its requirements need to be adjusted to the limits of agents *as* human agents, then it really is hard to get a grip on the notion of the ideal.)

14. E.g., obligations of individual beneficence replaced by private charities and social welfare institutions.

15. Issues of this sort have recently been raised concerning the rationales for preventive war and the need to curtail civil rights in order to fight terrorism.

We may be morally obligated to promote just institutions, so that given an appropriate conception of justice, and of the limits of social life, there is a well-formed notion of the ideal that nonideal theory is to promote. But we have no similar obligation to promote the institutions of morality (whatever that would mean).[16]

That morality must have ways of responding to the fact that ordinary agents may not always act well, or that we have practices that both require and resist adjustment, does not by itself point to an ideal condition where things would be otherwise. It seems equally sensible to think that the point of morality and such facts of human limits are in important ways co-determining. More malign failures do not in the same sense belong to morality: from its point of view, action that undermines the grip or sense of moral principle is always unexpected, even if not uncommon. That is why normal morality cannot prepare us for all the ways moral action may be subverted, or for what to do when we seem compelled to actions that morality (even strategically adjusted morality) does not permit. For different reasons, but to similar effect, normal morality cannot tell us how to respond to new circumstances or unexpected revelations about familiar ones. But of course we will have to respond in each kind of case.

This leads me to think that what is at issue in many cases is less about ideal and nonideal theory than about the need for principled ways to extend morality beyond the boundaries of normal moral action. For that we will require access to deliberative resources—fundamental principles of action and volition, or conceptions of our relations to one another—that support general standards of correctness for actions and practices. We don't appeal to such principles in ordinary judgment, but they provide the terms of justification for the obligations and duties we take ourselves to have and thus make possible, if anything can, the extension of our moral understanding into unfamiliar territory.

III

In most of the regions so far canvassed, contingency in obligation is handled in one way or another by additional rules (or action-guiding prin-

---

16. Even if there are better norms of friendship than those we have, our obligation is to be (or to help others be) better friends. The idea of an institution of friendship is no more than a *façon de parler*.

ciples). In some cases, the rules are socially or situationally specific determinations of higher-order principles; in others, they are reactive responses to kinds of failure that are frequent enough or serious enough to require set terms of response. But not all contingencies are susceptible to this sort of management. Whether because they are more extreme, and so disrupt the very idea of establishing rules (global catastrophes and the other "what ifs" of the overheated moral imagination), or because they are singular and seem to challenge our terms of justification, some moral contingencies require a different kind of resolution.

As noted earlier, one of the problems one might fear contingency in obligation would introduce is instability in the content of ground-level duties and obligations. Instability is to be distinguished from mere variability of moral requirement. That can be normal, a function of changing conditions that affect action and our relationships or commitments to others. Making a promise, I cannot know with certainty what I will have to do. Being a parent, I cannot know what will be required of me as my child develops, has unexpected needs, or extends my liability. In a sense, this form of uncertainty is already contained in the obligation taken on. If I am not prepared to adjust my activities as events develop, then I have not undertaken the obligations responsibly in the first place. Typically, in incurring an obligation, we accept an authorial position: a commitment to make the narrative of self and some others come out "just so."[17]

Among the things we learn quickly is that our authorial control over the happenings in the world, even in our immediate environment, is limited. It is not just that we have limited powers, our actions are hostage to the unexpected. In the face of this, a prudent agent takes steps to minimize vulnerability: we trim our projects and ambitions; we construct a social world that helps make the effects of others' actions more predictable, and our own intentions more likely to succeed. We do not obligate ourselves if there are too many intermediate steps, or our success is dependent on the unpredictable actions of others. Still, unexpected actions and events are inescapable, and if something significant hangs on it, they can alter what we may plausibly have committed ourselves to do.

---

17. We might use this metaphor as yet another way of marking the difference between negative and positive duties: negative duties tell us that the narrative may not unfold this way (by this means), or over there; positive duties set us on a path: to get Jamie into college, Joey out of harm's way, the package into Mary's hands.

However, while the normal moral agent cannot be assumed to know or anticipate what is happening right now halfway around the world, or what lies she is being told by authorities, or what increases in knowledge will show to be morally salient, things will happen, things probably are happening, that will make what she should do different, and even different in kind, from what she can now expect. This introduces a different order of uncertainty and contingency in the range and content of our obligations—not something that we can, with prudent foresight, prepare for. One curious effect of absorbing this is that it makes morality—at least, moral knowledge—more like science than we typically think. The problems and questions we are taxed to answer expand. We may uncover new moral particles or systems or facts about our psychology that our "old science" cannot accommodate. We revise the way we understand the connections (causal and moral) between material conditions and obligations. And we know that the expansion of our knowledge will continue.[18]

It will follow that although lived morality (our ethical life) is by its nature parochial, as it must be in order to play its role in anchoring the conditions of everyday life, morality itself is not parochially limited. This creates an in-principle tension between the moral facts, as it were, some of which are visible, others newly encountered or excavated, and the desired or desirable seamlessness and stability of ordinary life. While not all tensions are signs of something gone wrong—they are inherent in many normal processes of growth and development—the tension between the conditions of ordinary lived morality and the scope of morality *tout court* is not a piece of a natural process, though it is, or is now, a tension we cannot avoid.

We might then think of the morality we live as a working model—an expression of moral understanding at a time, articulated in terms that cohere with the social and political institutions in which most of our action will take place. The coherence is not primarily about cognitive consonance. Many social institutions—law, educational welfare agencies—are moral institutions: they exist to do moral work, or to make moral action and

---

18. One might think that the very idea of morality changing is suspect, or worse, an opening to some kind of relativism about moral claims and judgments. But even if we thought that fundamental moral principles were fixed—a priori or eternal—the conditions of their application are not, and that creates quite enough space for there to be pressure for change on the lived morality of individuals (this is easy to see for the principle of utility; I think it no less true for the morality of the categorical imperative).

relations possible.[19] Some moral practices are elaborated in terms that make little sense apart from local ways of life (the significance of the hand-shake). This degree of embeddedness partly explains why we cannot expect lived-morality to change easily, not even in response to increased moral awareness and discomfort. Because so much moral work is done without much thought, or done for us, even the appearance of something new to consider can be disorienting.

This is most easily seen at the outer limits of moral embedding, in the norms of manners and etiquette. It can be difficult to think of these norms as part of morality since they regulate modes of dress, patterns of socializing and eating, historically meaningful rituals of civility. These are not the kinds of prescriptions we think of when we bring "morality" to mind, yet they provide the visible form and many of the daily terms of a moral way of life. It is not far-fetched to say that manners and etiquette articulate the outward form of respect—moral business, if anything is.[20]

There are predictable costs at this end of the spectrum. The embeddedness of etiquette in the minute details of living partly explains why it can so easily devolve into high silliness; it goes seriously wrong when it vies for the content and not just the form of our (usually non-intimate) relations. And since etiquette is often also used to provide marks of class, it can seem important to reject it outright (or just ignore it); at the least we should not confuse this aspect of its concern with moral ones. Still, one needs to proceed with care in deconstructing etiquette's social pretensions: they are often ossifications of something with a point, and not as costlessly rejectable as we (or righteous adolescents) might think. The way we meet and greet one another, how we behave in groups and public meetings, what we signal with what we wear—all must have conservative inertia if they are to perform their function.[21]

19. Some of this is familiar: we cannot make promises or exchange goods without the institutions of promising and property. Some is less so: we may have obligations (e.g. of beneficence) that we cannot fulfill without moral risk or fault unless there is institutional mediation (see Jonathan Garthoff, *The Embodiment of Morality*, Ph.D. diss. UCLA, 2004). Of course, there is a danger on the other side as well: reliance on public devices of caring may make persons less morally sensitive, and less able to act well when they must act on their own.

20. For a useful discussion, see Sarah Buss, "On Appearing Respectful: The Moral Significance of Manners," *Ethics* 109 (1999): 795–826.

21. A function that includes in an essential way the possibility of its iconoclastic subversion.

Although ordinary morality is essentially conservative, it does change. What drives change is no one thing, and some of the sources of moral change can be both elusive and morally complex. Certainly not all moral change is for the good. And some changes only appear to make things morally different, especially when they are not well integrated into agents' moral understanding. On the negative side, we know that fear or trauma can cause persons or groups to regress. A strong shared emotion sometimes renders ordinarily decent individuals open to actions they could not straightforwardly countenance. What they then do may be hard to explain in terms of their standing intentions and goals—hard for them as well. Better explanations will appeal to psychological effects: some kind of causal mechanism that affects individuals when they are in group situations. Historical examples are all too common: mob violence, massacres, lynchings, various acts of religious and ethnic extremism, all participated in by ordinary persons. Such episodes may even attain a perverse kind of normality for some sustained time.[22] Positive change also can occur in the absence of a deliberative cause and without a sustained effect on moral life. Individuals, even whole communities, can rise to something that surpasses their own expectations of what is possible. Many of the best known examples of extraordinary actions are taken in response to actual or threatening eruptions of violence, human and natural.[23] They too can become normal for awhile, yet they rarely bring lasting change to the morally ordinary. Like their physical analogue, when the rush of moral adrenalin abates, the new powers and interests are lost and devolve into tales of heroism.[24]

From the point of view of moral theory, both kinds of alteration are matters of psychology that need to be monitored and managed. Lessons may need to be learned, cautions and barriers introduced. However compelling

22. One would like to think that when the frenzy is over and normal life resumes, there is shame. This does not always seem to be the case. There is ample evidence of pride (souvenirs kept in plain sight, stories told the children, a willingness to re-enact, if asked), and remorse, if it occurs, may take generations, or the externally imposed intervention of courts and tribunals.

23. Sometimes it is ordinary life that is temporarily transformed. The French village of Le Chambon during World War II is a famous example.

24. Interviews sometimes suggest after-the-fact puzzlement. In other cases, a possibility for human interaction is glimpsed and then mourned, and once again, inspiring stories are told. It would be interesting to know under what conditions change of this sort can enter ordinary morality through acts of retrospective integration.

at the time, they may not represent a route to moral change that morality itself can recommend. This can happen if the change relies on abilities and character traits that cannot survive the moment, or the actions are not ones that could flow from or even fit with agents' understanding of their obligations.[25] This is not to say there are no questions about obligations one might come to have when such temporary moral phenomena occur. It may seem easy to know what to do or avoid when the issue is others' evil, but it is less obvious what we are obliged to do when surrounded by members of our community caught up in a desire to do some extraordinary good. It seems unlikely that those not part of the emotional surge could be obligated to act in accordance with the new, temporary standard.[26] But I think they may not act in what were the old, ordinary ways, if this now would compromise the good attempted. Collective increases in public kindness, or a willingness to help strangers, or to rescue the persecuted, would seem to impose obligations on all in ways that even widespread acts of personal heroism do not.

The kind of change that morality can most readily welcome arises from deliberative responses to new or newly available (or newly effective) knowledge about events or changes (that may or may not themselves be the product of intention or plan). A new possibility of action is identified as a way through or around some moral difficulty that either the new conditions or the new knowledge generates. It may not matter *how* a possibility is identified; it matters a great deal that a connection be made with available resources of obligation and justification as a condition of affirming the possibility. Such interventions may then work their way into shared moral knowledge and practice. (School integration in the 1950s, partly as a response to psychologists' reports about the stigmatizing effect of racial segregation, is an example.) If, as we do with our knowledge of the physical world, we have reason to expect our moral knowledge to in this way increase and change—knowledge of what may be required of us, as well as of the possibilities and difficulties of successful action—then an openness to the ongoing intentional alteration of the landscape of obligation ought to

---

25. The comparison with supererogatory action is instructive. Supererogatory actions go beyond duty, but they do not surpass an agent's moral understanding and remain connected to the content of obligation; though they too may call on abilities and will that an agent cannot normally access.

26. Though they might become so obligated if it becomes permanent.

be an integral part of the morality we live, and itself a source of distinctive obligations. This kind of openness does not ignore the concern for stability. Only some forms of stability require conservation; others involve maintaining balance, or securing a new equilibrium. The question is then not about stability per se, but about the right kind of stability.

IV

This comparison with our physical knowledge might suggest a simpler theoretical account. Wanting to sustain the objectivity of moral judgments and the stability of practices, I have emphasized the role of deliberative continuity: we deal with moral contingency and change by reknitting the moral fabric, as it were. The focus is on how things are for *agents,* whose choices and responses, guided by deliberative principles, construct a moral world. But suppose one thought that moral theory could accommodate the full range of cases because all possible obligations and duties are, in quasi-Leibnizian fashion, already contained in the concept or extension of our moral principles. It is a tempting picture, for it treats contingency as of mainly practical interest, on a par with adjusting one's financial practices to the ongoing interpretation of the tax code. On such a view, although we do not and cannot know what all our obligations and duties will be, for any set of circumstances, what duties there are is determined by the moral principles that apply. Our efforts may be partial and approximate, but the epistemic norm for moral judgment and deliberation is getting something right in the matching sense.

There are many reasons to resist this picture, but chief among them is that it leaves no place for the (anti-rigorist) idea that individuals and groups can produce moral responses to circumstances that were neither epistemically nor in any other sense "already there"—that their choices and actions can enact new norms, something created or improvised. We might want to go further and say: not only can a new obligation not be conditionally contained in prior moral principle, it need not be a uniquely correct response in the circumstances. So, for example, the suspicion that judgments of merit were affected by gender bias in orchestral auditions or in the refereeing of academic journal articles led some to introduce blind review (hearing but not seeing a performer; excising identifying information from a manuscript). Once introduced, I think it was clearly obligatory to adopt such measures, whether or not there might have been other means of acknowledging equity concerns (point systems, quotas).[27] Partly this was because the remedy was compelling, but also, an improvised remedy will often transform the way past norms of action are understood, potentially changing the significance or content of known rules and principles, so that what might have been another means no longer seems so (e.g., once the problem is identified *by the solution* as one of bias in judgment, not of numbers). All of this adds to the reasons for thinking the explanation of contingency is not a matter of epistemic access. Even failed moral improvisations—ones that are not intrinsically flawed, but that fail, for example, because of bad timing, or lack of sufficient fit with prior values—can create new spaces of moral possibility.

The phenomenon of improvisation, though a bit mysterious, is not really exotic. Most of us are familiar with the moment in the work of a group when someone recalls a past strategy or looks something up that enables the group to solve a problem. Much more unusual is the person who can, at the same kind of impasse, see a novel way of acting that will not only solve the problem, but, through her grasp of the problem and its solution, transform a group's conception of its powers and even of its charge (even more rarely, this may happen collectively). Most forms of moral problem-solving are well understood in the first way: involving factual discovery and reliance on precedent, they pose no strain on any reasonable conception of how morality works. But not all are like this.

I think that morality, and so moral theory, must allow for improvisation, both in its sense of system (that it is open to change not only *at* the bottom, but *from* the bottom) and in the way it acknowledges (and educates) the abilities of agents to effect moral change. In this respect, morality is unlike other practices with which it is often, at least formally, compared. It is not like games, which typically involve fixed systems of rules; and it is not like the law, which can change, but only through the activities of designated authorities (judges, legislatures, etc.). No one has authority to change moral norms. Changes that morality can countenance come by way of the responses of individuals and groups that mark out a direction of action that is held open to challenge on grounds of correctness of fit (fit both with the problem to be solved and also with the rest of morality) and of the legiti-

---

27. This is why it will not do to say that all the moral business lies in a standing obligation to do what one (permissibly) can to remedy injustice. That misses the obligating nature of what is actually done.

macy of costs imposed. It may be that a novel response, once understood, will fit easily with familiar moral principles. But it may also happen that in appreciating the force of an improvisation, one is moved to rethink or reinterpret familiar principles and values. Sound methods of moral justification need not regard the prevailing understandings as fixed. A culture's reflective engagement with these challenges is one way an appropriate demand for stability can be met.

V

To demonstrate the fruitfulness of this approach, I want to turn to a more extreme kind of case, where contingent phenomena seem to require not just a revision of moral understanding but the partial abandonment of moral strictures. Explanations of a normative divide between morality and politics are often made in these terms: political necessities can give us reasons to do things that morality cannot countenance.[28] In times of war or civil upheaval, rights may not be upheld, commitments kept, or justice done. The rationale is the overarching need for peace and security, or social order, or a change in regime. Because the goal is of such weight in terms of human goods (or evils avoided), it supports a permissive stance toward means. When the crisis is over, this rupture between politics and morality is repaired.

It would be more than odd to regard this *realpolitik* as good in itself. It arises, when and if it does, because of the limits of morality, whose rules prohibit the actions deemed politically necessary. While I won't argue against the possibility of such necessities, I do want to suggest that with a more capacious understanding of morality's resources, and in particular the possibility of moral improvisation, the "necessity defense" might be less frequently needed. And that would be good in itself.

To explore this possibility, I want to examine the issues as they arose in the debate over the establishment of the South African Truth and Reconcil-

---

28. Some might argue that what I call political necessity is really a species of moral justification, at the limit, where morality condones or even directs the violation of its central standards. It's a view that doesn't so much beg as give up on the moral question. A different way of ducking the problem is to claim that political justification is of its own kind, so that given its distinctive subject, one should not expect congruence with morality. Though we should not expect states to operate on the principles that govern personal relations, that is a reason to extend our understanding of morality, not to leave it behind.

iation Commission (TRC)[29]—a set of temporary, extra-judicial commissions through which victims of apartheid's violence could formally register crimes committed against them, perpetrators could seek amnesty, and some amount of reparations would be provided to victims. The legacy of grievous injustices of apartheid presented a range of obstacles to the possibility of shared moral life that ordinary morality and existing institutions lacked resources to overcome. The TRC was designed to bridge that gap. It is an especially apt case for my purposes, since those who created the TRC explicitly intended by so doing to obligate others—specifically, to forgo redress for claims they had against perpetrators of immoral, criminal acts, and to accept the regimen of the TRC in its stead. Given the circumstances in which the obligations were to be introduced, the question of their legitimacy arose naturally, and political necessity was one immediate answer, though not one that the principals endorsed.

The TRC has been viewed variously as a baldly political compromise introduced to avert a civil war, or as a situation-specific transition stage in the institution of constitutional democratic rule, or as a local modification of the post-Nuremberg structures used to provide an accounting of state crimes. I think the record shows that it was no *bald* compromise; it is hard to imagine a more articulate or morally anguished public debate, regardless of the existence of some backroom deals. I also think its creation was a piece of a strategy for constituting civil society, but it was not for that an act of political necessity, or something to be subsumed under the rubrics of irregular or reparative justice (though the procedures were irregular and reparative). The costs imposed were morally significant, and it would be best to offer a moral justification, if there is one. The question is: of what kind? I will argue that the TRC can be understood as a moment of moral improvisation, and as such prompts an account of the moral costs and benefits that reframes the issues involved. Pragmatic considerations can figure in its justification, but not so as to make the brunt of the argument instrumental— doing what had to be done for some pressing end.

---

29. The TRC was created by an act of Parliament in 1995 (fulfilling the directive of the postamble of the 1993 Interim Constitution to establish some mechanism and criteria for granting amnesty for conduct "associated with political objectives and committed in the course of conflicts of the past"). The first hearings were in 1996. The work of the Commission officially ended in April 1998 (though the amnesty phase went on until July 2001); its *Final Report* was issued in November 1998. The moral question begins with the postamble.

There is always some danger in trying to do philosophical work with a historically specific event. However, the wariness that is in order when one is adducing as argument a flow of interconnecting events and actions is to a considerable extent addressed in this case by the great care the participants took to publicly acknowledge and justify the moral complexity of their decisions. And there is a related advantage. Distinctions that might seem artificial in a philosopher's example here lie on or close to the surface of the historical record. It is an unusual moment in which thoughtful efforts were made to use available morality to introduce moral change.[30] So if there is a risk, I think it is one worth taking.

To make the case for the TRC as an example of successful moral improvisation, I need to show three things: that the creation of the TRC is not to be regarded in purely political terms; that its origin was in an improvisation that created obligations not latent in the moral world (in ideal or nonideal terms); and that nonetheless these obligations could be justified in the moral terms of the world they changed. The contingency of the obligations was at both ends: the source is in no rule or principle, and the outcome is a set of obligations whose justification, though moral, is tied to time and place.

In the moral story of the TRC, the moral improvisation comes in two steps. First, there was an act of individual creativity. It is credibly claimed that Nelson Mandela's stunning refusal to seek retribution for the grievous wrongs he suffered did much to create the moral possibility of social order and democracy in post-apartheid South Africa.[31] What he did, and was seen to have done, is to offer himself as a model of moral self-transformation. In refusing both the natural desire for revenge and any formal claim for just retribution, he created a possibility of self-movement from the status of victim of unjust violence to the status of citizen of a state (one not yet fully existing) committed to an ethic of forward-looking civic benevolence. But Mandela's act was not of a kind that many others could repeat. It required

30. I don't claim that the debates got all or even most things right, or that it was the moral force of the deliberative conclusion that carried the day. But the public discussions leading up to the TRC were remarkably clear about what was at stake, morally, if less clear about how or whether they resolved the moral problems introduced by their decisions. One of the purposes of this discussion is to suggest that the moral resources they had available to them were in fact adequate to the task.

31. The nature of the circumstances in which a charismatic individual can be morally effective is a question for social science. How the change effected can be legitimate and correct is the business of moral theory.

unusual moral heroism, and its success depended on Mandela's special public position. What Mandela and others saw, however, was that *given* his example, an institution might be constructed, the TRC, that would make generally available a less heroic avenue to the same transformation of moral status, from victim to citizen. (And this would be so even if it was also true that some of the actual argument for and the resulting form of the TRC was a product of naked political bargaining.)[32]

The second step introduced the obligations. In particular, with the institution of the TRC, all persons would be obligated to forgo normal routes of judicial redress for a wide class of crimes committed against them. Instead, they would have access to the TRC, either directly through public testimony and/or confrontation with the perpetrators of wrongs before the Commission, or by filing affidavits, or, symbolically and indirectly (given the testimony and the affidavits) through the creation of a new history whose framing theme turned what had been merely private stories into a public moral narrative. For those friendly to the work of the TRC, it is this symbolic and indirect moral possibility, with its wide inclusiveness, that provided the key element in its justification.[33] (Accounts of the TRC that emphasize forgiveness thus mistake its grand ambition.)

Critics of the TRC argued that the obligation to forgo judicial redress was not a necessary condition of an important moral possibility, but, very much to the contrary, an additional injustice, one that undermined the legitimacy of the claimed obligation, and so also, of the TRC (perhaps the TRC could obligate, but it could not obligate the relinquishing of *these* rights). If neither the act of creating the TRC nor the TRC itself could impose this obligation, and the imposition of the obligation was not a morally necessary action (no

32. Chiefly, balancing the moral and personal costs of amnesty with the needs for public order, given that any viable future state would not only contain perpetrators and victims but would have to rely on the good will of both, especially if, as was reasonably believed, the police and military would not tolerate purging malfeasors.

33. Analogous claims are made about the need for international war crimes trials. The claim is not (or not just) that ordinary criminal trials might not be successful, or would be too dangerous. That risk could be seen as part of what makes the use of the criminal justice system necessary—a way of bringing horrific acts within the orbit of ordinary justice. The justification for these abnormal judicial activities is more commonly that some moral possibility needs to be opened (or closed) that exceeds the orbit of ordinary justice, some difference negotiated between criminal liability and accountability per se. It is exactly the nature and extent of this sort of justification that is in question in the case of the TRC.

one argued that it was), the contested obligation was at best genuinely contingent, and, absent further justification, vulnerable to the criticism.[34]

In fact, with the TRC came an array of new obligations. Victims (their families and allies) were obliged to forgo not only revenge but also retributive justice, accept not only the possibility of amnesty but also a future in which they would share a normal social world with the unpunished guilty. Perpetrators were obliged to accept the amnesty process as a condition of their peaceful inclusion in the social order, a process that carried risks: of the roughly nine thousand people who applied for amnesty, only a few hundred met its conditions—that the deed for which amnesty was requested had been politically motivated and that a full public account of it be given. Archbishop Desmond Tutu expressed the odd gravity of the first condition this way: "You are able to tell the amnesty committee that you are proud of what you did, albeit that it constitutes an offense under law." It did not matter what the actual intention of the torturer was, or his personal moral guilt. What did matter was the conceptualization and subsequent repudiation of the political motive and its legitimizing source. For those who did not receive amnesty—because it was not granted or because they would not apply for it—there was risk of civil suit and criminal prosecution. Last, there was something like a general obligation to participate in the construction of a moral history: to resolve conflicting memory and private story into an emerging public narrative that would provide a shared truth, if in parts a permanently contested truth, on which a morally sound politics could be built.

Even though the occasion for these obligations was a radical political transition, and the obligations were given specific content by a quasi-parliamentary process, I do not think their nature or their justification is best dealt with in political terms. If we take political obligations to be those whose main line of justification derives from political institutions, the justification of (basic) political institutions and the obligations incurred in establishing them is not political, but moral.[35] Since from the point of view of justification the TRC is not a political institution, but part of the formation

---

34. The issue of authority to introduce the change is unusual in this case, since the TRC was established through public and open discussion. And if that was done well, there may be no authority question that is not tied to the question of moral legitimacy (i.e., some things may not be changed or forgone, no matter what the process).

35. In this sense, the obligation to form or enter a state cannot be a political obligation, though obviously it has political content.

conditions of political institutions, its justification depends on the legitimacy of the obligations it imposes, and *their* justification will depend on showing *both* that they promote some vital social good *and* that they are continuous with first-order moral standards and principles. That is why it will not help to argue that there is a standing obligation, political or moral, to bear costs in order to establish or re-establish political order, for it is precisely the justification of being obligated to bear those costs that is in question.

The question of justification is most acute with the obligation to forgo retributive justice, since what it required innocent victims (or their families) to forgo does seem to be precisely what they had a fundamental right to in virtue of their violated innocence. Especially given the continued operation of regular courts, how could persons become obligated not only not to exercise but not to claim their legal rights? It is true that in emergencies a state may suspend some rights. But in this case, the additional fact that so many agents of the state were perpetrators of the crimes in question undermines its authority to justify the amnesty on those grounds. If the TRC was to be part of a process of legitimation and inclusion, its role would be compromised if the obligation to forgo retributive justice and accept the conditions of the amnesty could not be justified in a way that answered the moral complaint. The problem is particularly difficult because of features shared with more radically contingent obligations: the obligation was unforeseen and unforeseeable; it was not chosen or voluntarily adopted by all affected; and it was not the unique solution to a state of moral conflict.

Let us focus first on non-uniqueness. We have already seen one kind of non-uniqueness with two-level theory, where obligation follows from institutions that give form to a higher-level principle that could have been expressed differently. But the TRC was not such an expression; it introduced an obligation that altered the moral terrain, imposing significant burdens, and it was just one of a number of possible obligations that could do the moral work. Why couldn't victims rightly object if they were to be so obligated, at considerable cost, when some other obligation was available, morally equivalent, and would impose lesser burdens on them? In a different but related context of non-uniqueness, T. M. Scanlon offers a decision principle that is suggestive.[36] He argues that where there is a region of activity that requires moral regulation, and there is more than one legitimate principle that can do the job, the fact that one of these principles is gener-

---

36. T. M. Scanlon, *What We Owe to Each Other* (Cambridge, Mass.: Harvard University Press, 1998), pp. 339–340.

ally, even if not universally, accepted in a community can be sufficient for it to obligate all. Those who are inconvenienced by the accepted principle, or just prefer another, have no legitimate grounds to object to it, no reason based in its non-uniqueness to resist it.[37]

If there were a way to extrapolate to the TRC, we could then say that both principles—the principle of retributive justice and the principle of amnesty (requiring that retribution be forgone)—might be morally supported, and yet only one, though either one, could obligate. However, the conditions of Scanlon's principle are not satisfied by the TRC, since it is the option of retributive justice that is already in place. On its own, Scanlon's principle is conservative.

The attraction of thinking about the TRC using some analog of Scanlon's non-uniqueness principle is that we would not have to judge the decision for amnesty as legitimate only if so deciding tracked a balance (in which some fundamental claims are outweighed). Nor would we need to describe the contested principles as representing an underlying conflict of duties (in this case, one looking backward, one forward). That is, if there really were different routes or principles that were morally legitimate, each supported by equally sound moral considerations, then in choosing the amnesty condition, the value of punishing gross violators of human rights would not need to be judged less weighty than the forward-looking goals of reconciliation and the constitution (or reconstitution) of civil society. It is doubtful this would assuage feelings of outrage at losing the opportunity of "seeing justice done," but it would address the sense of moral offense that individual entitlements are being swept off the stage for the collective good.[38]

Now to do its work, Scanlon's principle, or any analogue of it, has to appeal to something to give reason to elect one of the competing principles. First-order reasons are exhausted in support of the principles. The reasons to favor one principle over the other are, in a broad sense, pragmatic. But pragmatic considerations cannot trump or outweigh either principle, so there is a puzzle about how they enter at this stage.[39] Moreover, not just any pragmatic consideration would do, as if there were a wide-open consequentialism at the level of principles. That the adoption of one of two morally legitimate principles concerning punishment, or privacy, would have a pos-

37. Uniqueness *is* necessary for the meta-principle legitimating the authority of lower-order principles.

38. This was vivid in the complaints of Steve Biko's family.

39. Moral arithmetic isn't straightforward: one can't argue that since the principles are equal, pragmatics just adds a little weight-of-reasons to one side. The objections to deciding against a basic moral claim by appeal to numbers or welfare or pragmatics would just re-enter.

itive effect on gross national product seems irrelevant to the decision between them, though the same effect would not be irrelevant with respect to a pair of principles about fair taxation.

Overall, what we need is a way to fully acknowledge all the moral considerations that are reflected in the competing principles, without weighing and balancing—an analogue of Scanlon's principle would do that—*and* find criteria of relevance for the introduction of pragmatic considerations. We do not want to say that individuals who would make a claim for retributive justice—claims that could be honored—not only are blocked from pursuing their claims but are also obligated to accept principles requiring them to forgo their claim, on grounds that just appeal to numbers, or even general welfare. Fundamental moral claims should not be discounted in that way.[40]

A more general way to think about an alternative to weighing and balancing is in terms of a revisionary casuistry: replacing moral arithmetic with a form of argument that leads to a rethinking of the way underlying values support specific claims and moral relations. The goal is to present the conflict in a different moral configuration from the one originally contested, while still maintaining the integrity of the moral reasons on all sides. The challenge is to proceed without an *ex ante or* fixed commitment to each reason's full moral significance or justificatory reach. When successful, a sound revisionary casuistry can create a path through moral conflict by partially disarming the contesting parties.

In the case of the TRC, what we need to be able to do is think differently about the moral significance of the majority. We will not resolve moral complaints against the amnesty principle so long as we see the choice for the TRC as a matter of majority preference or will—an inappropriate pragmatics. How else might we regard it? First, the object of choice is not merely an independently valid principle of obligation but also one whose supporting reasons offer a vision of a future accepted by those who will, by means of the principle, act for that future together. In such a case, one might almost argue, *can* implies *ought.* And second, in contrast to more familiar weighing and balancing situations, the agents here saw themselves faced with a novel situation, where, as I would put it, there was need for improvisation.[41] Now any valid moral improvisation will be constrained by, among

40. Scanlon's own use of his principle is left unclear: it might be that the pragmatic concerns are the values of stability or continuity, or merely the preference or comfort of the majority.

41. Even if an existing institution had been embraced, it would have been for new reasons, and so represent a decision for a different principle.

other things, shared moral history: those who are to act on its principle have to be in a position to experience it (hear it) as obligatory. That is why the mix of political, religious, and traditional experiences and values brought to the decision between principles does not make the decision other than moral, and certainly not impure. These beliefs properly inform the decision, for they partly constitute the abilities agents have for action and sacrifice, and so inform their vision of what is possible. This is one of the ways Mandela's exemplary action clearly made a moral difference. By drawing on shared values and experiences, his singular action revealed a creative potential in the abilities and values people already had. Absent Mandela's example, the institution of the TRC might not have been able to generate a legitimate collective obligation.

In a sense, then, the claim that the circumstances prior to the creation of the TRC supported more than one legitimate principle is not quite right. More than one principle could have been justified—that is, is supported by sound casuistry—but only one principle was in fact made viable, or became a real possibility. Even if the counterfactual were true (had the other principle been chosen, it would have served as well), real possibility is determined from the point of view of those making the decision, and not all possible futures can be imagined, or imagined all at once. The actual conditions of moral life are thus part of the argument determining moral possibility.

However, if this shows a different way to support the decision for the TRC, we still need to account for the status of the moral interests represented by the option forgone. In some resolutions of moral conflict, a correct judgment about what to do does not remove the competing source of obligation—there are remainders, and if we can act in light of them, we should.[42] In the case of the TRC, however, any reassertion or continuation of the forgone retributive claims would seem to be excluded by the amnesty

---

42. Suppose we can act to save either A or B, both drowning; we cannot save both. We decide to save A and allow B's fate to unfold as it will. If B drowns, there is no moral remainder. We did what we could. But if B miraculously hangs on, we have further obligations toward him. We cannot now let B drown, even though our earlier decision to let B drown was without fault. The obligation continues past the decision point of action. However, the continuing presence of the obligation need not warrant action of the same kind: there may be new considerations that bear, including the effects of the first action. If B hangs on, but A needs to get emergency care to survive, the earlier choice to save A seems to encumber decision, even when B's need to be saved reasserts itself. So the fact that the obligation continues does not return us to the original choice situation.

provision itself. And yet key elements that supported those claims remain. Vicious illegal acts will not be punished; guilty persons will circulate with impunity among not just the innocent but their victims. True, that just is the effect of an amnesty. But in these circumstances, it seems hard to resist the argument that because of the abiding moral cost in forgoing retribution for those who supported the path not taken, the amnesty violates *some* ongoing moral claim. At the time, some who were concerned about this issue argued that the conditions of the amnesty—that perpetrators come forward and publicly admit to wrongdoing in the pursuit of political ends—were weakly retributive insofar as they created vulnerability to shame and public censure.

I doubt that the forms of public censure available could have been an adequate response to the retributive claims. Moreover, it is not clear that this role was consistent with the reparative ambitions of the TRC. But neither of these point addresses the real issue. If any part of the retributive claim is met, or acknowledged, then the decision to forgo retribution is not effective. So either there is an abiding retributive claim, which undermines the legitimacy of the amnesty decision, or the amnesty decision somehow cancels the retributive claim.[43] That is, the claim cannot be acted on—conceptually cannot (nothing would count as satisfying it)—or the reasons that had supported it no longer do.

To this point, I have treated the retributive claim as self-evident. In the last stage of the argument, it will be helpful to think a bit about the values that support it, and to introduce a revisionary casuistry here as well. We say that a victim of a crime has a claim in justice to seek the punishment of the guilty perpetrator. Take this to be a legal fact. Behind the legal fact is a more complex story. Consider one familiar version of it.[44] In broad strokes, there are, on the one hand, social needs: for deterrence of harmful acts, for making the social fabric whole again, and for institutions that embody ideals of fairness and the rule of law. On the other hand, there are moral concerns: only the guilty should be punished; some notion of proportionality in punishment; and so on. But, morally speaking, there has to be more. If we suppose that the desire for revenge is a natural response to wrong or harm done, it is an open moral question whether such a desire should be turned

43. This is not a general claim about remainders and residues. It is a special feature of this case that if the retributive claim survives, the principle that blocks retribution fails.

44. To make a point, I borrow liberally from Chapter 5 of J. S. Mill's *Utilitarianism (1861),* ed. and introd. George Sher *(Indianapolis: Hackett, 1979).*

into or reflected in a moral reason or claim.[45] Now, a legal system that makes retributive claims possible can be seen as creating a moral substitute for, or a translation of, the desire for revenge. It both asserts a monopoly of force, blocking the natural expression of the desire, and offers an interpretation of what it is about the desire that matters: say, the recovery of the moral or social status of the victim. The interpreted desire can then be captured in a judicial system that gives a legal status to the victim, by treating her private harm as a legitimate cause of public action, through a system of trial and punishment for accused wrongdoers.

Suppose some such account is plausible. We could then see the (morally) improvisatory TRC (including the decision for amnesty) as introducing a competing method of capture for the interpreted desire, the effect of which is to cancel the retributive claim. That is, the decision for amnesty will give the desire for revenge no retributive expression. The truth about injury and moral harm will still be publicly acknowledged, and the victims' status regained, but not by way of the institutions of retributive and compensatory justice.[46]

It is a strength of this account that the considerations that favor the decision for an institution like the TRC do not support it as a permanent substitute for the formal systems of criminal and civil justice. They belong to conditions of transition where a break with the past is called for and normal institutions cannot accommodate that role. A well-founded legal system expresses a community's commitment to the rule of law. That is why enforcement of laws can restore a community. But where the commitment is what is at issue because the community needs to be constituted, and those who were not entitled to share in that commitment need to be enfranchised, there is moral room and reason for extraordinary or quasi-judicial action. For the TRC, the argument that seems most to the point is that in the circumstances of transition from a regime that routinely violated human rights to a democratic system of government, the restitutive moral function of retributive justice could not be realized. There was therefore a need, for a time, for a different way of publicly negotiating past wrongs

45. I say "turned into" rather than "acknowledged as" to reflect the idea that desires alone do not support reasons or claims.

46. This sort of argument led some who supported the amnesty from criminal liability to want there to be room for civil suits seeking damages. The third arm of the TRC, the Committee on Reparation and Rehabilitation, was partly designed to capture that aim.

done that managed the entry of disenfranchised victims into the class of citizens. Given the goal of securing equal moral status, the abridging or balancing of fundamental moral claims was not a morally possible means to this end.[47] By contrast, the public creation of a moral history through the testimony and affidavits received and broadcast by the TRC was an enfranchising act, in that it changed the basis on which moral status was acknowledged. Thus, given a justification for the TRC based on the absence of conditions of civility and trust that allow ordinary systems of justice to perform their status-securing function, its legitimacy depended on making a credible claim to (re)instate them—though once reinstated, they are different, since situated in a different moral history.

VI

There are several things to note by way of conclusion. First, I take the extended web of moral justification offered on behalf of the TRC to support the claim that legitimate collective obligations can be generated by morally improvisatory acts. In general, the resumption of normal moral life will close the arc of the improvisation. The contingent obligations it introduces are replaced or absorbed and are no longer experienced as anything new. In either case, what now counts as normal is no longer what it was; hopefully it is better;[48] and stably so. Retrospective reconstruction may seem to show that the change was latent in the community's core values. Inevitably, there will be such connections: improvisations are constrained by their starting points, and when they are to result in collective action, they are also constrained by the values and abilities of those who are to act. But all of this connectedness does not defeat the claim that what has been done is something moral, and something new.

Second, there is the role of what I have been calling "pragmatics" in making obligating decisions between contending principles: considerations such as stability, psychological fit, historical viability, and so also the sheer need to resolve political and social crises to create or restore moral conditions of ordinary life. I have argued that they can enter determinations of basic rights and claims, but only *after* their justification is complete, and

---

47. Thus, rather than setting a limit *for* morality, it is a task *of* morality to set the terms in which such a goal can be an obligating target of our individual or collective action.

48. Better from its own as well as from the prior point of view.

only so long as they fit or enhance the work of first-order values. In this way pragmatics can extend, not just compete with, moral justification.

Last, we have seen how the reach of morality extends beyond the norms of ordinary moral life. Political crises can introduce unexpected normative questions, but the political context does not necessarily make the questions political—in the sense of belonging to a special sphere of argument—or show that the resources of morality are inadequate to answer them. The discussion of the TRC shows one possible creative extension of these resources: the improvisatory intervention and the resulting reorientation of justificatory argument. It is really something we should expect. Fundamental moral values and principles have greater potential for organizing our affairs than can be realized or even appreciated at any given time. It is this potential that is tapped for new procedures of justification when contingencies might seem to outstrip moral argument.

Credits

Chapters 10–13 are published here for the first time. Permission from the publishers to reprint all or parts of the other nine chapters is gratefully acknowledged; the original titles and sources of those chapters are as follows.

Chapter 1. "Making Room for Character," in Stephen Engstrom and Jennifer Whiting, eds., *Aristotle, Kant, and the Stoics: Rethinking Happiness and Duty* (Cambridge: Cambridge University Press, 1996).

Chapter 2. "Pluralism and the Community of Moral Judgment," in David Heyd, ed., *Toleration: An Elusive Virtue* (Princeton, N.J.: Princeton University Press, 1996).

Chapter 3. "A Cosmopolitan Kingdom of Ends," in Andrews Reath, Barbara Herman, and Christine M. Korsgaard, eds., *Reclaiming the History of Ethics: Essays for John Rawls* (Cambridge: Cambridge University Press, 1997).

Chapters 4–5. "Moral Literacy," in Grethe B. Peterson, ed., *The Tanner Lectures on Human Values*, vol. 19 (Salt Lake City: University of Utah Press, 1998). Permission to reprint courtesy of the Trustees of the Tanner Lectures on Human Values and the University of Utah Press.

Chapter 6. "Training to Autonomy: Kant and the Question of Moral Education," in Amélie O. Rorty, ed., *Philosophers on Education: [New] Historical Perspectives* (London: Routledge, 1998).

Chapter 7. "Bootstrapping," in Sarah Buss and Lee Overold, eds., *Contours of Agency: Essays on Themes from Harry Frankfurt* (Cambridge, Mass.: MIT Press, 2002).

Chapter 8. "Rethinking Kant's Hedonism," in Alex Byrne, Robert Stalnaker, and Ralph Wedgwood, eds., *Fact and Value: Essays on Ethics and Metaphysics for Judith Jarvis Thomson* (Cambridge, Mass.: MIT Press, 2001).

Chapter 9. "The Scope of Moral Requirement," *Philosophy and Public Affairs*, 30, no. 3 (2001).

Index

Absolute prohibitions, moral judgments and, 88–89. *See also* Taboos

Absorption, deliberative unity and, 285–287

Actions: agent-relative evaluative descriptions, 87–91; choice and will in relation to, 239–241, 249–251; desire and, 3–6, 8–11; evaluation of, 83–87; faculty of desire and, 234–236; government by ends of, 263–266; group identity and, 34–38; hedonism and choice of, 187–191; justifications for, 116–121; moral education and role of, 133–134; moral law concerning, 194–198; moral motives for, 51, 71–72, 77, 87–91; obligatory ends and, 264–266, 277–280; pleasure and, 176–178, 180–183; public legitimacy of, 72n31; reason-responsive, 119–120; standards of correctness for, 257–260. *See also* Nonmoral actions

Aesthetic judgment: interpersonal validity and, 117n16

Aesthetic pleasure: hedonism and, 185–191

Affirmative action, different moral arguments for, 289–292

Agency: autonomy of, 71, 127–128; beneficence and, 209, 215–219; deliberative unity and, 283–287; efficacy of, 36, 42, 142; Frankfurt's view of, 159–161; hedonism and, 187–191; imperfect duties and, 295–299; moral adequacy of, 36–38; moral development and, 79–105; moral education and, 144–145; moral law and, 192–198; moral literacy and principle of, 81–82; obligatory ends and shape of, 277–280; rationality and, 157; social bases of, 63–64, 75; "two natures" view of, 197n34. *See also* Rational agency

Allen, James, 290n11

Allison, Henry, 248n29

Amnesty: retribution and, 324–331; social order and, 322n32

Animals and animal instincts: capacity/incapacity and, 248n28; choice and, 242n17, 243–246; faculty of desire and, 234–236; human *vs.*, 9, 138–143; means-ends principles and, 170n16; obligatory ends involving, 271–272; perceptual representations and, 237n10

Archetype: of happiness, 136n4; kingdom of ends and, 70–71

Aristotelian ethics: character and, 24–28; moral development and, 96–97; moral judgment and, 1; nonrational part of soul in, 10; virtue in, 112n10

Authority: of conscience, 113; content and, 260n9; cosmopolitan moral community and, 50n21; deliberative field and, 46, 126n29, 158; freedom and, 241; interests and, 47; justice and, 127; for moral change, 323; of moral change, 323n34; of moral criticism, 27; morality and, 11–12, 82–83, 98, 145, 271, 303–304; of moral law, 196; norms of, 56, 113, 143, 318; obligatory ends and, 263, 265–266, 299; over decisions, 211–212; parental, 93; of reason, 32n5, 163, 165, 175; reflection and, 160; in religion, 45; of rules, 310; self-interest and, 23; in society, 226; of state, 324; of values, 125; of will, 63

Autonomy: desire and, 127–129; dignity and, 52; identity and, 165–168; indirect motivation and, 85n6; institutional structure of value and, 121–129; kingdom of ends and, 60–61; moral education and, 128–153; morality and, 13–17, 51–52, 58, 61, 64; power of will and, 251n35; principle of, 13; will and, 160–164, 266, work as condition of, 151–153

Ideal: community of moral judgment and, 77–78; of imagination, 136*n*4; Kantian sense of, 61*n*12; kingdom of ends as, 51–78

Identity, autonomy and, 165–168

Imagination: happiness and, 181*n*8; moral education and role of, 135–143

Impartial spectator, moral motivation and role of, 87*n*13

Imperfect duties: latitude or leeway in action and, 213–215, 219, 273, 294; obligatory ends and, 205, 215, 252–253; perfect duties *vs.*, 296–297; social conditions of, 297–298

Improvisation. *See* moral improvisation

Incapacity *(Unvermögen),* freedom of choice and, 247–253

Incentive: for action, 232; desires as, 2*n*4; material, 196; moral law and, 13; nonmoral *vs.* moral, 132, 141, 187*n*17; norms of, 11–12; rational agency and, 18–24; of will, 140, 172*n*17

Incest, 88–89

Incorporation thesis, 239

Indirectness, moral motivation and, 82–83, 104

Individual agency: contingency of obligations and, 317–319; happiness and, 182–183, 186*n*16; inherited obligations and, 225–228; moral judgment and, 143–145

Inherited obligations, 222–228

Instrumental rationality, 135, 140, 145, 192–193, 279

Intentions: identification of, 44, 284, 303; rights and, 89*n*19; social meaning and, 114, 147, 156, 249*n*31

Internalist theory: moral motivation and, 5–6, 24, 179; reasons and, 158–159

Intimacy: friendship and dignity and, 198, 210; moral development and, 4, 10, 14; need for, 93–97

Judgment: aesthetics, 117*n*16; context-sensitive, 32; moral education and role of, 133–134; motivation, 20–24; practical, 125–126; representation of, 15; social determinants of, 42. *See also* Moral judgment

Justice: and moral improvisation, 297–299; moral triage concerning, 222–228; obligations concerning, 324–331; poverty and, 228–229

Justification, obligations and, 324–331

Kamm, F. M., 206*n*4

Kantian theory: of beneficence, 208–211; categorical imperative in, 71–78; character in, 2–7, 24–28; context-sensitive judgment and, 32; deliberative field and, 40–44; desires and, 2*n*4; genius and artistic activity and, 117*n*15; happiness defined in, 178–183; of hedonism, 176–202; kingdom of ends and, 51–78; limits of morality in, 52–54; local values and moral judgment in, 44–46; moral agency in, 52–54; moral change and, 303–305; moral education and, 130–153; moral literacy and, 80–82; moral motive in, 87–91; motive and desire in, 7–13, 84–87; objects of will in, 230–253; obligatory ends and, 211–219, 254–275; rational agent in, 18–24, 129; skepticism about, 168; system of desires in, 13–17; toleration in, 32*n*5; use of others and, 110–113; on voting, 150–153; will in, 155–159

Kingdom of ends: categorical imperative formulas and, 55–61, 72; constructivist interpretation of, 72–73; idea of an Ideal and, 66–69; law and role of, 62–63; membership conditions in, 62–65; member-sovereign distinction in, 62–64 ; moral judgment and, 69–72; moral law and, 55–78; private or personal ends in, 58–60, 71; social form of moral world and, 75–78

Korsgaard, Christine, 5*n*11, 135*n*3, 155, 157*n*4, 165–168, 242*n*18, 309*n*13

Labor, 151–153; moral importance of, 122*n*23

Latitude of duty, 213–215, 219

Life: faculty of desire and, 234–236; happiness in, 188*n*19; happiness of others and, 268–271; Kantian definition of, 180–183; moral improvisation and, 287–292; obligations for the end of, 298–299; will and choice in, 236–241

Local morality: deliberative field and, 44–46; history and, 292–293; inherited obligations and, 223–228; mediation of, 49–50; moral education and, 144–145; primacy of, 205–208; regulative principles and, 38–39

Love: happiness of others and role of, 270–271; value and, 162–164

CPSIA information can be obtained at www.ICGtesting.com
Printed in the USA
LVOW10s2335181213

365952LV00002B/45/P